MANUAL

OF

ANCIENT GEOGRAPHY AND HISTORY.

BY

WILHELM PÜTZ,
PRINCIPAL TUTOR AT THE GYMNASIUM OF DÜREN.

TRANSLATED FROM THE GERMAN.

EDITED BY THE REV.

THOMAS KERCHEVER ARNOLD, M. A.,
RECTOR OF LYNDON, AND LATE FELLOW OF TRINITY COLLEGE, CAMBRIDGE.

SECOND AMERICAN,

REVISED AND CORRECTED FROM THE LONDON EDITION.

NEW-YORK:
D. APPLETON & COMPANY,
346 & 348 BROADWAY.
M.DCCC.LV.

PREFACE

TO THE SECOND EDITION.

THE first edition of this work was a reprint of the English edition, with a few verbal alterations and occasional corrections. But the favor with which it has been received has induced the publishers to have it carefully revised, and it now appears with material improvements. The most important is in the references for a fuller course of study, English authorities having been substituted for the German, except where there was a translation of the German work. This, it is believed, will give the list a practical value which it could not have, so long as it was filled with works that few of those, into whose hands such a book will fall, would be able either to obtain or to understand. And it is with pleasure and pride that we have inserted among these references the "History of Roman Liberty," by Mr. Eliot—a work of singular beauty and of great learning, and which, by the purity and elevation of its views, is one of the safest and most useful guides to a correct estimate of the results and processes of ancient history.

C. W. G.

Brown University, May 21, 1850.

PREFACE

TO THE AMERICAN EDITION.

One of the most encouraging features in our system of education, is the attention which is given to the study of history. Other branches address themselves more directly to our personal interests, and are mixed up with the daily concerns of life. Every man must read and write, if it be only to read the newspapers or write an advertisement. Arithmetic and geography will be studied as long as there are accounts to make up, or products to send to market. And railroads, and steamboats, and the thousand arts of polished society will always insure the cultivation of the exact, as well as of the experimental sciences. These are the conditions of every well-organized state which man can no more refuse to fulfil, than he can refuse to obey any other law of his nature.

But history, as a serious study, stands upon different grounds, and addresses itself to a principle, which is neither developed so early, nor so universally acknowledged. Not but what most men acknowledge its importance as a record of the past, and feel something of the same kind of interest in it, that they do in any other exciting tale; but its connection with the present, the light which it throws upon what we ourselves are doing every day of our lives, its checkered narrative of human hopes and disappointments, and its manifold lessons of encouragement and of warning, are less generally accepted, and often not even understood. They are classed among doubtful things, which, study as much as we may, we can never make perfectly sure. Characters are said to be distorted by party prejudice, because no two men agree exactly in their judgments of them: and facts to be wholly unsusceptible of proof, because every witness tells his story in his own way. And yet, there is scarcely an important event of our lives, in which we do not look back to our own experience, or to that of others, for some example to go by; and the gravest questions of life are decided every day, by the same rules of testimony, that every judicious historian applies to history. If one man calls Napoleon a selfish usurper, and another, the greatest of the moderns, it is not history that is at fault. The landscape is none the less beautiful because you have no eye to see it with: nor is truth any the less sure, because your line will not reach to the bottom of the well. Raleigh is said to have burnt the unpublished half of his history, because of two or three persons who undertook to describe an occurrence in the Tower court, which he had also watched from his prison window, each gave a different version of it, and his own differed from them all. But what jury would dare to bring a verdict, if this were to be their standard? or what judge could pronounce sentence or instruct a jury, without dreading that he might be sending an innocent man to punishment, or letting a villain loose upon the world? Let us judge past events as we do those that are passing under our own eyes; let us try to give life to our conceptions by comparing them with our experience; and above all, let us remember that the master art of doubting, can never be learned by any but those, who are carefully trained in the science of belief.

It is only when we take partial views of history, that these objections seem unanswerable. Look broadly over it, not as a record of incidents, but as a connected series of developments, through which the human race has passed, in its progress from the incomplete civilization of the ancients, to that diffusion of knowledge, those higher conceptions, that earnestness of endeavor and that hopeful trust in the future, which characterize our own age, and you will readily find an answer to every one of them. For you will see, that although here and there, a detail may escape us, the general tenor of the narrative corresponds with the result: that what seems obscure while standing by itself, becomes clear and definite the moment that you put it in its proper place; that men and events look very differently when taken in that natural connection which gives you the motives of the one and the causes of the other: and that if one or two chapters only serve to sadden us, the whole volume will inspire us with trust and hope. Nothing makes worse citizens than despondency, and there is nothing which political despondency grows on, like those half-way views of life, which we are inevitably led to form, by only looking around us or only looking behind, without feeling how the past and the present work together in moulding the future. If you would make good citizens, firm, hopeful, and earnest, teach them their duties to the future by teaching them their obligations to the past. Life itself will tell them what they owe to the present; and what may not a country hope from men grateful to their fathers, true to themselves, and who know what a joy there is in making the future too our own.

Hence, we look upon the place which history has at last won in our elementary studies, as a peculiarly hopeful feature of them. We feel more confidence in the principles and the judgment of the rising generation, from knowing that they are to be formed by the lessons of this great teacher; and acknowledging, as we unhesitatingly do, the claims of every other branch of knowledge, we feel that our firmest hopes must be drawn from this, which is, at once, the judge and the recorder of them all.

But to do this, history must be studied as a science. She must not be considered merely as a record of phenomena, but as an exponent of laws. As a narrative of facts, no man would have the time to study even the history of a single nation thoroughly: but as the science of humanity, any man may read the world's history, and read it well. There have been a thousand insignificant things and insignificant men in every age: and with these, history has seldom any thing to do. They may serve to fill up a gap in chronology, or form a kind of stepping-stone from one point to another. But your passage over the stream would be very slow, if you were to stop and examine every stone that gave you a footing; and your history would be very dull, if you were to give every man and every thing a place in it.

Now to see what really deserves a place, you must see what relation the parts bear to one another: and to see what kind of a place you can give it, you must get upon some eminence, from which you can look down upon them all and see how much room the whole fills up. And as in geography you begin by marking out the great divisions of land and water, before you attempt to trace the course of mountains or rivers, or to fix the sites of towns and the boundaries of nations, so your true starting point in history, is by mapping out those great successions of empires and of races, which show the part which each has performed in the progressive development of society. Then every fact falls into its proper place, and events class themselves in your mind, according to their due proportions. You know what to look for, and where to go; and feeling yourself at home in the great world of history, can choose out for yourself the parts that you wish to study with greater accuracy, and study them by themselves without losing sight of their bearing upon the whole.

It is with a view to facilitate this method of historical study, that the series of which the present volume forms a part, is offered to the public. The first steps are strictly elementary. This little volume contains a clear and definite outline of the history of the principal nations of antiquity. To render it still more clear, a concise geography of each country has been added, in which, without entering into minute details, all the important features of its physical aspect have been carefully marked. The enumeration of the sources from which we derive our knowledge of them, will familiarize the student's mind with this interesting part of literary history, and show him, from the beginning, how many irreparable losses we have suffered, and how much labor it has required to form that which has been preserved to us, into a definite and instructive picture of the past.

It was neither consistent with the plan of the work, nor the stage of progress for which it was designed, to enter into a fuller narrative of events. The history of each nation is given with as much brevity as is consistent with clearness, and with as much detail as its relative importance required. Where the whole is treated upon so limited a scale, much is intentionally left for the instructor to supply; and something too for the student. For the former can never gain a firm hold upon his pupils by confining himself exclusively to his text-book; and the latter will lose all the discipline of historical study, unless they are early accustomed to carry out an inquiry and use books of reference for themselves. The admirable treatises of Bojesen on Greek and Roman Antiquities, should be taken in connection with those parts of the volume which relate to Greece and Rome; and a fuller historical narrative for consultation, or for a more advanced stage of study, will soon be laid before the public in the series which has already been announced.

GEO. W. GREENE.

Brown University, April 11, 1849.

CONTENTS.

INTRODUCTION.

FIRST DIVISION.—ASIA.

I. THE ISRAELITES.

II. THE INDIANS.

III. THE BABYLONIANS.

IV. THE ASSYRIANS.

V. THE MEDES.

§ VI. THE PERSIANS.

VII. THE PHŒNICIANS.

VIII. THE STATES OF ASIA MINOR.

SECOND DIVISION.—AFRICA.

A. GEOGRAPHICAL VIEW OF AFRICA.

1*

B. THE STATES OF AFRICA.

I. THE ETHIOPIANS.

II. THE EGYPTIANS.

III. THE CARTHAGINIANS (CARCHEDONII).

THIRD DIVISION.—EUROPE.

SECOND PERIOD—FROM THE MIGRATION OF THE DORIANS TO THE PERSIAN WAR, 1104—500.

THIRD PERIOD—FROM THE PERSIAN WARS TO THE DECLINE OF GRECIAN INDEPENDENCE, 500—338.

II. THE MACEDONIANS.

III. THE KINGDOMS WHICH AROSE OUT OF THE MACEDONIAN MONARCHY.

IV. THE ROMANS.

A. GEOGRAPHY OF ITALY.

cc) From the Gracchi to the autocracy of Augustus—Decline and Fall of the Republic.

CIVIL AND FOREIGN WARS.

THIRD PERIOD—ROME UNDER EMPERORS.

MANUAL

OF

ANCIENT

GEOGRAPHY AND HISTORY

INTRODUCTION.

UNIVERSAL history is the record of those facts, by 1
which the internal and external relations of human society A
have been *created* and *modified*.

The sources of history are either articulate or mute.

The articulate are divided into

1. *Oral:* such as legends, traditions, and historical ballads.

2. *Written:* as inscriptions on buildings, columns, B
stones, and tablets, especially those of Greece and Rome; coins, medals, seals; documents, such as treaties, articles of peace, proclamations, records of public transactions, &c. (these sources are especially available for *mediæval* and *modern* history); annals (the historical portions of the Old Testament; the annals of the Phœnicians, Persians, and Romans); chronicles (especially those of the middle ages); and historical works, either contemporaneous with the events which they record, or written subsequently.

The mute are pictures and statues, coats of arms, all C
sorts of buildings and works of art, columns, altars, military intrenchments, ruins, domestic implements, weapons, &c.

By the term historical investigation we under-

(1) stand the collection of facts from these various sources,
A together with a critical examination of their credibility.

The handmaids of history are, I. Geography, topical as well as physical and political, the last being further divided into ancient, mediæval, and modern.

II. Chronology, or the science of computing time, which teaches us to define, according to a settled standard, the duration and succession of events. This standard is partly natural (as the revolutions of the earth and moon, on which is grounded the division of time into years,
B months, and days), partly artificial and arbitrary, the commencing point for the calculation of those natural periods and their further sub-division having been settled by legislators. Hence the distinction between *astronomical* and *historical chronology;* the former defining the natural portions of time, and the latter giving us the artificial or civil divisions, as well as the events which have been adopted as landmarks to distinguish the commencement of different *æras.*[1]

The most remarkable forms of the year.

2 1. The variable solar year of the *Egyptians* consisted of twelve
C months (each of which contained thirty days), with five supplementary days. 1461 Egyptian=1460 Julian years or the Sothiac cycle, so called from Sothis or Thoth, the Egyptian name of Sirius, the heliacal rising of which marked the rising of the Nile, an important epoch in Egypt. Manetho's chronology is founded on the Sothiacal cycles.

2. The *Chaldeans* and *Babylonians* are generally supposed to have adopted the same form and commencement of the year as the Egyptians; it seems, however, by no means improbable that their civil year, like that of all the Semitic nations, Syrians, Arabians, and Hebrews, was divided into lunar months.

D 3. The *Greeks,* particularly the Athenians, the only Grecian nation with whose chronology we are fully acquainted, had a lunar year of twelve months, consisting alternately of thirty and twenty-nine days. Three months were intercalated every eight, or seven every nineteen years, in order to fix the commencement of the year at one uniform season, viz. the summer solstice. The month was divided into three decades. Their day began at sunset, like other nations (Jews and Mahometans), whose division of time was governed by the revolutions of the moon.

4. Until the year B. C. 45, the *Roman* mode of computing time was very unsettled and imperfect. Under Romulus they had the Etruscan

---

[1] Perhaps a Gothic word. [It occurs in a Latin form in Isidore's Origines.]

year of 304 days, or ten months, which was exchanged by Numa (2)
for a lunar year of 355 days, or twelve months. To this year the A
Decemviri added an intercalary month twice in four years (once of twenty-two and once of twenty-three days). In the year B. C. 45, Julius Cæsar, as Pontifex Maximus, established a settled method of computation by the adoption of the solar year, with an intercalary day once in four years (after the 23rd Feb.). The Roman month [2, D] was also subdivided into three portions: Calendæ (the first day of the month), Nonæ (the ninth day before the Idus), Idus (in months of thirty-one days the fifteenth, and in others the thirteenth day), from which the single days were reckoned backwards. They
reckoned also by weeks of eight days (Nundīnæ). The day began B
at sunrise [and was therefore of variable length], but afterwards at midnight.

5. The *Christians* availed themselves of the Julian calendar, but at the same time borrowed from the Jews the division of the year into weeks, and named their days after the saints. The council of Nicæa decided that the feast of Easter should always fall on the first Sunday after the full moon following the vernal equinox. In the middle ages, the beginning of the year varied in different nations, some reckoning from the 1st of January, others from the 1st of March, the
Annunciation of the Blessed Virgin, Easter, Christmas, &c.; nor was C
it until the end of the 17th century, that the 1st of January was adopted (by an ordinance of Pope Innocent XII.) as the invariable commencement. The Julian calendar, according to which every year had an excess of 11′, 14″, 30‴, was amended by Gregory XIII.; ten days (the aggregate amount of the excess) being left out in the year 1582, an arrangement by which the 15th October was made immediately to follow the 4th, it being also settled that in future three days should be left out in every 400 years.

The Mahometans neglecting the correspondence of the lunar and D
solar year, count by lunar years of 354 days, with 12 months of 29 and 30 days alternately, adding a day 11 times in 30 years. Week of 7 days—day begins at sunset.

Republican calendar of the French, first used Nov. 26, 1793; abol- E
ished Dec. 31, 1805. Dated from Sept. 22, 1792. Year began at midnight of the day of the autumnal equinox; divided 12 months of 30 days, with 5 additional days for festivals, and every 4th year, 6; months divided by decades; days into 10 hours of 100 minutes each.

Autumn, { Vindémiaire (Vintage month), Sept. 22 to Oct. 21.
Brumaire (Foggy month), Oct 22 to Nov. 20.
Frimaire (Sleety month), Nov. 21 to Dec. 20.

Winter, { Nivose (Snowy month), Dec. 21 to Jan. 19.
Pluviose (Rainy month), Jan. 20 to Feb. 18.
Ventose (Windy month), Feb. 19 to March 20.

Spring, { Germinal (Budding month), March 21 to April 19.
Floréal (Flowery month), April 20 to May 19.
Prairial (Pasture month), May 20 to June 18.

Summer, { Messidor (Harvest month), June 19 to July 18.
Fervidor or Thermidor (Hot month), July 19 to Aug. 17.
Fructidor (Fruit month), Aug. 18 to Sept. 16.

The most important historical æras.

3 1. Among the *Babylonians* the æra of Nabonassar, (26 Feb.) 747.

2. The *Hebrews* reckoned at first by the ages of their patriarchs,
A and afterwards by the years of their governors. The most remarkable æras are the destruction of the first Temple (586), the Seleucian (312), that of the Maccabees 143 B. C.), and the æra of the world (calculated by Rabbi Hillel in the fourth century). 'B. C. 3761.)

3. The Olympiad of the *Greeks*, a period of four years, beginning with the year 776. This mode of computing time did not come into general use until the fifth century before Christ, when it was employed by the historian Timæus of Sicily; it did not, however, supersede, but merely existed in conjunction with, the more ancient mode
B of naming the year after some person in authority; at Sparta, for instance, after the first Ephor, and at Athens after *the* Archon (Archon *Eponymus*).

4. Among the *Romans*, the only æra recognized in public proceedings was the Consular, which was retained even under the empire until the reign of Justinian (541). The æra *ab urbe conditâ* also came into general use among writers in the reign of Augustus. Its commencement is fixed by Varro in the year B. C. 753, and by Cato in 752.

5. In the *Syrian empire*, they had the æra Seleucidarum,
C (1 Oct.) 312, in which year Seleucus Nicātor overthrew Demetrius Poliorcētes, at Gaza, and occupied Babylon. This æra is still in use, at least for ecclesiastical purposes, among the Syrian Christians.

6. The *Christians of the West*, in the first centuries, were accustomed to distinguish the year either by the date of the emperor's accession, or still more frequently by the names of the Consuls; but as the Consular æra began about the fourth century to lose its importance, they adopted the Indiction-Cycle, a tax period of 15 years, begun Sept. 1, 312 (according to the Benedictines 313), and counted Ind. 1, 2, &c., up to 15, when it began anew. This æra was
D also in its turn abandoned by degrees, with the constitution from which it derived its origin. In conjunction with this æra, which appears in public documents as late as the 16th century, the æra *from the birth of CHRIST*, invented by the Roman abbot Dionysius Exiguus (†556), soon came into general use, and has been retained to the present day, although its commencement is fixed four, or perhaps six years too late. The *Christians of the East* observed partly the Seleucian, and partly the *æra Diocletiani* or *Martyrum*, (29 Aug.) A. D. 284, in commemoration of the persecution under Diocletian. This æra is still in use among the Coptic and Abyssinian Christians. We find,
E also, among the Orientals a variety of æras, such as the Alexandrine, that of Julius Africanus, the Byzantine, &c.

7. Among the *Mahometans*, since the death of the Caliph Omar, the æra has been the Hegira (Hedschra), commencing on the evening of the 14th or 15th of July, 622. It must be observed, however, that the flight of Mahomet (*Mohammed*) did not occur at that time, but in the third month of the first year of the Hegira.

8. The *French* method of reckoning by the years of the republic (3)
was abolished, after being in use twelve years (1793—1805). An A
attempt was made by Joseph Scaliger, in 1609, to reduce all the
various computations of time to one æra, viz., *the Creation of the
World*, according to which he proposed to arrange the events of all
nations and ages; a plan which has been also adopted by Petavius,
Usher, and others. But as these authorities were unable to agree
respecting the settlement of the epochal year, a more simple and
convenient method (*the computation of years before and after the
birth of CHRIST*), invented by Riccioli, has been in general use
since the middle of the eighteenth century.

III. Genealogy, or the record of the origin, multipli- B
cation, and affinities of different races.

History is divided with reference to

1. Its *contents:* into *political* history, and the history of *civilization*.

2. Its *extent:* into *universal* and *special*.

3. *The portions of time comprehended:* into 1. The history of *Antiquity*, from the earliest period of which we
have any notices, to the dissolution of the Western empire,
A. D. 476. 2. The history of the *Middle Ages*, to the dis- C
covery of America in 1492. 3. The history of *Modern
Times*, to the present day.

Methods of history. The annalistic, ethnographic, and synchronistic, or by years, by nations, or by classing contemporaneous events together.

FIRST DIVISION.

ASIA.

Asia, the largest quarter of the globe, and the cradle of 4
the human race, is universally recognized as the native
land of civilization, the most remarkable religious systems
(the Jewish, Christian, and Mahometan, with those of D
Buddha, Zoroaster, and Confucius [Kon-fu-tse],) having
originated there: as well as the most perfect and richest
languages, most of the arts, sciences, and inventions; trade,
industry, and political science. On the other hand, the
civilization which had commenced in Europe at a later
period, was almost annihilated by immigrations of Asiatic
hordes (Huns, Seldschuks, Mongols), none of whom,
except the Arabians, exercised a favorable influence on
the cultivation of the arts and sciences. Its enormous

(4) extent (five times that of Europe), and its situation in
A three distinct zones (chiefly however in the temperate), have rendered Asia superior to the other quarters of the world in wealth, magnificence, and variety of productions in the animal, and still more in the vegetable kingdom; a variety which is found not only in the space bounded by its northern and southern, but in that which lies between its eastern and western extremities.

India, its southern portion, has always been a field for the display of commercial enterprise, the result of which has been the discovery
B of new seas and a (so-called) New World. The operations of trade have been rendered comparatively easy by the great extent of sea-coast, as well as by the deep gulfs and mighty rivers of that important peninsula.

A. Geographical View of Asia.

§ 1. *Its Boundaries.*

5 Although the ancients were unacquainted with the extreme northern and eastern portions of Asia, they seem to have been aware (at least after the expeditions of Alexander the Great) that this quarter of the globe was washed by three different oceans, and on the western side by an inland sea, the most considerable in the world. Its boundaries on the land side are variously reported.

C Herodotus mentions the Phasis, as separating it from Europe; others speak of the Tanais (*Don*), as its boundary on that side. The older geographers considered Egypt sometimes partially, sometimes entirely as belonging to Asia. Strabo mentions the Arabian gulf as its western boundary.

§ 2. *The principal Mountains of Asia.*

6 The ancients mention as detached branches of the Ural chain (the greater part of which was unknown to them), the Hyperborei, Riphæi (Rhymnici, also Alani) Montes.
D They were much better acquainted with the southern chain, the Taurus, which commences in Asia, and after sending out a branch, the Caucasus, in Armenia towards the north, divides itself in Sogdiana into two main arms, which inclose a vast desert (now called Kobi), and are united by the Imaus (Mustag). One branch of this southern chain is the Paropamisus (Hindu-Khu), crossed by Alexander the Great, a western continuation of the Himalayan range (Emōdus).

§ 3. *The Waters of Asia.*

Seas, Gulfs, and Straits.

In the north the *Frozen Sea* (mare Scythicum). 7

In the east the *Eastern Ocean* (Oceanus Eōus). A

In the south the *Indian Ocean*, with the *Erythræan sea* (between the peninsulas of Arabia and India), the Persian gulf and the Arabian gulf, or Red Sea.

In the west the *inner sea* (called by Herodotus *ἥδε ἡ θάλασσα, ἡ καθ' ἡμᾶς θάλασσα, ἡ ἔσω θάλασσα, ἡ ἐντὸς θάλασσα*), now called the Mediterranean. The parts of it which washed the coasts of Asia were the Ægean Sea (now the Archipelago), the Hellespont (straits of Dardanelles), the Propontis (Sea of Marmora), the Thracian Bospŏrus (straits of Constantinople), the *Pontus Euxīnus* [=*hos-* B
pitable sea), called in ancient times *Axĕnus* [*the inhospitable*]; the Black Sea (in contradistinction to the other inland seas, which were named the White Sea by the Arabian geographers), the Cimmerian Bosporus (straits of Kaffa or Jenikale), the Mæōtis (called also the Palus Mæōtis and Lacus Mæōtis), now the Sea of Azov.

LAKES.

The *Caspian* Sea, the largest lake in the world, which probably once communicated with the Sea of Aral, for which reason no mention is made of the latter in ancient writers. The Lacus *Asphaltites*, or Dead Sea, and the Lake C
of *Genezareth*, or Sea of Galilee.

RIVERS emptying themselves

Into the *Indian Ocean:* the Ganges, Indus (Sind), and the twin streams Tigris (also Tigres) and Euphrātes, both of which discharge their waters into the Persian gulf.

Into the *Pontus Euxīnus:* the Halys (Kisil Irmak), the Phasis.

Into the *Caspian Sea:* the twin streams Oxus (Amu), D
and Jaxartes (Sirr or Sihon), both into what is now called the Sea of Aral; from Europe the Rha (Volga).

§ 4. *Ancient division of Asia.*

A. THE CONTINENT. 8

The Greeks and Romans divided Asia either into

1. *Upper* and *Lower* Asia (*ἡ ἄνω καὶ ἡ κάτω Ἀσία*),

(8) separated by the Halys; thence called also Asia within
A and without the Halys.

Or, 2, into Asia, *on this side*, or *within* the *Taurus*, and *on the other side*, or *without* the Taurus. The *former* was also called Asia *proper*. The name of Asia Minor first occurs (in Orosius) at the beginning of the fifth century.

B. The Islands.

In the Mediterranean: Cyprus; in the Ægean sea, Rhodus, the Sporădes, Samos, Chios, Lesbos, Tenĕdos.

B In the Indian Ocean: Taprobăne (Ceylon), Insula Bonæ Fortunæ (Sumatra), and Iabadii insulæ (Java).

The more distant southern, and most of the eastern and northern islands were unknown to the ancients.

B. Particular States.

I. *The Israelites.*

9 Sources of information.—*Hebrew:* The principal source of information is the Holy Bible, especially the books of Moses or the Pentateuch (Genesis, Exodus, Leviticus, Numbers, and Deuteronomy), the books of Joshua, Judges, Ruth, Kings, and Chronicles, the holy Psalmists, and the Prophets.—We have also the Talmud, or Jewish tradition.

C *Greek:* Flavius Josephus (Ἰουδαϊκῆς ἁλώσεως 7 B. Ἰουδαϊκῆς ἀρχαιολογίας 20 B.), in the first century after Christ.—Trogus Pompeius in the Latin extract of Justin. xxxvi. c. 2, 3.)

For Geography: Strabo (16, 2), Ptolemæus (5, 15—17), Plinius (H. N. 5, 13—19), and particularly the Onomasticon urbium et locorum Scripturæ Sacræ, written by Eusebius of Cæsarea, and still extant in the form of a Latin translation by Jerome.—Mod. Milman's Hist. of the Jews. Eliot's Hist. of Roman Liberty, ch. 7.

§ 5. *Geography of Palestine.*

10 Names. In the Old Testament, the country between
the Jordan and the Mediterranean is called *Canaan* (also
the land of the Hebrews, Jehovah's, as being the peculiar
D possession of Jehovah), Israel (the promised Land). The name of *Palestine* was given at first to the country of the Philistines in south-western Canaan, but by degrees it became the term most frequently employed in the West to signify the whole country; which was also denominated *the Holy Land*, as being the theatre of events recorded in sacred history. It received the name of *Judæa* after the Babylonian captivity, because Judah was the chief of the tribes.

Boundaries (in the time of the Judges): on the west (10)
the Mediterranean sea, N. Phœnicia and Syria, E. the A
Syrian desert (country of the Ammonites), S. Arabia
(country of the Amalekites, Edomites, and Moabites).—
David subdued Syria; and Solomon's dominions extended
from Thapsacus on the Euphrates to Gaza, and southwards as far as the Red Sea.

Mountains: the two chains of *Lebănon* [Libanon:
Λίβανος], which is 10,000 feet high, and clothed with a
forest of cedars. At a later period, this range was divided
into Lebanon and Anti-Lebanon [*Hermon*], between which B
lies the valley of the Leontes, or the ancient Cœle-Syria,
with the ruins of Baalbeck.

The northern part of Palestine, afterwards called Galilee, forms a table-land, on the southern side of which rises Mount Tabor; thence the traveller towards the south descends into a small plain (Jezreel). The centre of the country is traversed by the mountains of Ephraim, the southern by those of Juda, and the eastern by those of Gilead.

Waters. The Mediterranean (in the Bible the Great
Sea). The lakes of Merom (or Samochonītis), and C
Genezareth, or the Sea of Galilee; the Dead Sea (so
called, because, as it is said, no living being can exist in
it, or on its surface), or Lacus Asphaltites (on account of
the bitumen or asphalt found there), or Salt Sea (on account of the unusual saltness of its waters). This body of
water owes its origin to the judgment which overwhelmed
the cities of Sodom and Gomorrah (with Adama, Zeboim,
and Bela), and changed the fruitful valley of Siddim into a
lake. The river Jordan rises from three sources in the D
Anti-Lebanon, and flowing through a valley formed by a
wall of rocks on each side, finally loses itself in the Dead
Sea. Before the destruction of Sodom and Gomorrah, it
seems to have discharged its waters into the Atlantic.

Climate. As the soil of Palestine comprehends within a small area almost all the formations of the earth's surface, from the bright lively chalk to the black basalt; so does it possess every variety of climate, from the tropical temperature of the valley of Jordan, on the banks of the lake Genezareth, to the cold and raw atmosphere of the heights of Lebanon. By this great variety of climate a gradation of vegetable life is created, ascending regularly

(10) from the stunted productions of colder climates, to the
A palm-trees and tropical fruits of the south.

Agriculture and the cultivation of the vine, as well as the growth of fruit (especially figs and olives), and the rearing of silk-worms once flourished extensively in Palestine; and, in conjunction with pasturage and the keeping of bees, formed the chief wealth of the inhabitants. Forests of cedars, cypresses, palms, and oaks, furnished wood for building, whilst salt was supplied abundantly by the Dead Sea.—The scourge of Palestine was its swarms of locusts.

Its divisions were various at different times. Joshua
B portioned out the land among the twelve tribes of Israel (Judah, Simeon, Benjamin, Dan, Ephraim, Manasseh, Issachar, Zebulon, Asher, Naphtali, Gad, and Reuben), and after the death of Solomon, it was divided into the kingdoms of Israel and Judah. In our Saviour's time, a distinction existed between the parts on this side Jordan (Judæa, Samaria, and Galilee), and on the other side (Peræa).

CITIES

In *Judæa*. 1. JERUSALEM or Salem, originally Jebus,
C the capital of the Jebusites; in the Bible Jeruschalaim, τὰ Ἱεροσόλυμα (in Herodotus *Κάδυτις* ?); from the time of Hadrian Ælia Capitolina, and Jerusalem again under Constantine the Great; the chief city of Judæa, and, since the days of King David, capital of the whole country, was situated on four hills, viz., Zion, the southernmost and loftiest, on which a fortress was erected by David; Moria [*Moriah*], where Solomon built the temple; Akra (so named from the castle built on it by Antiochus Epiphanes), and at a later period Bezetha. The city was surrounded
D with a triple wall, strengthened by towers. 2. BETHLEHEM, southward of Jerusalem, a mountain city, the birth-place of David and of our Blessed Saviour. 3. JERICHO, destroyed by Joshua, and restored by David, the seat of the "schools of the prophets." 4. On the coast the sea-port of Japho or JOPPA (Jaffa).

To Judæa belonged also the cities of the Philistines, who were subject for a short time to the Israelites; viz., Gaza on the coast, Askălon, and Ashdod (seat of the idolatrous worship of Dagon).

In *Samaria*. 1. SAMARIA (Schomron), sometime capital of the kingdom of Israel, destroyed by Shalmanesar in 722, and afterwards rebuilt. 2. SICHEM, where the Ten

Tribes revolted under Jeroboam, who fixed his residence (10)
there. It was afterwards the chief city of the Samaritans. A
3. SILO [*Shiloh*]; where the tabernacle of the Lord rested
from the days of Joshua to Samuel.

In *Galilee*. CANA, where our Lord wrought his first miracle at the marriage-feast; NAZARETH, where He was brought up; CAPERNAUM, his usual place of residence. There were no very remarkable cities in *Peræa*.

§ 6. HISTORY OF THE ISRAELITES.

I. *From Adam to Noah.*

(1656 years according to the Hebrew chronology.)

The Bible teaches us, that God[1] created (probably 1
about 4000 years before the birth of Christ) a pair of B
human beings, Adam and Eve, whom He placed in a
garden, named Eden, the situation of which it is impossible now to ascertain. Here they continued to dwell,
until, having fallen by an act of disobedience from their
state of innocence ('*the Fall*'), they were expelled from
Paradise, and man was condemned to earn his bread by
the sweat of his brow. But this sentence was accompanied by a *positive* but *indefinite* promise, that some
'*seed of the woman*' should accomplish, though not without difficulty and suffering, a final victory over sin and
the personal Spirit of evil who had tempted him to his C
fall. We learn from the Bible history that the sons of
Adam employed themselves in agriculture and the feed-
ing of cattle; and that they offered *sacrifice*, a rite
which afterwards prevailed throughout the whole ancient
world, and was probably of Divine appointment.[2] The
union of the first *family* was soon dissolved by the
murder of Abel by his brother Cain, and the flight of

[1] Chronologists have found it difficult to agree upon this date. The Hebrew text, according to Moreri, gives 4003 B.C. as the date of the creation. Usher, 4004, which is generally adopted by English writers. The Septuagint, according to Riccioli, 5634. The Vulgate, according to Riccioli, 4184. Petavius (in Strauchius), 3983. The Benedictines, in the Art of verifying dates, 4963. The deluge—Hebrew and Vulgate, 1656; Samaritan Pentateuch, 1307; Greek, 2262.

[2] [Sacrifices of expiation were commanded the Jews, and obtained among most other nations, from tradition, whose original probably was revelation.—*Bp. Butler, Anal.* ii. 5.]

(11) the fratricide into the land of Nod (i. e. of *banishment*),
A where he built the first city. The posterity of Cain,
whose wickedness had filled the earth with murder and
violence, were destroyed, together with most of the descendants of Seth (Adam's third son), by the waters of a
Flood. The Bible account of this visitation is confirmed
by the traditions of other ancient nations, as well as by the
history of the earth itself. None escaped this destruction
except righteous Noah, his wife, and their three sons
(Shem, Ham, and Japheth), with their wives, in all eight
B persons. These were saved in the *Ark*, which finally
rested on Mount Ararat; and thus the human race a
second time sprang from *a single* family.

II. *From Noah to Abraham.*

v. Goguet, Origin of Laws, &c., among Ancient Nations.

(B. C. 2300—2000.)

12 The rapid increase of Noah's descendants compelled
them to settle on the banks of the Euphrates, in the fruitful plain of Shinar (*Babylon*).—Building of the tower of
C Babel. Dispersion of Noah's posterity.—The *Shemites*
(or descendants of Shem) spread themselves over Asia,
from the Mediterranean to the Oxus; north-western Asia,
and Europe were peopled by the descendants of *Japheth;*
Africa and a portion of south-eastern Asia[1] by the children of *Ham*. In consequence of the universal degeneracy
of Noah's posterity the knowledge and worship of the one
true God were entirely lost, except in the family of Abraham, a descendant of Seth in the tenth generation, who,
being called by God, received from Him a command to
D leave his own country and kindred, and seek for a new
home in a land, the very name of which was not to be
declared to him till a future time. He was required to
act *in faith*, the command being enforced by a promise,
that his obedience should be rewarded by his being made
the father of a great nation, from which a blessing should
be conveyed to all the nations of the earth. The faith of
the patriarch was equal to the trial: he quitted the land
of his fathers (*Ur of the Chaldees*), "not knowing whither
he went;" and from this time the original promise of a

[1] [Apparently the coasts of Arabia and the Persian gulf.]

Saviour was limited, and thus rendered more definite by (12)
the added specification, that He should proceed from the A
family of *Abraham*.

III. *From Abraham to the Conquest of Palestine.*
(B. C. 2000—1500.)

Abraham, who was called, by the native Canaanites, 13
Hebri, i. e. 'the man from the other side' (hence the
term *Hebrews*), had entered their country (the land of
Canaan) in company with his nephew Lot; but the rapid
increase of their flocks and herds soon compelled them to B
separate. Lot, to whom Abraham granted the privilege
of choosing his future abode, settled in the valley of Siddim, the rich and well-watered plain of the *Jordan*. The
inhabitants of its cities, Sodom and Gomorrah, were so
terribly wicked, that the Lord rained fire and brimstone
upon them from heaven, showing at the same time his
power to *deliver the godly out of temptation* by preserving
righteous Lot. When these guilty cities were overthrown,
the plain in which they stood became the *Dead Sea*. Lot
escaped into the mountains with his daughters, who (by C
incestuous intercourse with their father, whom they had
made drunk with wine) gave birth to *Moab* and *Ben-Ammi*,
the ancestors of the idolatrous *Moabites* and *Ammonites*.

On the other hand, Abraham, who, on account of the
barrenness of his wife Sarah, had had a son (*Ishmael*) by
her handmaid *Hagar*, received a promise that Sarah, in
her old age, should have a son. Accordingly he became
the father of *Isaac*, '*the son of promise*;' and, as a reward
for a great and mysterious trial of his faith, when he prepared to *sacrifice this son* at the command of God, was D
admitted to a more intimate communion with the Almighty
by the establishment of a covenant, into which every male
of his race was thenceforward to be incorporated by
circumcision. Ishmael, with his mother Hagar (who
had justly offended Sarah by her *mocking* behavior on the
festival of Isaac's weaning), had been driven forth into the
Arabian desert at the request of Sarah, but with the permission of God. *Isaac* became the heir of his father's
possessions, and having married Rebekah (the daughter of
Abraham's brother, Nahor), begat twin sons, *Esau* (or
Edom) and *Jacob*, afterwards named *Israel*.

Esau, having profanely sold his birthright to his bro-

(13) ther, travelled towards the south, and became the founder
A of a commercial race named *Edomites* (*Idumæans*).

After Isaac's death, *Jacob* became the head of the
Israelitish family, and continued to lead a pastoral life,
being assisted in the care of his flocks and herds by his
twelve sons. His favorite son, Joseph, was sold by his
envious brethren to a caravan of Ishmaelites, who carried
him into Egypt, where he became the property of Poti-
phar, and was thrown into prison in consequence of a false
accusation brought against him by his master's wife.
B Having interpreted the dreams of Pharaoh, he was created
viceroy of Egypt, and after severely proving his brethren,
who had come down from Canaan to buy corn, at last discovered himself to them. By the invitation of his son,
Jacob migrated with his whole family into Lower Egypt,
where he dwelt in the land of Goshen. After residing
there 430 years,[1] the Israelites (now a considerable nation,
numbering 600,000 fighting men) quitted Egypt under the
command of MOSES. This leader (a descendant of Levi)
had been exposed when an infant on the banks of the Nile,
C in consequence of a command issued by Pharaoh that all
the first-born male children of the Israelites should be
destroyed. Being rescued from the waters by Pharaoh's
daughter (hence his name), he was given to his own mother
to be nursed, and as he grew up received instruction in all
the learning of the Egyptians. Having slain an Egyptian,
who was persecuting one of his brethren, the children of
Israel, he fled for safety to the country of the Midianites,
in Arabia, where *Jehovah* appeared to him in the midst of
a burning bush on Mount Horeb, and commanded him to
D return and conduct the people from Egypt into the land of
Canaan. In conjunction with his brother *Aaron*, he endeavored to obtain from Pharaoh permission for the people
to make a three days' journey into the wilderness, that
they might sacrifice to the Lord their God: but Pharaoh's
heart was hardened, so that he refused to let them go,
until his land had been visited by ten miraculous plagues.
The army of the Israelites, guided by a pillar of a cloud
by day and a pillar of fire by night, marched through the
Arabian gulf (God having first "*caused the waters to go
back by a strong east wind*," and then to return and over-

[1] So Pütz: but the 430 years are to be reckoned from the promise in Gen. xv. to the Exode.

whelm their pursuers) towards Mount Sinai, in Arabia, (13)
where Moses delivered to the people a code of laws, A
written by the finger of God Himself. God punished their faithlessness and disobedience by condemning them to wander forty years in the wilderness: after which they conquered the whole of Palestine as far as the river Jordan. Aaron and Moses, having on one occasion failed to *sanctify Jehovah before the people*, were not permitted to enter the promised land, but died before the children of Israel crossed the river.[1]

The Mosaic Laws, by which the Jewish people were to be go- 14
verned, were given to Moses by God Himself, especially the two B
tables of stone on which the Ten Commandments were engraven, and the pattern of the tabernacle, with its furniture and ordinances of worship. It contained, however, many confirmations of ancient patriarchal usages (such as the worship of one God by means of sacrifices, prayers, and vows, the observance of the Sabbath, circumcision, oaths, the avenging of blood, and the patriarchal life under the government of heads of tribes and fathers of families): and some of the political and domestic institutions bear a strong resemblance to those of the Egyptians. The laws were—

1. Religious. The worship of *one God*, Jehovah, as King of his
chosen people. It was forbidden to make any visible representation C
of the Almighty; but his presence was indicated by the cloud which rested on the mercy-seat in the tabernacle. This tabernacle was a portable tent, consisting of a court and the sanctuary, properly so called, the innermost division of which (the Holy of Holies) contained the ark of the covenant with the Ten Commandments engraven on two tables of stone. The tribe of Levi (to which Moses belonged) were charged with the administration of every thing relating to public worship, but the priesthood itself was confined to the descendants of Aaron; the head of the family for the time being having the title of high priest, and acting at the same time as head of the tribe of Levi and spiritual chief of the whole nation. All
duties connected with the worship of God, unless expressly reserved D
to the priests, were performed by the Levites, with the exception of the lowest offices, which were discharged by the slaves of the sanctuary. They were also required to transcribe and explain the books of the law, administer justice, and conduct the registration of the tribes; and were generally versed in all the scientific learning of those days. They dwelt in forty-eight cities, dispersed among all the tribes, and were not allowed to possess any property, but received a tenth part of the possessions of the other tribes (the tithe of which they again gave to the priests), besides a share of the beasts offered in sacrifice, the firstlings of the flock and the first fruits of the land. The high priest was also supreme judge, and had the privilege of inquiring the will of God. He entered the Holy of

[1] Before his death, Moses, by God's direction, nominated *Joshua* to succeed him as the leader of the people.

(14) Holies once a year, on the great Day of Atonement, to offer sacrifice
A for his own sins and the sins of the people. In order to fix in the
minds of the children of Israel a perpetual remembrance of their
dependence on the Divine Ruler of their nation, periodical feasts
were appointed by the Mosaic law. To remind them that their
persons and property belonged to God, their bodies were to rest
every seventh day, or *Sabbath* (as a memorial also of the rest
of God on that day from the work of creation), and their land
every seventh or *Sabbatical Year;* and at the end of seven times
seven years, or the year of *Jubilee*, all contracts for the possession of
person or property were cancelled, domestic slaves emancipated, and
lands which had been sold or pledged, were restored, with the neces-
B sary farm buildings, to their original owners. Their three annual
festivals, at which all the males were required to visit the place
where the ark of God was deposited, were partly commemorative of
God's wonderful protection of his people, and partly seasons of
thanksgiving. 1. *The Passover* (*Passah*), in commemoration of the
deliverance of the Israelites from Egyptian slavery, and the sparing of
their first-born by the destroying angel when he smote the first-born of
the Egyptians. 2. *The Feast of Weeks*, or πεντεκοστὴ (ἡμέρα), a thanksgiving for the delivery of the law on Mount Sinai, as well as for the
commencement of harvest. The *Feast of Tabernacles*, a festival
commemorative of their living in tents and booths in the wilderness,
and a thanksgiving for the end of the fruit gathering and vintage.
Their dependence on Jehovah was also especially recalled to their
C minds by a yearly penitential observance, called the *great Day of
Atonement*. The new moon of the seventh month, or beginning of the
civil year, was likewise a festival, and was announced by sound of
trumpet, whence it was denominated the *Feast of Trumpets*. The
sacrifices, which were all offered up on an altar in the court of the
Tabernacle, and afterwards of the Temple, were either *bloody*, consisting of clean beasts without spot or blemish (oxen, goats, sheep, and
doves), or *unbloody*, such as meats, drink-offerings, and the daily
offerings of incense. Besides these sacrifices, the Israelites were
required to bring before the Lord the first-born of beasts, and the
first fruits of their fields and vineyards, as well as a double tithe
(half for the Levites, and the other half to form a fund for the
expenses of sacrificial feasts, hospitality to strangers, and relief of
D the poor). Among their religious observances may also be classed
vows, prayers, circumcision, and the purification of the unclean.

2. Civil. Their *political constitution* was a Theocracy. The people were divided into twelve tribes, which were governed by heads of tribes and families (named *elders*), and formed each a small republic: but the whole nation was subject to the dominion of the invisible Jehovah, who governed by his visible representative the High Priest assisted by the priests and prophets. On extraordinary occasions the people were all called together to decide questions of peace, war, alliances, &c., and to elect leaders. We find, also, in the Mosaic law special provisions for the case (which afterwards occurred) of the people desiring to choose a king.

Administration of Justice. After the conquest of Palestine a judge, chosen generally from the tribe of Levi by the heads of families and tribes, was stationed in every city. The punishments

were, ***death***, inflicted for offences against the Theocracy, such as (14)
idolatry, desecration of holy usages, blasphemy, prophesying falsely, A
&c. All crimes of this description were punished with death by the sword or stoning, as acts of high treason against the Sovereign Ruler of the nation. The same punishment was also inflicted for murder, robbery of an Israelite, adultery, incest, and cursing or ill-treating parents. ***Corporal punishment*** (stripes); ***fines*** (for theft and defamation); ***ecclesiastical penalties*** (sacrifices). Moses appointed three cities on the eastern side of Jordan, to which the slayer, who had killed his neighbor without malice prepense, might flee from the avenger of blood.

WAR. Every free citizen who had attained the age of twenty years was required to serve in the army, which was divided into battalions corresponding to the number of the tribes, each tribe
being commanded by its own heads and fathers of families. Terms B
of capitulation were to be offered to besieged places, but if these were refused, and the city taken by storm, all the male inhabitants were put to death.

DOMESTIC LIFE. For the avoidance of idolatry, the people were commanded to separate themselves strictly from foreign nations (with the exception of their relatives the Edomites and the Egyptians), and to root out the ancient inhabitants of Palestine. They were required to lead a peaceful life within their own borders, maintaining themselves by agriculture and pasturage, and neither seeking to enrich themselves by commerce, nor attempting to extend their
territory by conquest. Kindness to the poor, widows and orphans, C
justice to the hired laborer, and gentle treatment of their slaves, and even of beasts, were strictly enjoined by the Law.

The commission of Joshua was ratified by the miraculous interposition of *Jehovah*, who caused the waters of Jordan to retire at the first touch of the priests' feet, and the walls of Jericho to fall down before the *people of God*. This leader subdued thirty-one princes of the Canaanites, and consequently made himself master of the whole land, which he divided among the twelve tribes, ten of which were named after the sons of Jacob (with the
exception of Levi and Joseph), and two after Manasseh D
and Ephraim, the sons of Joseph. The Levites occupied forty-eight cities.

IV. *From the Conquest of Palestine to the establishment of the Monarchy. Period of the Judges.*

(B. C. 1500—1100.)

The twelve tribes, each under its own prince, were 15
united into one federal commonwealth by their worship of Jehovah (the tabernacle at Shiloh), and their common interest in the priestly race and the high priesthood, which

(15) was hereditary in Aaron's family, as well as by the Mosaic
A law and their general assembly (at Sichem).

The command of God, speaking by his servant Moses, to root out the ancient inhabitants of the land, had been in a great measure disregarded; and the people not only contracted marriages with the Canaanites, but added the idolatrous rites of their neighbors to the worship of Jehovah. These transgressions, the envious feeling of the weaker tribes towards the stronger, and their conflicts, generally disastrous, with their neighbors, the Philistines,
B Edomites, Midianites, Ammonites, and Moabites, to whom the Israelites were alternately either subject or tributary, would have put an end to the commonwealth, had not individual heroes (JUDGES, such as Gideon, Jephthah, Samson, and Eli) been raised up by God in the time of their sorest need to rescue the nation from complete subjection. When, however, the sons of Samuel (a Judge, and the founder of a School of Prophets, in which the young Israelites were instructed in the laws, religion, and music), who had been admitted by their father as his coadjutors in
C the priestly office, were known to have accepted bribes, the people, forgetting that God was their King, persuaded themselves that a union of the tribes under a single head would insure them more unanimity among themselves, and greater security against their enemies. Accordingly, they desired to have a visible king, like the nations around them. Samuel was highly displeased at this request, which he justly considered an act of rebellion against their Almighty Sovereign; but being commanded by God to accede to their demand (though not without pointing out
D to them its sinful character), he anointed Saul, the son of Kish, a Benjamite, to be king over Israel.

V. *From the establishment of the Monarchy to the separation of the two kingdoms.*

(B. C. 1095—975.)

16 Saul, after obtaining a victory over the Philistines, received the homage of the Israelites at a general assembly, where he swore to observe the constitution as defined by the terms of his compact with the people and the laws of the Jewish nation. After this he subdued the remainder of their heathen neighbors, the Philistines, Moabites, and Edomites, and rooted out the Amalekites, but, in defiance

of Samuel's prohibition, spared their king and the best of (16)
the cattle. He had on another occasion offered sacrifice, A
in profane violation of God's law; and for these acts of
disobedience Samuel, by God's command, privately
anointed David, of Bethlehem in Judah (a young man), to
be the future king of Israel. When a boy he had kept his
father's flocks, but had been admitted at the court of Saul
as a player on the harp and armor-bearer to Jonathan,
the king's son. After his victory over the giant Goliath
he was persecuted by the jealousy of the king, and took
refuge among the Philistines. Saul, being deserted by B
God, ended his life by falling on his own sword after a
disastrous conflict with the Philistines, in which three of
his sons were slain.

DAVID then returned to his own country, and was at
once acknowledged by the tribe of Judah; the other
eleven tribes declaring in favor of Ishbosheth, the son
of Saul, who was put to death eight years after his
accession, when David became king of all Israel. Having
chosen Jerusalem, which he had conquered from the Jebusites, to be the royal residence, David transferred the Ark C
of the Covenant to that city, and built a magnificent palace
on Mount Zion, by the aid of workmen furnished by his
ally Hiram, king of Tyre. The booty taken in his wars
was also set aside to meet the expenses of erecting a
Temple which he desired to build, but was commanded by
God to leave the execution of his plan to his peaceful
successor. By the subjugation of the Moabites, Edomites,
and Syrians (of Zoba and Damascus), David extended his
kingdom eastward as far as Thapsacus on the Euphrates,
and southward to the Arabian gulf. At the same time he D
took measures for the regular administration of his enlarged
dominions, surrounded himself with a brilliant court and a
body guard (Krethi and Plethi), appointed ministers and
officers for the administration of justice and military affairs,
divided the company of priests and Levites into courses,
gave a more settled form and greater magnificence to public worship, maintained a standing army of 300,000 men
in twelve divisions, each of which remained in turn a
month under arms, concluded a commercial treaty with
Hiram of Tyre, &c.

Deep religious feeling and unshaken confidence in
the Almighty were the distinguishing characteristics of

(16) David, whose fervent spirit of devotion is displayed in the
A Psalms. Under the influence of passion he committed two grievous sins (the seduction of Bathsheba and murder of Uriah), of which he sincerely and bitterly repented. On this repentance he was himself pardoned; but because he had given occasion to the enemies of the Lord to blaspheme, a sentence of punishment was pronounced against him, that the sword should never depart from his house. His son Absalom, who had deposed his father, was put to death by the commander-in-chief (Joab) as he hung by
B the hair from the branches of an oak. A short time before his death David abdicated in favor of his son SOLOMON (the son of Bathsheba), who had been educated by the prophet Nathan.

17 The *wisdom* of Solomon, which was renowned throughout the whole eastern world, was displayed in his judicial decisions (the determining, for instance, which of two claimants was the true mother of a child), proverbs, of which 3000 are extant, songs (1005), and enigmas.[1] His great work was the *erection of a magnificent national*
C *Temple*, and the *establishment of a splendid ritual.* The Temple was finished in seven years by artisans from Tyre, and profusely ornamented with gold, silver, and precious stones. The building was divided (like the Tabernacle) into the Holy Place and Holy of Holies, and solemnly dedicated to the service of the Almighty; the Ark of the Covenant being brought from Zion and deposited in the sanctuary. He built also a royal palace, the walls of Jerusalem, and several cities (as Tadmor or Palmyra, in the Syrian desert). Solomon renewed the *commercial league*
D with Hiram, king of Tyre, and, in conjunction with him, sent ships from the Edomitic harbors of Elath and Ezion-Geber to Ophir, probably an emporium on the Arabian gulf,[2] and to Tarshish (Tartessus in Spain?). *A love of magnificence and luxury* was manifested in the arrangements of the court, the sacrifices, the troops of strange wives and concubines introduced by the king after his perversion to idolatry, and the vast number of horses. To support this extravagant expenditure, heavy contributions were exacted

[1] The *hard questions* in which the Queen of Sheba came to prove him (1 Kings x. 1).

[2] Külb (Hist. of Travels and Discoveries in Africa, i.) supposes Ophir to have been Sofala, on the eastern coast of Africa.

from the people, without any adequate advantage being (17)
gained by the remoter provinces. A conspiracy was in A
consequence organized by Jeroboam (of the tribe of
Ephraim), who, on the discovery of his treason, fled into
Egypt. Syria revolted, and the Edomites remained merely
as tributaries under kings of their own.

REHOBOAM, Solomon's son, having rejected a petition 18
for an alleviation of the public burdens, ten tribes at
once chose Jeroboam, and formed the kingdom of Israel,
only the southern tribes of *Judah* and *Benjamin* remaining
faithful to Rehoboam: these two tribes composed the king- B
dom of Judah. This political separation produced also
an ecclesiastical schism, the tribe of Levi remaining
in Judah and celebrating the worship of Jehovah in the
national temple, whilst the tribes of Israel, renouncing
their allegiance to the priesthood at Jerusalem, as well as
to the throne of David, with its promise of perpetual
duration, offered sacrifices on the high places, and adopted
very generally the Egyptian worship of beasts, and the
adoration of the Phœnician idol Baal.

VI. *The Kingdoms of Judah and Israel.*

(FROM B. C. 975.)

From this period the KINGDOM OF ISRAEL, with its capi- 19
tal Samaria (formerly Sichem), became a prey to intes- C
tine commotions, and only lasted (under nineteen kings)
until the year B. C. 722. The kings, who sought, by
favoring foreign idolatry, to prevent the people from
visiting the Temple at Jerusalem, and thus to render the
separation of the two kingdoms permanent, were strenu-
ously opposed by a party of faithful worshippers of
Jehovah, headed by the divinely-commissioned prophets,
Elijah, Elisha, &c., who denounced the foreign rites and D
the worship of the high places, and endeavored to re-
establish the connection with Judah. These struggles produced revolutions, which were the more frequent, because,
since the revolt of the tribes from the chosen family of
David, the right of their kings to the throne had no better
foundation than national opinion. Hence, repeated wars
with their heathen neighbors (particularly the Syrians), to
which they were urged by the exhortations of the prophets.
The Assyrian king, Tiglath-Pileser, took most of the cities
of Israel by storm, and his successor, Shalmaneser, put an

(19) end to the kingdom of Israel, after the surrender of Sama-
A ria to his forces in 722. Most of the inhabitants were
transported to the interior of Asia, and their place in Palestine supplied by Asiatic colonists, the mixture of whom with
the Israelites at home produced the race of the Samaritans.

THE KINGDOM OF JUDAH, with its capital, Jerusalem,
lasted from B. C. 975 to 586, under nineteen kings and one
queen (Athaliah) of the house of David, most of whom
supported the *Aaronic* priesthood, and maintained the
worship of Jehovah, but there were some who persisted in
B favoring idolatry, and offering sacrifices on the high
places, in defiance of the rebukes, warnings, and lamentations of the prophets (Isaiah, Jeremiah, &c.). After a succession of wars, for the most part disastrous, with the kingdom of Israel and their heathen neighbors, Judah became
tributary to the Assyrians (who had formed an establishment in the adjoining country of Israel), and at a later
period (after the death of Josiah, who fell in battle against
Pharaoh-Nechoh) to the Egyptians; and lastly, after the
overthrow of that nation at Karkemisch (Circesium), to
Babylon.

C Zedekiah, who had been placed on the throne by the
Babylonians, having rebelled, Nebuchadnezzar stormed
Jerusalem, B. C. 586, plundered and burnt the Temple, and
carried off the greater part of the inhabitants to Babylon,
a few being left behind, under the government of a viceroy,
for the cultivation of the corn-land and vineyards.

VII. *The Israelites under the rule of the Persians.*

(B. C. 538—332.)

20 After the capture of Babylon by Cyrus, the Jews were
D not only permitted by that sovereign to return to their own
land after an exile of seventy years, but were presented
with the treasures which had been plundered from their
Temple, protection being also granted to them for the restoration of the building. At first, however, only a small
body of the exiles (50,000) returned to Palestine, which
now formed a district of the Persian satrapy of Syria.
The administration of civil affairs was left by the satraps
for the most part to the high priest, who was now, for the
first time probably, assisted by a council of seventy-one
elders. During the reigns of Cambyses and Smerdis, the
building of the temple was obstructed by the Samaritans,

who had been excluded from a participation in the work, (20)
and was not finally completed until the reign of Darius I. A
The Jewish colony, already established in Judæa, was joined by new settlers under the command of Ezra and Nehemiah.

§ 7. *Literature, Arts, and Sciences.*

LITERATURE.

The exclusive and sacred character of the divine oracles 21
was naturally an impediment to the growth of any *mere literature* among the Jews. Before the exile the arts of
reading and writing were confined to but a few, principally B
to the Priests, Levites, and Prophets. The commandments of God and the miraculous events of the national history were communicated *orally* by parents to their children, whose curiosity their religious institutions were calculated and intended to excite (*Deut.* vi. 7, *sqq.*).

POETRY.—The poetry of the Israelites is distinguished by a majestic simplicity, great strength of expression, elevation, and originality. It differs from all other national poetry, not only in its *substance*, derived from divine *inspiration*, and filled therefore with the spirit and power of religious
wisdom, but also in its *form*, being constructed without C
metre, and in a rhythm which consists merely of a correspondence in the length and structure of the *sentences*, that of the syllables being entirely neglected. Their poems are, 1. *Lyrical*, like the Psalms (almost all of which are of the time of David, and, generally speaking, his own compositions), and the Song of Solomon; 2. *Didactic*, either in short detached sentences, like the Proverbs of Solomon, or in the form of dialogues, like the book of Job; 3. *Lyrico-didactic*, like the Lamentations and prophecies of the four greater prophets (Isaiah, Jeremiah, Ezekiel, and Daniel), and the twelve lesser ones. v. Lowth's Hebrew poetry.

THE ARTS.—There was no opportunity for the attainment D
of *architectural excellence* among the Israelites, since they had only *one* Temple (built by Phœnician architects), the pattern of which had been prescribed by God Himself; nor do they seem to have possessed any other public building worthy of notice. Still less could *painting* and *sculpture* flourish among a people, who, being forbidden by their religion to make any carved or molten image as a representation of the invisible God, were restricted to mere decoration.

(21) On the other hand, *music*, on account of its use in the A Temple worship, especially from the time of David, seems to have attained a certain degree of perfection.

Their *trade* with foreign nations was intentionally prevented, by the Mosaic law against intercourse with foreigners; at a later period its development was impeded by the vicinity of the Phœnicians and Arabians, who shared the commerce of Asia between them: Palestine, nevertheless, exported a considerable quantity of corn, oil, honey, and balsam. The commerce established by Solomon in conjunction with Hiram at the ports of Elath and Ezion-B Geber (which had been added to his dominions by David), ceased with the loss of those provinces. Their internal trade was more important, Jerusalem being the scene of an animated traffic thrice a year at their great national Festivals.

II. *The Indians.*

22 *Sources of information.*—Neither *native* historians nor annalists. The authorities for Indian religion, legislature, and literature, are the *Vedas*, or four ancient collections of religious notices, neither belonging to *one* time nor compiled by *one* writer. The principal C authority, however, on legal questions, is Manu's (the first mortal, grandson of Brahma) code of civil laws, a compilation, gradually formed, of written or traditionary laws, with an immense mass ot commentary. Among *Greek* writers, the most credible accounts are found in Herodotus (iii. 94), Strabo, and Claudius Ptolemæus. On the other hand, the "Indica" of Ctesias is almost entirely fabulous, and the "Indica" of Arrian, with many fragments from the excellent accounts of Megasthenes and other eye-witnesses, contains also a great deal of exaggeration, introduced for the sake of flattering Alexander the Great. Among the *Roman* authorities is Pliny (Hist. Nat.), whose account, although copious, is disfigured by his love of the marvellous and exaggerated. The writings of Q. Curtius contain little that is new or worthy of credit.

D The best general view will be found in Heeren's Researches, 3d vol. of the Eng. tr. v. also an excellent ch. in Eliot's History of Roman Liberty, Introd. View, ch. 2. Ancient ana modern India are so closely connected that they may be studied together. v. Elphistone's Hist. of India, 2 vols.; Crawford's Researches concerning the Laws, Theology, &c., of Anc. and Mod. India; for the knowledge the ancients had of India, Robertson's Hist. Disquisition.

§ 8. *Geography of Ancient India.*

23 Name and Boundaries.—The name of India, which is derived from the river Indus, is generally employed by Greek and Latin writers to designate the countries of the South generally, but most frequently southern Arabia and

Ethiopia. The later division into India intra and extra (23)
Gangem, although still inaccurate, indicates a more correct A
knowledge of the country. The name of Hindostan,
first introduced by the Mahometans, is given to the tract
of country lying between the Indus and Burrampooter,
and between the Himalayan mountains and the Indian
ocean.

India, in the centre of the tropical peninsula of southern Asia, 24
the Italy of the eastern world, the goal of conquerors and settlers,
the emporium of the world's commerce, the exporter to all climes
and in all ages of the richest productions of nature (precious stones
and spices), extends 330 German miles in breadth (the distance from
Bayonne to Constantinople), and 400[1] in length (that of Naples from
Archangel).

Face of the Country and Rivers.—The continent of 25
India consists of an Alpine, a lowland, and a highland B
district, and is separated from the rest of Asia by almost
inaccessible mountains. 1. The *Alpine district* is in the
north, between the Himalaya, the highest point of which,
the Dhawalagiri (*i. e.* Mont Blanc) stands 27,000 feet
above the level of the sea, and a lower chain (7,000 feet
in height) which runs along the skirts of the valley. 2. C
The *Lowland* country stretches in the centre, between the
Alpine and highland districts, in the form of a triangle,
from the bay of Bengal to the Persian gulf, and is separated into two regions of very opposite character; viz. the
fertile plain of the sacred Ganges and Burrampooter, which
unite before they enter the sea, and forming a delta, discharge their waters by several mouths into the bay of
Bengal; and the plain, for the most part barren and waste,
of the Indus, the five tributary streams of which (the
Hydaspes, Acesīnes (*Acesīnus*), Hydraōtes, Hyphăsis,
and Satadrus,) water the Punjâb, or land of the five rivers,
which is fertile, and in parts well cultivated. 3. The *Table-* D
land of Deccan, surrounded on three sides by the sea, is
a uniform triangular peninsula, the eastern and western
borders of which are formed by the Ghaut mountains,
whilst the Vindhaya range, which forms its northern
boundary, slopes in terraces down to the valley, and the
middle consists of one unbroken tract of table-land.

The Islands.—That Ceylon and the more distant 26

---

[1] About 1200 and 1600 English miles.

(26) islands of the East Indian Archipelago, as Sumatra, Java,
A Borneō, Celĕbes, &c., were peopled and cultivated by Hindû tribes, is evident from the Sanscrit names of the mountains, cities, and rivers, and the complexion, manners, and institutions of the islanders, as well as from the stupendous vestiges of Indian architecture, with which the islands abound.

27 Productions.—No portion of the earth is equal perhaps in the riches and variety of its productions to India, which unites the characteristics of the tropical and polar regions.

B The chief of these productions are—in the vegetable kingdom, the cocoa-tree, the richest spices and southern fruits, rice, sugar, all sorts of aromatic woods, cedar, teak, the timber of which is almost imperishable, the cotton shrub, indigo, the sacred banyan-tree, and the equally hallowed lotus—in the animal kingdom, buffaloes, used for draught and riding, elephants, lions, tigers, jackals, large wild dogs, apes, serpents, peacocks, parrots, silk-worms, and innumerable insects—in the mineral kingdom, gold, silver, diamonds, saltpetre, &c.

28 Inhabitants.—The Hindûs, of Caucasian race, and an aboriginal negro tribe, the Parias, who are sometimes to a certain extent civilized, but as frequently savage, living on garbage, and sunk into the lowest state of degradation.
C The dialect in which the classical works of the Indians are written, and which has been a dead language since the time of the Mahometans, is called Sanscrita, *i. e.* "the perfect," in contradistinction to the popular dialects which have sprung from it, and which bear the general name of Prâkrita (common, vulgar).

§ 9. *Fragments of the Ancient History of India.*

29 As the expeditions of Semiramis and Sesostris belong to
D legendary lore, little is known respecting the history of India before the time of Alexander the Great, beyond the fact that certain nations on the banks of the Indus were subdued by Darius Hystaspes. Alexander the Great found several kingdoms already existing in the Punjâb, some of which he restored, after his conquest of the country, to their former kings (as Taxiles and Porus), and placed others under the jurisdiction of Macedonian satraps. His successors lost the Indian provinces during their disputes respecting the partition of the kingdom. Sandrocottus, king of the Prasians on the Ganges, having

expelled the governors appointed by Alexander, and (29)
founded, about the year 312, an empire, which extended A
from the Ganges over the whole of the Punjâb, and a
great part of Aria, Arachosia, and Gedrosia, but at a later
period was first circumscribed, and then entirely destroyed
by the Bactrian kings. The conquests of the Bactrians in
India were soon transferred to the Parthians, and from
them to the Scythians, who were utterly defeated by the
Indian king, Vikramâdityas, B. C. 56, and the Indo-
Scythian empire broken up. Then follows another period B
of darkness until the time of the Mahometan invasions
(about A. D. 1000), during which the peace of southern
India seems to have been grievously disturbed by the religious feuds of the Brahmins and Buddhists.

§ 10. *Religion, political Condition, Literature, &c. of the ancient Indians.*

1. RELIGION.

The Brahminical system. The original religion of the 30
Indians consisted in a veneration for nature, with some sort
of vague acknowledgment of a Supreme Being. This C
primary cause they termed Brahma, and honored the Sun
as his representative under the name of Brahman. Together with Brahmaism there arose in Northern India
two forms of popular worship,—the fierce *Sivaism*, or
worship of fire, and the milder system of *Vishnu*, which
venerated water and air as the great elementary powers.

Their three great deities, Brahman, Vishnu, and Siva, which form
the Trinity of Indian theology (the Trimûrtis), must be considered
like all their other gods, as nothing more than personifications of the
Supreme Being's power, as displayed in the creation, preservation,
and destruction of all things. The will of God that the world should D
be created was revealed through Brahman; that it should continue
to exist through Vishnu, and that the works of creation should be
destroyed through Siva. Vishnu ten times assumed the human form,
in order to revive the expiring virtue of mankind. Their religious
observances are,—prayers, purifications, sacrifices, of various sorts,
rejoicings at most of their religious festivals, severe penances, and
retirement in old age, generally accompanied by ascetic mortification
of the body. The practice of burning widows prevails only among
the followers of Vishnu, and is subject, even among them, to many
restrictions.

The *Buddhist Reformation* (about B. C. 1000). The 31
reformer of the stern Brahminical system, or founder of the

(31) milder religion of Buddha, was Gautamas, surnamed
A Buddhas, i. e. the Wise (son of the king of Magadha), who seems either himself to have given out that he was an incarnation of the god Vishnu, or in process of time to have passed for the manifestation of that deity in a human form. He rejected the system of caste (D); forbad bloody sacrifices and the burning of widows, whom he permitted to marry again; required the priests to lead a life of chastity, celibacy, self-denial, and renunciation of all worldly possessions: a system which led to the establishment of
B several Buddhist monasteries. The humane and tolerant worship of Buddha had spread itself in the fourth or fifth century before Christ over all the East Indian islands; and about the year B. C. 200 had reached China, and through the emigrations caused by the intolerance of the Brahmins, had extended as far as Korea, Japan, Tibet, and Mongolin.

32 2. CONSTITUTION. Their form of government was monarchical, and the succession to the throne hereditary, according to priority of birth. The king could make grants of land to any individual, and again withdraw them, except in the case of the priests, whose estates, granted to them in lieu of a money payment, were inviolable and
C exempt from taxation. In accordance with this practice, the king appointed governors over the larger provinces, who again made grants of the smaller districts to inferior officers and farmers, on condition of receiving a rent, which varied in amount according to the times and circumstances, and of being furnished in time of war with a certain contingent of young men, of the warrior caste, capable of bearing weapons.

D The king, sprung from this caste, seem to have been surrounded by a body of priests, but it does not distinctly appear what share they had in the government. He chose his ministers from the caste of Brahmins, and took counsel with his senate of gray-haired men; but seems, nevertheless, to have acted on all occasions according to his own discretion. His most important duty was the administration of justice; for which purpose a court, consisting of ten learned and aged Brahmins, was established in each province, the king himself being the supreme court of appeal.

33 From the earliest times the people have been divided into four CASTES:—

a. The *Brahmins* (i. e. descendants and worshippers of Brahma), who are sacred and inviolable, more highly edu-

cated than the other castes, exempt from taxation, and (33)
subjected to less severe punishment than others for any A
violation of the laws. They seem to be highly esteemed,
and to exercise considerable influence in all political affairs.
Only a fourth part of the caste are priests, the remainder
being employed as teachers, judges, physicians, or in some
other honorable office.

b. The *Warrior-caste*—Kshatriyas (*i. e.* averters of devastation). The king must be of this caste.

c. The *Visâs* (*i. e.* inhabitants), the agricultural and trading caste.

d. The *Sûdras* (*i. e.* fugitives); the people properly so B
called, divided into guilds, and employed in a variety of
trades, manufactures, arts, and even in commerce. They
are excluded from reading and hearing the Vedas, but are
not considered altogether unclean like the Parias.

3. Literature.—The literature of the ancient Indians, 34
the extent of which has not yet been fully ascertained,
consists of—

a. Their sacred writings, comprehended under the title
of *Sâstra* (*i. e.* the guide, the law), and divided into
eighteen classes. At the head of these stand the four C
Vedas, with their numerous commentaries and explanations.
The remainder treats of various arts and sciences
(music, dancing, military tactics, mechanical arts, grammar,
and lexicography, religious usages, and astronomy,
legislation, philosophy, &c.), and concludes with the
Purânas or antiquities, and the religious Epopee.

The practical sciences, such as geography, natural philosophy, and
medicine, seem to have been in their infancy among the ancient
Indians. Individual discoveries of considerable merit are overlaid
with poetical fictions and religious myths. Their labors in the D
abstract and speculative sciences, such as mathematics and philosophy,
are of a more respectable character. To them we are indebted
for the invention of numerals and algebra. Of their religious
epic poems, which in many respects bear a great resemblance
to the poetry of Homer, the two most ancient and famous are—
1. The Râmâyana (of Vâlmikis), which relates, in 24,000 double
verses, the seventh incarnation of Vishnu (Ramas) and his expedition
to Celone. 2. The Mâhâbhârata (of Vyâsas), which describes
in nearly 100,000 double verses a civil war between two kindred
races, with a great number of episodes.

b. Their *profane* writings, including their lyric and dramatic poetry.

(34) The Indian drama, which, like that of Greece, is a development of
A their ancient sacrificial hymns and rural dances, has chosen its subjects from the celestial world and the lives of heroes, as well as from the realms of philosophy and the domestic circle ; employing also, in most instances, the religious Epopee. The most renowned dramatic writer of Indian antiquity was Kalidasas, who flourished in the first century before Christ. The Sakuntalâ of this author was the first of his works known in Europe.

35 ART.

B *Architecture.* The monuments of Indian architecture, which are on a more stupendous scale than those of any other nation, may be divided into three classes. 1. SUBTERRANEOUS TEMPLES, hewn out of the solid rock; remarkable for their extent, the grandeur of the plan, and its careful execution, and the richness of the statues and relievos which cover the walls. They are found in different parts of the country, but the most magnificent are at Ellore, where the mountain of the gods, as it is termed, is hollowed out from its base to its summit into innumerable temples, forming a complete Pantheon.—
C 2. ROCK-TEMPLES, above ground, hewn out of the solid rock. Of these the most celebrated are the seven pagodas, or monuments of the rock-city Mahabalipuram, on the coast of Coromandel.—3. BUILDINGS, PROPERLY SO CALLED, formed of masses of stone. These edifices are partly of a religious character (as the temples, called by Europeans pagodas, which are generally in the form of pyramids and obelisks, and are often superior in magnitude and colossal architecture to the monuments of Egypt, which they almost invariably surpass in elegance of execution and arrangement of the details); partly erected for secular purposes, like the castles and fortresses which are seen in great numbers on insulated crags.

D The attainment of excellence in the art of *sculpture* was rendered almost impossible by a religious law, which prohibited any change in the existing form of their sacred images.

Of *painting* we find the earliest distinct traces in their dramatic representations.

That *music* attained perfection at an early period among the Indians, and was raised to the rank of a science, is manifested by the great variety of their instruments, as well as by the number of Sanscrit treatises on the theory of harmony.

COMMERCE. 36

Their *home traffic* was carried on, not so much by cara- A
vans as by individual traders, who employed tame elephants for the conveyance of their wares by land, and vessels for river and coast navigation. Their sacred stations, to which hundreds of thousands of pilgrims resorted, were the principal markets for the sale of domestic produce.

The *foreign trade* was in three directions:—1. To the B
North-East, especially to China, whence they imported silk. 2. To the *East*, or peninsula on the other side, named by the Greeks Chryse, in consequence of the great quantity of gold brought from its coasts. From the numerous harbors and commercial stations on the coasts of Coromandel and Ceylon, a brisk trade was carried on between the two extremities of India. 3. To the *West*, from the Malabar coast to Arabia, whence they imported frankincense, and by Arabian ships to the eastern or gold coast of Africa.

The principal exports were—spices, the sugar-cane, precious C
stones, especially diamonds, pearls, various sorts of Indian cloth, from the finest gauze and embroidered satin to nankeen and cotton stuffs, figured with grotesque representations of animals and plants in the brightest colors, &c., &c.

III. *The Babylonians.*

SOURCES OF INFORMATION.—*Native.*—BERŌSUS, priest of Bel and 37
astrologer at Babylon, wrote, about the year B.C. 268, a work, entitled Βαβυλωνικά (in three vols.), compiled from ancient records preserved at Babylon, and from stamped tiles. His book comprised the histories of Babylon, Assyria, and Media. (Fragments of this D
work are preserved in Josephus, Eusebius, and Syncellus.) 2. ABYDENUS, a scholar probably of Berosus, who wrote περὶ τῆς τῶν Χαλδαίων Βασιλείας. (Fragments in Eusebius, Cyrillus, and Syncellus.)

Hebrew.—The BIBLE, particularly the Books of Kings and the Prophets (especially Daniel).

Greek.—1. HERODOTUS; see particularly B. I. c. 178—199. 2. CTESIAS, a native of Cnidus in Caria, and body physician to Artaxerxes II., compiled from oral accounts and the annals of the Persian kingdom, a Persian history (Περσικῶν, 23 B.); of which nothing is extant except a quotation in Photius, and some fragments in Diodorus. His Babylonian history (in B. I—III.) contradicts in

(37) many particulars both the Bible and Herodotus. 3. DIODORUS
A SICULUS, in B. II. of his Βιβλιοθήκη 'Ιστορική. 4. EUSEBIUS, Bishop of Cæsarea (A. D. 300), wrote a Chronikon in two books, of which only fragments were known, until the discovery at Constantinople of an Armenian translation, which has also been rendered into Latin. v. Heeren, vol. 2, pp. 129 et seq. Grote, ch. 19.

§ 11. *Geography of Babylon.*

38 SITUATION. Babylon, called also Chaldæa, and in the Bible Sinear or Senaar, extended on both sides of the Euphrates southwards, from the central bend of the river and the Median wall (which separated it from Mesopotamia) to the Persian gulf.

B SOIL. An entirely flat alluvial land, which on account of the want of rain, is watered by canals by means of hydraulic machines, and then produces from two to three hundred fold. The only tree that flourishes in this soil is the palm, of which there are great numbers. Its fruit not only served for food, but produced also a sort of wine and honey.

The want of wood and stone is supplied by an inexhaustible abundance of clay for making bricks, and instead of lime they used naphtha or bitumen (of which there are large fountains in the neighborhood), with layers of reeds and palm-leaves.

39 RIVERS. The *Euphrātes* and the *Tigris ;* the last of
C which is very rapid ; hence its name Tigris, which signifies the arrow. Both rise in Armenia, and unite their streams fifteen miles above their entrance into the Persian gulf at Pasitigris (*Shut-ul-Arab*).

The Euphrates generally overflows its banks in winter, and still oftener in spring, when the snow begins to melt on the Armenian mountains. These inundations were restrained by dams, or carried off by canals (the largest of which, the royal canal, communicated with the Tigris, and was navigable for ships of considerable burden,) either into the Tigris, the bed of which is lower than that of the Euphrates, or into marshes and artificial lakes.

40 CITIES.—1. Babylon stood in the midst of a fertile
D plain on both sides of the Euphrates. It was surrounded by walls 337 feet 8 inches high, 75 feet thick, and comprising a square, of which each side was 120 stadia or nearly 15 English miles in length. Around the wall was a broad, deep moat, lined with bricks, and a hundred gates served for communication with the surrounding country. Each street was 15 miles long, 150 feet broad, except the half streets under the walls, which were 200

feet broad. There were besides, 296 squares used as (40)
gardens, &c., so that half the city, like modern Rome, A
was filled with cultivated ground. 2. Borsippa. 3.
Cunaxa (battle in 401).

Buildings of Babylon.—The most magnificent were—1. *The* 41
Temple of Bel, or *Babylonian Tower;* which consisted of eight towers
or stories, one above the other, diminishing gradually in size as they
approached the summit, which was crowned with a temple, containing
the couch and golden table of the god. Used for astronomical observations: a heap of ruins in Alexander's time. 2. Old palace, both
sides of the Euphrates. 3. New one by Nabopolassar and Nebuchadnezzar. Hanging gardens. Situate in the Pachalic of Bagdad, B
near Hella. East bank of the Euphrates, ruins of vast buildings—
none of the walls. *Birs Nimrud*, huge oblong edifice of brick, west
of the Euphrates—tower of Babel? v. Rich's Journey to Babylon,
&c.

§ 12. *History of the Babylonians.*

Establishment of the Empire.—According to the 42
express declaration of *Scripture*, Babylon was a more
ancient state than Assyria. It was founded by *Nimrod*
probably about the year 2000, and from it Assyria was
peopled.

The *Greeks* mention, as the founder of the Babylonian empire, C
Bel (i. e. Lord or King), to whom they ascribed all the ancient institutions, of which the founders and date were unknown. According
to the same authority, his son Ninus was founder of the Assyrian
empire. One writer alone, Ctesias, asserts that Assyria was the
mother country. The *native legends*, preserved by *Berosus*, speak
of ten kings who ruled Babylon before the deluge. In the reign
of the third, there arose out of the Erythræan sea a being named
Oannes, half man and half fish, who taught men the arts and sciences,
and communicated them a legend respecting the creation of the
world. The meaning of this fable probably was,—that the Babylonians were indebted for their civilization to a people who came
over the sea, from Egypt or Meroe. Under the last of these kings D
(Xisuthrus), there was a great deluge, from which the king and his
family were saved in a ship.

The history of the Babylonian empire, from the de- 43
luge to the Persian conquest, comprehends, according to
Berosus, seven dynasties, the sixth of which (of forty-five
Assyrian kings) continued, according to the same authority, 526 years; a statement which is confirmed by the
assertion of Herodotus (I. 95), that the Assyrian rule over
Upper Asia lasted 520 years. From this Assyrian domi-

(43) nation the Babylonians delivered themselves, in the year
A B. C. 747, under *Nabonassar*, with whom begins the seventh
dynasty of nineteen native kings. (The era of Nabonassar
reckons from the 26th of February, 747.) Repeated attempts were made by the Assyrians to repossess themselves of Babylon, which for a short period was again
subject to them. Under *Nabopolassar*, the fourteenth king
of this dynasty (625—604), happened probably the immigration of the Chaldæans from Mesopotamia; which they
were compelled, it would seem, to abandon by the Scy-
B thians, who had lately invaded their country. This sovereign, in conjunction with the Medes, put an end to the
Assyrian empire, destroyed Nineveh, and received for his
share the western portion of the empire (Mesopotamia,
Phœnicia, Syria, and Israel). When Necho, in his victorious progress from Egypt, advanced to the banks of the
Euphrates, Nabopolassar sent out his son Nebuchadnezzar, who overthrew the invader near Carchemish
(Circesium), and compelled him to disgorge Syria with
Palestine (B. C. 604). Meanwhile Nabopolassar died, and
was succeeded by *Nebuchadnezzar* (*Ναβουχοδονόσορος*)
C (604—561). In his pursuit of the *Egyptians*, this monarch
advanced as far as Pelusium, and carried off a number of
Jews to Babylon. The kingdom of *Judah* having refused
to pay tribute, and formed an alliance with Egypt, Nebuchadnezzar laid siege to the city of Jerusalem, which surrendered after being closely invested for one year and a
half. The city was plundered and destroyed (B. C. 586);
the king, Zedekiah, had his eyes put out, and most of the
inhabitants were carried away as prisoners to Babylon.
D Those who remained in Judah were subjected to the jurisdiction of a Babylonian governor. Nebuchadnezzar waged
a third war against the *Phœnicians*, because they had
formed an alliance with Zedekiah, destroyed Sidon, and
besieged Tyre thirteen years without success. Thus his
empire extended from the Nile to the Tigris. After his
return he built the new royal palace, with the hanging
gardens, for his wife Nitocris; and laid the foundations,
on the other side the Euphrates, of a second half of the
city, which he surrounded with a triple intrenchment.

44 During his seven years of madness the government was administered by Nitocris. This queen dug a lake, into which the waters of

the Euphrates could be conveyed, built a bridge over the river, and (44)
erected a monument, with a lying inscription, in honor of herself. A

His fourth successor, and the last king of the Babylonians, was *Nabonēdus*, called by Herodotus Labynētus, who supported Crœsus ineffectually against Cyrus, and on that account was besieged by the Persians in Babylon. The river Euphrates being diverted from its course into the lake constructed by Nitocris, the city was taken whilst the inhabitants were celebrating a feast, and Babylon reduced to the condition of a Persian province[1] (B. C. 538).

§ 13. *Religion, Literature, &c. of the Babylonians.*

1. RELIGION.—The religion of the Shemites,[2] and of 45
the ancient Asiatics generally, was that of nature; *i. e.* a B
deification of her powers and laws, and the offering up of
prayers to objects in which those powers were supposed to
exist. In this natural religion the Godhead is not, as in
the religion of the Hebrews, a distinct self-existent ruler
by whom nature is governed, but the innate powers of
nature herself, as she reveals them according to fixed laws,
sometimes in creation and preservation, and then again in
the destruction of her own works; thus exciting in the
minds of men at one time admiration, love, and adoration,
and at another, terror, and a desire to avert her anger. The C
most common idea of the Godhead among Asiatic nations,
who profess the religion of nature, is that it consists (after
the analogy of mortals) of a male and female. Thus Baal
is the active, and Baaltis the passive power of nature; the
one a creative, conservative, but at the same time destructive element, the other the concipient and productive principle. This sexual distinction, which extends to all the
powers and phenomena of nature, seems to have occasioned at an early period the grammatical distinction of
genders as applied to inanimate objects. A later step in D
the development of material religion was the representation
of gods with human characters and the human form. To

[1] According to Xenophon (Cyrop. vii. 5), and Daniel (v. 30), the king lost his life when the city was taken; but Berosus asserts that he escaped to Borsippa, gave himself up to Cyrus, and ended his life in Carmania.

[2] To the Shemites belonged the Assyrians, Babylonians, Phœnicians, Carthaginians, and Lydians.

(45) complete this notion, the gods were described as dwelling
A on earth, and as the founders of families, especially those
of kings and princes, suffering the trials of mortality, and
at last dying and reposing in sepulchres, which were still
to be seen. Thus we find, that wherever any divinity was
especially venerated, he or she had been in ancient times
the king or queen of the country, and that the guardian
deities of cities were generally their founders. The first
rank among the Shemitic divinities is assigned to Bel
(Belitan), their first king, who subdued the whole east,
beginning with Syria, and stands at the head of all the
B Shemitic royal pedigrees. From him the Babylonians
gave their city the name of Babel (*i. e.* the court of Bel),
and ascribed to him the erection of their famous wall, and
even of the tower of Babel. In this fortress he was accustomed to watch the movements of the heavenly bodies
from a lofty observatory, and communicate his discoveries
to the Chaldæans.

46 Of the five planets, two, Jupiter and Venus, were considered be-
C neficent powers by the Chaldæans, and all the other astrologers of
those days. Mars and Saturn were destructive, and Mercury sometimes good and sometimes malignant, according to his position. The Chaldæan priests believed that the will of the gods and the destinies of men might be learned from the position, rising, and setting of the planets, and in the course of their observations made many scientific discoveries.

47 2. The Constitution. "The King of kings," who
received divine honors from his people, and exercised uncontrolled and irresponsible power, resided in his tower,
surrounded by an immense multitude of officers and at-
D tendants. The empire was divided into satrapies, which
were governed despotically by the king's lieutenants.
Considerable authority was also possessed by the priestly caste of the Magi, who were termed pre-eminently "Chaldæans" (Kasdim), and were sole possessors of all the learning of those days, which they communicated by tradition to members of their own caste.

48 3. Trade. The favorable position of their country, midway between the Indus and the Mediterranean, in the neighborhood of the Persian gulf, and on the banks of two navigable rivers, rendered Babylon the centre of commercial communication between Upper and Lower Asia.

a. The *land trade* was carried on by means of caravans, *eastward,* (48)
with India (from which they imported precious stones, hounds, and A
coloring substances), and with Bactria (for gold); *westward,* with Asia and Phœnicia, up the Euphrates as far as Thapsacus, and thence by caravans. Their exports to these countries were Arabian and Indian produce.

b. *Trade on the Euphrates,* by leathern boats, which brought wine from Armenia.

c. *Maritime commerce* was carried on, not so much by the Babylonians themselves, as through the Phœnicians settled on the coasts of Arabia, and the Arabians beyond the Persian gulf: 1, with *Arabia* (especially with the Chaldæan colony of Gerra and the islands of Tylus and Aradus), whence they brought back pearls, cotton, frankincense, and timber for ship-building; and, 2, with the western coast of *India,* from which they imported spices, ivory, ebony, precious stones, pearls; and with Ceylon, which sent them cinnamon.

4. Arts and Manufactures. Woollen and cotton 49
stuffs and carpets, objects of luxury (perfumed waters, B
carved *walking-sticks,* cut stones).

IV. *The Assyrians.*

Sources of Information.—The same as those for Babylonian his- 50
tory. The most numerous, but at the same time most incredible and fabulous notices are found in *Ctesias* (B. 1—3). To these we may add *Trogus Pompeius,* a Gaul who flourished in the reign of Augustus. We have his universal history in the Latin extracts of
Justin (see the beginning of B. 1). *Herodotus,* in his history (i. 184; C
compare i. 106), refers to a separate history of Assyria, which has been lost. Grote, ch. 19. Layard's Nineveh.

§ 14. *Geography of Assyria.*

Name and Situation. By the term Assyria we un- 51
derstand—1, the *province;* comprehending all the country between the Tigris and Media, southwards as far as Babylon, and northwards to Armenia, corresponding to what is now termed Kurdistan; 2, the *empire;* which, besides the province of Assyria, comprised Mesopotamia, Babylon, with Chaldæa, Media, and Persia. Sometimes the names of Assyria and Syria were interchanged.

Soil. Mountainous in the north and east; well watered, D
and consequently for the most part productive; produces bitumen. Chief and boundary river, the *Tigris.*

Cities. *Nineveh* (ἡ Νῖνος), the earlier city built by Ninus, was situated on the Tigris, probably where the royal canal runs into the river; the more modern city of

(51) Ninus lay further north on the eastern bank of the Tigris.
A The old town was 480 stadia in circumference (150 in length, and 90 in breadth): its walls were 100 feet high, and broad enough to receive three carriages abreast, with 1500 towers, 200 feet in height. 2. *Gaugamēla τὰ Γ.*), in the vicinity of *Arbēla* (*τὰ A.*), the scene of Alexander's victory in 331.

§ 15. *History of the Assyrians.*

52 According to the Bible narrative, the Assyrian empire
B and its capital Nineveh were founded from Babylon, either by Nimrod himself, or by the emigration of the tribe of Assur.[1] Grecian writers ascribe the foundation either to Bel or to his son NINUS (a personification of the Babylonian colony), about 2000 years before Christ. To this monarch and his consort and successor SEMIRAMIS (daughter of the goddess Derkĕto), Ctesias ascribes expeditions on a magnificent scale in Asia and Africa (against Bactria, Libya, Ethiopia, and India), in which the forces on both sides amounted to several millions.

C Semiramis founded commercial cities on both sides of the principal rivers, with causeways, canals, dams, extensive gardens, &c.; besides erecting memorials of her expeditions, one of which is still seen at Ecbatana. According to Ctesias, she conquered the greater part of Libya and Ethiopia, and at last undertook an expedition on the Indus against an Indian king, with an enormous force consisting of 3,000,000 of infantry, 500,000 cavalry, and 100,000 chariots; and a fleet of 2000 ships. This multitude was met by a still more numerous army of Indians, who were vanquished by Semiramis; but the stratagem of her pretended elephants being discovered, the heroine was compelled to give way in her turn, and being wounded by the king, returned to Nineveh, where she soon afterwards died, and was numbered among the gods.

53 Semiramis was succeeded by her son NINYAS. This mon-
D arch and his successors (until Sardanapālus), whose number, names, and reigns are variously given, led for the most part an effeminate life in their palace, which was guarded by a standing army of 400,000 men, changed every year. During

---

[1] Whether Nimrod himself was the founder of the Assyrian empire is doubtful; for the passage (Gen. x. 11) may be interpreted—"From this country he (Nimrod) went to Assyria, and built Nineveh;" or it may signify—"From this country went Assur, and built Nineveh."

this period (according to Herodotus and Berosus) occurred (53)
the subjection of Upper Asia to Assyrian rule. After an A
interval of thirty generations, we find the throne occupied
by the effeminate TONOSKONKOLEROS, surnamed Sardanapālus (the Admirable), about the year B. C. 840. An
insurrection of the Babylonians and Medes against this
monarch produced the establishment of an independent
Median empire, whilst that of the Assyrians, so far from
being destroyed, continued to subsist under its own kings,
the Babylonian empire being also incorporated with it.[1]
There exists no record of the kings who succeeded Sar- B
danapālus until the period when the history of Assyria
becomes blended with that of Israel. We have then the
following succession :—

PHUL (about B. C. 770), who compelled the Israelites to pay tribute.

Under TIGLATH-PILESER the Babylonians revolted 54
(747); but the Assyrians were indemnified for this loss
by the acquisition of Syria and a part of Israel, which were
invaded and conquered by their king on the invitation of the
king of Judah. SALMANASSAR, 'Shalmaneser' (730), after C
the conquest of Samaria (in 722), destroyed the kingdom
of Israel, which had refused to pay tribute at the instigation of the Egyptians. The Israelites were transported to Assyria, and Assyrians sent to supply their places. The conqueror then advanced as far as Phœnicia, which he subdued, with the exception of the insular city of Tyre, the siege of which he was compelled to raise, after his fleet had been defeated by the Tyrians. The Assyrian empire was now exceedingly flourishing; but again declined under SENNACHERIB[2] (Sanacharibos, about B. C. 713), who subdued

[1] According to Ctesias, this revolt of the governor Arbaces and the priest Belesys of Babylon ended in the destruction of Nineveh, and the complete dissolution of the Assyrian empire. But as it is spoken of in the Bible as continuing to exist after this period, and the names of Assyrian kings are given, by whom the kingdom of Israel was overthrown, some writers have tried to reconcile the discrepancy by supposing a *second* or *new Assyrian empire*. It is, however, certain that such an empire never existed; the supposition being grounded on the error of Ctesias, who places the destruction of Nineveh and the dissolution of the Assyrian empire in the reign of Sardanapalus I. instead of that of Sardanapalus II.

[2] [Between *Shalmaneser* and *Sennacherib* we meet with *Sargon* in Is. xx. 1. Mr. Browne's dates are: *Shalmaneser*, 723; *Sargon*, cir. 718; *Sennacherib*, 713.]

(54) the Babylonians, took their king prisoner, and made his
A own son king of Babel; but in an attempt on Judah was not only compelled to raise the siege of Pelusium (the bow-strings of his soldiers having been gnawed through, it is said, by field-mice), but lost his army under the walls of Jerusalem [by the miraculous interposition of God, of which the tale just mentioned was probably a corrupted or disguised version], and after his return was slain by his two eldest sons. He was succeeded by his third son, ASSAR-HADDON ('Esar-haddon,' about 700), who warded off the ruin of the empire
B for a time. Under the last of the Assyrian kings, Sardanapālus II. (or Sarak), an alliance was formed between Nabopolassar, governor of Babylon, and Cyaxăres, king of Media (whose daughter Nitocris was given in marriage to Nebukadnezar, the son of his ally), for the conquest of Assyria; and the Assyrians were already overthrown in an engagement and siege laid to Nineveh, when the Scythians invaded Media, and kept possession of the country for twenty-eight years. It was not until after their expulsion that Nineveh fell, and was utterly destroyed, probably about the year B. C. 604[1] [606, Browne and Zumpt; Niebuhr, 625].

§ 16. *Religion, Literature, &c. of the Assyrians.*

55 Notwithstanding the fertility of their soil, the Assyrians
C never attained a high state of civilization. Their trade was in the hands of foreigners; nor do we find among them any traces of art or science, beyond the rough tactics of a half-savage warfare. Their *religion* consisted in the worship of the planets, like that of the Babylonians, but under different names, and in the offering up of human

[1] This statement follows exactly the words of Herodotus (I. 103—106). According to the historian, the war of Cyaxares against the Assyrians and the siege of Nineveh were interrupted by an invasion of the Scythians. The conquest of Assyria is mentioned as occurring subsequently to the expulsion of the Scythians, and being the last act of the reign of Cyaxares. Now if his reign began in 633, the expulsion of the Scythians, after twenty-eight years' occupation of the land, could not be earlier than 605 or 604, and the taking of Nineveh could not, therefore, have occurred previously to the year 604. That it did not happen *later* than that year is evident from the prophecy of Jeremiah (xxv. 18), delivered in the first year of Nebuchadnezzar (*i. e.* B. C. 604), which does not mention Assyria among the nations threatened by Nebuchadnezzar, because Nineveh had been already destroyed. [Cf. *Ordo Sæclorum,* § 491.]

victims. Their *political constitution* was similar to that of A
the Babylonian empire.

V. *The Medes.*

SOURCES OF INFORMATION. *Native.*—ZOROASTER's Zend-Avesta. 56
Greek.—Herodotus, i. 95—130. CTESIAS, B. 4—6 (in Diodorus, ii.
24—34). XENOPHON of Athens, in his Κύρου παιδεία, contradicts both
Herodotus and Ctesias. But this work is not generally received as
an authentic history. Grote, ch. 17.

§ 17. *Geography of Media.*

BOUNDARIES.—On the north the Caspian sea, on the 57
east Hyrcania and Parthia (in ancient times the domi- B
nion of the Medes seems also to have comprehended Aria
and Bactria), on the south, Susiana and Persis, and on
the west, Assyria and Armenia.

SOIL.—The *northern* part, afterwards named the *lesser* 58
Media or Atropatēne (now Aderbeidscan [Azerbijan]),
was a cold and barren tract of hilly country, whilst the
southern or *greater Media* was a fertile plain, which produced wine and all sorts of southern fruits. In this district, on the Nisæan plains, were reared the white horses
so famous for their size, sureness of foot, and swiftness.

The Κάσπιαι πύλαι was a narrow mountain pass which formed the
only means of communication with the north-eastern districts.

The capital, *Ecbatana* (Called by Herodotus, τὰ Ἀγβά- C
τανα, now Hamadan) was built without walls on the slope
of a hill, on the summit of which stood the royal castle,
surrounded by seven walls increasing in height as they
approached the centre, and crowned with battlements
painted seven different colors. As the residence of the
Median, and subsequently of the Persian, kings, as well as
on account of its situation on the great commercial road
between Babylon and India, Ecbatana soon became one of
the fairest cities of Asia.

§ 18. *History of the Medes.*

The first mention of the Medes is found in Berosus, 59
who speaks of Babylon being ruled by a dynasty of eight D
Median kings. At a later period they became subject to
the Assyrians, from whose dominion they emancipated

(59) themselves in the reign of Arbăces. For a succession of
A years, each tribe (of which Herodotus, i. 101, enumerates
six) was governed by its own prince or chieftain, until the
election of the judge Deiŏces to be king of the whole
nation. This sovereign (who reigned from 708—655)
built the city of Ecbatana with its castle, established a
body guard, and introduced a rigid court ceremonial.

He was succeeded by his son Phraortes (655—633),
who subdued the Persians and other nations of Asia, but
was slain in battle with the Assyrians. His son Cyaxares
(633—593) was the first who divided the army regularly
B into cavalry soldiers, spearmen, and archers. He subdued
western Asia as far as the river Halys. Having formed
an alliance with the Babylonian king, Nabopolassar, Cyaxăres commenced a war with the Assyrians, and laid siege
to Nineveh; but the Scythian Nomades (who had driven
the Cimmerians out of Europe into Asia Minor) advanced
into Media, defeated Cyaxăres, and remained masters for
twenty-eight years (633—605) of the whole of western
Asia as far as Syria, and even extended their conquests to
Egypt, where they were bribed by the king, Psammetichus,
to withdraw their forces from his country.

C Whilst the Scythians were thus dominant in Asia, that is to say
were driving their herds wherever they found pasture, and plunder-
ing the inhabitants, Cyaxăres was carrying on a war (which lasted
six years) against Alyattes, king of Lydia. The pretence for
this aggression was, that Alyattes had refused to deliver up some
Scythians, who had set before Cyaxăres at a banquet the body of a
murdered Median boy. The war, which was carried on for some
time, with various success, was suddenly terminated by an eclipse of
the sun, which had been foretold by Thales the Ionian (30th Sept.,
610).

60 A number of the Scythians having been treacherously
D murdered at a banquet, where they had drunk to excess,
the remainder returned to their own country, and finding a
new generation, the offspring of their wives and slaves,
attacked the intruders with whips instead of swords, and
completely vanquished them. After the departure of the
Scythians, Cyaxăres renewed the war against the Assyrians, destroyed Nineveh, and reduced Assyria itself to
the condition of a Median province (604), the western
districts of that empire being left to his ally Nabopolassar.
His son and successor, Astyages (593—558), lost Persia,

which revolted under his grandson Cyrus; and taking the (60)
field in person against the rebels, was defeated and made A
prisoner at Pasargădæ.

VARIOUS ACCOUNTS OF THE RELATION WHICH CYRUS BORE TO 61
ASTYAGES.—According to Herodotus (who had heard four different accounts) the king, having had a strange dream respecting a flood, married his daughter Mandane to a Persian named Cambyses, by whom she had Agradatus, afterwards called Cyrus. Astyages has a second dream concerning a vine—Cyrus, being exposed by Harpagus, is rescued by a herdsman and brought up as his son—is chosen king by his playmates—recognized by Astyages—Harpagus made to feast on the limbs of his own son—the Magi declare that the dream of Astyages is already fulfilled—Cyrus sent back to Persia to his own parents—receives a letter from Harpagus, conveyed in the belly of a hare—and in consequence incites the Medes to revolt—the two unequal days [*the day of toil and the day of feasting*;—the latter as a *type* of what *every day* would be, if they conquered the Medes]—Cyrus and the Persians rise against Astyages—Harpagus, being sent to oppose him, goes over to the rebels—Astyages overthrown, and taken prisoner in an engagement at Pasargadæ.

ACCORDING TO CTESIAS, Cyrus was not related to Astyages, but B
was urged to attack him simply by the lust of conquest. He stormed Ecbatana, took the king prisoner and then released him; but afterwards sent him into a desert to die of starvation.

XENOPHON'S story is, that Cyrus, so far from having obtained the crown by violence from Astyages, was not even his immediate successor, Astyages being succeeded by his son Cyaxăres II., at whose death the kingdom passed quietly into the hands of Cyrus.[1]

§ 19. *Religion, Literature, &c. of the Medes.*

The RELIGION of the Medes, even before the time of the 62
Median kings, whose names are given by Herodotus, was C
that of the ancient Bactrians or *Zend*-people, as they were called, who quitted their Nomadic life at the instance of a leader named Dsjemschid, and established themselves in the vicinity of the Oxus. This doctrine, of which Zarathustro or Zoroaster, who flourished long after Dsjemschid, was the author, was contained in the Zend-Avesta, in twenty-one parts, of which one (the Vendidad) has reached us entire, and the others only in fragments and tables of contents.

---

[1] As a confirmation of this account, it may be mentioned that Xenophon relates several acts of Cyaxares II., which cannot all be the offspring of a poetical imagination; and that the prophet Daniel (vi. 1; ix. 1), who lived at the Medo-Persian court, speaks (after Astyages) of a Darius the Mede, who answers to the Cyaxares II. of Xenophon.

63 *The principal doctrines taught in the Zend-Avesta are,* that there
A exists a kingdom of light (*i. e.* a good principle) in which Ormuzd reigns, who is the origin and promoter of all good—and a kingdom of darkness (*i. e.* an evil principle), the ruler of which, Ahriman, is the author of all physical and moral evil. Both these kingdoms are engaged in a perpetual warfare, but Ahriman will one day be overcome, and the kingdom of light alone remain. All things in the world belong either to Ormuzd (pure men, beasts, and plants), or to Ahriman (unclean, *i. e.* sinful men, and impure, *i. e.* poisonous or hurtful, beasts and plants). *Moral precepts.*—Every man should be pure and holy, and promote purity and holiness by every means in his power. On this principle are grounded his laws respecting the improvement of the land by agriculture and pasturage, and of the human race by marriage. His disciples are commanded to adore the sacred fire. The people are divided into four castes—priests, warriors, husbandmen, and mechanics; the king is absolute, and his ordinances irrevocable, but he is required to follow the precepts of Ormuzd, and command only that which is good and just.

64 This code of laws was intrusted to the Magi, to whom alone belonged the right of offering up prayers and sacrifices, and of interpreting the will of Ormuzd. They possessed great influence also over all public and private undertakings, on account of the universal belief in divination, especially by means of the stars. There were no temples.

Constitution.—At first, the different clans lived apart, each under a chief chosen by itself; but from the time of Deïŏces, the nation was governed by a king, to whom they paid divine honors, and whose will was law, but his ordinances, when once promulgated, could not be recalled.

Manufactures.—The Median stuffs (probably of silk), celebrated for the delicacy of their texture and the brightness of the colors, were the favorite dress of the Asiatic Greeks.

VI. *The Persians.*

65 Sources of Information.—1. *Native. The annals of the Persian*
D *empire* (διφθέραι βασιλικαί) were compiled by the scribes, who always attended the king, and preserved in the royal residences a Susa, Babylon, and Ecbatana. From these annals the Greek historians have drawn their facts. The Persian poets (Ferdusi, in the seventh century), and annalists (Mirkhond, in the fourteenth), of the middle ages, contain notices of ancient Persian history, which are utterly at variance with the accounts of the Greek writers.

2. *Scriptural.*—The books of Ezra, Nehemiah, and Esther (the last for a knowledge of Persian court life), and the contemporary Prophets.

3. *Greek.*—Herodotus, who in addition to the oral information

obtained in his travels, seems to have drawn largely from the (65)
Persian archives (*e. g.* in his description of the nations who com- A
posed the army of Xerxes, his account of the speeches delivered by the Persian kings, &c.). *Thucydides* the Athenian (born 371), Ξυγγραφή, in eight books. *Ctesias.* *Xenophon's* 'Ανάβασις, Κύρου παιδεία, and 'Ελληνικά. *Diodorus.* *Arrian's* 'Ιστοριῶν ἀναβάσεως 'Αλεξάνδρου, seven books, compiled from the journals of writers who accompanied Alexander. *Plutarch*, in the life of Artaxerxes I., and biographies of different Grecian Generals. Mod. Heeren, vol. 1. Grote, chs. 32—36. Eliot, ch. 4.

§ 20. *Geography of the Persian Empire.*

NAME.—The term "Persia" signifies either the *pro-* 66
vince, which was bounded by Media and the Persian gulf, B
or the *Persian empire*, which extended from the Mediterranean to the Indus, and from the Pontus Euxinus and the Caspian to the Indian sea, and at one time comprehended Egypt, Thrace, and Macedonia.

The Countries belonging to the Persian Empire were,

I. In Europe; Thrace and Macedonia.

II. In Africa; Egypt and the neighboring country of Libya.

III. In Asia.

A. *On this side the Euphrates (or the western part of* 67
the highland country of Asia). C

1. *Asia-Minor* (Anatolia), see 110, sqq. (p. 65).

2. *Syria* (in the Bible Aram), in the more restricted sense of the term, the country between the Mediterranean and Euphrates (sometimes with, sometimes without Phœnicia and Palestine), in its wider sense, the whole region as far as the Tigris (Assyria often used for Syria and *vice versâ*). FACE OF THE COUNTRY.—Partly mountainous
and partly desert. CITIES.—1. Thapsăcus on the Eu- D
phrates; 2. Tadmor or Palmyra in the Syrian desert, built by Solomon, afterwards the capital of a kingdom (under Odenathus and Zenobia); 3. Chalybon, famous for its excellent wine. The term of ἡ κοίλη Συρία, Cœlē-Syria, was first employed in the time of the Seleucidæ to designate the southern part of Syria, which lies between the chains of Libanon and Anti-Libanon [in Lat., *Libanus* and *Anti-Libanus*]; Damascus was the capital of this district, and at a later period Antiochia and Seleucia, both built by Seleucus Nicātor.

3. *Phœnicia*, see 97 (p. 60).

4. *Palestine*, see 10 (p. 8).

68 B. *Between the Euphrates and Tigris (or the Alpine*
A *country of Armenia and the lower terraces of the Euphrates and Tigris).*

1. *Armenia,* northward from Mesopotamia and Assyria, and westward from the Euphrates to the Caspian sea.

SOIL.—An elevated cold mountain soil, interspersed with warm fertile valleys, from which wine was conveyed by the Euphrates to Babylon, and horses and mules to Phœnicia. There were no cities here in the Persian times, but merely extensive open spots. At a later period we find Artaxata (τὰ 'A.) and Tigrano-certa.

B 2. *Mesopotamia* (a name unknown in the Persian times, and subsequently reckoned sometimes as belonging to Syria, sometimes to Arabia) extended southwards from Armenia to the Euphrates and the Median wall, which form the boundaries on the side of Babylonia.

SOIL.—In the north, mountainous, well-watered, and fertile; in the interior, barren, and inhabited only by Nomadic hordes. Cities, Karkemish [or Carchemish] (Circesium), &c.

C 3. *Babylonia,* always distinguished in the Persian times from the rest of Mesopotamia, the richest and most powerful of the satrapies. See 38, sqq. (p. 32).

69 C. *Countries between the Tigris and the Indus, or the eastern part of the highland district of Asia—Plateau of Iran.*

a. On the western border of the highland country.

1. *Assyria,* see 51, sqq. (p. 37).

2. *Media,* see 57, sqq. (p. 41).

D 3. *Susiana* (Louristan), between Babylonia and Persis on the Persian gulf; the entrance to the highlands; capital city, Susa (τὰ Σοῦσα).

b. On the southern border.

1. *Persis* (Fars *or* Farsistan), between Susiana and Carmania on the Persian gulf.

SOIL.—Various: in the north, lofty and rugged mountains; in the centre, fertile, undulating plains (especially on the rivers Cyrus and Araxes); in the south, the mountains end abruptly in a narrow, sandy, desert shore, of African character, rendered almost uninhabitable in summer by the simoom.

70 On these mountain ridges stood the CITIES of 1. Persepolis, not the residence,[1] but the burial-place of the Per-

[1] [The monuments show that the Persian monarchs must, even at the height of their power, *have resided there* from time to time.—*Neibuhr.*]

sian kings, and the national sanctuary. Since its destruction (70)
by Alexander the Great, there remain considerable ruins A
(with sculpture and inscriptions in arrow-headed characters), consisting partly of the fragments of a royal castle, partly of sepulchres hewn in the rock. 2. In the vicinity, Passargăda or Passargadæ [*Deh Minaur*. Arr.], founded by Cyrus in commemoration of his victory over Astyages at this place (on the river Cyrus), the capital of the whole kingdom, depository of the royal treasures, and burial place of the king.[1]

2. *Carmania* (K e r m a n), on the Persian gulf, between B
Persis and Gedrosia.

3. *Gedrosia*, between Carmania and India, the most barren of all the Persian districts (with its capital, P u r a); on the sea-coast, the Ichthyophăgi.

c. EASTERN BORDER. 71

1. *Arachosia*, a district situated northwards of Gedrosia, on the confines of India (with the city A r a c h ŏ t u s), and making with Gedrosia only one satrapy.

2. *The country of the Paropamisădæ*, between Arachosia and Bactriana.

3. *Indoscythia*, the eastern slope of the highlands, to- C
wards the valley of the Indus.

d. On the NORTHERN BORDER. 72

1. *Bactriana*, between the country of the Paropamisădæ and Sogdiana, from which it was separated by the O x u s (with its capital, B a c t r a, *τὰ Βάκτρα*, now B a l k), the residence of the Zend-people, who obey the law of Zoroaster.

2. *Margiana* belonged in the Persian times to Hyrcania, D
with Alexandria (built by Alexander, then destroyed, and rebuilt by Antiochus Soter, under the name of A n t i o c h i a.)

3. *Hyrcania*, on the Caspian sea (capital, Z e u d r a k a r t a [*Zadracarta : Goorgaun*]).

e. IN THE INTERIOR. 73

1. *Aria* (*Ἀρία* and *Ἀρεία*), an extensive steppe with some fertile spots, a lake named Aria, and two rivers (Arius), and a city (A r i a).

---

[1] Heeren (Ideen, i. 1. 269) and Tychsen (in his supplement to Heeren's Ideen, i. 2, S. 401) suppose Persepolis to be the translation of the name Pasargada.

(73) 2. *Parthia* under the Persian and Macedonian rule be-
A longed to Hyrcania. The capital of the Parthian kingdom, founded by Arsăces, was Hecatompy̆los.

3. *Drangiana*, between Aria, Gedrosia, and Arachosia.

74 D. *The Alpine country between Oxus* [*Jihon* or *Amoo*]
and Iaxartes [*Sir* or *Sihon*], or *Sogdiana*, the northern-
most Persian province, which forms the boundary between
the arable district and the pasture land of the Nomadic
tribes, and consequently was inhabited partly by Sogdianian
settlers, partly by Scythian Nomades. In the southern
B district, which was rendered fertile by numerous canals,
was Maracanda (now Samarcand ?), the royal city of the
Sogdianians. On the Iaxartes, as a defence against the
frequent inroads of the Scythian Nomades, Cyrus built
the fortress of Cyreschata (garrisoned with 18,000 men),
and Alexander the Great, Alexandria ultima.

§ 21. History of the Persians.

75 A. History of the Persians before Cyrus.

C The Persians, on account of the variety of their soil,
were partly Nomades, partly agriculturists. Herodotus
enumerates four Nomadic herdsmen castes, three agricultural, and three warrior castes, who governed the inferior and supplied the higher officers of state. The
most distinguished of these was the tribe of the Pasargadæ, its most illustrious family being that of the
Achæmenĭdæ, from which alone the kings were chosen.
The Persians had been subdued by the Median king
Phraortes (about 640), but retained their own kings, the
first of whom was named Achæmēnes. His descendant,
Cambyses, was the father of Cyrus, by Mandane, daughter
of the Median king, Astyages (see 77, sqq. p. 49).

76 B. History of the Persians from Cyrus to the
D dissolution of the Empire. 558—331.

1. Cyrus (originally Agradatus), 558—529, became
by a stratagem leader of all the Persian tribes, and in
consequence of his victory over Astyages, at Pasargadæ
(see 60, A.), lord of the whole Persian empire, extending
westwards as far as the river Halys, which divided it from
the kingdom of Lydia. The *Lydian king Crœsus*, hoping
to avenge himself on Cyrus for the expulsion of his
brother-in-law, Astyages, and interpreting in his own

favor the ambiguous response of an oracle, crossed the (76)
Halys, ravaged Cappadocia, and after an indecisive en- A
gagement (at Pteria, not far from Sinōpe ?) retreated to his
capital, which, after a second battle, was invested, stormed,
and sacked by Cyrus. After the destruction of the Lydian
empire, Cyrus sent Harpagus to subdue the *Greek cities
on the coast of Asia Minor*, which were ready to pay
tribute provided their constitution were respected. Most
of them received tyrants under the protection of the
Persians, but the inhabitants of Phocæa emigrated to
Corsica (where they had a short time before founded
Alalia), and being expelled thence by the Tyrrhenians and
Carthaginians, retired to Lower Italy.[1] At the same time,
the Teians colonized Abdēra, in Thrace. The Carians B
and Lycians were also subjugated by Harpagus ; so that
the whole of *Asia Minor* or lower Asia belonged to the
Persian empire.

Meanwhile Cyrus himself had subdued *Upper Asia*, 77
taken Babylon after a two years' siege (because that city
had formed an alliance with Crœsus), and put an end, in the
year 538 B. C. to the Babylonian empire, which comprised
also Syria, Palestine, and Phœnicia. The Jews were permitted by the conqueror to return to their own land (compare 20, p. 22.) For an account of the form of government established in the conquered countries see 94, B. (p.
59.)

There are three different accounts of the death of Cyrus, as well as C
of his origin. 1. *According to Herodotus*, he fell in battle with the
Massagĕtæ (northwards of the Iaxartes?), and their queen, Tomyris,
plunged his head into a vessel filled with human blood. 2. *Ctesias*
says that he was slain in a war with the Sacæ ; 3, and *Xenophon*
that he died a natural death.

Before his death he nominated his eldest son Cambyses to be his successor ; the younger, Smerdis, being appointed viceroy (under his brother) of the eastern portion of the empire, which now extended from the Hellespont to the borders of India. He was buried at Pasargadæ [or, Passagardæ].

---

[1] That Massilia (Marseilles) was not originally founded by the Phocæans, who emigrated at that period, but had been already in existence since the year B. C. 600, is clearly shown by Dederich, in the Rhenish Museum.

78 2. Cambȳses, 529—522, added *Egypt* and *Libya* to
A the countries already subdued by his father.

According to the narrative of Herodotus, the cause of his undertaking this expedition was a personal affront received from Amăsis, king of Egypt, whose daughter he had sought in marriage, but who had sent him in her stead the daughter of the former king. Full of indignation at this insult, Cambyses crossed the Arabian desert, under the guidance of a Greek mercenary named Phanes, and entering Egypt, overthrew Psammenitus, the successor of Amasis, at Pelusium, took Memphis, and made prisoners of the king and his family. The captive monarch was treated kindly for a time, but, in consequence of an attempted insurrection, was afterwards put to death by being compelled to drink ox's blood (?). The Libyans and Cyrenians bordering on Egypt, surrendered themselves voluntarily to the conqueror.

79 *Expedition against Ethiopia and Ammonium.*—The plan
B of Cambyses, for extending his conquests in Africa by the subjugation of the Carthaginians, Ammonians, and Ethiopians, was rendered abortive by the refusal of the Phœnicians to lend him a fleet for the attack on Carthage, and by the destruction of an army which he had sent against the Ammonians. This force was overwhelmed by the shifting sands of the desert; whilst another division, which he was leading in person against the Ethiopians, was compelled to return for want of provisions.

C After his return to Memphis, Cambyses, meeting a solemn procession of the worshippers of Apis, caused the priests to be scourged, wounded and overthrew the god, insulted his temples and sacred rites, and committed various other extravagant acts. Having dreamt that his brother Smerdis had usurped his throne, he caused him to be assassinated by Prexaspes, married two of his own sisters, and killed one of them with a kick; slew the son of Prexaspes with an arrow, ordered twelve of the principal Persians to be buried alive, commanded Crœsus, who had ventured to remonstrate with him, to be put to death, and slew his servants for neglecting to execute the sentence.

D *Return to Persis and death.*—The death of Smerdis having been kept a profound secret in Persis, a Magian, of the same name, who also closely resembled him in person, had ascended the throne. On receiving intelligence of this treason, Cambyses hastened his return to Persis, and died at Agbatana, in Syria, in consequence of a wound in the thigh. He left no children.

80 3. Pseudo-Smerdis, 522, who endeavored to render his usurpation popular by dispensing with military service and

remitting the taxes for three years, was discovered in the (80)
seventh month of his reign, (in consequence of having lost A
his ears ?) and, with many other Magi, put to death by a conspiracy of seven of the chief Persians. A festival, termed τὰ μαγοφόνια, was instituted in commemoration of this event. After a discussion among the conspirators respecting the best form of constitution, it was resolved to retain the monarchy, and

4. Darīus I. ascended the throne, by the contrivance, 81
says the legend, of his master of the horse. This king,
who was the son of Hystaspes, of the race of Achæ- B
mĕnes,[1] married two of the daughters of Cyrus and one of the real Smerdis (521—485). To him the kingdom was indebted for a better organization, the whole country being divided into twenty satrapies, each of which had a civil governor termed a *satrap*, and a *commander-in-chief* for military affairs.

These satraps, who were generally relations of the king, were 82
charged with the collection of the revenue, and the promotion of agriculture. They were assisted by royal secretaries (γραμματισταί), who received the commands of the king through messengers, and communicated them to the satraps. These messengers performed the journey very rapidly by means of *stations*, placed at the distance of a day's journey from each other. The civil and military administration of each province, as well as the cultivation of the land, were inspected every year either by the king in person, or by royal commissioners, and always at the head of an army,

Financial administration.—From each of the provinces, except C
Persis, a tribute was raised, which was paid in the precious metals, generally in an uncoined state. After providing for the expenditure of their own establishments (which were modelled on that of the king), the support of the standing army, and the maintenance of the various provincial officers, the balance was forwarded by the satraps to the royal exchequer. Another source of revenue were the pre-

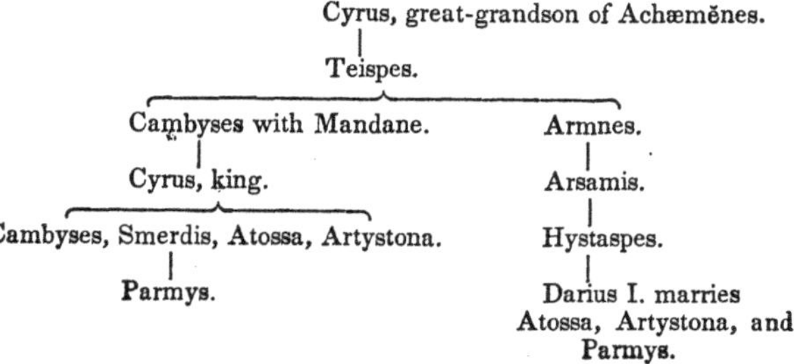

(82) sents made by the courtiers and satraps, consisting of costly objects
A of various descriptions. The inferior officials received their remuneration in kind, and those of a higher rank were rewarded with estates. Personages of the most exalted station, such as the wives and mothers of the kings, had a separate district assigned to them for the supply of their wants.

The conquests of the Persians having reached the ocean southwards, and been arrested on the north by the resistance of the inhabitants of the Steppes, Darius undertook the extension of his empire in a westerly and easterly direction.

Liberation of Samos.—Sylŏsōn of Samos, who had presented a purple mantle to Darius when he was at Memphis, obtained from him in return the power of delivering his native city from a tyrant (the secretary of the murdered Polycrătes, the brother of Syloson).

83 *Reduction of the revolted province of Babylon.*—After a
B siege of twenty months, Babylon was taken (through the cunning, it is said, of Zopȳrus); 3000 of the principal Babylonians were crucified; and Zopyrus, as a reward, was invested with the satrapy of Babylon, of which he received the whole revenue for the term of his life.

Expedition against the Scythians, on account of their former invasion of Media. Darius, at the head of 700,000 men, crossed the Thracian Bosporus into Europe, subdued the Getæ and Thracians, and passed the Ister, leaving behind him the Ionians to guard the bridge which he had
C built over that river. The Scythians retreated before him, laying waste the land as they went, so that Darius was compelled by want of provisions to return without accomplishing his purpose. Meanwhile the Scythians, supported by Miltiades (the Athenian), had been tampering with the Ionians who were left in charge of the bridge, which was only saved from destruction by the strenuous remonstrances of Histiæus of Milētus. On the march back, Megabazus, the Persian general, subdued the Thracian sea-coast, and received from Amyntas, king of Macedonia, earth and water in token of submission. (The Pæonians were transplanted from Thrace into Phrygia.)

D *Expedition to India.*—Darius, having previously dispatched Scylax (of Caryandes) on a voyage of discovery down the Indus, entered that country in person and subdued a part of it.

An expedition into Libya, undertaken by the Persian viceroy of

Egypt, ended in the capture of the city of Barca and the removal of A
its inhabitants to Bactria.

THE WARS WITH GREECE, 500—449. 84

Insurrection of the Ionians, 500—494.—Histiæus, tyrant of Miletus, who had been rewarded with a grant of land in Thrace, for his good service in preserving the bridge, had no sooner laid the foundations of a city in that quarter, than he became an object of suspicion to the king, and was recalled to Susa, his son-in-law Aristagoras being nominated tyrant of Miletus in his room. The failure of an attempt on Naxos having rendered the security of this appointment precarious, Aristagŏras, in conjunction with Histiæus, persuaded the Ionians to rise against the Persian government, and visited Greece in person, for the purpose of soliciting co-operation, but could only obtain a small subsidy of ships
from Athens and Eretria. Sardes, it is true, fell without B
striking a blow, and was utterly destroyed by fire; but the Ionians were overthrown by a Persian land force, and being abandoned by the Greeks, were gradually reduced (after the conquest of their fleet off the island of Lade, opposite Miletus), and the inhabitants of Miletus transplanted to the interior of Asia. Aristagoras was slain in Thrace. The participation of the European Greeks in this insurrection of the Ionians, hastened the commencement of the Persian wars, which were soon afterwards undertaken for the conquest of Greece.

The first expedition against Greece (in 492) was con- 85
ducted by Mardonius, satrap of Asia Minor, who subdued C
the Macedonians; but his fleet, after taking Thasos, having been wrecked off Mount Athos, and his land forces cut to pieces in Thrace, he was compelled to return. Darius, acting under the influence of the exiled Athenian Hippias, and the Spartan king Demarātus, having ineffectually called on the Grecian cities to acknowledge his authority, *a second expedition was undertaken* in 490, under the command of Datis and Artaphernes. These generals sailed to Eubœa with an enormous fleet, took Eretria by treachery, and having crossed the channel into Attica by the advice of Hippias, drew up their forces, which amounted to 100,000 men, on the plain of Marăthon, where they were completely defeated by a little army of 9000 Athenians and 1000 Platæans (29th of September), under the

(85) command of Miltiades, and after an unsuccessful attempt
A on Athens returned to Asia. Darius died in the midst of preparations for a fresh expedition, which had been interrupted by an insurrection of the Egyptians.

5. He was succeeded by XERXES I. (485—465), his son by his second wife, Atossa, one of the daughters of Cyrus. Having reduced Egypt to submission, the new king collected the forces of his immense empire for *a third expedition against Greece.* A land army of 1,700,000 men was assembled at Critala, in Cappadocia, and a fleet of 1207 ships of Phœnicia and Asia Minor, collected in the Ionian harbors of Cyme and Phocæa.

B A canal dug through the isthmus of Mount Athos (?)—the bridges over the Hellespont destroyed by a storm—the sea scourged—two new bridges constructed—Sardes revolts—first review of the troops at Abydos on the Hellespont—the bridges crossed by the army in seven days and seven nights—second review, and numbering of the army at Doriscus in Thrace. Thirlwall, chs. 15, 16. Grote, chs. 38 to 42, inclusive.

86 The land army continued its march through Thrace, Macedonia, and Thessaly, until it reached the pass of Thermopylæ, where Leonidas, king of Sparta, with 300 Spartans and 4900 other Greeks, courageously withstood the millions of Xerxes, but, being betrayed by Ephialtes, was slain, with all his Spartans and 700 Thespians, who had
C voluntarily remained with him. The Persian army then advanced without opposition into Attica, and burnt Athens. Meanwhile their naval commanders, after an indecisive engagement off the promontory of Artemisium with the Greek fleet, under the command of Eurybiades, had dispatched a fleet of 200 sail round Eubœa into the Eurīpus, for the purpose of inclosing the Greeks; but the ships of
D this detachment were scattered by a storm. A second indecisive engagement then took place off Artemisium on the same day as the battle of Thermopylæ; after which the Greek fleet retired to Salamis. Here, by a stratagem of Themistocles, the Greeks were forced into an engagement, which ended in the total defeat of the Persians (23d of September, 480) and their return to Persia. Xerxes hastily recrossed the Hellespont (induced by a fresh stratagem of Themistocles), leaving Mardonius in Thessaly with an army of 300,000 men.

87 *Campaign of Mardonius in* 479.—After fruitless nego-

tiations with the Athenians (through Alexander of Mace- (87)
donia), Mardonius advanced into Attica and took Athens, A
which had been abandoned by the inhabitants; but, on the approach of the Lacedæmonians, he retreated into Bœotia, where he was slain in an engagement at Platææ (25th of September, 479), in which the army of the Persians was utterly routed by the Athenians under Aristīdes, and the Lacedæmonians under Pausanias. The Persian camp fell into the hands of the allies.

On the same day the Persians were defeated at Mycăle, B
in Asia Minor (where they had formed a bulwark of their ships hauled up on the land), by the Spartan king, Leotychīdes, and the Athenian, Xanthippus. Their camp and fleet were utterly destroyed, and thus Ionia was delivered from her oppressors. After this victory the Greeks commenced a war of aggression against the Persians. Pausanias and Aristides subdued the greater part of the island of Cyprus and Byzantium; Cimon expelled the Persians from Thrace, Caria, and Lycia, and defeated both their fleet and army on the river Eurymĕdon, in Pamphylia[1] (469).

Xerxes was murdered by Artabanus, the captain of his C
body-guard, together with his eldest son, Darius. The crown, in consequence, descended to his second son.

6. Artaxerxes I. (μακρόχειρ [Longimănus]—also Artaxerxes), 465—424.

War with the Egyptians and Greeks.—Second revolt of 88
the Egyptians under the Libyan prince Inărus, who beat the Persian army with the aid of the Athenians, but, being soon afterwards conquered by Megabȳzus (son of Zopȳrus), Inărus capitulated, together with the Greeks, who were blockaded by the enemy in Prosopītis, an island of the Nile. One prince alone, Amyrtæus, still maintained his position in the marshes at the mouth of the Nile. The D
war was prosecuted by the Greeks under the command of Cimon, whose fleet and army were victorious (after his death) at *Salamis in Cyprus* (B. C. 449).

First revolt of the satraps.—Artaxerxes having put to 89
death Inărus and the Greek prisoners, for whose safety Megabyzus had pledged his word, the satrap threw off his

[1] The pretended *peace of Cimon* (placed by some in 469, by others 449), but which, if real, Thuc. i. 112, *must* have mentioned, has been fully discussed by *Dahlmann*, *Krüger* [and *Thirlwall*, iii. p. 37]. Grote, ch. 45, shows that a convention was actually made, and accounts on good grounds for the silence of Thucydides.

4

(89) allegiance, conquered the royal forces, and prescribed his
A own terms to the king. From this period there were frequent revolts of the satraps, occasioned by the overweening power of the governors of provinces, who not only united in their own persons the civil and military authority, but were sometimes lords of several satrapies. Their rebellious projects were also favored by the foreign wars. Hence arose new independent kingdoms (Cappadocia, Pontus). The employment at the same time of mercenary troops, chiefly Greeks, hastened the degeneration of the once-warlike Persians into luxurious and
B effeminate cowards. Artaxerxes, who during the whole of his life had been the slave of his mistresses, was succeeded by his only legitimate son,

7. Xerxes II., who was murdered, after a reign of forty-five days, by his illegitimate brother,

8. Sogdianus. This king, after reigning six months, was also assassinated by another illegitimate brother, who ascended the throne under the name of

C 9. Darius II.—Nothus (424—405).[1] During his reign there were repeated revolts of the satraps, in consequence of the king's subserviency to his wife Parysatis. The Egyptians, also, under Amyrtæus, for the third time renounced their allegiance, and retained their independence under kings of their own for a period of sixty-four years.

10. Artaxerxes II. Mnemon (405—362).

90 *War with his brother Cyrus.*—His younger brother, Cyrus, the favorite of his mother, and satrap of the whole of Asia, endeavored to establish his right to the succession, as being the first-born son of his father after he had ascended the throne; and for this purpose assembled in Asia a large body of mercenary troops, under pretence of leading them against the Pisidians, who were still unsub-
D dued. Being supported by the Spartans, to whom he had furnished subsidies of money during the Peloponnesian war, Cyrus advanced without opposition as far as the Euphrates, where Artaxerxes, who had received seasonable information from Tissaphernes, the deputy-governor of Ionia, met his brother with an army of nearly a million soldiers (?). Cyrus fell in the battle of *Cunaxa* in 401;

[1] According to Clinton (Fast. Hell.), Artaxerxes II. probably ascended the throne in Dec. 405.

and the Greek auxiliaries, who had successfully resisted (90)
the enemy, and still numbered 10,000 men, retreated in A
good order under the command of Xenŏphon, and, after encountering indescribable hardships, at last reached Asia Minor in safety.

War with Sparta.—Tissaphernes, who had been re- 91
warded for his fidelity with the province formerly governed by Cyrus, having punished the Ionians for their share in the rebellion, the Spartans prepared to support them. Considerable progress was made in the liberation of the Asiatic Greeks by the Spartan general, Dercyllidas, and particularly by their king, Agesilăus; but their plans were frustrated by the satrap Tithraustes (successor of Tissaphernes, who had been murdered at the instigation of
Parysatis). This crafty politician contrived, by bribing B
the democratical party in Thebes, Corinth, and Argos, to establish in those cities a league (which was afterwards joined by Athens), for the express purpose of resisting the Spartan *Hegemony,* and thus to transfer the war from Asia to Greece (see § 67—3). The Spartan general, Lysander, having fallen in an engagement with the allies at Haliartus, Agesilaus was recalled from Asia to take the command in this *Corinthian war.* In the year 394, the Persians, under the command of Conon, an Athenian refugee, having annihilated the Spartan fleet off Cnidus, in Caria, the Greeks of Asia Minor again gradually lost their independence, and in *the peace of Antalcĭdas* (387), were abandoned, with Cyprus, to the dominion of the Persians.

An attempt to reconquer Egypt miscarried through the disunion C
of the commanders, Iphicrătes and Pharnabazus. A general rebellion of the satraps of Asia was betrayed by one of their body, and crushed. Artaxerxes had nominated as his successor his eldest son, Darius; but this prince having been put to death for conspiring against his father, the king appointed Ochus, who soon poisoned his benefactor, and ascended the Persian throne, under the name of

11. Artaxerxes III. (362—338).

War with the Phœnicians and Egyptians.—The Phœ- 92
nicians having expelled the Persians from their cities and formed an alliance with the Egyptians, Artaxerxes took Sidon (through the treachery of their own king, Tennes), the inhabitants having previously set fire to the city. The rest of Phœnicia submitted voluntarily to his authority. Artaxerxes, then, with the assistance of his Greek auxi-

(92) liaries, overthrew the Egyptians at Pelusium, and com-
A pelled the country, after sixty-four years of independence, again to submit to the authority of Persia. Their king, Nectanebus, fled to Ethiopia.

Artaxerxes, whose cruelty had rendered him universally odious, was poisoned by the Egyptian Bagōas (by whom he was entirely governed), together with all his sons, except the youngest.

12. ARSES (338—336), who was placed on the throne by Bagōas, and murdered by him at the end of two years. A great-grandson of Darius Nothus,

B 13. DARIUS III. CODOMANNUS (336—330), was then made king, and Bagōas, who had intended to put him to death, was compelled himself to drink the poison which he had prepared for his master. The new monarch was unable to avert the ruin of the Persian empire, which, since the Greek wars, had been gradually falling into decay. He was vanquished by Alexander the Great in three battles—on the *Granīcus*, 334; at *Issus*, 333; and at *Guagamēla* in 331; and at last taken prisoner by his own satraps, and murdered by Bessus in 330 (see § 76).

CAUSES OF THE DECLINE OF THE PERSIAN EMPIRE.—1. The exhaustion occasioned by the expenditure of men and money in the expeditions against Europe. 2. The introduction of mercenary troops, and the consequent frequency of wars and degeneracy of the Persians. 3. The insurrections of the satraps, whose power had become enormous since the reign of Artaxerxes I. 4. To corruption of court morals, produced by the influence of women and eunuchs.

§ 22. *Religion, &c. of the Persians.*

93 1. The RELIGION of the Persians was a worship of nature,
C according in all essential particulars with the doctrine of Zoroaster. They adored the sky as the supreme godhead; together with the sun and moon, some of the planets (particularly Venus, under the name of Mitra), the earth, fire, water, the winds, &c. Like the Medes, they offered up their prayers, not in temples, but in the open air. The priestly caste of the Magi, after the conquest of Media, transferred itself, with all its influence, to the Persian court.

94 2. The CONSTITUTION was also borrowed from the Medes, and, like all other eastern governments, was despotic. The "Great King," whose power was circumscribed only by the laws of Zoroaster and a court ceremonial invented by

the Magi, was considered sole proprietor both of the land (94)
and people, and was entitled to receive tribute (called A
"a present" until the reign of Darius Hystaspes) from the conquered provinces. In his palaces (πύλαι) at Susa, Babylon, and Ecbatana, which were occupied alternately according to the season of the year, the king was surrounded not only by officers of the court (the king's 'eyes' and 'ears'), through whom all communications were conveyed to him, but also by a numerous army, consisting chiefly of cavalry. In addition to the power of the Magi, the ladies of the seraglio, and the eunuchs by whom it was guarded, exercised an influence not only over the administration of public affairs, but even over the succession to the throne.

To secure the possession of conquered countries—1. Standing B
armies were left, which were entirely supported by the inhabitants; 2, the people were transplanted into other countries; 3, warlike nations were compelled to become luxurious and effeminate, as in the case of the Lydians, who were thus treated by Cyrus at the instigation of Crœsus. The constitution in the conquered cities was suffered to remain unchanged; their dependence on Persia being recognized in the performance of particular services as vassals—viz., the payment of tributes in gold and silver for the use of the court and the satraps, the support of the standing army, contingents in time of war, and certain presents.

For the division and organization of the empire by C
Darius I., see § 21.

3. Of SCIENCE we find scarcely any trace among the 95
Persians, their whole literature being confined to the writings of Zoroaster, in the Zend language—borrowed from the Medes—and a few works, on the subject of his religion, in the Pehlevi language. On the other hand, the ruins of the royal palace at Persepolis display considerable remains of architecture, exceedingly perfect, as regards the mechanical part, and of sculpture, which seems, however, to have confined itself to works in relievo. Both are disinguished by great simplicity.

VII. The Phœnicians.

SOURCES OF INFORMATION.—*Native.*—In the larger cities were 96
archives, containing annals and notices respecting the most im- D
portant events, from which *Sanchoniathon*, about the year 1250 (?), compiled a Phœnician and Egyptian history in nine books, written in the Phœnician language, which was afterwards translated into Greek by Philo of Byblus. (Of this work only a fragment has been preserved by Eusebius.) *Hebrew*—the Bible, especially the prophet

A EZEKIEL. *Greek*—Menander of Ephesus, and Dius, a Phœnician, compiled a history of Tyre from Tyrian annals (of which fragments are found in Josephus and Syncellus), Herodotus, and Diodorus. [For Sanconiathon, see a Dissertation of Goguet, Origin of Laws, &c., vol. i.] Mod. Grote, ch. 18. Heeren, vol. 2. Eliot, ch. 5.

§ 23. *Geography of Phœnicia.*

97 Phœnicia (so named from the nnmber of palm-trees φοίνικες, on its coasts) consisted of a narrow strip of land on the Syrian coast, between Arădus and Tyre (twenty-five miles in length and four to five in breadth), abounding in harbors and full of lofty mountains; most of which are comprehended under the name of Libanon, and produced timber for ship-building and the construction of houses. A cluster of islands, lying close to the coast, were studded with towns as thickly as the continent itself.

B TOWNS from the north to the south.—1. Arădus, on an island, and opposite to it on the continent. 2. Antaradus. 3. Tripŏlis, consisting of three towns founded by Aradus, Tyre, and Sidon. 4. Sidon, the most ancient of the Phœnician cities, and the mother country of several foreign colonies. 5. Tyre (in the Bible Zor [*Tsôr* or *Tsur*], called by Virgil also Sarra), consisting of the old town built by the Sidonians on the continent, and the new city founded by the inhabitants of the old, with a double port. During the siege of the old town by Nebuchadnezzar, many of the inhabitants took refuge here; in consequence of which new Tyre increased in importance, whilst the old town gradually declined. After its conquest by Alexander, the new town also fell into decay. 6. Ptolemais, or Accon (now S. Jean d'Acre).

§ 24. *Foreign Settlements of the Phœnicians.*

98 The usual motives for founding colonies are—1. To
C establish a secure intercourse with distant and particularly with uncultivated countries. 2. To prevent too rapid an increase of the poor, and thus to anticipate violent revolutions. 3. When, during intestine disturbances, the weaker party emigrates, either voluntarily or by compulsion, and settles itself elsewhere.

GENERAL VIEW OF THE PHŒNICIAN COLONIES.

99 1. *On the Islands of the Mediterranean*, as well on the larger—viz., Cyprus and Crete—as the smaller—viz., the

Sporades and Cyclades—and northwards as far as the Hel- (99)
lespont, especially on Thasus, for the sake of its rich gold- A
mines. There were also still more distant settlements on
the coast of Sicily, especially Panormus and Motye, and
afterwards Lilybæum (at a later period Greek settlements
were formed in these islands); and on Sardinia and the
Balearic islands, which served for a harbor of refuge on
the voyage from Phœnicia to Spain. 2. *On the northern
coast of Africa*—Utica, Carthage, (Καρχηδών) Adru-
metum, the Greater and Lesser Leptis, &c. 3. *Spain*, B
especially its southern coast, was a favorite locality for the
establishment of Phœnician colonies; of which the most
remarkable were Tarsis, or Tartessus, Carteia,
Gadia, or Gades, the pillars of Hercules (two rocks now
occupied by Gibraltar and Ceuta), Malăca, and His-
pălis. There were, however, more than 200 places in
Spain which claimed a Phœnician origin. 4. *On the
western coast of Africa*, 300 cities, as it is pretended (?), all
founded by Tyre; on the Fortunate (*i. e.* Canary) islands
and Madeira. 5. *In the Persian gulf*, on the islands
Tyrus, or Tylus, and Aradus (the Bahrein islands).

In Egypt an entire quarter of Memphis was inhabited by Phœni- C
cian merchants. Whether the colony of Cadmus came to Thebes
from Phœnicia is still doubtful (compare 231, *b.* p. 115).

The date of these settlements can only be fixed generally. 100
Most of them were probably founded in the palmy days of the mother city, Tyre; that is to say, during the period from Hiram to Cyrus (1000—550).

Their relation to the mother country.—The Phœnicians, unlike their descendants the Carthaginians, do not seem to have possessed the art of retaining their colonies in a state of dependence. In consequence of this defect, which was the result of their extended colonial system, and the great distance of the colonies from the mother country, their mutual relation was limited to commercial intercourse, the celebration of feasts in honor of their common gods, and the offering of sacrifices by ambassadors sent for that purpose from the colonies to the mother city.

§ 25. *Fragments of Phœnician History.*

The Phœnicians belonged to that race of Shem which 101
spread itself over the whole of western Asia, and of which, D
long before the existence of historical records, individual
hordes had overrun Syria from the north, or Arabia from

(101) the south, straggling by degrees into Canaan, (*i. e. the*
A *low country* in contradistinction to Aram, *the highlands*,) where they established themselves in settled habitations. From these they were expelled by the invasions of Nomadic tribes, and especially by the immigration of the Israelites, and obliged to take refuge in the neighboring countries and islands, the inhabitants of the sea-shore alone being able to maintain themselves in their fortified cities and the little islands immediately adjoining their line of
B coast. In very ancient times, this little territory was governed by one king, who resided first at Tyre, and subsequently (after Hiram ?) at Sidon, but after the separation of Sidon from Tyre in the time of Salmanassar each city had its own king. The history of the two more powerful states or cities is very imperfect. Of the others we know nothing.

102 From the history of Sidon.—Sidon (named after the first-born son of Canaan) is mentioned as a great city in the days of Joshua, and is celebrated by Homer as the most renowned of all the cities of the earth for its works of art. It was already famous for its navigation and trade in amber, but notorious also for the piracy
C practised by its inhabitants. Among its earliest foreign settlements were Thebes (founded by Cadmus in 1500), and Utica (about 1100). About the year B. C. 700, Sidon surrendered to the Assyrian king, Salmanassar, (see § 15,) and after the dissolution of the Assyrian empire, became subject to Babylon, and was destroyed by Nebuchadnezzar as a punishment for having formed an alliance with Judah. Under the dominion of Persia it seems to have become again prosperous, and took the lead in an insurrection against Artaxerxes III., which ended in its ruin a second time; the city, which had been surrendered to the Persians through the treachery of its own king, Tennes, having been set on fire by the inhabitants themselves. After its restoration, it became subject to Alexander the Great, and received a new king at his hands.

103 From the history of Tyre.—Tyre was founded at an early
D period by Sidon, which it soon surpassed in wealth and power. Even in David's time it seems to have been the chief of the Phœnician cities. Its king Hiram sent workmen and timber to Solomon for the building of the Temple, and entered into a commercial treaty with him for the purpose of sending ships to Ophir (see 17, D. p. 20). King Pygmalion having murdered the husband of his sister Dido, the widow fled to Africa, where she founded the city of Carthage (830 ?). About the year 720, Sidon, old Tyre, and other cities, threw off their allegiance to Tyre, and were supported by Salmanassar, who invested the city, but was compelled to raise the siege at the end of five years. With equal success Tyre maintained its independence against Nebuchadnezzar, who besieged the old town thirteen years without effect.

Under the Persian dominion the Phœnician cities re- 104
tained their own kings, and were merely required to pay A
tribute and furnish contingents of shipping. The kings of Tyre and Sidon are mentioned as commanders-in-chief of the Persian fleet at Salamis. The Phœnician cities submitted without resistance to Alexander the Great, with the exception of Tyre, which refused to receive a Macedonian garrison, and after a siege of seven months was taken and almost entirely demolished. Although it was afterwards rebuilt, the establishment of Alexandria prevented its ever attaining its former prosperity.

§ 26. *Religion, &c. of the Phœnicians.*[1]

The RELIGION of the Phœnicians is a subject of unusual 105
importance, as relating to a people who were the most B
polished of all the Semitic tribes, and exercised the greatest and most lasting influence on the civilization of the ancient world, partly by means of their commercial relations, and partly through the extensive migrations of Phœnician tribes. Their religion, like that of the Shemites in general (comp. 45, p. 35), was that of nature, expressed in the worship of the heavenly bodies, their gods being mythical personifications of her powers visibly represented by the planets. The Sun (Baal), as the C
stronger and more vigorous light, was worshipped as the symbol of the male power of nature, whilst the Moon (Astarte), as the milder and feebler luminary, represented the female. The various effects of the sun's rays were also worshipped as divine beings, both the beneficial (as Jao, the vivifying power of nature), and the injurious, (personified in Typhon,) and his different phases at the various seasons of the year, and different parts of the day, suggested the idea of separate deities (*e. g.* the sun in spring was worshipped as Adonis), and, lastly, the planets (Venus, Mars, and Mercury), as deriving light and power from the sun, were considered emanations of his godhead. They believed, moreover, that the supreme Being acts in D
the world, not immediately, but by the intervention of a Mediator, who is like himself, and regarded as his son, because he is the visible manifestation of his essence.

[1] '*The Phœnicians*' (die Phönizier), by F. C. Movers, 1841, vol. i.

A This manifestation of Baal was the Tyrian Hercules, who in this character is partly a conservative principle (Chon or Saturn), partly a destructive one (Moloch).

106 2. INVENTIONS.—Necessity led the Phœnicians to invent ship-building, the alphabet, arithmetic, and, perhaps, also the coinage of money; but the discovery of their purple dye and the manufacture of glass seem to have been the result of accident.

107 3. COMMERCE.

B *Maritime trade.* To this they were driven by the position of their country, and the barrenness of its soil, as well as by the accumulation of articles of merchandise brought by caravans from the interior of Asia. The chief goals of their maritime enterprise were their own colonies, especially the south of Spain, from which they imported gold, silver, lead, and iron, wine, oil, wax, wool, fruits, and salt fish. From Spain they visited the "tin islands," (Cassiterides), the amber coast(?),[1] and the western coast
C of Africa; but these voyages were kept secret. From the Persian gulf they sailed to India, and from the Arabian, in company with the Israelites, to Ophir. Necho, king of Egypt, is said to have prevailed on them to circumnavigate Africa.

There was never any very considerable commercial intercourse between the Greeks and Phœnicians, partly on account of their mutual jealousy, and partly because the Greeks could obtain most articles of Phœnician produce in their own colonies in Asia Minor; partly also on account of the political relations of the Greeks to the Phœnicians, as subjects of the king of Persia. Frankincense, spices, and Tyrian cloths, seem to have been the only articles imported from Phœnicia by the Greeks.

D LAND-TRAFFIC.—aa. *Southward to Arabia,* from which the Nomadic people of that country, the Edomites and Moabites, brought to Phœnicia the productions of their own land (frankincense, which was obtained, not in Arabia, but from the opposite peninsula of Zuila, gold, and precious stones), as well as those of India and Ethiopia (cinnamon, ivory, and ebony), and *to Egypt,* whence they themselves imported cotton and embroidered stuffs in exchange for wine.

bb. *Westward to Palestine,* whence they imported corn, wine, oil, and balsam; *to Syria* (wine from Chalybon, and wool), and *to Baby-*

[1] *C. O. Müller* (die Etrusker, 287), proves that it does not follow from the early acquaintance of the Phœnicians with *amber,* that they visited the coasts of Prussia, by establishing the fact, that this production was conveyed through Germany, and thence to Greece, by means of the Etruscans in Upper Italy.

lon, on the great commercial road across the Syrian desert by A
Palmyra.

cc. *Northward to Armenia* (importations, horses and mules), and to *the Caucasian countries*, (importations, slaves and copper). The trade of Phœnicia was carried on principally by means of barter.

4. ARTS AND MANUFACTURES. The most celebrated were 108
their dyes. The Tyrian purple (a term used to express not a single color, but generally those produced by the liquor of the sea-muscle, especially the scarlet and violet), was among the chief articles of luxury purchased by the great. *Stuffs* (Sidonian garments are mentioned by Homer)
in Sidon and especially in Tyre. *Glass*, the manufacture B
of which was discovered by the Phœnicians, and for a long time confined to them. *Objects of luxury*, in gold, amber, and ivory.

VII. THE STATES OF ASIA MINOR.

SOURCES OF INFORMATION.—Our notices of the history of these states 109
are meagre and scattered. Most of them are found in Herodotus and Strabo, and (for the history of Troas) in Homer and Virgil. Xanthus of Sardes wrote a history of Lydia, in four books, of which only a fragment is extant. Cramer, Geog. and Hist. description of Asia Minor. Grote, chs. 16, 17.[1]

§ 27. *Geography of Asia Minor.*

NAME.—The peninsula (formed by the Black, Ægean, 110
and Mediterranean seas), which we name Asia Minor, had no general appellation among either the Greeks or Romans; the term "Asia Propria," as well as that of "Asia Minor," which is first found in Orosius (in the fifth century), being employed to indicate only the western half.

SOIL.—The interior of the peninsula forms a westerly 111
continuation of the Armenian highlands, separated from C
the coast on the north by the Taurus, and on the south by the Anti-Taurus, and broken towards the west into chains of lower mountains, such as the Tmolus, Sipўlus, Ida, and Olympus. The highest peak is the Argæus on the upper Halys, the point from which the rivers run in different directions into the Black and Mediterranean seas and the Euphrates.

RIVERS.—*a.* Flowing into the *Pontus Euxīnus*—the 112
Halys (now Kisil-Irmak); *b.* into the *Propontis*—the Granīcus (battle in 334); *c.* into the *Ægean sea*—the

[1] Fellowe's Lycia and Journals of excursions in Asia Minor will well repay a careful perusal.

A Hermus with the golden Pactōlus, the Mæander; *d.* into *the Mediterranean*—the Eurymĕdon (battle in 469), and the Cydnus.

113 Divisions and Cities.

A. *On the northern coast.*—1. Pontus with Trapezūs (now Trebizond), and Amīsus, the residence of Mithridates.

2. Paphlagonia, with Sinōpe on the Euxine (the birthplace of the Cynic Diogenes).

B 3. Bithynia, with the cities of Chalcēdon on the Bosporus, opposite Byzantium, Nicomedia on the Propontis (death of Hannibal), Nicæa in the interior (first council in 325).

114 B. *On the western coast.*—1. Mysia, divided into, *a. Lesser Mysia*, the northeastern part, wi.h the cities of Cyzĭcus, on the isthmus of the promontory known by the same name; Lampsăcus and Abȳdus (*or* os) on the Helles-
C pont (battle in 410). *b. Greater Mysia* comprehending—*aa.* Troas or the Trojan kingdom (from Abȳdus to the promontory of Lectum), the capital of which, Ilium (ἡ Ἴλιος and τὸ Ἴλιον), afterwards called Troja, with its citadel Pergăma, stood on a hill between the rivers Simois and Scamander. (In the place of the Ilium of Homer, which was destroyed, the Mysians and Phrygians founded a second Ilium, and after the death of Alexander a third city of the same name was built nearer the coast.) *bb.* The district of Dardania, or kingdom of Æneas, situated north of Troas, with its city, Dardania (to be distinguished from the Æolian colony of Dardania, where Sulla con-
D cluded a peace with Mithridates). *cc.* The territory of *Pergamum*, at a later period the capital of a distinct kingdom. *dd.* The twelve Æolian cities (reduced to eleven after the secession of Smyrna). See § 57, 1.

115 2. Lydia, originally Mæonia, with Sardes (αἱ Σάρδεις) on the Pactōlus, the capital of the kingdom of Lydia, afterwards the residence of the Persian satraps, and Magnesia on the Sipylus (defeat of Antiochus in 190), with the Ionian towns. See § 57, 2.

3. Caria, with several promontories, among which Mycăle is famous for the defeat of the Persians in 479.

116 C. *On the southern coast.*—1. Lycia (with Patăra and Xanthus, renowned for the oracle of Apollo Patareus).

2. PAMPHYLIA. (116)
3. CILICIA, divided into western or mountainous (τρα- A
χεῖα, aspera), and eastern or champaign (πεδιάς, campestris) Cilicia. In the latter were the cities of Soli (οἱ Σόλοι), afterwards Pompeiopolis (Solœcismus), Tarsus on the Cydnus (birth-place of the Apostle Paul), and Issus on the Issic gulf (Alexander's victory in 333).

D. *Mountain districts of the Taurus.*—1. PISIDIA. 117
2. ISAURIA.

E. *Elevated country of the interior.*—1. PHRY- 118
GIA, at various times a district of considerable extent, B
divided into the Greater Phrygia, to which Lycaonia and Galatia originally belonged, and Lesser Phrygia or Phrygia on the Hellespont. City, Ipsus (battle in 301).

2. GALATIA or GALLOGRÆCIA formerly a part of Phrygia, occupied since the third century by the Gauls, and divided into twelve tetrarchies. City, Gordium (the Gordian knot).

3. LYCAONIA, with the city of Iconium.

4. CAPPADOCIA, which in the time of the Persian empire C
comprehended also Pontus, was divided into two satrapies, the Greater Cappadocia (which afterwards alone retained the name of Cappadocia), and Cappadocia on the Pontus, which at a later period was known simply by the name of Pontus.

F. The *islands*.—See § 52. D. ii. c.

§ 28. *History of the Kingdom of Lydia.*

The original inhabitants of Lydia, the *Mæonians* (pro- 119
bably Pelasgians), were subdued by the *Lydians*, a Carian race, who invaded the country at a later period. The history of the Lydians is divided, according to the three consecutive dynasties of the ATYDÆ, HERACLĪDÆ (1200—700 ?) and MERMNADÆ (700—546), into three periods, the two first of which are entirely fabulous. The fourth D
of the Mermnadæ, CRŒSUS (560—546), subdued the whole of Asia from the Ægean sea to the Halys (with the exception of Lycia and Cilicia according to Herodotus), but having crossed the river and invaded the Persian dominions, he was conquered and deprived of his kingdom in 546.—See § 55.

Conversation between Crœsus and Solon the Athenian, 120
in which the latter pronounces the happiest of men to be one Tellus, an Athenian, on account of his son's and his

120) own death on the field of battle; and next to him the
A brothers Cleŏbis and Biton, on account of their filial affection, and the love borne them by their mother. Crœsus, before his invasion of Persia, consults the oracle at Delphi, and receiving a response which he deems favorable, crosses the Halys, and after an indecisive battle at Pteria, returns to Sardes, which is taken after a siege of fourteen days, and destroyed by Cyrus, who had previously in a second engagement obtained a victory for which he was
B chiefly indebted to his camels. Crœsus, whose life had been saved first through his dumb son's sudden recovery of speech, and afterwards (when placed on a funeral pile with fourteen Lydian youths), through his mention of the name of Solon, sends his fetters to Delphi, and advises Cyrus to secure the subjection of the Lydians, by compelling them to lead a life of enervating luxury.

121 Of the history of the remaining states, we possess nothing beyond a few legends and detached notices. For the war of the Greeks against Troy see 237. 4. (p. 118).

SECOND DIVISION.

AFRICA.

PRELIMINARY REMARKS.

122 Africa, of which only the northern part was known to the
C ancients, was called by the Greeks simply Libya (*Λιβύη*). Of all the quarters of the globe this is the most uniform, both as regards its line of coast, which is scarcely diversified at all by gulfs, isthmuses, or promontories, and its interior, which presents merely an alternation of hill and valley, with a narrow strip of sea-coast. Its insular form separates it from the other quarters of the old world; whilst the division of the whole region by the equator into two portions, differing but little in climate, and lying nearly under the same parallels of north and south latitude, produces a sameness of phenomena in the animal and vegetable kingdoms. Communication with other parts of the world is rendered difficult by the want of harbors and roadsteads, and by the small number and insignificant extent of its rivers, in most of which navigation is impeded

by cataracts. Of its two most important streams the one (122)
communicates merely with an inland sea, whilst the mouth A
of the other has only been discovered within a few years. At the same time, the vast extent of its trackless deserts, and the small number of navigable rivers, present almost insuperable obstacles to communication with the interior. In consequence of these disadvantages, Africa, with the exception of Egypt, has made very little progress in civilization, as compared with the other quarters of the globe.

A. Geographical View of Africa.

§ 29. *Its Boundaries.*

On the west the Atlantic ocean, or outer sea; on the 123
north the inner, Libyan, or North sea (Mediterranean); B
on the east Asia (of which the boundaries on that side were exceedingly vague, see 5), the Arabian gulf, and the Erythræan sea; and on the south (as the Greeks supposed) the ocean which united the Erythræan sea to the Atlantic.

§ 30. *The Soil of Africa.*

Mountains.—The *Atlas*, the summit of which, enve- 124
loped in eternal clouds, was regarded by the ancients as C
the supporter or pillar of heaven—the *Libyan* and *Arabian* chains, which inclosed the valley of the Nile—the *mountains of the Moon*—*Sandy deserts*—the sea of sand between the Libyan mountains, the Mediterranean, the Atlas, the Ocean, and Nigritia (now called Sahāra), the most extensive desert in the world. In its eastern portion, which is the smaller of the two, there are a few scattered springs of water and oases; but the western division consists entirely of a mass of shifting sand, which is every year extending its limits.

§ 31. *The Waters of Africa.*

Seas.—On the north the *Mediterranean*, or *North sea* 125
(a part of which was called the Egyptian sea); on the D
east the *South*, or *Red sea*, with the Arabian gulf; on the south the *Ethiopian* sea; on the west the *outer*, or *Atlantic* ocean, connected with the Mediterranean by the Straits of Hercules (fretum Herculeum or Gaditanum).

(125) Lakes.—Tritonis and Mœris.

A Rivers.—Flowing into the Mediterranean—the Nile (see 133, p. 73); into the interior of Africa—the Niger, or Nigris (Niger, Dschòliba [*or*, Joliba], Quorra); the embouchure of which, in the Bight of Benin, was discovered by Richard and John Lander in the year 1830.

§ 32. *Division of Africa.*

126 The continent of Libya is divided by Herodotus, ac-
B cording to its physical character, into three regions. 1. *Habitable* Libya, on the shores of the Mediterranean (from Egypt to the promontory of Solœis), inhabited partly by an indigenous race (Libyans and Ethiopians), partly by Greek and Phœnician settlers. 2. The Libya *of wild beasts*, or region of Mount Atlas; and, 3. *Desert or sandy* Libya. The interior of Africa he designates by a general name, as the country of the *Ethiopians*.

The Islands.—Insulæ Purpurariæ (the northern Canary islands); Insulæ Fortunatæ (the southern Canary islands); Hesperidum Insulæ (Cape de Verd islands?).

B. The States of Africa.

I. The Ethiopians.

127 Sources of Information.—Herodotus (B. III.), Fragments of
C Eratosthenes B. C. 250), and Agatharchides (about 120), Diodōrus (B. III.), and Strabo. Ethiopians—Modern accounts:—**Heeren, vol. 4, pp. 285 et 199. Russell, Nubia and Abyssinia, comprehending their civil history, antiquities, arts, religion, literature, and natural history. Edin. Cab. Cyc. For travels, v. Bruce's Abyssinia Burckhardt's Nubia, Hoskin's Ethiopia.**

§ 33. *Geography of Ethiopia.*

128 Name and Extent.—The name of Ethiopians (in the
D Bible Cushites) was originally given by the Greeks to all people of a black or swarthy complexion (*αἴθω* and *ὤψ*), but afterwards the term was applied exclusively to the inhabitants of the country lying southwards of Egypt on the Upper Nile (now Habesch and Nubia).

Soil.—In the south a table-land, traversed in all directions by chains of mountains; further northwards, towards the middle of the Nile's course, an undulating country, interspersed with rocks, over which the river forms cataracts. (128)

RIVERS.—The Astăpus and Astabŏrus, the union of A
which forms the Nile. The inundation, which renders the valley of the Nile so fertile, is occasioned by the Astăpus, but repeated attempts to discover its sources have been hitherto unsuccessful. Probably (as suggested by Ptolemy) it rises in the Mountains of the Moon. The Astabŏras flows out of a lake (Tzana) in Abyssinia.

INHABITANTS.—The Ethiopians of the state of Meroe; the Troglodȳtæ and Ichthyophăgi, both on the shores of the Arabian gulf; the Macrobii, on the Indian ocean (?), the Egyptian Warrior-caste, which emigrated in the reign of Psammetichus, and, settling in the southern part of Meroe, founded a city dependent on that kingdom.

§ 34. *The State of Meroe.*

1. GEOGRAPHY.—On the large *island*, or rather penin- 129
sula of *Meroe*, formed by the Astăpus and Astabŏrus, B
stood the *city of Meroe*, the exact position of which cannot now be ascertained. *Inhabitants*.—Tribes of hunters, herdsmen, and agriculturists, united by their common worship of Ammon and commercial relations.

2. HISTORY.—Meroe, which seems to have been the 130
founder of the most ancient Egyptian states, and, in conjunction with Thebes, to have planted the little colony of Ammonium in the Libyan desert, had attained considerable importance as early as the year B. C. 1000, through the celebrity of the oracle of Jupiter Ammon; and its situation, as a central point for the caravan trade, which was protected by the priests, and carried on by the surrounding Nomadic tribes. Its most flourishing period was between C
the years 800 and 700, when Sabăcus subdued Egypt. From this country the worship of Ammon and Osīris, the colossal style of architecture, and probably the hieroglyphic characters, found their way into Egypt. The power of the priests was destroyed in the third century before Christ by king Ergamenes, who put them to death with the aid of the warrior-caste, and changed the theocracy into a monarchy. As early as Nero's time the kingdom had ceased to exist, and the country was a desert.

131 3. Religion, &c.

A *a. Religion.*—They worshipped the sun as the god Amun, or Jupiter Ammon, in connection with his oracle. The great similarity between the Ethiopian and Egyptian systems of worship is testified by their architecture. Both seem (like the religion of Brahma) to have been founded on astrology.

b. Constitution.—The sovereignty of a priestly caste, who chose a king from their own body. The power of this monarch was restricted within very narrow limits by a variety of sacred laws and a rigid priestly ceremonial.

B *c. Art.*—In Ethiopia, as well as in Nubia, we find numerous ruins of magnificent temples, decorated with sculpture and inscriptions; the most ancient of which are either entirely (like those of India) or partially hewn out of the solid rock; whilst the more recent, the Nubian for instance, are distinct monumental buildings, often with alleys of sphinxes and colossal statues. The relievos on the walls represent historical scenes, partly of a religious character (such as solemn supplications, with offerings and distributions of alms), partly political and warlike; the former, as the more important, being placed in the sanctuary, the latter on the outside. There is a remarkable similarity between Egyptian and Ethiopian works of art.

C *d.* Trade.—Meroe was the centre of the great traffic between *India*, *Arabia*, *Ethiopia*, *Egypt*, *Libya*, and *Carthage*.

This traffic was carried on by Arabians from India by sea to Arabia Felix, or Yemen, across the Arabian gulf to the eastern coast of Africa; and thence by caravans of the Nomadic tribes on that side (Troglodytæ and Icthyophagi),[1] through Meroe, which was also the emporium for the products of central Africa. Thence the merchants conveyed their goods through Thebes down the Nile into Egypt, and by caravans, which touched at Ammonium, and thence continued their progress through the country of the Garamantes, by the greater Leptis, to Carthage: thus visiting the three principal establishments of the priestly caste (Meroe, Thebes, and Ammonium); to which they were attracted partly by the prospect of greater security, and partly by the concourse of persons who flocked to the national sanctuaries.

II. The Egyptians.

132 Sources of Information.—Manĕtho, high priest of Heliopolis, compiled (about the year B. C. 260), by command of King Ptolemy II., a work, entitled *Αἰγυπτιακά* (in three books), from copies of the

---

[1] Tribes mentioned by the ancients as living in caves, but of whom we know little or nothing.

hieroglyphical inscriptions preserved in the temples. Fragments of (132)
his work are found in Josephus, Eusebius, and Syncellus. A

Hebrew.—Principally the books of Moses.

Greek.—Herodotus, in Book II.[1] His information was derived from the priests at Memphis; whose accounts, collected from pictorial records, admitting a variety of interpretation, and from the ill-understood hieroglyphical inscriptions on the public monuments, were of necessity imperfect and unsatisfactory. Diodorus, in B. i., partly from the older Greek writers, partly from oral and written communications made to him by the priests at Thebes.—STRABO. Heeren's 5th volume is devoted to Egypt. Grote has a valuable chapter, 20—Eliot, ch. 3. For a full view, v. Wilkinson's Manners and Customs of the Ancient Egyptians. The great work (when completed) will be Bunsen's "Egypt's Place in the World's History." Hawks's "Egypt" contains an interesting view of the connection of Egyptian and Biblical history.

§ 35. *Geography of Egypt.*

NAME AND BOUNDARIES.—Egypt, in the Bible Mizraim, 133
and thence still called Mesr by the Arabians, described by B
the ancient geographers as belonging either partially or entirely to Asia, was bounded on the north by the Mediterranean, on the east by Arabia and the Arabian gulf, on the south by Ethiopia (so that the islands of the Nile, Elephantine, and perhaps Philæ, belonged to Egypt), and on the west (without any definite frontier) by Libya. In ancient times, however, the name of Egypt was generally understood as belonging only to the valley of the Nile; nor was it until the time of the Ptolemies that its boundaries were extended eastward and westward.

SOIL AND CLIMATE.—The valley of the Nile is inclosed 134
by the *Libyan* and *Arabian* mountain chains; both of C
which are pierced with a number of valleys crossing them obliquely, and leading on the one side to the Red sea, and on the other to the greater and smaller oases of the Libyan desert. The western chain forms a monotonous barren dam, by which the valley of the Nile is protected from the sand-waves of the Libyan desert; the eastern, which fills the whole country as far as the Red sea, has in Upper Egypt three distinct formations—viz., in the south (from Philæ to Elephantine) rose-colored granite (the material of which the obelisks, entire temples, and colossal statues, were formed), in the centre (from Syēne to Esne) sand-

[1] v. Kenrick's valuable edition of this book.

(134) stone of various colors (material of the temples), gradually
A merging in the limestone formation of the mountains in the north, or in Lower and Middle Egypt (material of the pyramids). Of this region the only fertile portion is the valley (from two to three miles in breadth), which is inclosed between these chains, and watered by the Nile. This valley becomes wider as it approaches the north, and, with the Delta (excepting the sandy and marshy ground on the coast), forms a tract of rich alluvial soil, which is manured every year by the overflowings of the Nile. Rain is known only in the Delta. The Chamsin. Ophthalmia —plague.

135 WATERS.

B *Seas.*—The North sea (also the Egyptian sea); the Arabian gulf (in the Bible the sea of weeds), the north-western part of which, at a later period, was called the gulf of Heroopolis.

Lakes.—1. The lake Mœris (formerly forty, now only twenty-five leagues in circumference, and extending even within the last 200 years two leagues further southwards than at present), was fed by a canal from the Nile; to which alone the remark of Herodotus applies, that the lake Mœris was excavated by human hands. In the middle are two pyramids. 2. The lake Mareōtis, connected with the Nile and the Mediterranean.

C *Rivers.*—The Nile (ὁ Νεῖλος), called by Homer Αἴγυπτος (in the Bible Jeor, Nahal Mizraim, and Sihor), is formed by the confluence of the Astăpus and Astabŏras (see § 33); and, after descending in two cataracts[1] (a greater in Ethiopia and a lesser on the confines of Egypt), passes Syēne in Egypt, and twenty miles above its mouth divides itself into two principal channels, which inclose the Delta (probably in ancient times a gulf), and flow into the Mediterranean. In the time of Herodotus the Nile had seven mouths; of which the easternmost was at Pelusium, and
D the most western at Canopus. Of these only two—at Damietta and Rosetta—are now navigable. The constant rains which prevail in Upper Ethiopia during the wet season (from May to September) cause the Nile to rise annually (from June[1] to September), and, when the water is at its full height, to inundate the whole of the valley. In

[1] From end of June to end of September at the rate of about four inches a day, and falls at the same rate.

order to distribute this body of water (on which the fer- (135)
tility of the land entirely depends) equally over the A
country, and, at the same time, to facilitate inland communication, artificial lakes (Mœris) and canals were formed, the latter being furnished with sluices and hydraulic machines. The most extended of these canals (that of Joseph) was forty miles in length, and ran parallel to the Nile. Most of them were in the Delta. Two ancient canals communicate with the Red sea.

Natural Productions.—The crocodile, esteemed sacred, 136
and after death embalmed and inclosed in a coffin by some B
Egyptian tribes, and eaten by others—the hippopotamus, or river horse—the ichneumon—the ibis, which devours winged serpents—the trochĭlus. Corn (even in the days of Abraham and Joseph, Egypt was a place of refuge for the neighboring nations in seasons of scarcity, and subsequently became the granary of Rome and Constantinople)—cotton—the papȳrus shrub—the lotus (from which they made bread). There is a deficiency of wood and metals, but an abundance of stone.

Division into—1. Upper Egypt, or Thebais (from C
Syēne to Chemmis; 2. Central Egypt, or Heptanŏmis (as far as the division of the Nile); 3. Lower Egypt, or the Delta, and the lands on each side of it belonging to Egypt. Each of these districts was subdivided into a number of Nomes (see § 37).

Cities.—All standing on elevated ground. Herodotus, 137
ii. 177, calculates their number in the time of Amāsis at 20,000.

A. In *Upper Egypt.*—1. Philæ, on a little island above 138
the smaller cataract, visited by pilgrims on account of the D
grave of Osiris (only 2700 feet in circumference), the richest and best preserved group of ruins in all Egypt, principally remains of temples. 2. Elephantine, also on an island, with some architectural remains, demolished in 1818. 3. Syene, on the Nile (now Assuan), opposite Elephantine, the frontier town on the side of Ethiopia; where Juvenal died in exile. 4. Thebes, or Diospŏlis, on both sides of the Nile, capital of the Thebais, and the most ancient residence of the Egyptian kings. This city, called by Homer the hundred-gated (ἑκατόμπυλοι, Il. ix. 383), was richer than any other city of the earth in

138) architectural specimens, the ruins of which now fill the
A whole of a valley two miles in breadth.

The most remarkable monuments of antiquity in Thebes are—

a. ABOVE GROUND. *aa.* On *the western side*, the race-course, used for foot-, horse-, and chariot-races—innumerable ruins of ancient temples and palaces in Medinet-Abou—a crowd of colossal fragments—two colossal figures of Memnon, represented in a sitting posture, one of which is reported to have sent forth a musical sound at sunrise—gigantic remains of the sepulchre of Osymandias, with an enormous granite rock, which looks at a distance like a
B statue of Osymandias. *bb.* On *the eastern side:* the two Obelisks, in front of the temple of Luxor, one of which has been set up at Paris (since 1834)—the torsos of lions, with rams' heads, being the remains of an avenue of 600 colossal sphinxes in the village of Karnak—and the temple of Karnak, with a mass of dilapidated walls, broken columns, mutilated colossal statues, and overthrown obelisks;[1] and between them enormous halls (one of them according to Wilkinson, 170 feet by 329), the roof-plates of which are supported by a forest of columns. In the largest building there are 134 of these pillars, 12 of which are 66 feet high and 12 feet in diameter: in front of them are the loftiest gates and porticos in the world. The whole is covered with sculpture, and the interior decorated with paintings in fresco, the colors of which are still exceedingly brilliant.

C *b.* UNDERGROUND.—Opposite Thebes the Libyan range of mountains, to the extent of two leagues, and to the height of 300 feet, is pierced with innumerable Catacombs, which, in number, dimensions, and beauty, excel all the grottos of a similar description in Egypt, India, and Italy. In ancient times they served as places of burial for the dead; and at the commencement of the middle ages were occupied by the anchorites of the Thebais. They are now inhabited by Troglodytæ. (See § 37—4, *c.*)

A separate cleft of this Libyan chain contains the sepulchres of the kings of the Thebais, sunk into the rock (one of them is 341 feet deep), with long galleries, which gradually descend to a greater depth), interrupted by innumerable halls, corridors, and chambers, in which stood the sarcophagi which contained the mummies; the whole decorated with the most exquisite sculpture and
D painting. In one of them there was found a sarcophagus of the most beautiful alabaster, only two inches thick, and consequently transparent. It was covered within and without with 2000 hieroglyphic figures, varying in height from one to six inches, with others of the natural size. In the catacombs, near the uncoffined mummies, rolls of papyrus have been found, covered with hieroglyphics and Egyptian characters.

139 B. *In central Egypt* the monuments of antiquity were destroyed at a much earlier period, and more completely,

---

[1] Here once stood the largest monolith in the world, ninety-one feet in length.

than in Upper Egypt. The catacombs, however, still (139)
point out where the demolished cities once stood. The A
most important of these was Memphis, on the western side of the Nile, near to which stood the pyramids. See § 37—4, *e*.

C. *In Lower Egypt*—*a. In the Delta*. 1. Naucrătis, 140
where the Greek merchants established themselves, by permission of Amāsis. 2. Sais, from the time of Psammetichus, the royal residence. 3. Busīris, with the chief temple of Isis. *b. Westward of the Delta*—Canōpus, called by Herodotus Canobas (now Aboukir), on the western bank of the Nile at its mouth, and at a later period Alexandria, founded by Alexander the Great, with its four ports; before the largest of which lay the island Pharos, with its famous lighthouse. *c. Eastward of the Delta*— B
1. On (*Ἡλιούπολις*), with the celebrated temple of the sun. 2. Pelusium (perhaps the Avaris of the Hyksos), on the eastern side of the Nile, near its mouth, surrounded by swamps (hence Pelusium from *πήλυς*), and considered the key of Egypt on the side of Asia. It was besieged without success by Sennacherib. Defeat of Psammenitus, and subsequently of Nectanebus.

D. On the *shores of the Arabian gulf* arose, at a later 141
period, the cities of Heroopolis (on the canal of Ptolemy), Arsinoe, Myoshormos, and Berenīce.

§ 36. History of the Egyptians.

1. *Fabulous period to the reign of Sesostris, or*

(about 1500 years B. C.)

The most ancient states (Nomes) of Egypt, that is to 142
say those of Upper Egypt, were settlements founded by C
the priestly caste of Meroe (comp. § 34), whose rallying point was the temple with its privileged priesthood. The more powerful states soon began to exercise authority over the weaker. The most ancient and mightiest was *Thebes*. During the period anterior to Sesostris, the throne, according to Manĕtho, was occupied by eighteen dynasties.

The first king is generally supposed to have been *Menes*, to whom the building of Memphis (a Theban colony) is ascribed. According to Herodotus he was followed by 330 sovereigns (answering to the eighteen dynasties of Manetho), of whom the priests knew only the names, no memorials of their deeds being extant. Among the

(142) successors of Menes, Diodorus mentions Busiris as the builder of
A Thebes and Osimandyas, on account of his sumptuous monument with its library. As early as the year 2000, Abraham found a kingdom established in Upper Egypt. The Pharaoh at whose court Joseph lived, resided probably at Memphis.

143 The most important event of the first period was the invasion of the H y k s o s[1] (name of their leaders ?), a Nomadic tribe from Arabia, who fortified Avaris, *Αὔαρις*: (Pelusium ?) and spread themselves over lower and central Egypt, ravaging the country, and destroying every vestige of civilization. This accounts for the blank in the early history of
B Egypt. These invaders destroyed the power of the priesthood, but were themselves, after a lapse of many centuries(?) expelled by the Egyptians under the command of Thutmossis, king of Thebes. The religion, which had been suppressed by the Hyksos, was then re-established, and the great temple erected (under the auspices of Amenophis II., called by the Greeks Memnon, whose statue used to send forth musical sounds at sunrise).

According to Herodotus, the last of these kings was Mœris, to whom the historian ascribes the excavation of the lake Mœris and the building of its two pyramids. Exodus of the Israelites, establishment of colonies by Cecrops in Attica, and Danaus in Argos.

2. From Sesostris to the Autocracy of Psammetichus.

(B. C. 1500—656.)

144 The mighty conquests ascribed by tradition (following,
C perhaps, some Egyptian heroic poem) to S e s o s t r i s (on the monuments, Ramases: in Diodorus, Sesoosis) are limited by Herodotus to an expedition on the Arabian gulf for the subjugation of the nations on the Erythræan sea, and a campaign (through Syria and Asia Minor, where the historian himself saw memorials of his exploits) against the Scythians and Thracians; but with the increase of geographical knowledge, the range of his reputation became so extended, that Diodorus speaks of all the nations of Asia, to the very shores of the Pacific, as being his tributaries. Herodotus also mentions him as the only Egyptian king, who ever ruled over Ethiopia. He divided the country into thirty-six Nomes (comp. § 37. 2),

[1] [Supposed to be the Israelites by *Josephus* and many modern writers. See Browne's *Ordo Sæclorum*, p. 578.]

each under a governor (Nomarch), distributed in equal (144)
proportions the land capable of cultivation, allowed A
architects from the conquered nations to build temples to the principal divinities in all the cities of Egypt, erected obelisks, intersected Lower Egypt with canals, and built a wall 1500 stadia in length from Pelusium to Heliopolis, to protect the country from invasion on the side of Syria and Arabia. Under his successors, who probably resided at Memphis, the territory acquired by conquest in Asia and Europe was soon lost, the authority of the later Pharaohs extending only over Nubia (as far as Meroë), and over Libya.

RHAMPSINĬTUS (about 1200), story of the robbery of his treasury. 145
CHEOPS closed the temples and prohibited the offering of sacrifices, B
that he might exact the full amount of compulsory labor from the people, for the building of the pyramids (compare § 37). His brother acted in a similar manner.

CHEPHREN continued the building of the pyramids.

MYCERĪNUS reopened the temples and distinguished himself by his justice. During the period from Mycerīnus to Sabaco (about 300 years), only two kings are mentioned by Herodotus; viz. *Asychis* and the blind *Anysis,* who was driven by Sabaco into the marshes. In the Bible, mention is made of an Eyptian king named *Sisak*, who, in the year 970, made war on Rehoboam, and stormed and plundered Jerusalem.

About 760, the Ethiopians under Sabaco invaded 146
the country, and governed Upper Egypt[1] during a period C
of fifty years, the dynasties of Bubastis and Tanis still maintaining their authority in Lower Egypt. Soon after the departure of the Ethiopians, the reins of government were seized by SETHOS or Sethon, a priest of Phtha at Memphis. The warrior-caste having been treated with great contempt by this sovereign and robbed of their estates, refused to meet the Assyrian king Sennacherib, who had advanced as far as Pelusium. Nothwithstanding this backwardness on the part of the army, the invader was compelled to raise the siege (by an army of field-mice,
according to the legend). After Sethos, the sovereign D
authority was restored to the warrior-caste, and Egypt divided into twelve states, the DODECARCHY (671—656),

[1] According to Manetho, Egypt was governed during these fifty years by three Ethiopian kings, of whom the Bible recognizes only the two last.

(146) which were destroyed by a civil war after continuing
A fifteen years. One of these twelve princes, PSAMMETI-
CHUS, who reigned at Sais, and opened Lower Egypt to
the Greeks and Phœnicians, was banished to the marshes
by the other eleven, on account of his fulfilment of a prophecy (by pouring a libation from a brazen helmet); but
with the aid of Greek and Carian mercenary troops, he
succeeded in expelling the eleven princes and re-establishing the monarchy.

3. FROM THE REIGN OF PSAMMETICHUS TO THE PERSIAN CONQUEST.

(B. C. 656—617.)

147 1. PSAMMETICHUS (656—617) having offended the
B warrior-caste by granting estates to his mercenaries, the
greater part of the former body (240,000) migrated from
Egypt to Ethiopia (comp. § 33). From this period the
flower of the Egyptian army, and even the royal body-
guard, was composed of Greek mercenaries. At the head
of these troops the Egyptian kings made several attempts
on different parts of Asia, especially Syria and Palestine.
C These expeditions were commenced by Psammetichus, but
his progress was stopped by the obstinate resistance of the
Syrian frontier city of Azŏtus (Ashdod), which was taken
after a blockade of twenty-nine years, and by the advance
of the Scythians into Syria. Memphis still continued to
be the capital, but the usual residence of the sovereign
was Sais. Psammetichus having caused Egyptian youths
to be instructed in the Greek language by Greeks who
had settled in Europe, from them sprang the caste of the
interpreters. His son
148 2. NEKOS (also Necho, 617—601) continued the favor
D shown by his father to the foreign mercenaries, at whose
suggestion probably he began a canal intended to unite the
Red and Mediterranean seas, by communicating with the
latter by the Pelusian branch of the Nile; but this project
was never completed. He also carried out the plans of
conquest set on foot by his father, stormed Jerusalem, and
advanced as far as the Euphrates, where he was overthrown by Nebuchadnezzar, near Circesium (in 604), and
deprived of all his conquests in Syria and Palestine. The
circumnavigation of Africa by the Phœnicians (see § 26).

3. Of his son Psammis (601—595), Herodotus records 149
only one short expedition against Ethiopia, of which the A
issue, as it was related to him by the priests, was unfavorable. His son

4. Apries (in the Bible, Hophra, 595—570) revived 150
Necho's plans, and marching with a land force against Sidon, carried that city, and at the same time overthrew the Tyrians in a naval engagement. But the anti-national system of government of the Asiatic dynasties was cut short in consequence of an accusation brought against Apries, that he had undertaken an expedition against Cyrēne, for the purpose of wearing out the remnant of the
warrior-caste. The army, after sustaining a defeat from B
the Cyrenians, rose against the king, and called to the throne Amăsis, who had been sent to put down the insurrection. Apries, with his Greek mercenaries, was vanquished near Momemphis, taken prisoner, and subsequently strangled.

5. Amasis (570—526), who at the commencement of 151
his reign was lightly esteemed, as belonging neither to the priestly nor warrior-caste, endeavored to propitiate the priesthood by building and embellishing several temples and other edifices, and established his authority on a firm basis by the conquest of the island of Cyprus, as well as by alliances with Cyrene, Polycrătes the tyrant of Samos, and the Greeks, to whom he granted Naucratis for
a settlement. His reign was the most flourishing period C
of Egyptian history. He died whilst Cambyses, whom he had insulted, was advancing against him with an army (comp. § 21). His son

6. Psammenitus (525) was vanquished by Cambyses, 152
near Pelusium, Memphis taken, and Egypt reduced to the condition of a Persian province (see § 21).

4. Egypt under Persian rule.

(B. C. 525—332.)

The insults offered by Cambyses to the priesthood (still 153
an influential caste) and to the Egyptian religion, had D
excited a spirit of national hatred, which on *three* occasions led the Egyptians to throw off their allegiance to Persia, a proceeding which was rendered comparatively easy by the distance of the seat of government from their

(153) country. The first revolt was in the reign of Darius I.,
A and suppressed by Xerxes I. The second under Artaxerxes I., by whom they were compelled to return to their allegiance, with the exception of Amyrtæus, who maintained himself in the marshes at the mouth of the Nile. Third revolt under Darius Nothus. Amyrtæus assumed the sovereign authority, and the Egyptians remained sixty-four years (414—350) an independent nation, subject to their own kings, in spite of the attempts of Artaxerxes II. to reduce them. This object was at length accomplished by Artaxerxes III., the last Egyptian king, Nectanebus, being compelled to take refuge in Ethiopia. Egypt a Macedonian province in 332.

§ 37. *Religion, &c. of the Egyptians.*

154 1. Religion.[1]—*Objects of worship* different in different
B Nomes. 1. *Beasts*, either individual animals (*e. g.* Apis at Memphis, the he-goat at Mendes, &c.), or species, such as the crocodile, hawk, cat, dog, ichneumon, hippopotamus, serpent, &c., which in one Nome were accounted sacred, and the killing of them forbidden on pain of death, whilst in the others they were killed and eaten by the people. Individual animals among the sacred beasts were attended by guardians specially appointed to that duty, and after death were embalmed and placed in consecrated coffins amidst the lamentations of their worshippers. 2. *Inanimate objects*—the Nile, Osiris (the sun ?) and Isis (the
C moon ?) 3. *Local divinities*—Ammon (Zeus) at Thebes, Phtha (Vulcan) at Memphis. On (the sun) at Heliopolis, Neith (the goddess of fate) at Sais. The religion of the priests was essentially different from that of the people, embracing more exalted conceptions of the divinity, and furnishing other views of the life after death. Feasts, sacrifices, and religious practices, varied according to the locality and the deity worshipped; but the belief in the immortality of the soul seems to have been universal, its existence however being supposed to depend on the preservation of the corpse, the soul passing, after the decay of its habitation, into the body of some beast. Without embalming and the performance of funeral rites

[1] [Mr. Brown thinks, that the hated *Typhon* is "the mythological impersonation of Israel." *Ordo Sæclorum*, p. 606.]

the deceased could not be admitted into the realms of the (154)
blessed. His right to these honors was ascertained by A
an inquest consisting of forty members, by whom his former life and conversation were strictly investigated. There were oracles at the principal temples (of Ammon at Thebes, Latona at Buto, &c.).

2. CONSTITUTION.

DIVISION OF THE COUNTRY INTO NOMES.—The number 155
and names of these Nomes are variously reported. They seem originally to have been independent priestly states, each settlement of the priestly caste forming a Nome of its own, until the gradual amalgamation of the whole into *one* kingdom.

DIVISION OF THE PEOPLE INTO SEVEN CASTES (γένεα): 156
a. The *priestly caste*, which emigrated from Meroe, and B
spread over the whole of Egypt, had its principal stations at the chief temples, viz. at Thebes, Memphis, Heliopolis, and Sais. The priesthood and high priesthood were hereditary, the sons being compelled to remain in the same temple, and attached to the service of the same god as their fathers. Scientific knowledge being exclusively in the hands of the priesthood, all judges, physicians, interpreters of signs, and officers of state, were taken from that body, which was honored as the ruling caste. Their revenue consisted of the income derived from the farming out of the tax-free estates belonging to the temples. They were rigid monogamists, and observed the strictest cleanliness in their persons and dress.

b. The *warrior-caste*, hereditary, settled generally in C
Lower Egypt (on account of the frequent wars with Asia), and paid by grants of land. No cavalry, only war chariots and infantry. The emigration in the reign of Psammetichus did not extend to the whole caste.

c. *Caste of the herdsmen*—not Nomades, but tribes settled in the mountains and swampy lands of the Delta, where there was no arable land, but abundance of excellent pasture.

d. *Caste of the swineherds*, an indigenous, unclean, D
and despised tribe, prohibited from mingling with the other castes, and even excluded from the temples. Indispensable, however, on account of the use made of swine in sacrifices and for treading in the corn.

(156) e. *Caste of tradesmen* (κάπηλοι), comprising artists,
A merchants, shopkeepers, and artificers. Each of these employments was probably hereditary.

f. *Caste of boatmen on the Nile,* of especial importance during the inundations.

g. The *caste of the interpreters,* which formed the medium of communication with foreigners, was established by Psammetichus (see 147, c. p. 80).

Diodorus, who comprehends all the herdsmen in one caste, mentions also a caste of agriculturists, who perhaps were the farmers of estates belonging to the kings, priests, and warriors. Whether these formed a portion of the "tradesmen caste" described by Herodotus, is not very clear.

157 The kings or Pharaohs were probably chosen from the
B warrior-caste by the priests. Their power was circumscribed by the influence (arising principally from their control over the oracles) of the priests by whom they were surrounded, and from whom they were obliged to choose all the officers of state. They resided at Thebes, afterwards at Memphis, and lastly at Sais. Their revenues were derived from their estates, the gold mines of Nubia, the fisheries, and the tribute paid by conquered nations. The kings commanded the army in time of war; but judicial questions were investigated by courts of which the members were all priests (the supreme court of justice consisted of thirty members). The proceedings were conducted in writing, and sentence given according to written laws.

158 3. Sciences, which were exclusively in the hands of
C the priests.

a. *Astronomy,* applied either to the settlement of the seasons, the arrangement of the calendar, and the agricultural operations dependent on it, or to astrology, which in Egypt, more than elsewhere, exercised an influence over the public and private life of the people.

b. *Geometry,* a science introduced by the necessity of re-measuring the fields after every inundation of the Nile. The erection of their magnificent buildings also required mathematical knowledge.

c. *Medicine.* Each part of the body and every disease had its own physician, who could not depart from the rules laid down in the six books of medical instructions.

d. *Jurisprudence*. Legislation being connected with religion, their priests were also judges. (158) A

e. *Historical learning* consisted in an acquaintance with the public monuments and sacred writings.

4. ART. The monuments of Egypt exhibit proofs of great mechanical skill, and gigantic solidity of construction; but the dependence of art on religion and politics, and the rigid prohibition of any alteration in the established forms, although no impediment to the production of grand and magnificent effects, rendered it impossible for Egyptian artists to rise to the repsesentation of the beautiful. 159

ARCHITECTURE and SCULPTURE were closely connected among the Egyptians, the latter being employed partly in the production of hieroglyphics, partly of figures representing, with the aid of painting, religious ceremonies, the affairs of private life, and historical events. 160 B

THE OBJECTS OF ART were: 161

a. The *Temples*, the walls, pillars, and roofs of which were covered with figures representing for the most part objects of religious worship, and with hieroglyphical inscriptions.

b. The *Palaces*, with representations of historical events.

c. The *Catacombs* or sepulchres in the Libyan mountains, especially near Thebes, with a great number of chambers, side-closets, halls, staircases, corridors, and perpendicular wells, adorned with hieroglyphics and painted sculpture, representing every possible circumstance and employment of life. C

d. The *Obelisks* were pillars, square at the base, and terminating in a point. They were generally formed out of a single block of granite from 50 to 180 feet in height, with a base of from 5 to 25 feet; hewn and polished in the mountains of Upper Egypt, and transported by the Nile and its canals to the place of their destination (principally Thebes and Heliopolis), where they were set up at the entrances of the temples and palaces and covered with hieroglyphical inscriptions.

Several of these obelisks were brought in the time of the Roman emperors to Rome and Constantinople, where they were erected, but afterwards thrown down. Sixtus V., and some of the other popes, caused several of them to be replaced at Rome. The Luxor obelisk is in the Place de la Concorde at Paris. Cleopatra's needle in Waterloo Place, London. D

(161) e. The *Pyramids* (also Piramyds), only found in central
A Egypt, are quadrilateral buildings (the horizontal length of the sides being gradually diminished as the building ascends), often ending at top in a flat superficies. They were built of various heights (the largest, that of Cheops, originally 480, now 460 ft. 9 in. high, was completed in thirty years by 100,000 laborers; a canal from the Nile was brought to the spot, and on the island formed by its waters was the burial place of the king), of limestone cased externally with granite or marble, with few inscriptions. On the
B inside were chambers and passages. There are still about forty pyramids near Memphis, standing in five groups, the most celebrated of which is the group of Ghizeh. Their four sides are turned towards the four cardinal points of the compass. Various conjectures have been hazarded respecting the use for which they were intended. Probably they were either themselves sepulchres, or erected over burial places to mark the entrance.

f. *Colossal Sphinxes.*—Couchant lions, with human heads, representing (perhaps) distinguished men and sovereigns.
C Thus the double rows of 200, and even 600, of such sphinxes at Luxor and Carnac might represent the long line of Theban kings.

g. The *Labyrinth*, erected (according to Herodotus, II. 148) by the Dodecarchs (146, D.), in the vicinity of the lake Mœris, consisted of twelve covered courts, with 1500 chambers above ground; and the same number, it is said, of subterranean rooms, with the coffins of the twelve founders and the sacred crocodiles. The ruins which have been discovered do not enable us to trace the ground plan of this extraordinary work.

162 THE ART OF WRITING.[1]—Of the Egyptian inscriptions
D only a few detached sentences and single letters have been hitherto deciphered.

163 According to the opinion of Champollion, they had three distinct modes of writing. 1. The *hieroglyphic*, or sacred text, which was

[1] The interpretation of the Egyptian hieroglyphics is the great critical discovery of our age. Champollion's claims are allowed to be better than Young's. The great work is Champ Précis du Système Hierog. des Anc. Egypt. Its application to Scripture history is given by Greppo, whose essay was translated by Isaac Stuart, and commented by Prof. S. Lieber's article in the Am. Enc. contains an admirable general view, and the whole subject of the Egyptians is thoroughly discussed in Bunsen's Egypt, now in course of publication. Good summary in Hawks's Egypt.

employed on their public monuments, and comprehended three sorts (163)
of characters, viz.—*a*. Figures, representing the actual object; *b*. A
Symbolic signs, indicating abstract conceptions, through the medium of analogous natural objects; *c*. A sort of alphabet, consisting of 100 letters (phonetic hieroglyphics), which represented different sounds by the figures of those objects of which the name began with the sound in question in the ancient Egyptian tongue, which is interpreted through the Coptic; a language no longer spoken, but preserved in their literature. 2. The *Hieratic*, or characters employed by the priesthood; an abbreviation of the hieroglyphic form. 3. The *demotic*, or popular character, consisting almost entirely of phonetic signs, and employed in the common intercourse of life.

5. The want of timber for ship-building compelled the 164
Egyptians for a long time to confine themselves to inland B
and river traffic. Its position, midway between Africa and Asia, in the vicinity of the gold of Nubia and Abyssinia, and the facilities for transport afforded by the Nile, the only navigable stream of northern Africa, rendered Egypt, especially Upper Egypt, the centre of an extensive commerce by means of caravans. (Compare § 34.) (Corn and cloth were transported into Arabia and Syria by caravans of the Nomadic tribes.) The commercial relations of Egypt were extended by Psammetichus, who opened the ports to the Phœnicians and Greeks, and by Amasis, who
permitted the Greeks to form a settlement at Naucratis C
(the Hellenion). The increase in the consumption of Egyptian produce, consequent on these arrangements, gave a fresh stimulus to agricultual and manufacturing industry.

6. Our knowledge of Egyptian HANDICRAFTS, as well 165
as the employment of their every day life, is obtained from pictures, especially those found in the tombs. They possessed the art of weaving garments, tapestry, and carpets; of dying in various colors; of producing a great variety of elegant articles in metal, and of manufacturing earthen vessels for domestic use, and for the reception of the sacred mummies.

III. The Carthaginians (Carchedonii).

Sources of Information.—The works of their *native* writers 166
(alluded to by Sallust, Bell. Jug. 17) are all lost; nor is any mention D
made of Carthaginian history by the Greek and Roman historians, except in so far as it coincides with that of their respective countries. We possess, it is true, accurate accounts of the wars of Carthage with Syracuse and Rome in the works of Polybius, Diodorus, Livy, and Appian; but none of them treat the history of that country as a primary subject. The only notices which we have respecting the

early history of Carthage are found in Justin (from Theopompus). The constitution is also described by Aristotle in his Politics. Heeren, vol. 4. Arnold's Rome, chs. 22, 39.

§ 38. *Geography of the kingdom of Carthage.*

167 The kingdom of Carthage, at its most flourishing period,
A was bounded on the north by the Mediterranean, on the east by the state of Cyrene (the boundary stone was called aræ Philænorum), on the south by the lake Tritonis, and on the west by Numidia; the frontier on that side being very vague and unsettled, on account of the Nomadic tribes by whom the country was inhabited.

168 DIVISION AND CITIES.
B *a.* The *northern* part, or *Zeugitana*, with the cities of—1. CARTHAGO, on a peninsula, in the bight of a gulf formed by two promontories (the Hermæan and that of Apollo), was protected by the citadel of Byrsa, and on the land side by a triple wall (thirty yards high and thirty feet in breadth), with two ports; the outer for trading vessels, and the inner (in the city itself) for ships of war. 2. Utĭca, a more ancient city than Carthage, and, after its fall, the capital of the province of Africa (Cato Uticensis).

C *b.* The *southern* part, or *Byzacium* (from the people of the Byzantines); of which the fertile region, bordering on the lesser Syrtes and the lake Tritonis, is sometimes further distinguished by the name of *Emporia* (on account of the number of commercial towns). Cities:—1. Adrumētum; 2. The Lesser Leptis; 3. Thapsus (Cæsar's victory over Juba, B. C. 46).

c. The *eastern* part, or the *regio Syrtica*, between the two Syrtes; a flat district, inhabited by Nomadic tribes, with a few colonies, such as the greater Leptis and others.

§ 39. *Foreign Possessions and Settlements of the Carthaginians.*

169 A. FOREIGN PROVINCES, governed by lieutenants (στρα-
D τηγοί).

1. *Sardinia*, the most ancient foreign possession of the Carthaginians. This province, which was ceded to the Romans at the end of the first Punic war, was important, partly on account of its natural productions (grain, metals?), partly as the key of the Mediterranean, and the emporium of their commerce with western Europe. Capital city, Calăris (Cagliari), built by the Carthaginians.

2. *Corsica* (Cyrnos), of which only a part belonged to (169)
Carthage; ceded to the Romans at the same time as A
Sardinia.

3. *Sicily ;* never entirely in their occupation. The Carthaginians took possession of the settlements founded by the Phœnicians (see § 24); and through the attempts which they made to extend their conquests, were involved for 200 years in quarrels with the Syracusans.

4. *The smaller western islands of the Mediterranean.*—The Balearic isles (inhabited by Troglodytes, who served in war as slingers), with Ebŭsus (Ivica), and Melīte (Malta).

5. In *Spain*, the Carthaginians at first had only a few B
detached settlements on the southern and western coasts. It was not until after the loss of Sicily and Sardinia that they endeavored to make themselves masters of the whole country.

B. Foreign Settlements on the *northern* and *western coasts* of *Africa*, and the *western coast* of *Spain*. These, as well as the provinces, were kept in a state of complete dependence on the mother country, which was enabled to retain her supremacy by her position almost in the centre of her colonies, and her large military and naval force. Establishment of the worship of Melkarth in the colonies.

§ 40. History of the Carthaginians.

1. *From the Building of Carthage to the Wars with the Greeks in Sicily.*

(B. C. 880—480.)

The Phœnicians having already founded Utica, and per- 170
haps other cities on the northern coast of Africa, partly on C
account of the fertility of the soil, partly for the sake of commerce with the native Nomadic tribes, and intercourse by sea with Spain, the establishment of Carthage was effected about the year 878 (?) by a party who had emigrated from Tyre in consequence of a civil war.

Legend of its establishment.—Dido, a Tyrian princess (according to 171
Virgil and some historians a contemporary of Æneas), fled from her D
brother Pygmalion, the murderer of her husband, and having purchased as much land in the district of Utica as she could cover with an ox's hide (βύρσα?) cut it into strips sufficient to inclose a space of half a mile (?), and built the fortress of Byrsa, which was gradually surrounded by a city.

This state, which from its foundation was independent 172

(172) (except in religious matters), soon extended itself. 1. By
A the subjugation of the neighboring tribes, who were kept in a state of dependence by the establishment of Carthaginian colonists. The amalgamation of these with the natives produced the nation of the Libyo-Phœnicians. 2. By foreign conquests and settlements.—Voyages of discovery undertaken by Hanno and Himilko beyond the pillars of Hercules.—Abortive attempt of Cambyses against Carthage (see § 21).—First commercial treaty with Rome.

2. From the beginning of the Wars with the Greeks in Sicily to the Wars with the Romans.

(B. C. 480—264.)

173 First War in Sicily (480).—The first step towards
B the downfall of the Carthaginian state, which had risen so rapidly into importance, was the unsuccessful attempt of the Carthaginians entirely to subdue Sicily, where they had already taken possession of the colonies formerly established by the Phœnicians. Although they chose for this purpose the very moment when Greece, occupied with the Persian war, was straining every nerve to preserve her own independence, their immense army (300,000 strong ?) was nevertheless utterly defeated near Himĕra (480) by Gelon, tyrant of Syracuse, on the same day as the battle of
C Salamis. In this engagement Hamilcar, their commander-in-chief, was slain, and their fleet burnt, nor were terms of peace granted to them until they had consented to pay a considerable tribute.

174 Second War in Sicily (410—339).—After an intermission of hostilities for seventy years, the war with the Greeks was renewed, in consequence of the assistance given to the people of Egesta against Selinus by the Carthaginians, who destroyed Selinus, Himera, Agrigentum, and Gela, and concluded a peace with Syracuse, by which
D they became masters of the western part of Sicily. The Syracusans, however, under their tyrant Dionysius I., and afterwards under the Corinthian Timoleon, made repeated attempts to expel the Carthaginians from Sicily ; and succeeded so far as considerably to circumscribe their possessions on the island.

175 Third War in Sicily (317—375).—The tyrant Agathŏcles had hardly ascended the throne of Syracuse, when he endeavored to subdue the rest of Sicily, and, in

consequence of this attempt, became involved in a war (175)
with the Carthaginians, who afforded an asylum to the A
people whom he had expelled, wrested his conquests from Agathŏcles, and laid siege to Syracuse itself. The tyrant then effected a landing in Africa, stormed most of the Carthaginian cities, ravaged their territory, and even threatened the capital itself, which at that time was in a state of commotion on account of Bomilcar's attempt to make himself absolute. Meanwhile, the Syracusans overthrew and B
annihilated the besieging army of the Carthaginians. No sooner, however, had Agathŏcles quitted Africa for the purpose of crushing the opposition of the Sicilians, than the army which he had left to carry on the siege of Carthage began to melt away, and Agathŏcles himself was compelled to concede to the Carthaginians the peaceable occupation of their former possessions in Sicily, on condition of their becoming tributary to Syracuse. After the C
death of Agathŏcles (280), the victorious Carthaginians advanced to the walls of Syracuse, which was weakened by intestine struggles; but were twice beaten back as far as Lilybæum by Pyrrhus, who had been invited over from Italy, and was already on the eve of embarking for Africa, when several cities, disgusted at his extreme severity, again joined the Carthaginians, and overthrew him in a naval engagement on his return from Sicily in the year 275.

3. From the beginning of the Wars with the Romans to the destruction of Carthage.

(B.C. 264—146.)

First War with Rome, 264—241. See § 119. 176
War with the Mercenaries (240—237).—The first D
war with Rome not only ended in the loss of Sicily, but so completely exhausted the exchequer of the Carthaginian government, as to leave no funds for discharging the arrears of pay due to the mercenary soldiers. A mutiny of these hired troops being immediately succeeded by an insurrection of the Carthaginian provincial towns, which availed themselves of this opportunity to throw off the oppressive and often bloody yoke of the Carthaginians, Hanno was appointed commander-in-chief; but, being unsuccessful in his endeavors to crush the insurrection, was

(176) superseded by Hamilcar Barcas, who, by great exertions,
A brought the war to a satisfactory termination. During this war the Romans deprived the Carthaginians of Sardinia, and soon afterwards of Corsica. Proceedings having been commenced by his enemies against Hamilcar, on the ground of his having occasioned the mercenaries' war, and the consequent loss of Sardinia, by promises made to the soldiers on his own responsibility, the accused appealed to the people, and having succeeded in gaining over their leaders, the process fell to the ground. Thus there arose an *aristocratical party* under *Hanno*, and a *democratical*, headed by *Hamilcar*,—the first step towards the destruction of the constitution.

177 In order to indemnify his country for the loss of her
B best provinces, Sicily and Sardinia (the guilt of which was laid to his charge), and for the purpose of recruiting the finances, Hamilcar, without consulting either the people or senate, undertook the conquest of Spain. Hamilcar was succeeded in the command by his son-in-law Hasdrubal; and during the nine years of its occupation by the former general, and eight by the latter, the whole of southern Spain was brought into subjection to the Carthaginians, partly by negotiation and partly by war; until a period was put to their conquests in that quarter by the conclusion of a treaty, by which Hasdrubal pledged himself not to cross the Iberus, and to respect the
C Saguntines as allies of Rome. Hasdrubal, who, besides other cities, had founded Carthago Nova (Carthagena), which he had destined to be the seat of Carthaginian government in Spain, fell by the hand of an assassin in the year 221, and was succeeded in the command by Hannibal, the son of Hamilcar, then in his twenty-sixth year; whose appointment was sanctioned both by the senate (where the party of Barcas was predominant) and the people. The capture of Saguntum by Hannibal occasioned the

178 SECOND WAR WITH ROME, 218—201. See § 122. The
D tyrannical authority of the 100 (104 ?) (an order of judges, according to Livy) was restricted by the new dictator to one year, and several improvements were adopted in the administration of the finances. He also, in conjunction with Antiochus the Great, king of Syria, formed a plan for commencing a fresh war with Rome; but his project being

betrayed by his opponents, Hannibal fled for safety to the (178)
court of Antiochus, and subsequently to Prusias of Bithy- A
nia, where he withdrew himself from the persecutions of
the Romans by taking poison. Masinissa, king of Numidia, and an ally of the Romans, deprived the Carthaginians (who by the terms of the last peace were not permitted to undertake any war without the consent of the
Romans) of two of their provinces (Emporia and Tyska),
and, at the same time, secured a party at Carthage by
means of bribery. This party being expelled from the
city, a war broke out, and Masinissa, after defeating the
Carthaginian army, shut them up in their own camp, and
compelled them to surrender. This war having been un- B
dertaken without the permission of the Romans, afforded
them a welcome pretext for the renewal of hostilities.

THIRD WAR WITH ROME (150—146), AND RUIN OF 179
CARTHAGE.

A colony of Roman settlers having been established in Africa twenty-four years after the destruction of Carthage, a new city was founded by Augustus (on the southern extremity of the peninsula), which rose into considerable importance as a Roman colony, and at a later period became the capital of the kingdom of the Vandals. Afterwards it was the residence of a Byzantine governor, and in the year 706 was destroyed by the Arabs. Modern Tunis was built from its ruins.

§ 41. *Religion, &c. of the Carthaginians.*

1. The RELIGION of the Carthaginians was, generally 180
speaking, the same as that of their mother country, Tyre C
—adoration of the heavenly bodies, in conjunction with a
dark and blood-thirsty superstition.

The chief divinities of the Carthaginians (as of the Phœnicians) D
were—1. Baal (sometimes a general term for God, Lord, &c., sometimes signifying the sun), who, as the guardian and patron of the nation, was addressed by the distinctive title of (2) Melkarth, or Melkar. His peculiar residence being supposed to be at Tyre, embassies were sent yearly to that city with offerings of tithes and first-fruits from Carthage, and all the other provinces. 3. In conjunction with Baal, they worshipped a female deity named Astarte [Ashtaroth], probably the moon. Both of these divinities were beneficent, and opposed to (4) the malignant Moloch; who could only be propitiated in seasons of calamity by human sacrifices, especially of children. Another beneficent deity was (5) Esmûn, the Asclepios or Æsculapius of the Greeks and Romans. In addition to these gods of the mother country, the Carthaginians, at a later period,

(180) adopted in some instances the worship of foreign nations; for ex-
A ample, that of the Sicilian goddesses, Ceres and Proserpine. The adoration of Dido, and of the brothers Philæni, was peculiar to Carthage. The Carthaginians, like the Phœnicians, had no hereditary priesthood.

181 2. Constitution.—The government was in the hands of two *suffetes*, or kings, chosen by the people from the principal families, and holding their office probably for life, and of the *senate*, which was composed of representatives from all the guilds of the citizens, and divided into the greater (γερουσία) and lesser council (ἡ σύγκλητος), both of which are often comprehended under the common
B term of συνέδριον. In this assembly the kings presided, and proposed the questions for discussion. In the event of a difference of opinion between the kings and the senate, the decision was referred to an assembly of the people. As a general rule, the kings possessed the supreme, civil, but not the military authority. Apprehensions being entertained that individual families—the warlike race of Mago, for instance—might become too powerful, a second power was created, by the selection from the council of a body termed the college of 100, who were invested with the right of calling the commanders
C and other public officers to account. They were also required to take measures for upholding the existing constitution, and probably acted as judges in cases of high treason. This college must be distinguished from the court of 104, appointed for the decision of civil causes. The inhabitants of the Carthaginian dominions were mere vassals, without any of the rights of citizens in the capital. Their magistrates were partly chosen by themselves, partly sent from Carthage. The colonies of Phœnician origin, however, seem to have been allies rather than subjects of Carthage.

182 *Sources of revenue.*—1. The tributes of the African and foreign
D provinces, partly in specie (from the commercial cities), partly in produce (from the low countries); 2. Duties levied in the ports of the capital and the colonies; 3. The profits of the mines, especially in Spain; 4. Piracy.

183 *Warlike resources.*—Their *naval force*, before their wars with the Romans, consisted generally of 150—200 triremes. In the sea-fight with Regulus 350 quinqueremes were engaged, each manned with 120 armed marines and 3000 slaves to work the oars. 2. The *land force* consisted, for the most part, of mercenary troops, composed of

soldiers from different countries of the west. The Carthaginians (183)
themselves formed what was termed the sacred band. The van con- A
sisted of Balearic slingers, and the centre of the African vassals; the chief strength of that division being the light Numidian cavalry. They had also elephants.

3. In Carthaginian LITERATURE we hear of historical works, 184
and a long treatise on agriculture (in twenty-eight books), by Mago, which was translated into Latin by command of the Roman senate. Fragments of this work are still extant. The Romans, when they stormed Carthage, found several libraries, which they presented to the Numidian kings. Architecture, mechanics, hydraulics, &c., attained a high state of perfection at Carthage.

The LANGUAGE of the Carthaginians (the Punic, of B
which we find remains in the Pœnulus of Plautus) was a dialect of the Phœnician.

4. TRADE. 185

a. *Commerce by sea.*—The Carthaginians, in their anxiety to monopolize the commerce of the west, opened only the ports of their capital to the vessels of foreign nations, excluding them as much as possible from those of their colonies, in order to avoid a competition which they considered prejudicial to their interests. The intercourse with foreign countries was facilitated by friendly connections between individuals belonging to different countries, and by leagues with the states themselves. Their navigation C
extended to almost all the coasts and islands of the Mediterranean, especially on the western side; to Sicily, southern Italy, Malta (a principal emporium of Carthaginian manufactures, chiefly stuffs), Corsica, Æthalia D
or Elba, the Balearic islands (*Majorca* and *Minorca*), and especially Spain; probably also to Gaul. Beyond the pillars of Hercules, they shared with the Phœnicians the trade carried on between Gades and the tin[1] and amber islands; and on the western coast of Africa their traffic not

[1] The tin islands are generally supposed to have been Britannia and Hibernia. Heeren, however, imagines that they were the Sorlingin or Scilly islands, on the western coast of England; and Vogel (Encyclop. von Ersch. und Gruber) states their existence to have been simply an invention of the Phœnicians, devised for the purpose of satisfying inquirers, and withdrawing their attention from the real tin countries, Hispania and Britannia.

A only extended to their colonies, but was carried on secretly on the rich gold coast of Guinea.

186 Chief Articles of Commerce.—a. *Exports*—Black slaves, precious stones, gold, manufactured goods. b. *Imports*—Oil and wine from India, honey and wax from Corsica, iron from Elba, fruit and mules from the Balearic islands, metals from Spain.

b. Internal traffic, by means of caravans of the Nomadic tribes, between the two Syrtes, from the district of Emporia, *eastwards*, to Ammonium and Egypt (compare § 34, 3, *d*), and *southwards* to the country of the Garamantes (now Fezzan); and still further into the interior of Africa; whence they brought black slaves, salt from the salt lakes, pits, and mines in the desert, dates from Biledulgerid, gold, and precious stones.

THIRD DIVISION.

EUROPE.

PRELIMINARY REMARKS.

187 Of all the quarters of the globe, Europe, although the
B smallest, is unquestionably the most powerful, civilized, populous in proportion to its extent, and remote from extremes of every description. Its position, for the most part in the temperate zone, renders it inferior to Asia and America as regards the number, variety, and beauty of its productions, but the happy union of a continental and maritime climate, and the consequent facilities afforded to agriculture in almost every part, dispose the inhabitants to habits of regular industry, without encouraging them to lead what, in strictness of speech, may be termed a
C Nomadic life. Commercial intercourse is also greatly facilitated by the extent of coast, the islands lying within an easy distance of the continent, the numerous inland seas, and the equal distribution of navigable rivers. In addition to these advantages, it excels all the other quarters of the globe in the productions of the intellect; for it cannot be denied, that if the seeds of political knowledge, the sciences, manufactures, and trade were to a great extent first sown in the east, they attained their full per-

fection on European soil, at first in the south, and subse- (187)
quently in the north. Through this intellectual excellence, A
added to their immense superiority in the art of war, the Europeans have been enabled not merely to bid defiance to foreign invaders, but to extend their dominion, and the civilization which has always followed in its train, to all the other quarters of the globe, by means of their discoveries, conquests, colonies, and commerce.

The great chain of the Alps, which is united by its western and B
eastern branches with the Pyrenees and the Hæmus, divides our quarter of the world into two unequal parts, each distinguished from the other by the difference of productions indigenous to a northern or southern climate, as well as by a variety in the character and appearance of the inhabitants. These mountains also in ancient times formed a barrier between the civilized and uncivilized world. There exists another distinction between eastern and western Europe, the former being remarkable for its monotonous character and the extent of its plains, the latter for the greater variety and form of its mountain districts.

A. Geographical view of Europe.

§ 42. *The boundaries of Europe.*

On the north the Frozen Ocean (mare congelatum, 188
pigrum, Cronium, &c.), on the west the Atlantic or outer C
sea, on the south the Mediterranean or inner sea, on the east the Tanăis, the Palus Mæŏtis, the Cimmerian Bospŏrus, the Pontus Euxīnus, the Thracian Bospŏrus, the Propontis, the Hellespont, and the Ægean Sea.

§ 43. *The principal mountains of Europe.*

1. The Pyrenees (*τὰ Πυρηναῖα*, Pyrenæi montes); 2. 189
The Alps (*αἱ Ἄλπεις*, Alpes); 3. The Apennines (*τὰ* D
Ἀπεννῖνα, Apennīnus); 4. The Hæmus (*ὁ Αἶμος*) or Balkan; 5. The Carpathian mountains (*ὁ Καρπάτης*); 6. The Ural or Hyperborean mountains; 7. The Kjölen [Koelen, *or* Fiell] mountains (Sevo mons ?). The Hercynian forest.

§ 44. *The waters of Europe.*

SEAS AND GULFS.[1]

1. The Frozen Ocean. 2. The Atlantic, which at 190

[1] No mention is made here of those waters for which names are not found in *ancient* authors. The titles which often appear in maps have no classical authority, and are generally borrowed from such writers as Cellarius or Cluverus.

(190) once divides and connects the two most civilized quarters
A of the globe; with its several divisions, viz.—

a. *Not surrounded by land:* 1. The Cantabrian or Aquitanian Sea (now bay of Biscay); 2. The Britannic Sea (la Manche, or Straits of Calais); 3. The Caledonian Sea (now also Minsh); 4. The German Ocean (Γερμανικὸς Ὠκεανός) or North sea.

b. *Inland seas:* 1. The Suevian or Sarmatian sea[1] (now the Eastern Ocean); 2. The Mediterranean or Inner Sea, which at the same time separates and unites the three continents of the old world, is divided into a western basin,
B and an eastern almost double the size of the other. The first of these comprehends the Ligurian gulf (Gulf of Genoa), and the Tuscan or Tyrrhenian sea (between Italy and its three great islands), the *other* comprises the Adriatic Sea with the Tergestine bay (bay of Trieste), the Ionian Sea with the Tarentine and Corinthian gulfs (gulf of Lepanto), and the Ægean Sea (now Archipelago), with the Thermaic gulf (gulf of Salonichi); 3. The Propontis (sea of Marmora); 4. The Pontus Euxīnus (Black Sea), entirely without islands; 5. The Mæōtis (sea of Azov).

191 STRAITS.

C 1. Fretum Gaditanum or Herculeum (straits of Gibraltar); 2. Fretum Siculum (Faro di Messina); 3. Hellespontus (straits of Dardanelles); 4. Thracian Bospŏrus (straits of Constantinople); 5. Cimmerian Bospŏrus (straits of Kaffa or Jenikale).

192 LAKES.

D 1. In Greece, the Copais; 2. In Upper Italy, Lacus Verbānus (Lago Maggiore), Lacus Larius (Lago di Como). L. Benācus (Lago di Garda); 3. In the country of the Helvetii; L. Brigantinus (Boden-See, or Lake of Constance), L. Lemānus (Lake of Geneva).

193 RIVERS.

a. Flowing into the *Atlantic*—1. The Bætis (Guadalquivir); 2. The Anas (Guadiana); 3. Tagus (Tago); 4. Durius (Duero); 5. Garumna (Garonne); 6. The Liger (Loire); 7. The Sequăna (Seine).

---

[1] The Eastern Ocean was considered by the ancients, not as a Mediterranean, but as a portion of the Oceanus Septentrionalis; Tacitus Germ. c. 40. 43 and 44, names it the Ocean. The term "Suevicum mare," indicates the southern portion of the eastern sea.

b. Into the *German ocean*—1. The Taměsis (Thames); (193)
Scaldis (Scheldt); 3. Rhenus (Rhine); 4. Visurgis A
(Weser); 5. Albis (Elbe).

Tributaries of the Rhine—On the right hand the Nicer (Neckar), Mœnus (Main), and the Lupia or Luppia (Lippe); left, the Mosella (Moselle), and the Mosa (Maas or Meuse).

c. Into the *Suevian sea*—1. The Viădus[1] (Oder); 2. The Vistŭla.

d. The *Mediterranean sea* receives but few great rivers B
—1. The Ibērus (Ebro); 2. Rhodănus (Rhone), with the Arar (Saone); 3. The Arnus (Arno); 4. Tibĕris (Tiber); 5. Through the *Adriatic* sea, the Athĕsis (Adige) and Padus (Po).

e. The *Pontus Euxinus* receives within its narrow limits four of the greatest European streams—1. The Ister, the upper part of which was called Danubius (the Danube); 2. The Tyras (Dniester); 3. The Borysthĕnes (Dnieper); 4. (Through the Mæotis) the Tanăis (Don).

Tributaries of the Ister—*a.* On the *right* the Isarsa (Isar), Ænus C
(Inn), Arăbo (Raab), Dravus (Drau), Savus (Sau); *b. left,* Cusus (Waag), Tibiscus (Theiss), Hierăsus (Pruth).

f. Into the *Caspian sea*—The Rha (Volga), the most considerable river of Europe.

§ 45. *The countries of Europe.*

A. On the Continent proper—1. Gallia; 2. Ger- 194
mania; 3. The southern Danube countries (Vindelicia, Rhætia, Noricum, and Pannonia); 4. Dacia; 5. European Sarmatia.

B. The Peninsulas (or limbs of Europe)—1. The D
four southern, Hispania, Italia, the Greek peninsula (Illyria, Mœsia, Macedonia, Thrace, and Greece), and the Tauric Chersonesus (now Krim [*Crimea*]), the first being the entrance from Europe into Africa, the third into Asia. 2. The *two northern:* the Cimbrian peninsula (Jutland) and Scandinavia (also Baltia, now Sweden and Norway, the last of which was also called Nerigos).

[1] The *Οὐίαδος*, mentioned by Ptolemy, for which the name of Viadrus has been unmeaningly substituted by modern geographers, is generally taken for the Oder. Other writers, however, (Reichard, Giesebrecht, and von Spruner), take the *Σουΐβος* (Suevus) for the Oder, and the Viadus for the Wipper.

195 THE ISLANDS.

A 1. *In the Atlantic*—Britannia or Albion, Hibernia or Ierne (Ireland), the Hebŭdes or Ebudes (Hebrides), the Orcădes (Orkney islands), Thule (Iceland?).

2. In the *Suevian sea*, the island of the goddess Hertha (Rügen?).

B 3. In *the Mediterranean*—The Pityusæ (among these was Ebŭsus or Ebŭsus, hod. Ivica) and the Baleāres (also called *Γυμνήσιαι*), of which the largest are the Balearis major and minor (now Majorca and Minorca), Sardo or Sardinia, Cyrnos or Corsica, Æthalia or Ilva (now Elba), Trinacria or Sicilia, Melĭte (now Malta).

4. *In the Ionian sea*—Corcyra or Kerkyra (Corfu), Leucadia (now S. Maura), Ithaca (Theaki), Cephallenia (Cephalonia), Zakynthus (now Zante), Cythera (now Cerigo).

C 5. In the *Ægean sea*—Creta now (Candia,) the Cyclades, Eubœa (now Negropont).

B. INDIVIDUAL STATES OF EUROPE.

I. The Greeks.

Sources of Information.

196 Their historical writers, strictly so called, were preceded by: *a.* the CYCLIC POETS, who used to repeat in a continuous form the various legendary ballads (κύκλους), and the *Logographi*, who first related the legends in prose (λόγους). Such were Hecatæus, Charon, Hellanicus, and others, of whose works only detached fragments have reached us.

197 THE HISTORIANS.

D 1. HERODŎTUS (pater historiæ), born at Halicarnassus, B. C. 484. He wrote, after his great journey (through Greece, Macedonia, Thrace, Asia, Egypt, and Libya), a history of the Persian wars to the retreat of the Persians from Europe—with episodes concerning the early history of that people, and the nations who came into contact with them, in nine books (ἱστοριῶν), which he revised and completed at Thurii. He is said to have read his work in public at the Olympic games (?). 2. THUCYDIDES, born at Athens, B. C. 474, a commander in the Peloponnesian war—superseded in his command. In his place of banishment on the Thracian Chersonesus, he collected materials for his history (ξυγγραφή in eight books) of the Peloponnesian war, reaching to the year 411. 3. XENOPHŎN, born at Athens in 443 (?), a disciple of Socrates, banished from Athens for Laconism; he wrote, *a.* 'Ελληνικά (seven books), a continuation of the history of Thucydides to the battle of Mantinea; *b.* 'Ανάβασις (seven

books) ; *c.* Κύρου παιδεία (eight books) ; *d.* λόγος εἰς 'Αγησίλαον. (197)
4. Polybius of Megalopŏlis (205—131), author of a practical uni- A
versal history ἱστοριῶν 40 B.), from the commencement of the second Punic war to the conquest of Macedonia by the Romans. 5. Diodorus Siculus, in the reign of Augustus, wrote a βιβλιοθήκη ἱστορική (in forty books). 6. Plutarch (born A. D. 50 at Chæronea): he wrote forty-four βιοὶ παραλληλοί, and five separate biographies. Of Diodorus, only books 1—5=11—20 remain.

Geographers.

1. Strabo (in the first century of the Christian era), in book 8—10 198
of his γεωγραφικά. 2. Pausanius (born at Rome in the second cen- B
tury), in his description of Greece ('Ελλάδος περιήγησις, in ten books). 3. Claudius Ptolemæus (an Egyptian who flourished in the second century), wrote γεωγραφικὴ ὑφήγησις (in eight books).

The chronicle of the Parian marbles is a tablet, discovered in the island of Paros, and now preserved at Oxford, containing a chronological list of the principal events in the history of Greece, and particularly of Athens; 1381 years, from 1450 B. C. to 264 B. C.

Of Latin historians, who have written upon Grecian history, we have Cornelius Nepos [or the lives that go under his name] and Justin. Besides the historians, we have, for the first mythical period, the library of Apollodorus, for the third, the orations of Isocrates, Æschynes, and Demosthenes, and for constitutional history, the politics of Aristotle ; for geography, Pomponius Mela, first cent. A. C.

Modern Books of Reference.

a. Geography. Cramer, A geographical and historical description 199
of Ancient Greece ; 3 vols. 8vo. Thirlwall, History of Greece, ch. 1. C
Geographical outlines of Greece. Grote, part 2, ch. 1, General geography and limits of Greece. Gell, Itinerary of Greece ; *id.* Journey in the Morea. Leake's Travels in Northern Greece. Wordsworth's Classical tour in Attica, &c.

b. History—The best general histories of Greece are in English, D
although particular parts have been treated with great success by other nations, and especially by the Germans. Grote's is the only work in which the "Legendary Period" is satisfactorily treated, without which Grecian character and half of the subsequent history is almost unintelligible. The vast learning, sound judgment, liberal views, statesmanlike sagacity, critical acumen, and classical taste of this writer, must give his work the first place among the histories of Greece. (Grote's Greece. 6 vols. are published down to the peace of Nikias.) Next in merit is Thirlwall (8 vols. 8vo.), deficient in grouping and judging the legendary history, inferior in learning and philosophy to Grote, but far superior to all his predecessors. These works have entirely thrown out Mitford, who had but little relish for antiquity, and wrote ancient history with the pen of a modern partisan ; and Gillies, who though more readable than Mitford, is every way unequal to such a subject. Eliot has a very interesting chapter on Grecian liberty, in his Liberty of Rome ; v. also Greene's Historical Series, vol. 1.

(199) *Chronology*—Clinton's Fasti Hellenici, or Civil and Literary Chro-
A nology of Greece; a valuable work, when the author once gets on historical ground.

Religion, Politics, Commerce, &c.—Heeren, vol. 6 of the English edition, originally translated by Mr. Bancroft and published in the United States. Herman, Political Antiquities of Greece, 1 vol. 8vo. (from the German), Oxford, 1836. St. John's History of the Manners, Customs, Arts, &c., of Ancient Greece, 3 vols. 8vo. Potter's Grecian Antiquities. Bojesen's Manual of Grecian Antiquities, Appleton's edition, 1 vol. 12mo.

A. Geography of Greece.

§ 46. *The name of Greece.*

200 In the most remote times there was no general name for
B the whole of Greece, any more than for Italy and Asia Minor. The name of *Hellas* had various significations at different periods. Originally it indicated merely the city of Hellas in Thessaly; at a later period, the term comprehended the greater part of Thessaly, and afterwards it was applied to the whole of midland Greece, which was called Hellas proper in contradistinction to Peloponnesus.
C After the Persian war Peloponnesus itself was also included, and at length (after the Macedonian war) the term was understood as designating every country inhabited by Hellenes.

The term Achæan Land ('Αχαΐς γαῖα in Homer), is applied in strictness of speech only to a small portion of southern Thessaly, where Achæus, the son of Xuthus, reigned; but in a secondary sense it is employed also to indicate the rest of Greece, especially Peloponnesus, of which the descendants of Achæus had made themselves masters.

In like manner Argos, originally the name of a town in Argolis, was used for Peloponnesus, and at last for the whole of Greece.

D The term Græcia (*Γραικοί*) was never employed by the Greeks themselves, but was the only name given by the Romans to the whole of the country. Originally it was limited to the district of Dodōna in Epīrus.

As a Roman province, Greece (with the exception of Thessaly, Epirus, and Acarnania), was distinguished by the name of Achaia.

§ 47. *The boundaries of Greece.*

On the north the Macedonian (or Cambunian) and Ceraunian mountains; east, the Ægean and Myrtoan seas;
201 west and south, the Adriatic and Ionian seas.

No country of Europe presents, in proportion to its size, such an A
extent of coast, or such facilities of approach.

§ 48. *The mountains of Greece.*

A. 1. In NORTHERN GREECE, the Pindus (a continuation 202
of the Scardus, from 7000 to 8000 feet in height) forms B
the line of separation from which the rivers flow in different directions either into the Ionian or Ægean sea. Its branches are: *a. westwards*, the *Ceraunian* chain, the northern boundary of the half Grecian tribes in Epirus; the steep promontory in which it terminates (called Acroceraunia), marks the division of the Ionian sea from the Adriatic. *b. Eastwards: 2. Chains at right angles with the Ceraunia:* 1. The CAMBUNIAN in the north (6000 feet), the continuation of which, Mount OLYMPUS [now *Elymbo*][1] (6000 feet), was supposed to be the habitation of the gods; 2. The Othrys in the south, forming with Pelion [*Plesnia*] and the round-headed Ossa [*Kissovo*] (5000 feet), the eastern frontier of Thessaly. The last C
of these is separated from the southern slope of Olympus only by the narrow pass of Tempe. Thessaly, therefore, is a basin surrounded on all sides by mountains, the waters of which are conveyed by the river Peneus through the narrow channel of Tempe into the sea.

B. In CENTRAL GREECE: *a.* in the north, continuations 203
of the Pindus, such as the Œta [*Catavothra*, &c.] (4000 feet), with the famous straits of THERMOPYLÆ, once a very narrow pass along the shore; *b.* in the south, detached groups of mountains and hills, for the most part barren and D
inhospitable; *e. g.* PARNASSUS [*Lyakoura*] (7500 feet), with its three abrupt peaks, HELICON [*Zagora*, or *Paleo Vouni*] (5300 feet), covered with forests, the rugged CITHÆRON [*Elatea*] (3900 feet), the HYMETTUS [*Trellovouno*] (2700 feet), the PENTELICUS [*Pentele*], &c.

C. The PELOPONNESUS forms a table-land (2000 feet 204
above the level of the sea) the flattest part of which (Arcadia) is by no means level, but broken into isolated groups of mountains (some of them 6000 feet above the sea), and surrounded on all sides by still loftier chains, the branches of which form the four isthmuses of the peninsula.

---

[1] [Arrowsmith gives: *Olympus*, 6250 feet; *Ossa*, 4000; *Pelion*, 4000; *Pindus*, 8500; *Taygetus*, 8000.]

(204) The most steep and lofty is the northern border (Achaia), which
A reaches its greatest height (7200 feet) in the mountain of CYLLENE, the continuations of which stretch west towards Elis, and southeast into Argolis. The eastern (Parthenius) sends out a spur as far as the promontory of Malea, the southeastern extremity of Laconia, whilst the more broken western ridge (Erymanthus) slopes very gradually down to the level coast, its southern continuation intersecting the isthmus of Messenia. The southern is connected with the Taygetus, the highest ridge (7400 feet) in Peloponnesus. It traverses the western isthmus of Laconia to the promontory of Tænarum (Cape Matapan).

B PROMONTORIES: Actium on the Ambracian gulf (battle 31). Rhion and Antirrhion [or, Rhium and Anti-Rhium] opposite each other on the Corinthian gulf. Malĕa [also, Malēa] and Tænarum, the extreme points of Laconia. Sūnĭum, the southernmost point of Attica. Artemisium, the northern point of the island of Eubœa (battle 480).

§ 49. *The Waters of Greece.*

205 SEAS.—1. The *Ægean* sea; 2. The *Myrtoan* sea, be-
C tween the eastern coast of Peloponnesus and the islands; 3. The *Ionian* sea. The currents of the two last meet at the promontory of Malĕa, which on that account was notorious for shipwrecks.

GULFS.—1. The Thermaic (hod. gulf of Salonichi); 2. The Pagasæan and Malian bays; 3. The Saronic gulf (now the gulf of Egina); 4. The Argolic (gulf of Napoli); 5. The Laconic (gulf of Kolokythia); 6. The Messenian (also the Coronæan, now gulf of Koron); 7. The Corinthian (now gulf of Lepanto), with the Crisæan bay; 8. The Ambracian (gulf of Arta).

D STRAIT.—The Eurīpus, between Eubœa and Bœotia.

LAKES.—1. Acherusia, in Epirus; 2. The Copāis, which communicates with the Eubœan sea by long subterraneous channels.

The RIVERS, as in every mountainous country, are numerous; but on account of the close vicinity of the sea on all sides, and the consequent narrowness of the continent, they are very insignificant, and so ill-supplied with water, as to be for the most part dry in summer. 1. Penēus [*Salembria*], flowing into the Thermaic gulf; 2. Achelōus (now Aspro-potamo), between Acarnania and Ætolia, flowing into the Ionian sea; 3. Cephissus, into

the lake Copais; 4. Alphēus [*Rouphia*], into the Ionian A
sea; 5. Eurōtas [*Iris. Basilopotamo*] into the Laconic gulf.

§ 50. *Climate and products of Greece.*

In no country, perhaps, is the contrast of climate so 206
great as in Greece. The temperature varies with the difference of soil; so that whilst Laconia is enjoying spring, and Messenia summer, the winter has scarcely ended in Arcadia. The months from May to September, inclusive, are extraordinarily dry, scarcely any rain falling except in winter, when it descends in torrents, generally on the lands of moderate elevation, in the form of squalls, with thunder and lightning. The highest peaks of the mountains are covered with almost perpetual snow.

PRODUCTS.

1. *Mineral kingdom.*—The precious metals were, for the most part, B
rare. There were gold mines on Thasos (and Siphnos), silver mines in the mountains of Laurium [Λαύριον, or Λαύρειον] in Attica, copper and iron near Chalcis in Eubœa, marble in Pentelicus and Paros.

2. *Vegetable kingdom.*—The most productive grain was barley (of which they made ἄλφιτα). Among the varieties of trees were the silver poplar, the Greek cedar, the evergreen cypress, and the majestic plane. Besides an abundance of fruit of other sorts, they had grapes, figs, and olives, the last especially in Attica.

3. *Animal kingdom.*—Bullocks, sheep, goats, hogs, and mules. C
The rearing of horses was rendered very difficult by the mountainous character of the country. Pigeons on Cythēra, owls at Athens, bees, especially on Mount Hymettus, fish, dolphins. The country was grievously plagued by locusts.

§ 51. *Divisions of Greece.*

A. NORTHERN GREECE contains—1. Thessaly; 2. 207
Epirus.

B. CENTRAL GREECE, or Greece Proper, is divided into —1. Acarnania; 2. Ætolia; 3. Doris; 4. Locris; 5. Phocis; 6. Bœotia; 7. Attica; 8. Megaris.

C. SOUTHERN GREECE, or Peloponnesus (formerly D
'Απία, now the Morea), comprises—1. Corinthia; 2. Sicyonia; 3. Phliasia; 4. Achaia; 5. Elis; 6. Messenia; 7. Laconia; 8. Argŏlis; 9. Arcadia.

D. The ISLANDS.

§ 52. *Topography of Greece.*

A. NORTHERN GREECE.

1. THESSALY (named also Hellas, compare 200), the 208
largest district of Greece, and the cradle of all the Grecian

(208) tribes, consists principally of two caldron-shaped basins,
A the greater of which (according to Herodotus, vii. 129) in early ages was a lake, until Ossa was separated from Olympus by an earthquake, and an outlet made for the river Peneus through the narrow valley of Tempe. High mountains (see 202, c.) inclose a plain, well adapted for agriculture and the rearing of cattle; the only outlet for he waters being, as we have mentioned, the narrow fissure called the valley of Tempe (described by Ovid. Met. i. 569).

B This district was divided by the ancient geographers into four circles (Tetrades or Tetrarchies): Hestiæotis in the north (the Peneus forms, generally speaking, its southern boundary); Phthiotis in the south; Thessaliotis between the two first-mentioned; Pelasgiotis in the east, between Ossa and Pelion.

209 Cities.—1. Phthia, the ancient capital, the birth-place of Achilles. It disappeared at an early period. 2. Lamia (the Lamian war, 323). 3. Pharsālus (battle in 48); in the vicinity was the hill of Cynoscephăle (battle in 197). 4. Pheræ (the tyrants). 5. Larissa on the Peneus.

C The district of Magnesia on the sea-coast, with Iolchos (the rendezvous of the Argonauts), in all probability did not belong to any of the tetrarchies of Thessaly, not having been subject to the Thessalians when that division was made.

2. Epirus (ἤπειρος=the continent), in the Odyssey, means that part of the continent which lies immediately opposite to Ithaca; nor was it until a later period that the name was used to distinguish the country bounded by the Acroceraunian mountains, Pindus, the Ambracian gulf, and the
D Ionian sea. On account of its volcanic soil, this district was supposed to communicate with the infernal regions; the river Achĕron [*Mauro*, or *Souli*], which flows through the lake Acherusia, and, after receiving the Cocȳtus [*Bassa*], empties itself into the Ionian sea, being placed in the lower world by the poets.

Epirus was inhabited by fourteen distinct Pelasgic tribes, ranked as *Greeks* by Herodotus, but called barbarians by Thucydides and every other writer. The most considerable of these tribes were the Chaonians, Thesprotians, and Molossians; after whom the country was divided into three parts—Chaonia, Thesprotia, and Molossis.

Cities.—1. Ambracia (now Arta), the residence of Pyrrhus; 2. Dodōna, with the most ancient Grecian oracle (of Zeus).

B. Central Greece, or Hellas, in its more restricted sense.

1. Acarnania; bounded by the Ambracian gulf, the 210
Achelōus, the Corinthian gulf, and the Ionian sea. *Cities.* A
—1. Stratus, the largest city of the district; 2. Actium, founded by Augustus on the promontory of the same name, where there formerly was only a port with a temple (of Apollo).

2. Ætolia. *Boundaries.*—On the north, Thessaly and 211
Epirus; east, Locris and Doris; south, the Corinthian gulf; west, the Achelous. Capital city, Thermon (also Thermus), seat of the Ætolian league (Panætolium).

3. Doris.—This rugged little state contained four cities, 212
named the Dorian Tetrapolis. B

4. Locris—was divided into two districts, inhabited by 213
three tribes:—

a. That on the Corinthian gulf, which was surrounded by Phocis, Doris, and Ætolia, was inhabited by the Ozolian Locrians, a savage predatory tribe. *Cities.*—1. Amphissa (destroyed in 339). 2. Naupactus (now Lepanto); place of embarkation of the Dorians when they passed over into Peloponnesus—given by the Athenians to the Messenians, who were again expelled after the Peloponnesian war.

b. The rest of the district on the Eubœan sea and the C
Malian gulf was inhabited by the Opuntian Locrians, with their capital Opus; and northwards from these, as far as Thermopylæ, were the Epicnemidian Locrians, so named from the mountain Cnemis, at the foot of which stood the city of Cnemides.

5. Phocis. *Cities.*—1. Delphi (in Homer Pytho), on 214
the southwestern declivity of Parnassus, between its two principal peaks. Here was the "infallible" oracle of Apollo Pythius, so renowned even among foreign nations.
Its responses were delivered by the Pythia, seated on a D
golden tripod, placed in the temple over the prophetic cavern. In the court which surrounded the temple were votive offerings of various nations. Individual cities had also each their own treasury. The reputation of the oracle was further increased by the choice of Delphi as the place of meeting for the Amphictyonic council, and the celebra-

(214) tion of the Pythian games. 2. Crisa (also Crissa), or
A perhaps (Cirrha ?), was destroyed in the time of Solon, and its territory assigned to the Delphic god. 3. Elatēa, in the valley of the Cephīsus, the key of Phocis and Bœotia.

215 6. Bœotia. This fertile basin is formed by the mountains of Parnassus, the Helicon (the seat of the Muses), with its numerous springs; the savage Cithæron, and the rugged rocky chain of Parnes; and comprehends within itself several plains of greater or smaller dimensions,—a circumstance which rendered Bœotia the battle-field of
B Hellas, as Arcadia was that of the Peloponnesus. The more considerable of the Bœotian cities formed a confederacy under the Hegemony of Thebes. *Cities*.—1. Thebæ; also Thebe (ἑπτάπυλος); the acropolis of which was founded by the Phœnicians under Cadmus, and thence called Cadmea. According to the legend, the walls of the lower city were raised by the notes of Amphīon's lyre. It was destroyed by Alexander the Great (335), and restored by Cassander. 2. Orchomĕnus, formed with its district, which in the earliest times comprehended the whole of western Bœotia, a distinct country, not attached to Bœotia
C until after the Trojan war. Its inhabitants were called Minyæ or Minyans (also Phlegyans). Victory of Sulla in 86. 3. Platæa, or Platææ (on the northern declivity of Cithæron), which separated itself from the Bœotian confederacy (battle in 479). 4. Thespiæ, at the foot of Helicon (obstinate courage of the Thespians in the battle of Thermopylæ). Between Thespiæ and Platææ lay probably the hamlet of Leuctra (battle in 371). 5. Tanăgra (battle in 457); in the district belonging to which were Aulis (rendezvous of the Grecian fleet for the Trojan war), Delium (battle in
D 394), and Œnophyta (battle in 456). 6. Haliartus, on the lake Copais (battle in 394). 7. Coronēa (battle in 394). 8. Chæronēa, a frontier fortress on the side of Phocis (battles in 338 and 86).

216 7. Attica (Ἀττική). *Boundaries*.—On the north, Bœotia; west, Megăris; south, the Saronic gulf; east, the Ægean sea. *Division* into four, from the time of Cleisthenes ten, and at a still later period twelve Phylæ; which were subdivided into demi, the number of which amounted at one time to 174. *Cities*.—1. Athens (Ἀθῆναι), consisted of two principal parts, viz., the city, and its three

ports, Phalēron [*or* Phalērum], Munychia, and Piræus [in (216)
Greek, *Πειραιεύς*], which were united to the city by two long A
walls (*τὰ σκέλη*). After its demolition by the Persians, Themistocles rebuilt Athens in a more magnificent style, surrounded it with walls, and joined it to the Piræus.

The city, which stood in the plain Cecropia, on the banks of the 217
river Ilissus, consisted of—*a.* the *Acropolis* (called also Cecropia), on a steep rock, crowned with the Parthĕnon, or temple of Minerva, built entirely of white Pentelic marble (by Ictīnus and Callicrătes), and approached by a portico termed the Propylæa (erected by Mnesicles). In this temple stood a statue of Pallas Athēnē (by Phidias), thirty-seven feet in height, and carved in gold and ivory. On the frieze was a model in relievo of the Panathenaic procession, B
and in the tympanum the victory of Athene over Poseidōn, exquisitely represented in a group of colossal statues. On the side of the Propylæa stood a bronze statue, seventy feet high, of Athene Promăchus, cast by Phidias. *b. The lower town.*—In the western quarter of the city, on an elevation, was the Pnyx, where the assemblies of the people were held; and on another eminence, the Areopagus, from which there was a thoroughfare through the street of Hermes, by the Poikile [*or,* Pæcile] (adorned with frescoes of the battle of Marathon by Polygnōtus) to the new Agora; and thence along the Tripod street, by the Prytaneum (where ambassadors and meritorious citizens were entertained at the public cost), to the great theatre of Dionysos [Bacchus]. In the southeastern quarter of the city, after- C
wards called Hadrian's town, stood the Olympieion, or temple of Zeus, with a colossal statue of the god, in gold and ivory. *Without the city* were three Gymnasia, viz.—*a.* the Academy [Academia], where Plato taught; *b.* the Cynosarges; *c.* the Lyceum, where Aristotle used to walk with his disciples (hence the term Peripatetics). On the other side of the Ilissus was the stadium (of Herodes Atticus) for public games.

2. Eleusis, with its temple and mysteries of Demētēr [*Ceres*]. 3. Sūnium; a fortress on the promontory of the same name, with the temple of Athene Sunias, of which the D
ruins are still visible. 4. Marăthon, on the plain of the same name, with monuments (still in existence), erected in commemoration of the battle in 490. 5. Phyle, where Thrasybūlus assembled the opponents of the thirty tyrants. 6. Decelēa, fortified by the Spartans in the Peloponnesian war.

8. Megaris. *Boundaries.*—On the north, Bœotia; 218
east, Attica, and the Saronic gulf; south, the isthmus of Corinth; west, the Corinthian gulf. In the *city* of Megăra (*τὰ* M.), which at an earlier period belonged to Attica, the Dorians, on their return from the war against Codrus, founded a colony.

C. The Peloponnesus.

219 1. Corinthia, with the city of Corinth (formerly
A Ephȳra), at the foot of a steep mountain, on which stood the Acro-Corinthus, the strongest fortress in Greece, and key of the Peloponnesus. The situation of Corinth rendered it the emporium of the maritime traffic, not only between northern and southern Greece, but between Italy and Asia, as well as the chief seat of manufacturing industry and the arts (the Corinthian order of architecture, vases, Corinthian brass). The successful cultivation of these various branches of commerce rendered it the most populous (300,000 inhabitants) and wealthy, but at the
B same time the most dissolute, of all the Grecian cities. It was demolished (with the exception of the citadel) by Mummius in 146, and rebuilt by Cæsar. On the isthmus stood a temple, a stadium, and a theatre of Poseidōn [*Neptune*], where the Isthmian games were celebrated.

220 2. Sicyonia, with the city of Sicyon (also Ægialia), near the coast of the Corinthian gulf, was also famous for Grecian manufactures and works in metal, as well as for painting and sculpture.

221 3. Phliasia. The city of Phlius, with its little ter-
C ritory, formed an independent state.

222 4. Achaia (also Achaïa, formerly Ægialos), extended from Sicyonia along the northern coast of Peloponnesus. Here, as in all the settlements of the Ionians, we find a confederacy (of twelve hamlets), with a democratic constitution. *Cities.*—1. Helĭce, the ancient capital, ingulfed in 373 by one of the earthquakes so frequent on this coast. Its territory fell into the hands of the neighboring state. 2. Ægium, the station of the Panegyris. 3. Patræ (now Patras), a sea-port.

223 5. Elis (also Eleia), divided by mountains into three
D portions, viz.—1. Elis *proper*, or the "hollow," with the capital Elis, a city without walls, and its port of Cyllene. 2. Pisatis, with Olympia. This was not, strictly speaking, a town, but ranked as such on account of the multitude of buildings, groves, altars, and places for public games and combats, belonging to the temple of Zeus Olympius, and occupied at the Olympic games. In a grove of olives (named Altis) stood the temple, with a statue of the god

in a sitting position, carved by Phidias, in gold and ivory, (223)
and reaching to the ceiling of the temple. The length of the A
stadium (one-fortieth of a geographical mile) was the Greek
standard measure of distance. 3. Triphylia, with Pylus.

6. MESSENIA (also Messene). *Cities.*—1. Pylus (now 224
Navarino), the residence of Nestor, with a harbor protected by the island of Sphacteria; 2. Ithōme, a fortress
on a high hill, at the foot of which Epaminondas built (3)
Messene; 4. Ira, defended for eleven years by Aristomĕnes.

7. LACONIA (*Λακωνική*). *Boundaries*, in the more con- 225
fined sense—Messenia, Arcadia, Argolis, the sea. From B
the second Messenian war to the battle of Leuctra, Messenia was reckoned as belonging to Laconia. *Cities.*—1.
Sparta (*Σπάρτη*), Lacedæmon; on several eminences
on the declivity of Tāÿgĕtus and the banks of the Eurōtas;
without walls, until it was fortified by the tyrant Nabis.
2. Helos (*τὸ Ἕλος*), on the low lands at the mouth of the
Eurotas. Its inhabitants were reduced to the condition of
bondsmen by the Spartans. 3. Sellasia (battle in 222).

8. ARGOLIS (also *τὸ Ἄργος* and *ἡ Ἀργεία*). *Cities.*— 226
1. Argos (in Latin also Argi), the most ancient city in Pelo- C
ponnesus, gave its name to the whole district. Its acropolis, named Larissa, was a Pelasgian building, with Cyclopian walls. 2. Nauplia (near what is now called Napoli
di Romania), the sea-port of Argos. 3. Mycēnæ; of
which the Cyclopian walls, the lions'-gate, and what is
called the treasury of Atreus, still remain. The residence
of Agamemnon. 4. Tiryns, with its Cyclopian walls, of
which remains still exist. 5. Lerne (the Lernæan Hydra); D
Nemĕa, not a city, but merely the name of a valley, and
of the temple of Zeus, which stood there. (The Lion, the
Nemean games.) The three smaller districts of Her-
mione, Trœzēne, and Epidaurus.

9. ARCADIA, from the most ancient times the pasture 227
country of Nomadic herdsmen, never formed a whole, po-
litically speaking. *Cities.*—1. Mantinēa (battles in 418
and 362). 2. Tegĕa; which, with its district (Tegeatis),
formed one of the most considerable cantons of Arcadia. 3.
Megalopolis, the most modern and largest of the Arcadian cities, founded by the advice of Epaminondas in 371,
and peopled by the inhabitants of the (38) circumjacent

(227) hamlets. It was destroyed by the Spartans under Cleo-
A menes, and only partially rebuilt, with the largest theatre in Greece (native city of Philopœmen and Polybius).

D. The Greek Islands.

228 I. In the Ionian Sea.—1. *Kerkyra*, or Corcyra (now Corfu), in Homer; the Scheria inhabited by the Phœnicians. *Capital*—Corcyra, a colony of Corinth, in the time of the Persian war, the most considerable naval power
B after Athens. 2. *Leucadia* (now S. Maura), so called from its chalky soil, was originally a peninsula, mentioned by Homer as belonging to Epirus. The isthmus was dug through by the Corinthians, and Leucadia made into an island. *Capital*—Leucas (in Homer Nericon). 3. The *Cephallenic islands*, or islands belonging to the dominions of Odysseus [*Ulysses*], viz.—*a*. Ithăca (now Theaki), which consists of two rugged mountain masses, united by a narrow isthmus, on which stood the city of Ithăca, with an acropolis, containing the palace of Odysseus (the ruins of which are still called by the islanders the castle of St. Pene-
C lope). In front of the isthmus was the port of Rheithron. *b*. Cephallenia; in Homer Samos, or Same (now Cephalonia), with the city of Same. *c*. Zakynthus (now Zante), with its single city Zakynthus. 4. The *Teleboides*, or islands of the Taphians, the largest of which, called Taphos, lay between Leucadia and the continent. 5. *Sphacteria* (or Sphagia), opposite Pylus. 6. *Cythēra* (now Cerigo), at the entrance of the Laconic gulf. *City* of the same name, with a temple of Aphrodīte Cytherea.

II. In the Ægean Sea.

229 *a*. In the *western part*—*aa*. in the *Saronic gulf*. 1.
D Calauria; temple of Poseidōn, with an asylum, where Demosthenes died. 2. Ægina. The Æginetan sculptures (from the temple of Zeus Panhellenios), discovered in 1811, now in the Glyptothek at Munich. 3. Salamis, or Salamin, taken from the Megarians by Solon (battle in 480). *bb*. In the *Ægean sea*. Eubœa (now Negroponte), probably separated from the continent by one of the earthquakes common in those parts, with the promontory of Artemisium (so named from a temple of Artemis—battle in 480), and the cities of—1. Chalcis (now Negroponte),

joined to the continent by a bridge over the Euripus—a (229)
strong fortress, and place of considerable trade; the A
mother-state of Cumæ and Rhegium. 2. Eretria; the inhabitants of which were transplanted into Asia by Datis.

b. In the *northern part*—1. Lemnos. Its most ancient inhabitants, according to Homer, were the Sintians, who practised piracy, and received Hephæstus [*Vulcan*] when he was thrown down out of heaven. 2. Samothrāke, *or* Samothrace. 3. Thasos, formerly famous for its gold mines.

c. In the *eastern part*—1. Lesbos, celebrated for its B
excellent wine. *Cities.*—*a.* Mitylene (also Mytilene), renowned for the contests of poets; many of whom were natives of the city (Terpander, Arion, Alcæus, Sappho). *b.* Methymna, which remained faithful to the Athenians (428). 2. The Arginusæ (battle in 406). 3. Chios (now Skio), famous for its wine; *Capital,* Chios—minstrel-school of the Homerides. 4. Samos, with its capital of the same name, the native city of Pythagoras, at the height of its reputation and power, under Polycrates (532). 5. Rhodus, renowned for its nautical enterprise and cultivation of the sciences. In the port of the city of Rhodes stood the brazen colossus, seventy yards in height.

d. In the *southern part*—*aa.* the twelve *Cyclades;* C
among which the most important were—1. Delos, in the centre, the birth-place of Apollo and Artemis (on the mountain of Cynthus). Near the temple of Apollo solemn games were celebrated every five years. 2. Naxos, the largest of the islands, sacred to Dionysus—Ariadne. 3. Paros, famous for its white marble—the marble chronicles. *bb.* Creta (now Candia), in the vicinity of three quarters of the globe, and the centre of a much frequented sea, with a mountain chain, split into four parts, and intersecting the island. Its highest peak is Mount Ida (7200 feet).
The island was inhabited at a very early period (thence D
called by Homer ἑκατόμπολις), and well cultivated. *Capital city,* Cnossus, the residence of Minos, with its labyrinth, built by Dædălus (probably nothing more than the extensive and partly subterraneous quarries in that part of the island).

B. History of the Greeks.

First (Mythical) Period.

From the earliest Notices to the Migration of the Dorians, B. C. 1104.

§ 53. *The earliest Population of Greece.*

230 1. Aboriginal Inhabitants.—The most ancient in-
A habitants of Greece seem to have been the Pelasgi, one of the most numerous clans of southern Europe, who spread at the same time over Italy, Macedonia, Thrace, and even over a part of Asia Minor.

They had already acquired a certain degree of civilization (for we read of them as the founders of the most ancient Grecian states, Sicyon and Argos), practised agriculture and the rearing of cattle, and founded cities, with strong fortresses (called Larissa), in fertile valleys (named Argos), manured by streams, which at certain seasons overflowed their banks. Some of these cities (as Argos, Mycenæ, Tiryns, Orchomenus, &c.) were surrounded by Cyclopian walls. The Pelasgi had also an oracle of Zeus at Dodona, and sent out colonies to Asia Minor, Crete, and Italy.

B The appellation of Hellenes was used originally, and even in the days of Homer (Il. ii. 684), to designate the inhabitants of the district of Hellas in Thessaly, or the Myrmidons; the names of Achæi, Argēi [᾿Αργεῖοι], and Danai, being applied to the people collectively. It was not until after the time of Homer that Hellen,[1] the son of Deucalion, was mentioned (first by Hesiod ?) as the founder of the Grecian race, and of its principal tribes—the Æolians, Dorians, Achæans, and Ionians—derived from his sons Æolus and Dorus, and his grandsons Achæus and Ion. Since that period the name has no longer been restricted to the Myrmidons of Achilles, but applied collectively to the whole Greek nation.

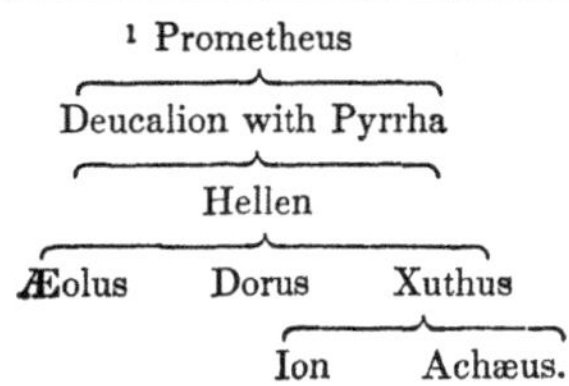

2. Foreign immigrations, as early as the sixteenth 231
century, B. C., are said to have contributed to the peopling A
and cultivation of the land.

a. Cecrops is said to have planted an Egyptian colony in Attica, and married the daughter of the king (Astæus), to whose throne he succeeded. He built the Acropolis (Cecropia), established the worship of Zeus and Athēnē, introduced lawful marriages and the interment of the dead, and divided the country into twelve demi.

b. Cadmus, son of Agēnor, king of Sidon, being sent B
(according to the legend) by his father in search of his sister Europa, who had been carried off by Zeus (a myth expressing the migration of the Phœnicians into Europe), arrived in Bœotia with a band of colonists, laid the foundation of the Cadmēa in Thebes, and taught the natives the Phœnician alphabet, metallurgy, and the worship of Dionȳsus [*Bacchus*].

c. Danaus, with his fifty daughters, migrated, it is said, from Chem, in Upper Egypt, to Argos, where he was called to the throne. The introduction of the Thesmophoria, and the worship of Athene and Aphrodīte [*Minerva* and *Venus*], are ascribed to this monarch.

The fifty sons of his brother Ægyptus, who followed him, and ob- C
tained his daughters in marriage, were all murdered by their wives; with the exception of Lynceus, who was spared by Hypermnestra, and having slain his father-in-law, became king of Argos. The daughters of Danaus were condemned to draw water for ever in the infernal regions.

d. Pelops, about the year 1320 (his father Tantalus, king of Sipylus, having been expelled by the Troes), came from Phrygia, and made himself master of Pisatis and Arcadia. His sons extended their dominion over the greater part of Peloponnesus.

§ 54. *Myths concerning the Migrations of the Hellenic Tribes,*

(between B. C. 1500 and 1300.)

Deucalion, the son of Prometheus, of the race of those 232
Titans who fought against the gods, landed, after the gen- D
eral deluge, on one of the summits of Parnassus, and, with the assistance of his wife Pyrrha, created a new race of men by throwing stones (λᾶς). Hence the word λᾶοι, people.

(232) With these followers he migrated to Phthiotis, where he
A was succeeded on the throne by his son Hellen, and he by his eldest son Æŏlus. From Phthiotis the Æolians spread themselves, under the command of his successors, over Thessaly more especially, and the western portion of central Greece (Ætolia, Acarnania, Phocis, and Locris), as well as over parts of the Peloponnesus (Elis, Corinth, Messenia,) and became amalgamated with the aboriginal inhabitants of those countries.

B Dorus expelled the Dryopes of Mount Œta, and founded the Doric Tetrapolis. Another division of the Dorians migrated to the island of Crete, which received a Doric constitution through their king Minos.

Xuthus, the youngest son of Hellen, went into Attica, where king Erechtheus gave him his daughter Crëūsa, as a reward for military services. By her he had two sons, Ion and Achæus. From Ion's four sons the legend derives the division of the inhabitants of Attica into four phylæ, according to their mode of life, viz., the Hopletes (warriors), Teleontes, or Geleontes (peasants who paid rent?), Ergadeis (handicraftsmen), and Agikoreis (goatherds).

C Xanthus, being expelled by the sons of Erechtheus, went to Ægialos, which was named Ionia (afterwards Achaia), after his eldest son, who remained behind in that country; whilst the younger, Achæus, proceeded into Thessaly, and took possession of his ancestral kingdom of Phthiotis, whence the Achæans, under the command of his sons, returned to the Peloponnesus, and spread themselves over Argolis and Laconia.

§ 55. *The heroic Age.*

(1300 to 1100.)

233 The wanderings of the Hellenic tribes had awakened at
D a very early period a passion for bold and extraordinary undertakings; which were at first confined to their native land, but soon extended into foreign countries. At first they were merely the enterprises of individual heroes, such as Hercules, Theseus, &c.; but at a later period expeditions were undertaken by numbers, who united for that purpose. In this manner Greece endured a period of the most fearful disorganization and supremacy of brute force, the natural consequence of its political division into separate nations, and the absence of popular rights.

Hercules is described in mythical history as the ideal of human (233) perfection, dedicated to the service of its fellow-creatures. All that A is excellent in him is of divine origin: thus he consists of a godlike and a human nature; is the son of Jupiter and Alcmēne, the wife of Amphitryon; and even in the cradle manifests his superiority over his merely human brother Iphicles by strangling a couple of serpents. As a youth he is tempted (fable of Hercules at the place where the roads divide), and overcomes the temptation. He is persecuted during the whole of his life by the relentless malice of Hērē [*Juno*], but protected by Pallas. His enemy Here avails herself of the assistance of Eurystheus, at whose command Hercules undertakes his *twelve labors;* which, in accordance with the object of the myth, consist in the destruction of noxious and violent animals (the Nemean lion, the Lernæan hydra, the Erymanthian boar, the hind of Artĕmis, the Stymphalian birds, the Cretan bull, the horses of Diomēdes in Thracia), or in the acquisition of treasures belonging to foreign lands (the zone of the queen of the Amazons, the cows of the three-headed Geryon, the golden apples of the Hesperides), or, most of all, in superhuman exertions (purification of the Augean stable). The B list of his toils closes with his triumphant return from the lower world, bringing with him the three-headed dog Cerberus. But to render the story fully instructive, the poet speaks also of his madness, and of his love for the Lydian queen Omphăle; and, in due course, of his return to the path of virtue. The myth concludes with a magnificent description of the hero's self-immolation on a funeral pile, and his assumption into heaven, where he is reconciled to Here, and marries her daughter Hebe.

Theseus, son of the Athenian king Ægeus, appears also in C mythical history as a benefactor to the human race, especially in his native country. He slays robbers, relieves Athens from the necessity of sending to Crete an annual tribute of seven boys and seven virgins, by putting the Minotaur to death in the Cretan labyrinth (with the assistance of Ariadne), and fights with the Amazons and Centaurs. He, as well as Hercules, is under the protection of a deity, Poseidŏn (whence he is said to be his son, and a native of Trœzēne, the city of Poseidon). By the aid of his patron, he returns safely from Crete and from the lower world, which he had visited in company with his friend Peirithous, for the purpose of abducting Persephŏne. He puts to death his son Hippolytus, who had been accused by his step-mother Phædra of an attempt to dishonor her. For his establishment of a constitution in Attica, see § 61.

Myths concerning Expeditions undertaken by the Geeeks conjointly.

1. The Argonautic Expedition.—Phrixus, son of 234 Athamas, king of Orchomenus, flying with his sister Helle D from the persecutions of his step-mother Ino, attempted to cross the sea to Colchis on the back of a ram, with a golden fleece. Helle, being unable to keep her seat, was

(234) drowned in the waters of the strait called from her the
A Hellespont; but Phrixus, having landed safely on the
shores of Colchis, offered up the ram in sacrifice, and presented its fleece to king Æētes, who placed it in the sacred
grove of Ares, under the guardianship of a dragon. To
recover this fleece, Jason, son of the king of Iolchus,
with the most renowned heroes of his time—such as Hercules, Theseus, and his friend Peirithous, Castor and Pol-
lux, the minstrel Orpheus, and the fathers of the heroes
who fought before Troy (Peleus, Telamon, Oīleus, Neleus,
and Menœtius)—embarked on board the ship Argo, and,
after various adventures, landed at the mouth of the Phasis, and effected his purpose by the aid of Medea, daughter
of Æetes, whom he carried off into Europe.
235 2. The War of the Seven Chiefs against Thebes.—
B In consequence of an oracle, Laius, king of Thebes, had
caused Œdĭpus, his son by Jocasta, to be exposed on
Mount Cithæron; whence he was rescued, and brought
up by Peribœa, queen of Corinth. Œdipus inadvertently
slays his father, unriddles the enigma of the Sphinx, mar-
C ries his mother, and becomes king of Thebes. On discovering his twofold crime, he puts out his own eyes, and,
guarded by his daughter Antigŏne, wanders in the guise
of a beggar to Colŏnos, in Attica, where he casts himself
down as a suppliant before the altar of the furies, is protected by Theseus, and soon afterwards dies. Jocasta falls
by her own hand. Their twin sons Eteŏcles and Polynīces dispute the succession to the throne; and Polynīces being expelled from the city, persuades six heroes
(Adrastus, Tydeus, Amphiarāus, Capăneus, Hippomĕdon,
and Parthenopæus) to join him in an expedition against
D Thebes. Both the brothers are slain, and of the other
leaders only Adrastus escapes. After the death of Eteŏcles, the guardianship of his infant son Laodamas is undertaken by Creon, the brother of Jocasta and uncle of the
deceased princes.
236 3. War of the Epigŏni.—Ten years after these events,
Thebes was again besieged by the sons of the fallen heroes,
who carried the city by storm, and placed Thersander, the
son of Polynīces, on the throne.
237 4. War against Troy (B. C. 1194–1184).—The angry
feeling which had long existed between the kings of Troy

and the race of Pelops, in consequence of the expulsion of (237)
Pelops by the Trojan king Dardanus, was brought to a A
crisis by the abduction of Helĕna, wife of Menelāus, king
of Sparta, by Paris, one of the sons of Priam, king of Troy.
At the instigation of Menelaus and his brother Agamemnon, the most powerful monarch of Greece, an expedition
against Troy is undertaken by most of the Grecian princes,
viz.—Nestor of Pylus, Odysseus of Ithaca, Achilles, chieftain of the Myrmidons in Thessaly, Diomĕdes of Argos,
the two Ajaxes (the one the son of Telamon of Salamis,
the other the son of Oïleus, and leader of the Locrians),
Thersander of Thebes, Idomĕneus of Crete, &c. Whilst B
the Grecian fleet, consisting of 1186 vessels with 100,000
men on board, was riding at anchor in the port of Aulis,
Artĕmis [*Diana*], who was angry with Agamemnon for
having slain a fawn, sent a calm, which continued until
the king, by the advice of Calchas, consented to offer up
his daughter Iphigenīa as a sacrifice to the offended goddess. Artĕmis, nevertheless, released the victim, and conveyed her to Tauris. After a siege of ten years the city
was taken (myth of the wooden horse, constructed by
Epēüs), and burnt.—Migration of Æneas to Italy.

Mode of Warfare.—Their armies were composed entirely of C
infantry and war-chariots, without cavalry.—Duels or single combats of the heroes.—The Greek camp protected by walls and ditches.—Achilles, enraged at the abduction of Brisēïs by Agamemnon, refuses to take any part in the war, until he resumes his weapons to avenge the death of his friend Patroclus, and kills Hector. Achilles himself also slain.

Fate of the Grecian Princes after their return.— 238
1. Agamemnon was murdered by his wife Clytemnestra,
and her paramour Ægisthus; both of whom were afterwards slain by Orestes, the son of Agamemnon, with the
assistance of his friend Pylădes. Orestes, who was per- D
secuted for a long time by the furies, on account of his
matricide, obtained the sovereignty of Argos and Mycenæ,
and, as son-in-law of Menelaus, became also king of Sparta.
His son Tisamĕnus was expelled by the Dorians (see p. 121, A). 2. Menelaus, accompanied by Helĕna, wandered for eight years about the coasts of Cyprus, Phœnicia, &c. 3. Diomedes, finding his wife Ægialea married again, quitted Argos, and fled to Italy. 4. A variety
of adventures were experienced by Odysseus [*Ulysses*].

(238) THE CONSTITUTION OF THE HEROIC AGE was hereditary
A monarchy. The kings, who were supposed to be allied to the gods ((ἐκ δὲ Διὸς βασιλῆες—thence called by Homer διογενέες, διοτρεφέες, δῖοι,) were judges, commanders, and the representatives of their people in offering public sacrifices. Their revenue consisted of an estate (τέμενος), a larger share of the booty and victims offered in sacrifice, and voluntary gifts (γέρατα, δῶρα). As counsellors of the kings, we find individual nobles, sometimes bearing the title of princes and leaders (ἡγήτορες ἠδὲ μέδοντες), sometimes of elders (γέροντες). There were also assemblies (ἀγοραί) of the people (δῆμος), who were, however, called together, not to express any opinion, but simply to decide.

B In many of the Grecian states the king seems to have been merely the first man among the nobles. Thus Attica was divided by Theseus into twelve districts, each under a separate dynasty; the twelve rulers being presided over by the king. Similar constitutions, according to Homer, existed in Scheria and Ithaca. These princes are also called βασιλῆες, and perform all those official duties which are not necessarily (like the command-in-chief of the army) intrusted to one person. As these chiefs gradually threw off the yoke of the sovereign, the supreme monarchical power came into their hands, and hence arose aristocratic constitutions.

SECOND PERIOD.

FROM TEE MIGRATION OF THE DORIANS TO THE PERSIAN WAR, 1104–500.

§ 56. *The Migration of the Dorians, or Heraclĭdæ.* (1104.)

239 Some fifty years after the Trojan war the Thessa-
C lians, a branch of the Thesprotians, wandered from Epīrus to the valley of the Penēus, and gave the name of Thessaly to the district which had been hitherto called Pelasgicon. The ancient inhabitants (Æolians) either became serfs (πενέσται), or went into exile, as in the case of the Bœotians, who conquered the country named from them Bœotia; the aborigines of which (as the Minyans in Orchomĕnus, the Cadmēans in Thebes, the Thracians, &c.) scattered themselves over the neighboring states, and founded several colonies. From this period we find no further mention of them in history.

THE CONQUEST OF PELOPONNESUS BY THE DORIANS

is represented in the myth as having been undertaken for (239)
the purpose of establishing the ancient hereditary claims A
of the Heraclīdæ. Amphitryon, we are told, the father of
Hercules, was deposed from the throne of Tiryns by
Sthenelus, king of Mycēnæ. The endeavors of his posterity to recover their inheritance were for a long time
ineffectual; but, eighty years after the Trojan war, three
of the descendants of Hercules (Temenus, Cresphontes,
and Aristodemus), at the head of the Dorians, who had
hitherto dwelt between Œta and Parnassus (see § 54),
and accompanied by the Ætolians under Oxȳlus, crossed
the Corinthian gulf near Naupactus, overthrew the Achæans under Tisamĕnus, the son of Orestes (who resided at
Mycenæ, and thence ruled the districts of Laconia, Argos,
and Messenia), and divided the conquered lands of the
Atrīdæ. Temenus received Argolis for his portion, Cres- B
phontes Messenia; Procles and Eurysthenes, the sons
of Aristodēmus (who had been struck dead by lightning),
obtained Laconia, and the Ætolians Elis. At a later period
Doric kingdoms were also founded in Sicyon, Corinth,
Megaris, &c. Attica lost Megaris, and only retained her
independence through the magnanimous self-sacrifice of
Codrus, the last Athenian king, 1068. Thus much seems
to be historically certain, that about the year B. C. 1100,
Dorians, under various leaders, after a great battle, settled
in Peloponnesus, and made themselves masters of the
greater part of the peninsula; not all at once, but gradually, and after a long and severe struggle. The Arca- C
dians alone continued to occupy their ancient habitations.
Of the Achæans some were subdued, and others took possession of the northern coast of the Peloponnesus, inhabited by the Ionians, who retired before the invaders, and
took refuge in Attica, the islands, and Asia Minor.

§ 57. *The Greek Colonies on the western coast of Asia Minor, and the adjacent islands.*

The movement of the Heraclidæ was followed by the 240
establishment of colonies in the islands and coasts of Asia
Minor, partly by the conquerors, who were compelled to
emigrate on account of the superabundant population, and
partly by the vanquished aborigines.

1. Æolian Colonies.—After losing the sovereignty of

(240) the Peloponnesus, the expelled Achæans (under the com-
A mand of Penthilus, a son of Orestes) migrated, in company with the Bœotian Ætolians, to Mysia and Lydia (hence the name of Æŏlis), where they founded twelve cities, or states; among which the most important were Cyme and Smyrna. The latter was taken at an early period of its history by the Ionians (expelled from Colophon). At the same time, they spread over Lesbos, where they founded Mitylēne and Methymna, and took possession of several other islands.

241 2. Ionian Colonies.—The same Ionians, who, when
B they were expelled by the Achæans from the northern coast of Peloponnesus, had fled to their kinsmen in Attica, migrated (under the younger son of Codrus), in company with the remnants of other Greek clans, to the Cyclades, Chios, and Samos, as well as to the southern coast of Lydia and to the north of Caria (hence the name Ionia), where they also founded twelve cities. Of these states, which were united by the bond of a common sanctuary (the Panionium at Mycăle), the most important were—1.
C Milētus; which founded more than eighty colonies, principally on the shores of the Pontus Euxinus and the Propontis (see § 62). 2. Ephesus, with the famous temple of Artĕmis, which was burnt by Herostratus (359), and restored on a more magnificent scale. 3. Phocæa, the inhabitants of which emigrated to Massilia (compare § 55). 4. Smyrna, formerly an Æolian city.

242 3. Dorian Colonies.—Dorians, from different cities of
D Peloponnesus and from Megara, emigrated to the islands of Crete (see § 54), Rhodes, Thera, and southern Caria (hence Doris), and founded a confederacy of six cities (the Doric Hexapŏlis); two of which, Halicarnassus (the birth-place of Herodotus and Dionysius), and Cnidus (battle in 394), were on the main land. From Thera a colony was sent out, about the year 632, to Cyrene, in Africa.

§ 58. *Origin of Republican Constitutions.*

243 With the heroic age expired also the absolute sovereignty of individuals, partly through the extinction of royal families, and partly through the restrictions imposed on the authority of the crown, or the violent expulsion of

their kings. Instead of monarchical, most of the states (243
adopted aristocratic, and at a later period republican, con- A
stitutions, with various modifications; and except at Sparta,
where two kings, a Eurysthĕnid and a Proclid (247, D) continued to reign, the monarchical constitution was retained only
in Argos, and that under considerable restrictions, until the
Persian war. Greece was split into almost as many independent states as there were cities with a territory attached
to them, only a few districts, such as Laconia, Megaris,
and Attica, forming each a confederate state; although in
many, perhaps in all the other districts, the different independent cities were united by a league. By this arrangement, which existed especially in Achaia, each city re- B
tained its own constitution, or sometimes a particular city
was invested with the Hegemony, or presidency over the
others, as Thebes over the states of Bœotia, and Sparta
over those of the Peloponnesus.

In most of the Grecian states, as well at home as in the
colonies, the struggles of the people against an arrogant
oligarchy occasioned, in the seventh and sixth centuries
B. C., the establishment of TYRANTS, as they were called, that
is, of individuals who assumed a supreme and irresponsible
authority, which they endeavored to render hereditary in
their families. In those states, especially, which were not
exclusively Dorian (*i. e.* in all those of the mother country C
except Sparta and Argos), the establishment of this kind of
tyranny was the result of the struggles between the ancient
inhabitants and the Dorians; the leaders of the popular
party, in their resistance to aristocratic oppression, generally retaining their power after the victory was gained,
and assuming the authority and name of Tyrants.

The most numerous changes of constitution were experienced by 244
Corinth, where, after the Doric immigration, the sovereign power E
was at first in the hands of the Heraclidæ, then of the Bacchiadæ, who for a time retained the monarchical constitution, but subsequently established an oligarchy under the presidency of a Prytaneus, elected annually—(during this period most of the Corinthian colonies were founded, such as Syracuse, Corcyra, Potidæa, &c.)—then a tyranny was established in the person of Cypsĕlus (657), who was succeeded by his son Periander, one of the seven sages of Greece, and he by his nephew Psammetichus, until the expulsion of their tyrants by the Corinthians (584) and the restoration of the oligarchical constitution.

There were two institutions which served, no less than

the confederacies of cities in the same district, to unite the little independent states into which Greece was divided.

245 1. The Amphictyoniæ (properly Amphictioniæ) or
A unions of people living in the vicinity of a sanctuary, established for the purposes of mutual security, and of celebrating their festivals in common. They differed from the ordinary confederacies, in not being directed against any third power. The most celebrated was the DELPHIC AMPHICTYONIA, originally a confederacy of Hellenic tribes in Thessaly, who acquired new settlements in their wars with the Pelasgians. The term was subsequently used in a more
B extended sense to express a union of the several nations of Thessaly and central Greece, comprising at an early period twelve districts (with their colonies), the number and privileges of which remained unchanged until the time of Philip II. of Macedonia. The reception of several Pelasgian clans into the confederacy, naturally altered its original character of a defensive alliance against the Pelasgians, and from that time the union assumed a more peaceful form. To the Amphictyons belonged the privilege of protecting the Delphic oracle and the treasures deposited in the temple, of arranging the festivals and providing for the security of pilgrims. Through this connection with the
C Amphictyons the Delphic oracle obtained such an influence, that at one time nothing of importance was undertaken without its command or sanction: but as faith in its prophetic powers declined, the Amphictyonia fell also into disrepute, and was superseded by the Hegemonia, first of Sparta, and subsequently of Athens.

From this period the duties of the confederacy were restricted to the protection of the oracle, and the superintendence of the Pythian games, until the Phocian war, when it again assumed a political character. So far was it, how-
D ever, from recovering the influence which it had possessed in the sacred war against Crissa, that its exertions were now of little avail, except to increase intestine discord, and hasten the downfall of Grecian freedom.

At the two meetings, which were held annually, in the Spring at Delphi, and in the Autumn near Thermopylæ (at Anthēla), the multitude of citizens who attended from the cities of the league composed the greater assembly. There was also a council of deputies, who, besides arranging the questions to be brought forward for dis-

cussion in the assembly, and carrying its decisions into effect, were (245)
charged also with the superintendence of the sanctuaries belonging A
to the league, and the worship connected with them; and more particularly with the management of the Delphic temple, and the Pythian games.

THE CONGRESSES (πανηγύρεις) at the four great 246
National Games, which, with few exceptions, were open to all Greeks, and to them exclusively.

a. The *Olympic*, the most renowned of all, were founded, according to the legend, by Hercules, and after a long in- B
terruption, revived by Iphitus of Elis (a descendant of Oxȳlus), and Lycurgus of Sparta (300 years after the destruction of Troy; consequently in 884?). It would seem, however, that what is called their revival, was, in reality, the first establishment of these games. From the year B. C. 778 (Olymp. i. 1), a regular record was kept of the conquerors, and from that date until A. D. 392. The games at the commencement of the first year in each Olympiad were celebrated at Olympia, in honor of Zeus, with gymnastic contests and horse-races, during a general amnesty, which lasted five successive days; the ceremonial being closed by sacrifices, a banquet, and a grand procession.

The gymnastic combats of men (at a later period of boys also)
consisted, at first, simply of races in the stadium: but gradually the C
programme was enlarged by the addition of the Pentathlon (or union of five exercises), viz., leaping, throwing the discus or javelin, running, and wrestling; and the Pancration, or union of wrestling and boxing. The other combats consisted of races on horseback, and in chariots drawn by two or four horses. The presence of so many Hellenes from all parts of the country, and the difficulty, in those days, of making any general announcement, rendered the Olympic Panegyris an occasion peculiarly favorable for public advertisements, and the exhibition of works of art. The victors were rewarded on the spot with crowns of wild olive branches, and statues in the grove of Altis, and still more substantially on their return to their own cities; at Athens, for example, with a triumphal entry, *Proedriæ*, and maintenance for life in the Prytaneum.

b. The *Pythian*, in honor of the Pythian Apollo, were D
held in the third year of each Olympiad, on the plain of Pytho between Delphi and Cirrha.

c. The *Nemean* were celebrated in a cypress-grove near the village of Nemea, in Argolis, in honor of Zeus (in the winter of the second, and summer of the fourth, year of each Olympiad).

d. The *Isthmian*, in the grove of pines on the Corin

A thian isthmus, in honor of Poseidōn (at the beginning of the first, and end of the third year in each Olympiad).

§ 49. *Sparta.*

247 Laconia, in the division of Peloponnesus, having fallen to the lot of Eurysthenes and Procles, the throne of Sparta was thenceforth always occupied by two kings, a Eurysthenid and a Proclid. The contest with the Achæans, who still occupied parts of the country, continued for about 300 years, and even in the eighth and seventh centuries, B. C., we find that Achæan colonies were sent out from Lacedæmon. Of all these struggles the most obstinate was
B with the inhabitants of Hĕlos, who, after the destruction of their city, became bondsmen of the Spartans.[1] Thus the population assumed a threefold character, viz.: 1. The dominant Dorians, or SPARTANS. 2. The PERIŒCI, or LACEDÆMONIANS, a title given to the conquered Achæans, who enjoyed personal freedom, and retained their property in the land. They paid taxes, but had no share in the administration of public affairs. 3. The Helots, or bondsmen of the state, who were the inhabitants of places formerly stormed by the Spartans. Their lands were forfeited
C to the conquerors, whose property they farmed, paying them a proportion of the annual produce by way of rent. They served in war, either as attendants on their masters, or as light-armed soldiers; but were considered the property of the state, and consequently could not be sold out of the country, or put to death.

LYCURGUS, a member of the family of Procles, and guardian of king Charilāus, was compelled by the opposite party to withdraw from Sparta; but returned about the year 880, after having visited Crete, Asia Minor, and Egypt. At the
D request of his fellow-citizens, and with the approbation of the Delphic oracle, Lycurgus gave his native city a constitution, partly new, but for the most part merely a legal confirmation of ancient practices, recorded by oral tradition in the form of proverbs (ῥῆτραι). THE TWO HEREDITARY KINGS were retained. They presided over the public sacrifices, and in war had the uncontrolled command of the army; but in

[1] [The term *Helots* is much more probably connected with ἑλεῖν than with *Helos* and this tale of its capture, which was probably invented to ***account for*** the term.]

time of peace were distinguished merely by the privileges (247
which they enjoyed (a dwelling, estates, perquisites of A
beasts offered for sacrifice, and skins, booty, precedence,
a double portion at the public meals, and a public funeral).
The government was administered by a γερουσία, consisting of the two kings, and twenty-eight men who had reached, at least, their sixtieth year. They were elected by the people and were irresponsible. The duties of this council were to propose measures to the general assembly of the people, discharge the highest functions of government, sit in judgment as the supreme criminal tribunal, and in conjunction with the Ephors, to watch over public morals.

The Popular Assembly, at which every Spartan above 248
thirty years of age had the right of voting, was regularly B
assembled every full moon in the open air, and decided by acclamation on the adoption or rejection of the propositions successively laid before it by the Gerusia, which related principally to the passing or repealing of laws, the choice of public officers, war and peace. It is uncertain, whether Lycurgus himself introduced the five Ephori, who originally, as presidents of the popular assembly, acted the part of judges in civil matters, and, at a later period, as representatives of the people from whom they were taken, formed a standing opposition to the kings and Gerusia, and enjoyed
almost unlimited power. They exercised a strict control C
over the public morals, education, and the behavior of foreigners, enforced observance of the laws, conducted all public negotiations, particularly with regard to foreign affairs (the σκυτάλη[1]), inquired into the manner in which the magistrates performed their duties, and even possessed the power of arresting the kings. To the legislation of Lycurgus is ascribed also the introduction of an equal partition of the land, in accordance with which the whole country was divided into 39,000 inalienable and indivisible lots or properties, 9,000 greater, of which each Spartan family (at least after the acquisition of Messenia) possessed one, and 30,000 smaller for the Lacedæmonians; but this arrangement was probably subsequent to the first Messenian war.

The regulations of Lycurgus with respect to educa- 249

---

[1] [See the description of it in the 'Handbook of Grecian Antiqq.' (p. 139), or in the 'Dict. of Greek and Roman Antiqq.']

(249) tion and domestic life had reference principally to the
A qualification of every free citizen for military service, and the subjection of all private interests to those of the state. Every new-born child, if weakly or deformed, was exposed on Mount Tāÿgĕtus, the strong children were brought up by their mothers until their seventh year, and from that time, until the age of thirty, were publicly educated in troops or classes (ἀγέλαι and βοῦαι) instructed in gymnastic accomplishments, music, and dancing, and accustomed to practise the resources and endure the pri-
B vations of warfare. That the citizen's life might be perpetually that of the soldier in his camp, exempt from household cares and occupations, Lycurgus instituted public meals (συσσίτια, in Lacedæmon φειδίτια; the black broth), in separate messes of fifteen persons, and required the greatest simplicity in dress and lodging. For the removal of every temptation to avarice or foreign luxury, the only circulating medium allowed was an iron coinage; and commerce, travelling, and the residence of foreigners at Sparta, were strictly prohibited. The chief occupation of the free citizen was the practice of military exercises, in which all persons between the ages of twenty and sixty were required to join. The Periœci devoted themselves exclusively to trade and manufactures, whilst the cultivation of the soil and all mechanical labors devolved on the Helots.

Lycurgus, after exacting from the king, the senate, and the people, an oath that none of his laws should be changed during his absence, quitted the city and never returned.

§ 60. *The two first Messenian Wars.*

250 1. First Messenian War (743—724).

C Legend concerning the cause of the war.[1] Some Spartan virgins, who had come to worship at a temple of Artemis common to both Lacedæmonians and Messenians, were carried off by Messenian youths, and the Spartan king (Telĕclus) slain in an attempt to release them; soon after this outrage, a noble Messenian (Polychāres), being unable to obtain satisfaction from the Spartan senate for the driving away of his cattle, and the assassination of his son, (by a Lacedæmonian named Euæphnus,) avenged himself by the murder of some Spartans.

Their demand that the murderer should be delivered up

[1] According to an intimation in Tacit. Annal. iv. 43, the real cause of the war seems to have been a dispute respecting the boundaries of the two states.

to them, being treated with contempt, the Spartans at once (250)
commenced the war, by making several incursions into the A
Messenian territory. Many bloody, but indecisive, battles
were fought. The Messenians threw themselves into the
strong fortress of Ithōme, and, during the lifetime of their
king, Aristodēmus, with the assistance of the Achæans,
Arcadians, and Sicyonians, made head against the Spartans;
but after his death, Ithome was taken, and many of the
Messenians escaped into Argos and Arcadia, whilst those
who remained became tributary to the Spartans, under the
name of Periœci.

The despised Parthenii (children of slaves?), as they were called, being detected in a conspiracy with the Helots, emigrated to Italy, where they founded the city of Tarentum (708).

2. Second Messenian War (685—668). The hard 251
conditions on which peace had been granted to the Messe- B
nians, and their contemptuous treatment by the Spartans,
roused the next generation to insurrection, in which they
were assisted not only by their former allies, but also by
the Eleans. Under the command of the Heraclid Aristomĕnes, the Messenians defended themselves against the
Spartans (who were led by the lame Athenian minstrel
Tyrtæus), and for eleven years kept possession of the fortress of Ira, from which successful incursions were often
made into the Spartan territory. In one of these sallies C
Aristomĕnes himself was taken prisoner, but escaped from
his prison (the Cæadas) by following, it is said, the footsteps
of a fox (?), and returned to Ira. At length, through the
treachery of a Spartan deserter, the enemy were admitted
during a tempestuous night; and the Messenians, after
bravely contesting the possession of the city for three days
and nights, were at last compelled to abandon their post.
Aristomĕnes, placing the women and children in the centre
of the army, fought his way into Arcadia, but his plan of
surprising Sparta from this point was frustrated through the
treachery of the Arcadian king, Aristocrătes. Most of the
Messenians emigrated to Sicily, where they took possession
of Zancle, which thenceforth was called Messāna. The
few who remained became Helots.

§ 61. *Athens.*

1. Period of the kings to the year 1068. The whole 252
catalogue of Athenian sovereigns until the reign of Theseus D

(252) is a mere unconnected tissue of mythical personages, inter-
A woven with personifications of local events. The historical period of Athens begins with Theseus, who collected into one city the scattered communities of Attica, and in addition to the old partition of the country into four Phylæ, and twelve Phratriæ, introduced a fresh division (based on the condition and employments of the people) into εὐπατρίδαι (nobles), γεωμόροι (husbandmen), and δημιουργοί (handicraftsmen). The last sovereign of the line of Theseus lost his crown to Melanthus, a descendant of Nestor, who, flying from Pylos, arrived in Attica, whilst that country was engaged in a dispute with Bœotia concerning their boundaries, and accepted a challenge to meet the king of Bœotia in single combat, which had been de-
B clined by the Athenian monarch. He was succeeded by his son Codrus, after whose voluntary death (239) the contest of his two sons for the throne afforded the Eupatrĭdæ an opportunity of entirely abolishing the kingly office. Neleus, disgusted at the preference shown to his brother, emigrated to Asia Minor, as leader of the Ionians; whilst Medon and his descendants became mere chief magistrates, responsible for their administration to the aristocracy, the title of king being at the same time exchanged for that of ARCHON.

253 2. ARCHONS FOR LIFE (1068 to 752), of the family of
C Codrus. They differed from the kings merely in name, and in being responsible for their administration.

254 3. ARCHONS FOR TEN YEARS (752—682). Only the four first were of the family of Codrus: afterwards the Archonship was open to all Eupatrids.

255 4. NINE JOINT ARCHONS ANNUALLY ELECTED (from the year 682). The first of these, who had the title of *Eponymus*, because the year was *named after* him, was originally at the head of the civil administration, the second, or *Basileus*, was the chief-priest, and the third, or *Polemar-*
D *chus*, commanded the army in time of war. The remaining six, who were called Thesmothĕtæ, were charged with the administration of criminal justice.

As the Archons were chosen only from the Eupatrids, and, in the absence of statute law, were guilty of great partiality and oppression in the discharge of their office, a system of written laws was loudly called for by the dis-

satisfied plebeians. In the year 624 one of the Archons, (255)
named *Draco* [Δράκων], was commissioned to draw up such A
a code, but the extreme severity of his δεσμοί only increased the discontent of the people. Draco fled to Ægina, where he died, and most of his laws fell into disuse.

256 THE INSURRECTION OF CYLON (612). At the head of the malcontents was one Cylōn, who attempted to make himself absolute at Athens. With some troops belonging to his father-in-law, (Theagĕnes, tyrant of Megăra), he seized on the Acropolis, but was soon expelled by the Archon Megăcles of the family of Alcmæonidæ), at whose instigation the partisans of Cylon, who had fled for refuge to the altar of the Eumenides, were all put to death. The Alcmæonidæ, laden with a curse on account of this murder, were compelled, at the suggestion of Solon, to quit the city, which was purified from the pollution by Epimenides of Crete.

257 In order to remove the misunderstanding between the Eupatrids and the Demos [or *people*], two measures were B
proposed by Solōn, a descendant of Codrus, who was already well known to the people. 1. *The recovery of Salamis.*—This island had been lost to the Megarians, and all attempts to retake it having proved ineffectual, it was forbidden on pain of death to propose an expedition for that purpose. Solon, however, by means of an elegy, C
delivered under the influence, as he pretended, of insanity, prevailed on the Athenians to renew the war. He himself acted as their leader, and the Megarians having been inveigled into Attica, were put to death by soldiers disguised as women. The settlement of the dispute having been subsequently referred to the Lacedæmonians, Solon secured the possession of the island to his countrymen by interpolating a verse in the Iliad (ii. 558). 2. *The first Sacred War.*—The Crisæans had not only extorted heavy payments from the merchants and pilgrims who passed through their territory on the road to Delphi, but had even plundered the temple of Apollo, and put to death the foreigners who happened to be present. Solon having induced the D
Amphictyons to make war on Crisa [Κρῖσα rather than Κρίσσα]; the city was demolished, its inhabitants sold into slavery, and its territory, in obedience to an injunction of the oracle, consecrated to the Pythian Apollo. Meanwhile, three factions had sprung up in Attica: 1. The Eupatrids, who possessed rich estates on the plains of Attica (οἱ ἐκ τοῦ πεδίου), and advocated a rigid oligarchy. 2. The proprietors in the mountainous districts, who were poor and in debt;

(257) these wished to establish a democracy. 3. The Demiurgi
A on the coast (πάραλοι), who desired a mixed form of government. With the view of reconciling these various factions, the sovereign authority was offered to Solon, and on his refusal to accept the crown, he was chosen Archon Eponymus (in 594), and commissioned to draw up a new code of laws.

258 SOLON'S LEGISLATION.

The measures adopted by Solon for meeting the present emergency and reconciling the contending parties were: 1. The repeal of all Draco's laws except those against murder. 2. The *Seisactheia*, as it was called [i. e. the *shaking off of burdens*], by which claims were rendered more moderate, and the means of liquidating debts facilitated by raising the standard of the coinage (about $\frac{27}{100}$).[1] At the same time Solon abolished the ancient law of arrest for debt, and restored their civil rights to all citizens (except actual felons), who had been pronounced ἄτιμοι [Antiqq. 139].

259 The persons excluded from civil rights were: 1. The μέτοικοι [*resi-*
B *dent-aliens*], for the most part foreigners, who were permitted by the state to exercise their trades at Athens in consideration of a fixed payment and an undertaking to bear their share of all the public burdens (even military service). In all legal proceedings they were represented by a citizen as their advocate or patron (προστάτης). 2. The slaves (purchased foreigners and their descendants), whose lives were protected by Solon's code, and a right of complaint against their masters allowed in cases of undue severity. Emancipated slaves were admitted to the same privileges as the Metœci, and were required to choose their former masters as patrons.

260 A democratic character was given to the constitution of
C Solon by the substitution of property for birth as a qualification for the higher offices of state. In accordance with this plan, the citizens were divided into four classes: 1. The πεντακοσιομέδιμνοι, who obtained yearly from their estates 500 measures of dry and liquid produce. 2. The
D ἱππεῖς, who had 300 measures, and were able to maintain a war-horse. 3. The ζευγῖται, who had 200 measures, and kept a pair of farm-horses. 4. The θῆτες, who possessed a smaller income. None but citizens of the first class were eligible to the Archonship; and by consequence no others were admissible into the court of Areopăgus. The other offices of state were open to the three first classes,

[1] ["— making the mina be counted at 100, instead of its previous value, 73 drachmas."—*Keightley's Greece*, p. 62.]

and all enjoyed the right of voting in the popular assem- (260)
blies and acting as judges. In this manner, Solon con- A
trived to reconcile the conflicting claims of the nobility and the people; the former continued for a long period to monopolize all the most important offices, whilst at the same time the personal equality of all free-born citizens was fully recognized.

The citizens of the first and second classes served as cavalry soldiers, those of the third as hoplites, and those of the fourth (only in cases of necessity), as light-armed troops, and at a later period as marines on board the fleet.

The NINE Archons were retained. They were chosen 261
annually by lot from the first class; and before entering B
on their office, were required to undergo a formal examination, and to swear that they would neither go beyond the law nor receive bribes.

The Senate (βουλή), which from the time of Solon 262
had consisted of 400 members (above thirty years of age), 100 for each Phyle, was increased to 500 when Cleisthĕnes divided the nation into ten Phylæ, and subsequently to 600, on the addition of two new Phylæ. The members were chosen annually by lot (after a previous scrutiny) from the three first classes. The senate was not only required to investigate all questions previously to their discussion in the general assembly, but was also charged with the superintendence of all public functionaries, and the various branches of the administration, especially as regarded financial arrangements, such as the farming out the produce of the public lands, and the income arising from the mines, import duties and personal taxes paid by the *μέτοικοι*, as well as those exacted from them for permission to exercise their trades. The collection of rents from individual farmers was also intrusted to the Senate.

The ASSEMBLY OF THE PEOPLE (ἐκκλησία), which con- 263
sisted of all classes of citizens, was held regularly four C
times in each Prytany (thirty-five or thirty-six days), on the Pnyx (at a later period also in the theatre), and after formal debate decided such questions as were proposed to it by the senate, respecting the enactment or repeal of laws, he election of magistrates, war and peace, political offences, &c. They voted sometimes by holding up their hands, and sometimes (as in the Ostracism) by throwing pebbles into an urn.

264 The COURT OF AREOPAGUS, composed of ex-Archons
A who had discharged the duties of their office unblamably, held its sittings by night on the hill of Ares [" *Mars' Hill*"]. To them was committed the trial of grave offences, as well as the superintendence of public morals and the education of youth. They possessed also the right of investigating and annulling the decrees of the popular assembly.

For the lower courts of justice 6000 men, above thirty years of age (ἡλιασταί), were annually selected by lot from the assembly of the people, and from them were chosen the Thesmothĕtæ (generally from 500 to 600) required for the trial of each cause.

B After engraving on tables of wood and setting up on the Acropŏlis his code of laws, which the people swore to observe for 100 years, Solon travelled into Asia Minor, Crete, and Egypt: but on his return he found the nation still split into three factions, neither of which was satisfied with the privileges which it had obtained.

265 PISISTRATUS, a mountain chieftain, of the race of Codrus, having persuaded his countrymen that the wounds inflicted by himself on his own person were the work of his enemies, obtained a body-guard of club-bearers for his protection, and with their assistance seized the Acropolis, and became absolute sovereign of Athens (560). He was twice expelled from the city, but each time returned: and having at last obtained the confidence of the people, embellished the city, founded the first library, and made a collection of ancient poems, especially those of Homer.

266 The government was carried on in the same spirit by
C his eldest son HIPPIAS (527—510), who allowed a considerable share in the administration to his brother HIPPARCHUS. This prince, who was an enthusiastic admirer of poetry, was assassinated by Harmodius and Aristogeiton (from motives of private revenge, because the sister of Harmodius had been excluded by the Pisistratidæ from the Panathenian procession). After this event the administration of Hippias became insufferably severe: and at length, after putting many persons to death, he was expelled by the Alcmæonĭdæ, who had returned from Macedonia, and were assisted by the Spartans,[1] the enemies of all tyranny, and by the disaffected Athenians. In the year 510, Hippias abandoned his country and

[1] Under Cleomenes.

sought an asylum at the court of the Persian king, Darius I.

About the same time the DEMOCRACY was completely 267
established by the Alcmæonid Cleisthĕnes, who A
endeavored to obliterate all historical family reminiscences by dividing the people into ten local Phylæ, to which he gave entirely new names, and admitted into them many foreigners. At the same time the number of senators was increased to 500 (fifty for each Phyle), who were now chosen by lot. An ineffectual attempt to overthrow the new constitution was made by Isagŏras, at the head of the aristocratic party, supported by the Spartans, who were always favorable to the aristocratical form of
government. Cleisthenes and his party were compelled to B
retire from Athens, but soon returned. To him is ascribed the invention of the Ostracism, a popular mode of banishing from the city (generally for ten years) any person who, in the opinion of the people, had become too powerful, even although he was charged with no overt act. By this arrangement, the democratic party possessed the power of setting aside all whose wealth, talent, or merit rendered them objects of jealousy.

§ 62. *The Grecian Colonies.*

During this period (particularly from 750 to 650), a 268
number of Grecian colonies were established on the islands C
and coasts of the Mediterranean, the Propontis, and the Black sea, partly for purposes of commerce, and partly as a means of relieving the mother country from a superabundant population, or in consequence of political disturbances. These settlements adopted for the most part the constitution, manners, and institutions of the mother country, and at a very early period had oligarchical or aristocratical forms of government; which, however, degenerated, even sooner than in Greece proper, into democracies or tyrannies. They were entirely independent of D
the mother country, except in so far as they were induced by piety to accord to her certain privileges and distinctions.

I. ÆOLIAN, IONIAN, and DORIAN COLONIES on the 269
western coast of Asia Minor, see § 57.

II. DORIAN COLONIES in Lower Italy, or Magna Græ- 270
cia: 1. Tarentum (see § 60); 2. Locri Epizephyrii

(founded in the first instance by the Ozolian or Opuntian Locrians, and afterwards re-settled by Messenian Dorians).

271 III. ACHÆAN COLONIES, in Lower Italy. 1. Croton;
A 2. Sybăris. After the destruction of this settlement by the Crotoniates (510), another city named Thurii was founded in the neighborhood by the Athenians (446).

The Sybarites founded Metapontum and Poseidonia, the latter of which, under Lucanian rule, obtained the name of Pœstum.

272 IV. CHALCIDIAN COLONIES: *a. On the Thracian coast* (where the whole peninsula between the Thermaic and Strymonic gulfs had the name of Chalcidicē) were thirty-two places (Olynthus, Chalcis, &c.) all of Chalcidian origin. *b. In Lower Italy:* 1. Cumæ [or Cyme; in
B Greek *Κύμη*], the most ancient of all the Grecian settlements in the west, and the mother-city of Neapŏlis; 3. Rhegium. *c. In Sicily:* 1. Naxos (afterwards Tauromenium), with the daughter-cities of Leontini and Catăna; 2. Zancle (afterwards a Dorian city under the name of Messana); 3. Himĕra.

273 V. DORIAN COLONIES: *a. In Sicily,* 1. Syracuse
C founded about the year 735, by Archias, a Corinthian, on the island of Ortygia. It subsequently became four cities: 2. The Hyblæan Megara (destroyed by the Syracusan tyrant, Gelon, about 480), with its daughter city Selīnus; 3. Gela, with its daughter city Agrigentum (destroyed by the Carthaginians in 405, and restored by Timoleon). *b.* A chain of *Corinthian* settlements *on the coast of the Ionian sea, viz.* Leucas, Anactorium, Ambracia, Apollonia, Epidamnus, and particularly Corcyra. *c. On the Thracian coast:* 1. Potidæa (founded by Corinth); 2. Byzantium (by Megara); *d. On the Thracian Bospŏrus,* Chalcēdon.

D *Outline of the History of Syracuse.*—Syracuse underwent more numerous changes of constitution than even her mother country, Corinth (see § 58). *a. Aristocracy* from the establishment of the colony to the time of Gelon (735—484). During this period the supreme authority was lodged in the hands of a few rich families (Gamoroi), who were expelled by the democratic party and an insurrection of the slaves, but restored by Gelon, lord of Gela. *β. Tyranny* (488—466), under three brothers, who succeeded each other in the following order—Gelon, who overthrew the Carthaginians at Himĕra on the same day as the battle of Salamis (480), Hieron, and Thrasybūlus. The last was deposed, after a reign of eight months, on account of his cruelty. *γ. Democracy* (466—405),

introduction of the Petalismus, for the purpose of expelling citizens (273) A
who had become objects of suspicion. Attempt on Syracuse by the Athenians (415—413). δ. *Tyranny* (405—343), Dionysius I. and his son Dionysius II. thrice waged war against Carthage; Timoleon being invited from Corinth to take the command of the Syracusans, overthrew the Corinthians, expelled the tyrants, and re-established ε. the *democracy* (343—317). ς. *Tyranny* (317—269), Agathocles (317—289), took most of the Grecian cities in Sicily, and waged a fresh war with the Corinthians (comp. § 40. ii.). He was succeeded by Mænon and Icetas. η. *Kings* (269—212). The reign of Hiero II., who was chosen king on account of his victory over the Mamertines, and carried on war for a short time against Rome (see § 118), was the most flourishing period of Syracusan history. His great grandson, Hieronymus, made an alliance with the Carthaginians, which occasioned the siege and capture of the city by Marcellus, in 212. For Dionysius, v. Arnold's Rome, ch. 21.

VI. Colonies of Miletus.—*a. On the Hellespont*— 274
Abȳdus and Lampsacus. *b. On the Propontis*— B
Cyzicus. *c. On the Pontus Euxinus*—Sinōpe (with its daughter city Trapezus), Phasis, Tanais, at the mouth of the river Tanais, Panticapæum, Olbia, at the mouth of the Borysthenes, Tomi, &c.

VII. Colonies of the Phocæans: Aleria on the 275
island of Corsica, and Massilia, on the southern coast of Gallia.

VIII. Colony of Zacynthus: Saguntum, on the east- 276
ern coast of Spain. C

The establishment of two colonies by Athens (Amphipolis in Macedonia, and Thurii in Magna Græcia), occurs during the next period. For the colony established in Cyrene, see § 57.

Third Period.

From the Persian wars to the Decline of Grecian Independence, 500—338.

§ 63. *The Persian Wars.*

(500—449.)

For the causes of the Persian wars (the participation 277
of the Athenians and Eretrians in the revolt of the D
Ionians), see § 21, b. 4.

A. Defensive war against the Persians, 492—479. 278
First campaign of the Persians under Mardonius (492); *second* under Datis and Artaphernes (490). See § 21, b. 4.

After the victory of Marathon 29th Sept. 490),

(278) Miltiades formed the design of chastising those islands
A of the Ægean sea which had revolted to the Persians
during the war. This project succeeded as far as regarded Lemnos, but his attempts to carry Paros being unsuccessful, he was condemned on his return to pay a pecuniary fine, which his son was compelled to raise after the death of his father. The fate of Athens, after the decease of Miltiades, was almost entirely in the hands of Themistocles, and of Aristides, surnamed the "Just."

Themistocles having espoused the popular cause as the
B most likely mode of carrying out his ambitious views,
succeeded in obtaining the ostracism of his rival by spreading a false report, that Aristides wished to exclude the common people from the privilege of sitting as judges. At the same time, he prevailed on them to pass a decree authorizing the expenditure in ship-building of the revenue arising from the silver mines of Laurion (thirty to forty talents), which had hitherto been divided annually among the people. This measure, dictated, as he pretended, by
C obedience to the oracle, which had counselled the Athe-
nians "to seek for shelter behind their wooden walls," was in reality the result of that sharp-sighted policy, which foresaw the preservation and future aggrandizement of Athens, in the establishment of a naval power as a counterpoise to the superiority of Lacedæmon by land.

279 Third Campaign of the Persians in 480.—Even the advance of an immense Persian army (comp. § 21, B. 5) scarcely awakened the Greeks to a sense of the necessity of combined exertions. Thebes and the greater
D part of Bœotia openly took part with the barbarians, whilst
Sparta, at the head of the Peloponnesian league, was supported only by Athens and her allies, the cities of Thespiæ and Platææ. An attempt to dispute the entrance of the invading army into Thessaly by the pass of Tempe having failed, the Spartan king Leonidas was detached, with 300 Spartans and 4900 Greek soldiers of other nations, to defend the pass of *Thermopylæ;* a Greek fleet, under the command of Eurybiades, a Spartan, being at the same time stationed off the headland of Artemisium. As soon as he heard of the treachery of Ephialtes, Leonidas dismissed all his allies except the Medizing[1] Thebans, and a

[1] [To Medize = *to favor the Medes.*]

little band of 700 Thespians who voluntarily remained at (279)
their post. After a brave resistance, the patriot army, A
consisting of these Thespians and 300 Spartans, was entirely cut to pieces. The Thebans laid down their arms; and the Persian army, advancing without opposition, traversed Attica, and burnt the city of Athens, which had been abandoned by the inhabitants. Meanwhile, the Grecian fleet having been twice engaged with the Persians off Artemisium, without obtaining any decided advantage, had retired to Salamis, where Themistocles (who had already bribed Eurybiades to continue at his post, and now, by means of a stratagem, compelled the Peloponnesians to risk another engagement) obtained a splendid victory over the Persian fleet on the 23d of September.

By a second stratagem of Themistocles (the destruction 280
of the bridge over the Hellespont), Xerxes was induced to B
hasten his return into Asia, leaving behind him in Thessaly Mardonius, with 300,000 men. After fruitless negotiations with the Greeks, carried on through the intervention of Alexander king of Macedonia, Mardonius invaded Attica in the year 479. The Athenians, abandoning their city for the second time, fled for refuge to their ships and to the island of
Salamis. The Spartans now sent an army to the assistance C
of their allies; and Mardonius, falling back on Bœotia, was utterly defeated near Platææ (25th of September) by the united forces of the Athenians under Aristides (recalled from banishment to take the command), and the Spartans under their king Pausanias. In this action Mardonius was slain, with the greater part of his army. The rich camp of the invader was plundered by the conquerors, and the city of Thebes closely besieged, until the leaders of the Medizing faction were delivered up to Pausanias,
who put them all to death (at Corinth). On the same day D
the Persians (who had intrenched themselves behind a bulwark, formed partly of their ships, which they had hauled up on land near the promontory of Mycăle, in Asia Minor) were defeated by the Spartan king Leotychides, and the Athenian Xanthippus. This battle, followed by the destruction of the Persian camp and fleet, was the first aggressive movement on the part of the Greeks, and prepared the way for the liberation of the islands and the restoration of independence to the Greeks of Asia Minor.

(280) Under the administration of Themistocles, Athens was
A rebuilt on a more extensive scale, and the fortifications completed with astonishing rapidity, notwithstanding the remonstrances of the Spartans, who viewed with distrust the increasing power of their rivals. At the same time, the commodious harbor of Piræus was also completed and fortified. As a reward for their bravery, Aristides obtained the enactment of a law, by which citizens of the fourth class were rendered eligible to all offices of state.

281 B. Aggressive Maritime War against the Persians
B under the Hegemony of Athens (478—449).—The war was continued by the allied fleet, under the command of Pausanias, Aristides, and Cimon, with the view of expelling the Persians from Thrace, the Greek islands, and the colonies of Asia Minor. The greater part of Cyprus was subdued, together with Byzantium; but the haughty arrogance of Pausanias so disgusted the allies, that they transferred the maritime Hegemony from Sparta to Athens (477 ?). The Spartans hereupon recalled Pausanias, and refused to take any further part in the war against the Persians, which was now carried on with considerable success by the Athenians and their allies.

C The Hegemony of Sparta over the other Peloponnesian states consisted in this—that in all wars undertaken by general consent a Spartan should take the command in chief of the allied army; and that all congresses and councils of the allies should be held at Sparta. Until the Persian war this Hegemony was confined to the Peloponnesus, but, in consequence of the almost universal participation of the Greeks in these wars, the system was so far extended, that at the battle of Mycale Sparta found herself at the head of a confederacy, which, in addition to most of the states of the mother country, comprehended also the colonies on the coast of Asia Minor. Athens, on withdrawing from this Hegemony, naturally found allies in the colonists (for the most part democratical), whom she had delivered from the Persian yoke, and over whom she already exercised
D a species of Hegemony, as the chief maritime power. The tyranny of Pausanias soon compelled, as we have seen, the rest of the allies to withdraw from the Spartan Hegemony, and seek protection by placing the Athenians at the head of the confederacy. The proposal being willingly accepted, Aristides drew up a plan, in which the relative duties of the allied powers were distinctly defined. Each state was to furnish a contingent either of ships or money; and the island of Delos was to be the place of meeting for the congress, and the depository of the common chest, the administration of which was committed to the Athenians.

282 From this period commences the development of a

fierce antagonism between the aristocratic and democratic (282)
states of Greece, which gradually split into two parties; A
of which Athens and Sparta were respectively the heads
and representatives. But even in Athens itself there still
lingered a restless aristocratic faction, which persuaded the
people that danger was to be apprehended from the popu-
larity of Themistocles; and being aided by the secret
co-operation of Sparta, at length obtained his banishment by
ostracism in the year 473 (?). Themistocles retired, in the
first instance, to Argos; but being accused of maintaining
a treasonable correspondence with the Persians, in conjunction with Pausanias, he quitted that country, and
sought the protection of Artaxerxes I., who granted him
for his support the revenues of three cities (Magnesia,
Myus, and Lampsacus.) He died (it is said, by drinking B
ox's blood?) without attempting any thing against his
native country. Pausanias, who had been engaged in
secret negotiations with the Persians for the abolition of
the Ephorate and increase of the kingly power at Sparta,
escaped arrest by taking refuge in a temple, where he was
starved to death. Aristides died about the same time
(468?) in extreme poverty. After the banishment of
Themistocles, and the death of Aristides, Pericles seems
to have been the leader of the democratic party, and Cimon, the son of Miltiades, of the aristocratic; the policy
of which was to keep the people employed by continuing
the war. Cimon, being appointed commander-in-chief C
of the army of the league, expelled the Persians from
Thrace, Caria, and Lycia; defeated them, by sea and land,
on the river Eurymedon; and expended the booty obtained by these victories in beautifying Athens, and joining Piræus to the city by means of the long walls.

§ 64. *The third Messenian War.*

[465 (or 464)—456 (or 455).]

The Spartans were on the eve of invading Attica, for 283
the purpose of defeating the designs of the Athenians on D
the island of Thasus, when their preparations were arrested
by a tremendous earthquake, by which 20,000 persons lost
their lives. The oppressed Helots availed themselves of
this opportunity to make an attempt on the city, whilst it

(283) lay in ruins, but finding the Spartans drawn up in arms,
A under the command of their king Archidāmus, they retreated to Ithome, which they occupied in conjunction with
the Messenians. Through the influence of the aristocratic
party, particularly of Cimon, aid was afforded to the
Spartans by the people of Athens. Cimon himself marched
twice into Messenia, but as the place continued to hold out,
and he no longer possessed the confidence of the Spartans,
he was dismissed; and in consequence of this disgrace
was banished by the ostracism, at the instance of the
B democratic party, headed by his rival Pericles. At length,
after sustaining a siege of ten years, the Messenians were
permitted to depart uninjured, and occupy Naupactus,
which had been taken by the Athenians a short time previously from the Locri Ozolæ.

§ 65. *The age of Pericles.*

284 A. Degeneracy of the Athenian Democracy.

From the banishment of Cimon may be dated the commencement of democratic supremacy, the people being
entirely governed by the influence of its leaders; among
whom the most powerful was Pericles, the son of Xanthippus,—a man who, although he had never filled the
office of Archon, exercised almost unlimited control as a
popular orator and commander during a period of forty
C years (468—429). The means of carrying out his various
innovations were principally afforded by the removal of
the exchequer of the league from Delos to Athens. Ever
since the Athenians had supplied shipping and troops, for
the purpose of carrying on the war, in return for the pecuniary contingents of the allies, they had been in the
habit of looking on the common treasury as their own
property, and instead of employing the finances against
D Persia, had applied them to their own purposes. To such
an extent was this abuse carried, that the funds contributed
by the allies of Athens were even used as an instrument
for destroying the independence of those who had supplied
them; it being, of course, requisite that all lawsuits connected with these finances should be decided at Athens by
the Heliasts. Besides this, all the allies (among whom
were now included all the Grecian cities on the coasts of

Macedonia and Thrace, as well as those on the western (284)
and southern shores of Asia Minor, as far as Pamphylia, A
and the islands of the Ægean sea) were not only compelled, after the conclusion of the Persian war, to continue the payment of war-taxes, but these contributions were gradually raised to double the original amount. With such resources at his disposal, Pericles not only embellished the city with the most magnificent buildings, but also found means of inducing the poorer citizens to take a greater interest in public affairs, by granting them a remuneration for their attendance at the public assemblies and in the
courts of justice. He also introduced the practice of B
paying the army, and discharged out of the public exchequer the fees required from the poorer classes for admission to the theatre. As the only obstacle to his design of raising the lower orders, and by consequence increasing his own power, was found in the Areopagus, now the sole representative of aristocratic interests, Pericles obtained (on the motion of one Ephialtes) a decree that the right of deciding certain causes, as well as the guardianship of public morals, and the superintendence of the public treasure, should be withdrawn from that court.

B. Foreign and Domestic Wars during this period. 285

1. The participation of the Athenians in the 286
Insurrection of the Egyptians, and of the Satrap C
Inarus (460—455) against the Persians, ended with the blockade of the Athenian fleet in the Nile, off the island of Prosopitis (see § 21, B. 6).

2. War of the Athenians with the Spartans 287
and Bœotians (457—450).—In order to establish in Bœotia a counterpoise to the power of Athens, by restoring the influence formerly possessed by the aristocratic government of Thebes, the Spartans, under pretence of expelling the Phocians who had invaded the Doric fatherland, sent an army into central Greece. But all the ad- D
vantages which they and their allies, the Bœotian and Athenian oligarchs, expected to have gained by the victory of Tanagra (457), were soon neutralized by a victory obtained by the Athenians, under Myronides (near Œno-

(287) phyta); in consequence of which, the Bœotians, Phocians,
A and Opuntian Locrians, joined the Athenian confederacy. As a severe struggle with Sparta was apprehended, Pericles consented to the recall of Cimon, and, through his intervention, obtained an armistice for five years with the Peloponnesians (450).

288 3. After their reconciliation with Sparta, a fresh campaign against the Persians was undertaken by the Athenians, at the instance of Cimon, who engaged to reduce the island of Cyprus, but died whilst blockading Citium. On their way home, his fleet and land army overthrew the Egyptians at Salamis of Cyprus (449).

289 4. War of the Athenians against the Bœotian
B Aristocracy (447).—A number of aristocratically disposed citizens, exiles from those Bœotian cities which had been compelled to join the Athenian confederacy, having united for the purpose of expelling the Athenians, a battle was fought at Coronēa (447), where Tolmides was slain, and the Bœotians gained such a victory as enabled them to attain their object. The Peloponnesians, after the expiration of the five years' armistice, having invaded Attica, for the purpose of embarrassing Pericles in his endeavors to reconquer the revolted island of Eubœa, the Athenian commander, in order to secure the island, concluded a truce
C with the Peloponnesians for thirty years (445). The conditions of this treaty were, that all places taken from the Peloponnesians during the war should be given up; and that Athens and Sparta should each confirm and respect the Hegemony of the other; but unfortunately permission was, at the same time, granted to the neutral states to join the alliance or not, as they might think fit,—an arrangement which laid the foundation of fresh disputes.

§ 66. *The Peloponnesian War.*

(431—404.)

290 Causes.—1. The opposition between the aris-
D tocratical party and that democratic element, which was rapidly acquiring the ascendency, in spite of the resistance offered by Lacedæmon and the other aristocratic states. One of the most prominent signs of this antagonism was the *jealousy* between Athens and Sparta,

created by the transfer of the Hegemony to Athens, and (290)
the fortification of that city; a feeling which had been A
aggravated by the insult offered to Athens in the dismissal of her troops during the third Messenian war, and by the active participation of the rival powers in the political disputes of other states. 2. The *discontent* of the *allies*, who were treated as vassals by Athens, and had made several ineffectual attempts to throw off the yoke.

IMMEDIATE CAUSES OF HOSTILITIES—1. *A War be-* 291
tween Corcyra and Corinth (434—432).—Epidamnus, a B
colony of Corcyra, being hard pressed by her banished nobles in conjunction with the Illyrian barbarians, and having applied in vain to the mother-country for assistance, had admitted troops sent by Corinth, the mother-country of Corcyra. Hence the war between Corcyra and Corinth. The Corcyræans obtain a victory (off Actium), blockade Epidamnus, and conclude an alliance with the Athenians, who take part in a third, but indecisive, engagement; and through this alliance extend their authority to the
coasts of the Ionian sea. 2. The *revolt of Potidæa,* C
a Corinthian colony, from Athens, in disgust at a command issued by the Athenians, that they should pull down the walls of their city. The Potidæans, although supported by Corinth, are conquered, and their city blockaded. At a congress of the Peloponnesian powers, held at Sparta, by desire of the Corinthians, war against Athens is resolved on, principally at the instigation of the Corinthians and Megaræans, in opposition to the advice of king Archidāmus.

ALLIES.—*a. Of Athens.* Thessalian cavalry—Acarnanians—the 292
Messenians in Naupactus, Platææ, almost all the islands of the D
Ægean sea, and in the Ionian sea Corcyra and Zacynthus; most of the Greek cities on the western coast of Asia Minor, the Hellespont, and the shores of Thrace. *b. Of Sparta.* The whole of Peloponnesus, except Argos and Achaia, which remained neutral, Megara, Bœotia, Phocis, Locris, the island of Leucas, and the cities of Ambracia and Anactorium.

I. TEN YEARS' WAR [ὁ δεκαετὴς πόλεμος] TO THE FIFTY YEARS' TRUCE OF NICIAS.

(431—421.)

The war commenced with the invasion of Attica by the 293
Peloponnesians, under Archidāmus, which was regularly repeated every year; the Athenians making reprisals by sending a fleet to ravage the coasts of Peloponnesus. As the

(293) Athenians evaded their enemies by land, and the Spartans
A shrank from a naval engagement, neither party obtained any decided advantage. The inhabitants of Attica, by the advice of Pericles, sought refuge within the walls of the city; where a pestilence [the famous *Plague*] broke out, which, among its numerous victims, carried off Pericles himself (B. C. 439). After his death the democracy of Athens degenerated into an unbridled oligarchy. The blockaded city of Potidæa was reduced in 430; and the island of Lesbos, the whole of which, with the exception of Methymna, had also thrown off its allegiance to Athens, was compelled (the relief promised by Sparta having arrived
B too late) to surrender at discretion (427). By the advice of Cleon, sentence of death was passed on all the inhabitants of Mitylene, but on the following day it was commuted into an order for the execution of the principal conspirators. One thousand of the most distinguished Lesbians were nevertheless put to death, their ships of war taken away, and the whole island (with the exception of Methymna) assigned to the Athenians in 3000 lots.

294 In the year 429 the Athenians sent a fleet to the assistance of the
C Leontines, who were engaged in war with Syracuse. Demosthenes, who accompanied a second fleet destined for the same service, landed in the dismantled port of Pylos, which he fortified, but was soon blockaded by the Spartans, both by sea and land; a situation from which he was delivered by Eurymĕdon. The Spartans stationed on the island of Sphacteria, opposite Pylos, being cut off from the main army by Eurymĕdon, were taken prisoners by Cleon [the demagogue, to whom the command had been given, as a practical joke, that he might make good his frequent assertions, that if the generals were *men*, the Lacedæmonians might be captured with ease] (425).

295 In the year 424 the Athenians took the important island of Cythēra, and ravaged the Laconian coast; but their good fortune had now reached its greatest height, for the next year they were defeated by the Bœotians at Delium (where Alcibiades saved the life of Socrates); and about the same time several of their colonies in Chalcidice, including Amphipolis itself, were wrested from them by the Spartan commander Brasĭdas (Thucydides rescued
D Eion, but was nevertheless banished). For the purpose of reconquering these cities, Cleon was dispatched with an army to the Macedonian coast; but being forced by Brasidas to risk an engagement, he was defeated at AMPHIPOLIS

in 422. Both generals having fallen in the engagement, (295)
a truce for fifty years was negotiated by Nicias; it A
being stipulated that each party should be placed in the position which it had occupied before the commencement of the war.

II. From the Renewal of the War to the Issue of the Expedition against Sicily.

(418—413.)

As some of the Dorian states were dissatisfied with the peace of 296
Nicias, a confederation for its maintenance was formed between Athens and Sparta, which produced the establishment of a counter-league between Argos, Elis, and Mantinēa. But presently complaints arose on both sides respecting the non-fulfilment of certain articles of the treaty; and Alcibiades, availing himself of the misunderstanding thus created between Athens and Sparta, persuaded the Athenians to renounce their alliance with Sparta, and join the Argive confederacy. The Lacedæmonians and their allies, although they obtained a victory over the army of the league at Mantinea in 418, were unable to prevent a renewal of the treaty between Argos and Athens.

The Expedition Against Sicily (415—413).—The 297
Athenians, being invited to aid the inhabitants of Egesta, B
in Sicily, against Syracuse and Selinus, were persuaded by Alcibiades (in opposition to the advice of Nicias) to send thither a fleet of 134 ships, under the command of Alcibiades, Nicias, and Lamăchus. The expedition had scarcely landed, and commenced the blockade of Catăna, when the Salaminia (the vessel employed for conveying sacred embassies) arrived, with dispatches to Alcibiades, commanding his immediate return to Athens, that he might defend himself against a charge of mutilating the statues of Hermes, and profaning the Eleusinian mysteries. Alcibiades escaped by landing at Thurii, whence he proceeded to Argos, and being condemned to death at Athens, sought an asylum at Sparta, where he persuaded the government to support the Syracusans. Meanwhile, Nicias C
was victorious in a battle fought under the walls of Syracuse; and the city, being closely invested, was on the eve of surrender, when Gylippus came to its assistance with a Spartan fleet. Nicias also received a reinforcement, commanded by Eurymedon and Demosthenes; but the Syracusans, who were now supported by all the Greek cities in Sicily, except Agrigentum, obtained a victory over the Athenian fleet, which they blockaded in the port.

(297) A last attempt to break through the blockading line having
A entirely failed, the crews abandoned their vessels, and commencing a retreat by land, were taken prisoners by the enemy. Nicias and Demosthenes were put to death, the prisoners thrown into the stone quarries, and after seventy days of suffering, the survivors (with the exception of the Athenians, Siceliotes, and Italiotes) were sold as slaves.

III. The Decelean War.

(413—404.)

298 Following the advice of Alcibiades, the Spartan army,
B under the command of their king Agis, invaded Attica, and fortified Decelēa, which thenceforward became the stronghold from which parties were sent out to ravage the country. At the same time, 20,000 runaway Athenian slaves joined the expedition. The resources of their allies being utterly exhausted, the Athenians were compelled to substitute for the direct tax hitherto paid a duty of five per cent., *ad valorem*, on all articles imported and exported; a grievance which occasioned the revolt of many
C of their allies in Asia Minor. Whilst Athens was thus deprived of all those resources which secured to the Demos a majority in the courts of justice and public assemblies, Sparta was receiving subsidies for the war from Tissaphernes, the Persian lieutenant in Caria. Every disaster was now laid to the charge of the democracy; and the oligarchical faction, whose secret intrigues had been long preparing the way for such a revolution, availed themselves of the absence of those sturdy burghers who were serving in the fleet, and of the utter despair of the multitude, to
D overthrow the existing constitution. The supreme authority was vested in an oligarchical council of 400, by whom the number of citizens allowed to be present at the popular assemblies was limited to 5,000. As the election and convocation of these representatives was entirely dependent on the will of the council, the authority of the people became merely nominal, whilst that of the oligarchy was unlimited. By the advice, however, of Thrasybūlus, the men who were serving on board the fleet stationed off Samos, pledged themselves to support the democracy, and recalled Alcibiades, who persuaded Tissaphernes to renounce the league with Sparta. It was with difficulty that

the general restrained his army from marching upon (298)
Athens; but such a measure was rendered unnecessary by A
the overthrow of the oligarchical faction, after a reign of
four months, in consequence of a suspicion that they had
been engaged in a treasonable correspondence with Sparta.
The ancient senate resumed its functions; but as the
government no longer possessed the means of remunerating
a large number of citizens for their attendance at the popular
assemblies, the supreme authority still remained in
the hands of the 5,000.

ALCIBIADES A SECOND TIME COMMANDER-IN-CHIEF, 299
411–407.—The Spartan fleet, under Mindărus, which had B
sailed for the Hellespont in order to join Pharnabazus,
satrap of Bithynia, was twice defeated in the neighborhood
of Abydos (off *Κυνὸς σῆμα*), and annihilated off
CYZICUS by Alcibiades in 410. After subduing the coasts
of the Hellespont and Propontis, and taking Chalcēdon
and Byzantium, Alcibiades returned in triumph to Athens
(407), where he revived the celebration of the Eleusinian
mysteries, but was soon deprived of his unlimited command,
in consequence of the defeat, during his absence, of
his lieutenant Antiŏchus by Lysander (near Notium).
Alcibiades retired to the Thracian Chĕrsonese; and ten C
generals, of whom Conon was one, were appointed to
succeed him. At Sparta, also, there was a change of commanders-in-chief.
Lysander was succeeded as Nauarch
by Callicratidas, who, with a superior force, blockaded
Conon in the harbor of Mitylēnē, but was defeated by a
newly-equipped Athenian fleet off the Arginusian islands,
and lost his own life in the engagement.

Of the ten Athenian generals, eight were condemned to death for having neglected to save the shipwrecked seamen after a storm, and to collect the bodies of those who were drowned. Six of them were executed, and the remaining two banished.

Lysander, being again appointed admiral of the Spartan 300
fleet, annihilated that of Athens at Ægospotamos (oppo- D
site to Lampsacus), in 405. Of the whole force only nine
ships were saved, with which Conon effected his escape to
Cyprus. He also subjugated all the allies of the Athenians,
except Samos, introduced aristocratic constitutions
with Spartan magistrates (Harmostæ), and blockaded the
Piræus; whilst Athens was beleaguered, at the same time,

(300) on the land side by the garrison of Decelēa, under Agis,
A and a Spartan army, under Pausanias. After a siege of four months, Athens was compelled by famine to capitulate, deliver up her fleet (except twelve ships), dismantle the long walls and the fortifications of Piræus; recall her banished citizens, receive an aristocratic constitution, engage to furnish assistance to the Spartans in all their wars, and place her armies under the command of a Spartan general-in-chief. With the fall of Athens perished also the democratic principle; and for a long period we hear no more of the struggles between the aristocratic and popular parties.

§ 67. *The Hegemony of Sparta.*

301 As many of the Athenian allies during, and in conse-
B quence of, the war, had placed themselves under the protection of Sparta (an example which Athens herself was obliged to follow, now that peace was established), the whole of Hellas was in effect subject to an authority, which was soon found to be as odious as it was oppressive, on account of the favor shown to a despotic oligarchy, as well as the establishment of garrisons and Harmosts in all those places which had formerly been in alliance with Athens; and also on account of the extortion practised by
C the Spartan government. Those states, especially Thebes and Corinth, which had taken a part in the war simply with the view of crushing the dangerous power of Athens, had never intended that Sparta should acquire through their exertions a decided preponderance in Greece. When, therefore, the demand of the Thebans, that Athens should be demolished, was rejected by Sparta, on the ground of her intending to retain it under her own influence, as a barrier against Bœotia, they so far changed their political creed as to advocate the restoration of Athenian democracy and independence, which had previously been the objects of their bitterest hatred.

302 1. The Supremacy of the Thirty at Athens,
D 404—403.—A change in the constitution was effected by the election, at the instance of Lysander, of thirty men, all taken from the former body of 400, and invested, according to the practice of antiquity, with supreme power during the continuance of their office. As soon as these persons

considered their authority firmly established by the admis- (302
sion into the acropolis of a Spartan garrison, and the dis- A
arming of all citizens, except 3000 who were known to
be oligarchically inclined, there followed a number of im-
peachments, executions (1400 ? it is said), and banishments, at the instigation principally of one Critias, a rene-
gade disciple of Socrates. One of their own number,
Theramĕnes, who had been the first to suggest more humane measures, was condemned to death, and compelled to
drink poison in prison. Alcibiades, having also become
an object of suspicion to the Spartans, was attacked and
slain in Phrygia by Pharnabazus, at the instance of Lysander. Happily for Athens, the Spartans and Thebans B
were now at variance, and Thebes received the Athenian
exiles, notwithstanding the prohibition of the Spartans.
Under the command of T h r a s y b ū l u s, these exiles made
themselves masters of the frontier fortress of Phyle, and,
having overthrown the troops of the oligarchs, took possession also of Piræus, where a battle was fought, in which
the Thirty were defeated, and Critias lost his life. The
places of the Thirty, most of whom had fled to Eleusis,
were supplied by ten oligarchs (one from each Phyle), who
were supported by Lysander, and manifested a disposition
to reign as despotically as their predecessors. But the C
Spartan king Pausanias, being jealous of the reputation of
Lysander, now entered into a compact with Thrasybūlus;
in consequence of which both the Thirty and the Ten were
set aside, a general amnesty proclaimed (from which, however, the Thirty were excluded), and, in place of the degenerate democracy, the laws of Solon were restored in
all their purity, with such modifications as a commission
appointed for that purpose should deem necessary to meet
the wants of more modern times.

2. War of the Spartans with the Persians.—At 303
first for the support of the younger Cyrus, and afterwards D
for the liberation and protection of the Greeks in Asia
Minor (see 90, p. 56).

3. The Corinthian War, 394—387.—For the pur- 304
pose of rendering abortive the plans of Agesilāus against
the Persian empire, the Persian satrap Tithraustes, successor of Tissaphernes, availing himself of the universal
discontent, succeeded, by means of bribery, in persuading

(304) the democrats in Thebes, Corinth, and Argos, to promote
A a war with Sparta; the Athenians, although they had received no subsidy from Persia, declaring themselves ready to join the confederacy. That there might be a pretext for the war, the Thebans incited the Opuntian Locrians to make a predatory incursion into the territory of Phocis, and supported them in their undertaking. The Phocians applied for aid to the Lacedæmonians; and Lysander, having joined their army in Bœotia, fell in a skirmish under the walls of Haliartus. As the confederation against the unpopular Hegemony of Sparta was rapidly
B extending itself, Agesilaus was recalled from Asia. Meanwhile the Lacedæmonians had obtained a victory over the confederates, who had drawn together their forces at Corinth for the purpose of enabling the wavering Peloponnesians to liberate themselves from the Spartan yoke; but their fleet was annihilated by that of Persia, under the command of the Athenian exile Conon (off Cnidus, in 394); in consequence of which almost all the maritime
C powers joined Pharnabazus and Conon. Agesilāus, concealing this disaster from his army, traversed Thrace without sustaining any considerable interruption on the part of the allies, and obtained a victory at Coronea, whither the allies had detached only a portion of the army which they had assembled at Corinth. Conon and Pharnabazus, having expelled the Spartan Harmosts from the Greek cities of Asia Minor and the islands, sailed for Greece, and ravaged the coasts of Laconia. By means of Persian gold, Conon was enabled to rebuild the walls of Athens, and to restore for a short time to his native city the maritime supremacy which had been lost by Sparta and abandoned by the
D Persians. To withdraw the Persians from their alliance with Athens, the Spartans sent their Nauarch Antalcidas to the Persian court with proposals of peace, engaging to leave the Persian monarch in possession of the Asiatic continent, provided the islands and other Greek states were permitted to be independent. On these terms, the PEACE OF ANTALCIDAS, as it was called, was concluded in the year 387; by means of which Sparta obtained the dissolution of every kind of supremacy exercised by one Grecian city over others [e. g. the Thebans over the Bœotian cities].

In the island of Cyprus, which had been assigned to king Arta- A
xerxes II., king Euagoras maintained himself in Salamis; and the Athenians continued to hold Lemnos, Imbros, and Scyros, which they had taken in the Persian war.

4. THE OLYNTHIAN WAR (383—379.)—Olynthus having induced 305
several Greek and Macedonian cities in Chalcidice and Thrace to form a confederacy, into which she was endeavoring to force the recusant cities of Acanthus and Apollonia, the Spartans sent an army into that country; and after carrying on the war for three years (during which they sustained considerable losses), compelled the Olynthians to abandon their conquests, and join the Spartan Symmachia, on condition of retaining their independence.

§ 68. *The War between Thebes and Sparta.*

(378—362.)

In Thebes, where the oligarchical and democratical par- 306
ties were at that time equally balanced, there stood at the B
head of affairs, as Polemarchs, in the year 383, the democrat Ismenias, and the oligarch Leontiades. In order to annihilate the democracy, the latter of these leaders persuaded the Spartan general Phœbidas, who had encamped in the vicinity of Thebes, on his march to Olynthus, to attack the city in time of peace, and take possession of the Cadmēa [or citadel of Thebes], which Leontiades was willing to surrender into his hands. Ismenias was put to death; and the rest of the democrats, among whom was Pelopidas, fled to Athens, where they found the same hospitality which the fugitive Athenian democrats had experienced from the
Thebans twenty years before. Pelopidas, having called C
on his companions in exile to assist him in delivering their native city from the dominion of the aristocrats and Spartans, twelve conspirators entered Thebes in disguise, and assassinated the leaders of the aristocratic party during the celebration of a festival; Leontiades being put to death in his own house by his rival Pelopidas. The Spartan garrison in the citadel were compelled, by want of provisions, to capitulate, on condition of being allowed free egress; and the democratic ascendency was re-established. Soon afterwards the Spartan kings Cleombrŏtus D
and Agesilāus appeared in Bœotia at the head of an army, which made repeated incursions into the Theban territory, but with so little success, that the Spartans were advised by their confederates to try their fortune by sea. Here, however, the Spartans found themselves opposed by an Athenian force far superior to their own (the Athenians

(306) having succeeded in forming, on equitable terms, a new
A Symmachia of seventy cities). Two victories, gained by the Athenians (at Naxos, under the command of Chabrias, and off the promontory of Leucadia, under Timothĕŭs, the son of Conon), annihilated the Spartan fleet, and secured the adherence of those maritime powers which had been previously wavering. Having thus established her authority over the maritime states, Athens now sought to secure it by a general peace, which the Thebans refused to recognize, because they were not permitted to sign the
B treaty in the name of the Bœotians. In consequence of this refusal, Bœotia was again invaded by Cleombrotus, who was defeated and slain by Epaminondas (who had concentrated all his strength against the wing commanded by the king), and the sacred band of Pelopidas, on the plain of Leuctra, in **371.** This defeat of the Spartans having hastened the defection of their allies in Peloponnesus, the Thebans, in the hope of promoting this movement, and raising a supremacy of their own on the ruins of Sparta, invaded Peloponnesus, and, in conjunction
C with the Arcadians, Argives, and Eleans, prepared to attack Sparta itself. Their cavalry had already advanced as far as the Hippodrome, when the unexpected opposition which they encountered, in addition to the want of provisions and unfavorable season of the year, compelled them to abandon the attempt, in order that their entire force might be available (according to the terms of the peace of Antalcidas), for the re-establishment of Messenian independence. The newly-built cities of Messēnē and Megalopŏlis were intended to form with Tegĕa and Argos a chain of fortresses, sufficient to restrain the Spartans from any further encroachments on Peloponnesus; but on the advance of the Athenians, who were unwilling that either Sparta or Thebes should become too powerful, the Theban army was compelled to retire.

D A second invasion of Peloponnesus had no effect beyond securing the accession of Sicyon, an ally it is true of some importance; and a third ended in the temporary subjection of Achaia.

307 In the north the Thebans undertook three several expeditions (368—364) against Alexander, the ferocious tyrant of Pheræ, for the purpose of delivering the Thessalians. In the first campaign their leader Pelopidas was

made prisoner, but was rescued in the second by Epami- (307)
nondas, and in the third fell in the moment of victory at A
Cynoscephale. The Thebans exerted themselves manfully to avenge the death of their beloved leader, and compelled the tyrant to conclude a humiliating peace. Soon after the death of Pelopidas, a fourth campaign in Peloponnesus was undertaken by Epaminondas, in consequence of dissensions among the Arcadians. Their chief magistrates had begun to employ the treasures of the temple at Olympia for the purpose of paying their mercenary troops; and when a portion of the Arcadians, among whom the Mantineans were most forward, protested against this dishonest practice, had applied for
assistance to the Thebans. After a second unsuccessful B
attempt on Sparta, Epaminondas fell in the battle of Mantinea, where his troops were victorious (362). In the confusion consequent on the death of their leader, the Thebans made so little use of their victory, that both parties erected trophies. The Greek states were now so thoroughly exhausted, that they were compelled to conclude a peace, to which Sparta for a long time refused to accede, on account of her unwillingness to recognize the independence of Messenia. Agesilāus died as he was returning from an expedition into Egypt, undertaken for the purpose of putting down an insurrection against the Persians.

§ 69. *The War of the Confederates against Athens.*

(357—355.)

The exaction of a larger amount of tribute from the 308
allies provoked the most powerful among them, Chios, C
Rhodes, Cos, and Byzantium (supported by the Carian king Mausōlus II.), to renounce their allegiance to Athens. After a struggle, which lasted three years, the Athenians (who after the death of Chabrias had been commanded by Iphicrătes and Timotheus), when they found themselves threatened also with war by Artaxerxes III., (against whom Chares had supported the revolted satrap Artabazus,) and saw Philip of Macedonia advancing in his career of victory, were compelled to recognize the independence of their revolted allies, and remit the tribute. Thus their newly established (since 377) naval supre-

(308) macy was a second time annihilated, and Greece lost the
A assistance of the only state which could have protected her liberties.

§ 70. *The Phocian or Sacred War.*

(355—346.)

309 CAUSES.—Many years before the breaking out of this war, the Phocians had been sentenced by the Amphictyonic council at Delphi to pay a pecuniary mulct, as a punishment for having occupied a tract of land near
B Cirrha, belonging to the temple of Apollo at Delphi. None however had ventured to enforce the sentence, until the Thebans, who viewed the Phocians in the light of enemies, as being allies of the subjugated Bœotian states, persuaded the Amphictyons to demand payment of the fine. The Phocians, in conjunction with the Spartans, who had also been condemned to pay a fine for their occupation of the Cadmea, now took forcible possession of the temple at Delphi, the superintendence and guardianship of which had formerly been wrested from them by the Delphians, and, as soon as war was declared against them by the Amphictyons, applied the treasures of the
C temple to the payment of hired troops. On the other hand the Thebans were joined by the Locrians, and almost all the nations of northern Greece.

310 Under the command of their general Philomēlus, the Phocians made head against the Locrians and Thessalians, but were defeated by the Thebans in an engagement in which Philomelus, to avoid falling into the hands of the enemy, threw himself headlong from a rock. His brother and successor Onomarchus, was enabled to continue the war by means of fresh funds drawn from the treasury at
D Delphi. The principal theatre of hostilities was now Thessaly, the Phocians having formed an alliance with the tyrants of Pheræ, the ancient enemies of Thessaly, and the Thessalians on their part having applied for assistance to Philip king of Macedonia. After many vicissitudes, the Phocians were at length compelled to yield to the Thessalian cavalry and Macedonian tactics; Onomarchus was slain in attempting to escape, and the prisoners were thrown into the sea. The treasures of the temple how-

ever were not yet exhausted, and hostilities were still (310)
carried on against the Thebans, by the Phocians, under A
Phayllus, the brother of their two former leaders, un-
successfully at first; but subsequently with such decided
advantage, that the Thebans were compelled to call in
Philip II. of Macedonia. This crafty monarch so completely deceived the Phocians, who had also applied to
him for assistance, that many of the Phocian cities
voluntarily placed themselves at his disposal, and others
were reduced with very little difficulty. By a decree of B
the Amphictyonic council (pronounced, it would seem,
only by the Thebans, Locrians, and the Thessalian tribes),
the Phocian cities were deprived of their walls, the inhabitants dispersed, their arms and horses taken from
them, restitution of the Delphic treasure enforced, and the
two votes of the Phocians in the Amphictyonic council
given to Philip, who was also, in conjunction with the
Thessalians and Thebans, charged with the superintendence of the Pythian games.

§ 71. *The War against Philip II. of Macedonia.*

1. On the Macedonian coast. 311

In order to obtain possession of the entire coast of his C
country, a portion of which was still in the hands of the
Athenians, Philip, as long ago as the war of the confederates, had captured Amphipŏlis and Pydna. Potidæa,
which fell into his hands at the same time, was given up
to the Olynthians, to prevent the formation of an alliance
between Athens and Olynthus, the most powerful city of
the Chalcidic peninsula.

2. In Thessaly. 312

The first pretext which Philip found for interfering in
the affairs of Greece, was an application of the Thessalians for aid against the tyrants of Pheræ. Philip com- D
plied with this request, so far as to co-operate with the
Thessalian cities in their attempts to recover their freedom,
but permitted the tyrants to remain, that there might still
be a necessity for his assistance. The Phocians having
formed an alliance with these tyrants, Philip occupied
Thessaly, successfully resisted an attack of the Phocians
under Onomarchus, held the places which he had captured,
and at a later period, after the ruin of the Phocians, and

(312) the consequent expulsion of the tyrants, treated the coun-
A try in every respect as a Macedonian province (343).

After his victories over the tyrants and the Phocians, Philip, unable any longer to resist the importunity with which his allies, the Thessalians and Thebans, urged him to annihilate the Phocians, advanced for that purpose as far as Thermopylæ; but finding the pass occupied by an Athenian army, he avoided a battle, contenting himself with having found an excuse for suffering the Phocians to remain, that his friends might still stand in need of his assistance.

313 3. ON THE COASTS OF MACEDONIA AND THRACE.

B Allowing the parties in Greece to wear out one another, Philip directed his chief attention to the conquest of the Grecian maritime cities on the Thracian coast from Byzantium to the borders of Macedonia, and to the creation of a Macedonian navy. The most obstinate resistance was offered by the powerful city of Olynthus, but after the defeat of the weak and ill-appointed force sent out from Athens to its assistance at the instance of Demosthenes, the city was betrayed into the hands of Philip (348), who demolished it with many others, amusing the Athenians meanwhile, through the agency of the bribed orator Æschines, with propósals for the conclusion of a
C peace. It was not until the end of the Phocian war (comp. § 70), and after Philip had effected a landing in Laconia, and compelled the Lacedæmonians to abandon their design of reconquering Messenia, that he recommenced his plans of conquest on the Thracian coast with the blockade of Perinthus and Byzantium (341). The capture of both these cities was however prevented by the arrival of an Athenian fleet under the command of Phocion (341).

314 4. THE SACRED WAR AGAINST AMPHISSA (339).

D That he might have a fresh excuse for marching an army into Greece, Philip persuaded the Amphictyons (through his agent Æschines), to impose a fine on the Locrians of Amphissa for an alleged desecration in ancient times of a piece of ground belonging to the temple at Delphi, and to intrust him with the execution of their sentence. In consequence of this arrangement, Philip entered Greece at the head of a considerable force, and put an end to the war (by what means does not distinctly appear). The occupation however of Elatēa, the key of

Bœotia, plainly indicated that he had ulterior objects in A
view.

5. THE DECISIVE STRUGGLE IN BŒOTIA (338).

When the astounding intelligence of the occupation of 315
Elatea reached Athens, none but Demosthenes had the
courage to propose the equipment of a fleet and a land
force. Proceeding to Thebes, he called on the government to form an alliance with Athens, and pleaded the
cause of his country so eloquently, that the Macedonian
party and the orator Python (who had been bribed by
Philip), were compelled to abandon their opposition.
Several other states also joined the confederacy, but the B
allied army (the Athenians were commanded by Chares
and Lysicles), after two successful engagements, was at
length overmatched by the Macedonian phalanx (338)
near Chæronea, where the young Alexander exterminated the sacred band of the Thebans, and thus decided
the fortune of the day. In the first moment of alarm
Thebes surrendered to the enemy, and was compelled to
receive a Macedonian garrison; Athens, which still held
out, was enabled to make terms with the invader, whilst
the smaller states hastened to purchase his forbearance;
and Philip, at a great national assembly of the Greeks held
at Corinth, was elected generalissimo of their armies
against the Persians.

§ 72. *Religion, Literature, &c. of the Greeks.*

The erroneous notion of antiquity, that Greek civilization was 316
derived from Egypt, had its origin partly in the assertions of the C
priests, who represented the gods of Greece as descended from
those of Egypt, in order that they might be themselves considered
the instructors of the Greeks, and partly from the propensity of the
Greeks to give Grecian names to foreign divinities. There seems
to have been no intimate connection between the two countries until
the reigns of Psammetichus and Amăsis, nor do we find in Greece
the slightest vestige of hieroglyphics, of Egyptian arts, or of the
Egyptian race.

RELIGION. The religion of the Greeks consisted ori- 317
ginally in the worship of natural objects and influences; D
but by degrees they began to represent the gods as sentient
beings, subject to human passions, and engaged in the same
pursuits and occupations as the inhabitants of earth. This
prosopopœia, which in a great measure owed its existence

(317) to the poets Homer and Hesiod, as well as to the artists
A of Greece, formed the popular religion; whilst the ancient
symbolical system existed almost exclusively as a priestly
religion in the mysteries, *i. e.* in those secret acts of
worship to which none but the initiated were admitted.
Yet even in the midst of this polytheism, we find some
traces of a belief in one supreme being; as exhibited in
the notion of an inevitable fate (*αἶσα*, *μοῖρα*), to which the
gods themselves are subject, and of the supreme dominion
B of Zeus. According to popular belief the residence of
this god was on the summit of Mount Olympus, which
pierces the brazen vault of heaven (*οὐρανός*), the lower
peaks of the mountain being occupied by the rest of the
gods. The various national divinities of the different
tribes were amalgamated at a very early period into
one body composed of twelve OLYMPII or NATIONAL DE-
ITIES.

318 1. *Zeus* [*Jupiter*], the supreme, most powerful, and wise being
C (*ὕπατος*, *ὕψιστος*.—*μητιέτης*), the king and father of gods and men,
watches over all the concerns of mankind, especially over hospitality,
oaths, and the relief of suppliants (hence called Ζεὺς *ξένιος*, *ὅρκιος*,
ἱκέσιος, &c.), and holds in his hands, as god of heaven, the ægis, and
the lightning. Tradition represents many heroes as descended from
Zeus, for the purpose of increasing their renown—hence the legends
of his numerous wives and children, and of the jealousy of Hērē [*Juno*].
To this god of the heavens was united, but not as a being of the same
rank, a goddess of the earth, named by the Dorians 2. *Here*, and by
the Ionians 3. *Demētēr* or *Γαῖα*, who bears him Persephŏne (that
is, the earth, rendered fruitful by the sky, brings forth corn). This
daughter, being carried off by Pluto, passes one half of the year
with her husband, the other with her mother (*i. e.* the corn is at first
concealed in the bosom of the earth, then springs forth and ripens).
Demeter herself teaches the art of agriculture to Triptolemus, son
of the king of Eleusis, to whom she also gives a code of laws—hence
D her feast is called Thesmophoria. The gods of heaven and earth
are accompanied by the deities of light, who were believed to be
children of Zeus; 4. *Athēnē*; 5. *Apollōn*; 6. *Artĕmis*. ATHENE
bears some relation to fire and light, physical (hence *γλαυκῶπις*) as
well as moral—hence she is named the goddess of understanding and
wisdom, and in that character springs from the brain of Zeus. She is
also connected with the element of water, whence her name Tritoge-
neia, and the legend of her contest with Poseidôn [*Neptune*]. Both
these elements, the warm and the moist, are employed in making the
earth bring forth: thus Athene becomes the goddess of the harvest
and of fertility, and her son is named Erichthonius. She is also the
goddess of war, and presides over works of female skill. APOLLON and
ARTEMIS, twin children of Zeus and Leto (*i. e.* darkness), born on
mount Cythnus in Delos, are the deities of light, the sun and moon.

Hence Apollon is called Phœbus, and an eternal fire is maintained on (318)
his altar. Artemis is drawn with a torch and crescent. Their rays A
were compared to arrows, and for that reason they were represented
also as deities of the chase (hence 'Απ. ἑκηβόλος, αργυρότοξος). Apollon is not only the god of destruction, but also of healing, (hence
παιών, ἀλεξίκακος, the father of Asclepios). In reference to the
effects of light, the destruction of grain by smut ('Απ. ἐρυθίβιος),
and even by mice (Σμινθεύς), is ascribed to Apollon. He is the
god of intellectual, as well as physical, light; hence to him is ascribed
the gift of prophecy, but as a deliverer of oracles he is ambiguous
(hence λοξίας). He is also the god of poetical inspiration, of song
and music, and the leader of the Muses. In this view of the universe,
the elements of fire and water have of course their place. Thus B
Poseidon (7) denotes both the sea and the fresh water in the deep
recesses of earth; and *Hephaistos* [*Vulcan*] (8) the terrestrial fire (on
and in the earth), the origin of which from celestial fire is poetically
represented by the hurling down of Hephaistos from heaven to earth.
The fertility of the vine on volcanic soils gave occasion to the fable
which connects Hephaistos with wine as the cup-bearer of the
gods; and on account of the agency of fire in the working of metals,
he is represented as a blacksmith famous for the production of works
in steel (the shield of Achilles). 9. *Hermes* [*Mercury*], perhaps, originally, a symbol of the generation of animals, is known as protector
of the herds, and especially of flocks of sheep; and also as messenger
of the gods and guardian of the streets (hence the Hermæ). In an
intellectual sense, he is represented as the inventor of the lyre and
of gymnastics, and the protector of trade; and in the last of these
characters is shrewd, cunning, and even inclined to theft. 10. *Hestia* C
[*Vesta*], or the deified conception of the hearth, as the centre of the
house, and place of assemblage for the family. 11. *Ares* [*Mars*], or
the personification of war. 12. *Aphrodītē* [*Venus*], or the personified
idea of love and enjoyment; a divinity borrowed from the Phœnicians. Different classes had their respective deities; thus the goatherds and vine-dressers paid especial honor to Dionysos [*Bacchus*],
who, as god of the Spring, clothes the fields with flowers, and makes
the herds bring forth their young; and, as god of Autumn, fills the
vats with wine, a union of the two legends respecting his birth (from
the thigh of Zeus, and from Semēle, the daughter of Cadmus.)
Hence he is called Dithyrambus. In his spiritual character, he
appears as a prophet, as the god of the dead (Zagreus), and the protector of democracy.

The inferior classes of deities were: 1. The *Dæmŏnes*, 319
who were either aboriginal local divinities; deified natural D
objects, the gods of the river, the mountain, and the forest;
or abstract ideas personified, as *Τύχη*, *Ψυχή*, *Ἥβη*, *Αἰδώς*,
Φήμη, *Εἰρήνη*, *Θάνατος*, *Φόβος*, the Erinnyes, or Eume-
nĭdĕs, &c. 2. The *heroes*, or mortals deified after death,
and termed demi-gods. These were either founders of
entire tribes, who were also believed to be the sons of

(319) gods, as Hercules, &c., or patrons of particular crafts, as
A Dædalus, the hero of architects, &c. The notion of a life after death produced the deities of the lower world, Pluton or Hades, and the three Mœræ (Clotho, Lachĕsĭs, and Atrŏpos).

The worship of their gods consisted principally in sacrifices, which were either offerings of prayer and thanksgiving, or sin-offerings, and were celebrated by the priests either in the open air, on the tops of mountains, in forests and groves, or in temples, especially on the occasion of certain festivals, such as the great national games, the Panathenæa, Thesmophoria, Eleusinia, Dionysia, &c.
B The offerings were either living victims, sometimes single, sometimes in great numbers (Hecatombs), or inanimate objects, as fruits, wine, honey, milk, frankincense, &c., and in the earliest times, human victims, for which, however, beasts were very soon substituted. Their other modes of honoring the gods were by short forms of prayer, uttered standing and with outstretched arms, by votive offerings, solemn processions, and religious dances. Besides these modes of propitiating the gods and turning away their wrath, men believed also that they could obtain revelations of the Divine will, either immediately from the oracles, of which the most renowned were those of Zeus at Dodōna, and of Apollo at Delphi: or mediately through the *ἱερεύς*, from the inspection of entrails, through the *μάντις*, from the flight and song of certain birds, and from atmospheric phenomena, and through the *ὀνειροπόλος*, from dreams.

320 2. Constitution.

C For the constitution of the heroic age see § 55; and for that of the second period, § 58.

In the third period both the external and internal relations of Greece received from the Persian wars a character which they retained during the succeeding age. The line of demarcation between Greeks and barbarians was more distinctly traced, the necessity for adopting common measures of defence produced offensive and defensive alliances, and in place of the old loose unions, more extended Hegemonies were introduced; the effect of which was, that in all political movements each nation bore a part either voluntarily, or by compulsion. In their internal policy great changes were produced by the almost contemporaneous expulsion of tyrants

from the different states. At Athens the constitution of (320)
Solon was restored (with a few alterations by Clisthenes, A
see § 61, and Aristides, § 63. In many states (as Argos, Mantinea, Elis, Megara, Corinth, Syracuse, &c.) democracy was for the first time introduced; in others, the aristocracy degenerated into oligarchy, as, for example, in Sparta and Thebes, the two strongholds of the oligarchical system; and also in Thessaly, Corinth, Sicyon, &c. From the breaking out of the Peloponnesian war these two forms of government were placed in a state of antagonism, which not only produced wars between different states, but also
created civil disturbances in many of the Grecian cities. The B
oligarchical system was at its greatest height during the Hegemony of Sparta, at the conclusion of the Peloponnesian war, oligarchical constitutions being introduced by the Spartans wherever they had any influence (in the western parts of Asia Minor, and at Athens, Elis, Corinth, and Thebes). These constitutions, however, lasted a very short time. The expulsion from Thebes of the oligarchical party and the Spartan garrison, and still more the battle of Leuctra, were the signal for a general rising against Sparta; and the extension of democracy became, at the same time, an essential part of the policy of Thebes, which was now straining every nerve to obtain the Hegemony. In the end, C
discord, cowardice, treason, and supineness prepared Greece to receive the yoke of a foreign master.

3. Literature. 321

A. *Poetry*.

Epic poetry, and then lyric, first flourished in the colonies of Western Asia Minor; dramatic poetry first developed itself about the year 500, in the mother country, chiefly at Athens.

Epic Poetry. Before the days of Homer the only 322
poems of this description were short ballads, descriptive of D
single deeds or adventures. By him the plan of the epic poem was fully developed, so as to comprise, in addition to the story of the principal heroes, the characters and actions of a large circle of the most remarkable secondary personages. The *Iliad* and *Odyssey*, the most perfect epic poems ever produced, were made known to the world by the Rhapsodists, a school of minstrels at Chios, and at a later period (in the time of Pisistratus) were copied out

(322) and edited by the Diaskeuastæ at Alexandria. The so-
A called Homeric hymns, employed by the Rhapsodists as introductions to their poetical recitations, are, for the most part, the work of the *Homeridæ*. The poetry of Homer produced a crowd of imitators, *cyclic poets*, as they were called (between 800 and 500), some of whom sang the other events of the heroic age (for example, the war against Thebes), whilst others wrote continuations of the Iliad and Odyssey. Contemporaneously with the minstrel school of the Homeridæ at Chios, there flourished another in Bœotia, at the head of which was Hesiod of Ascra.
B Three of his epic poems are still extant; two of which are mythological, viz., 1, θεογονία, a work of the highest importance in a religious point of view, as being the standard authority for all representations of the gods, their peculiarities, family connections, &c.; and 2, the ἀσπὶς Ἡρακλέους; and one of a didactic character, ἔργα καὶ ἡμέραι.

323 *b*. Lyric poetry, intended to be sung with a lyre or
C flute accompaniment, developed itself in the seventh century, B. C., contemporaneously with the rise of republicanism. It comprehends a variety of species, and many different metres. The invention of the *elegiac* measure, which differs very little from the epic, is generally ascribed to Callīnus (about 660), who, like his contemporary Tyrtæus, was chiefly famous for his warlike elegies. In proportion as the Ionians, among whom this style of poetry flourished, became less warlike and more effeminate, so did the elegy lose its political character, which is feebly exhibited in the poems of Mimnermus, but resumes its
D original strength in the elegies of Solon at Athens. To the elegy belong, as regards their contents and form, the remains of Theognis, which consist of mere fragments cited from his works by other writers without any regular connection. The last of the great elegiac poets is Simonides of Ceos, whose elegy in honor of the Greeks who fell at Marathon, was preferred to that of Æschylus. The elegiac is also the metre most commonly employed for the *Epigram*, perhaps because monumental inscriptions (the most usual form of epigrams among the Greeks) were intimately connected with songs of lamentation. Those of the most distinguished epigrammatic poet Simonides of Ceos, were, in fact, principally inscriptions

for the tombs of the heroes who fell in the Persian wars. (323)
The custom observed at certain religious festivals of attack- A
ing one another in scurrilous lampoons, called iambi, gave occasion to ARCHILOCHUS (a contemporary of Callinus) to frame a new species of poetry, which received the name of *Iambic*. It was distinguished from the epic and elegiac, not only by its different metre, but by a style more nearly approaching to prose. The *Lyric poetry* of the Greeks, in its more restricted sense, is divided into the *Æolic*, which was intended for recitation by a single performer, with the accompaniment of a stringed instrument, and appropriate movements of the body; and the *Doric*, which was sung
to the dancing of the chorus. The latter had its strophes. B
which were often very elaborate, together with its antistrŏphes and epodes; whilst the former had either no strophes at all, or only such as were of a very simple character, containing a few verses, all in the same metre, and uninterrupted by epodes. The subject matter was also different; the choral lyric endeavoring to bring before the audience, by means of the whole chorus, objects of public and general interest, whilst the Æolic gave expression to
individual feelings and opinions. The most distinguished C
poets of the Æolic school were Lesbians. ALCÆUS (about 600), and his contemporary SAPPHO, to whom we may also add ANACREON. The Doric choral poetry developed itself under ALCMAN and STESICHŎRUS, and attained perfection under IBYCUS and SIMONIDES (also elegiac poets) and especially under PINDAR (522—442). Of the various styles of lyric poetry, strictly so called, in which Pindar distinguished himself, nothing has reached us except his hymns of victory or Epinīcia, which are well calculated, by the richness of invention which they display, the elegance of their composition, and the variety of form and style, to create a favorable opinion of the writer's poetical talent.

c. DRAMATIC POETRY.—The choral hymns (Dithy- 324
rambs), chanted at the Dionysia, first assumed the form of D
tragedy, when Thespis (of Athens, about 540) intermingled with them the representation (*δρᾶμα, ἐπεισόδιον*) of a story or plot by a single actor (*ὑποκρῑτής*), who was separated from the chorus, and played many parts successively in the same piece. This action or Epeisodion was made the principal feature of the entertainment by Æschy-

(324) lus an Athenian (525—456), who added a second actor,
A and thus became the founder of the dramatic dialogue. At
every dramatic contest in which he was engaged, Æschylus
brought forward three tragedies, which formed a whole,
and were succeeded by a satyric drama. In these trilogies
we find the most striking myths dramatically worked out
in such a manner as to excite the astonishment and delight
of the Greeks, as they became aware of the part played by
the gods in their early history. SOPHŎCLES (495—406),
introduced a third actor, and made the action, even more
than Æschylus had done, a principal part of the drama, by
shortening the songs of the chorus; his object being to represent the feelings of the personages actually engaged in
the plot, rather than the impression made by its events on
B mere spectators. He also followed the custom of introducing three tragedies and a satyric drama at each representation; but these, as far as their subject matter was
concerned, were in fact not one long poem, but four distinct works. EURIPĬDES, who, according to the received
account, was born in the island of Salamis on the day of
the battle (more probably in the year 482, or 481), and
died a few months before Sophŏcles, introduced a twofold
innovation as regarded the form of the tragedy. In the
first place, the audience, by means of a *prologue*, were informed of previous events down to the very moment at
which the action of the tragedy begins; and secondly, the
knot of dramatic entanglement, instead of being unravelled,
was severed by the appearance of a "*deus ex machinâ*."
C The mythical traditions of antiquity, in which Æschylus
recognized the exalted workings of divine power, and
Sophŏcles discovered matter for the most profound re-
flections on human events, were treated by the philosophical
Euripĭdes almost as if he desired to expose their folly, by
stripping his heroes of all ideal greatness, and representing
them with the petty passions and weaknesses of ordinary
mortals.

325 One degenerate offspring of tragedy was the SATYRIC
D DRAMA, which formed a sort of connecting link between
it and comedy; and was generally introduced, with its
chorus of satyrs and Silenuses, after the conclusion of the
tragic trilogy. Although this practice was antecedent to
Æschylus, and retained its place as long as tragedy

flourished at Athens, only *one* complete piece is extant (325)
in the Cyclops of Euripĭdes. The OLD COMEDY, as it is A
called, which derived its origin from songs sung during the revels (κῶμοι) of the Dionysia, was moulded into a more artistical form in the fifth century, B. C., by the exertions of Epicharmus in Sicily, and Cratīnus, Eupŏlis, and especially ARISTOPHANES, at Athens. The last of these poets, who flourished between 427 and 338, has left us in his comedies (of which eleven out of fifty-four are extant) a very correct representation of Athenian manners, couched in bitter and often ribaldrous satire. During the reign of B
the thirty at Athens (404) all satirical notice of living characters, as well as the representation on the stage of contemporaneous events, was strictly prohibited; a regulation which produced what is called the Middle Comedy. In this species of drama the poet exposed, in the form of a mythic plot, the follies of different ranks and classes, or exercised his wit on the literary absurdities of the day.

B. *Prose.* 326

a. History. That so intellectual a people as the C
Greeks remained for so many centuries without feeling the want of an accurate record of their history, is explained by the fact, that between the occurrence of those events of the mythical age which were celebrated by their epic poets, and the breaking out of the Persian wars, no enterprise whatever was undertaken by the combined nations of Greece. As in epic and lyric poetry and philosophy, so also in history, the first ground seems to have been broken by the *Ionians;* hence the most ancient prose dialect is the Ionic. The compilers of history, antecedent to Herodotus (generally termed Logogrăphi), contented themselves with giving the results of their geographical and statistical researches, especially in the east, without any attempt at arrangement, or historical description. Hero- D
dotus, on the contrary, by interweaving episodical notices of oriental countries, and their inhabitants, with his history of the great struggle between the east and west, has succeeded in producing an animated picture of the two contending masses. Throughout the whole work we recognize also the pervading idea of a just Providence, which assigns to every man his path of duty, and the limits within which it behooves him to confine himself; and punishes

(326) with ruin and destruction the inordinate acquisition of
A riches or power. The first, and, at the same time, the most complete, description of contemporaneous events, is that given by Thucydides, in his history of the Peloponnesian war,—a work unrivalled for perspicuity, truth, and accuracy, as well as for the admirable delicacy and acuteness displayed in its delineations of character. His successor, Xenophon, is inferior to Thucydides as a descriptive writer; but there seems little or no foundation for the heavy charge brought against him by modern critics, of being intentionally a partisan of Sparta.

327 *b.* Eloquence.—Although addresses to the people were
B common at a very early period of Grecian history, as we learn from the speeches of Homer's kings, eloquence seems to have been cultivated as a political science only at Athens. The orations of Perĭclēs are especially worthy of remark, for the extraordinary depth and vigor of thought which they display, as well as for the manner in which single events are reduced to general principles. The grandeur of his conceptions, their ready adaptation to every possible contingency, and the majestic repose of his style, obtained for him the epithet of "the Olympian."
C The cultivation of rhetoric as an art originated with the sophists; among whom those of Hellas Proper aimed principally at correctness, whilst those of Sicily (as Gordias) considered elegance of style the chief excellence of an oration. The union of natural power (possessed in the highest degree by Pericles), with the rhetorical studies of the sophists, produced that elaborate eloquence of the senate and the bar of which we find examples in the *ten Attic orators.* Among these, Lysias, by his Epitaphios, created a new style of eloquence, viz., the oratory of display, as it has been termed (*ἐπιδεικτικὸν* or *πανηγυρικὸν γένος*), distinguished from all other sorts by having no
D practical object. The composition of these panegyrical orations was rendered more elaborate, and their style improved, by Isocrates, a distinguished teacher of eloquence. The powers of judicial and political oratory are exhibited in their fullest development in the contest between Æschines, the advocate of Macedonian interests (393—317), and his irreconcilable adversary Demosthenes (385—332), who for fourteen years employed the art, which he

had acquired with so much labor, in resisting the aggres- A
sions of Philip II.

c. PHILOSOPHY was first cultivated in the colonies of western Asia Minor and Lower Italy; in the former, in 328
the Ionic school of Thales, one of the seven wise men, whose reputation seems to have been founded rather on their practical activity, as statesmen and advisers of the people, than on their philosophical speculations; in the latter, in the Pythagorean and Eleatic schools (those of Pythagoras and Xenophanes). The ancient or *natural* philosophers (οἱ φυσικοί), as they were termed, were succeeded by the Sophists, who taught principally the art of dialectics invented by Zeno the Eleatic, and its application to rhetoric. Their abuse of this art was resist- B
ed by Socrates (469—399), who employed the peculiar (*interrogative*) method termed from him the Socratic. This philosopher endeavored by precept and example to stem the torrent of immorality, and to give men, by means of familiar conversations, more just conceptions of themselves, their knowledge, and their duties (hence he is known as the founder of Ethics). Notwithstanding, however, his endeavors to promote the welfare of mankind, he was held up to ridicule by Aristophanes, in his comedy of 'the Clouds,' as the representative of the Sophists; and being accused of corrupting the Athenian youth, was sentenced to drink poison. His doctrines are preserved in the C
writings of his disciples Xenophon and Plato (429—347), the founder of the Academic school. For their development in a scientific form we are indebted to the philosophy of Aristotle (384—322), the founder of the Peripatetic school (at the Lyceum at Athens); by which the first outline of a system of logic was traced, and a philosophical terminology created.

d. The earliest traces of MATHEMATICAL SCIENCE are found in the D
geographical and astronomical labors of several philosophers.

e. MEDICINE, being closely connected with religion, was for a long time entirely in the hands of the priesthood. Pythagoras, indeed, made an attempt to introduce it into ordinary life; but this object was not fully attained until the time of Hippocrătes (460—370), the real founder of the healing art.

4. ART.

a. The *architecture* of the Greeks was at first of the 329
rudest character—colossal blocks of stone, which in the

(329) most ancient times were not even hewn, were piled on one
A another, without mortar, until they formed massive walls. This style was called the Cyclopian. Vestiges of it may still be seen in the remains of walls at Tiryns and Argos, and in the gate of the lions at Mycēnæ, which is set in a wall of this description. Our notices of the sacred architecture of the heroic age are few and obscure; but, on the other hand, we are fully acquainted with the arrangements of their palaces from the descriptions of Homer (e. g. that of the palace of Odysseus [*Ulysses*]), and there still exist fragments of the *treasuries* that were con-
B nected with such palaces; for instance, those of the treasury of Atreus at Mycenæ. The most important architectural monuments of antiquity are the temples of the gods, in which we discover the development of the Grecian column, for the most part in two forms, the Doric and Ionic. Immediately in front of the temple were the Propylæa, forming an entrance to the sacred inclosure, by which the temple was surrounded; then succeeded colonnades appropriated to different objects (e. g. halls of justice, gymnasia, &c.), and at a still greater distance were
C inclosures for sports and combats, stadia, hippodromes, theatres, music-halls (ᾠδεῖα), &c.

The most ancient of the architectural monuments still in existence are found in the Doric colonies in Sicily (Selīnus and Agrigentum), in Magna Græcia (at Pæstum), and in the Ionic colonies of Asia Minor (the temples of Juno at Samos, and of Diana at Ephesus). Those of the most flourishing period of Grecian architecture may be seen at Athens (the Parthĕnon, the Propylæa, the Erechthēum), at Eleusis (the temple of Demēter), at Olympia (the temple of Zeus), and in the Ionic colonies of Asia Minor (the temples of Athēnē at Priēnē, and of Apollo at Milētus).

330 *b. Sculpture* produced at a very early period orna-
D mental works in metal (the shield of Achilles); earthen vessels with paintings burnt into the clay; and, above all, statues of the gods, which at first were of wood, covered with real garments, then of brass and marble, and at the period of their greatest perfection (after the Persian wars) also of gold and ivory. The ornaments of the temple afforded also an ample field for the sculptor's art. These at first consisted of splendid votive offerings, vessels and

other furniture with relievos, some of which were of co- (330)
lossal dimensions and rich materials; and, at a later period, A
of groups of statues, representing mythological scenes. When art no longer confined itself to religious representations, but selected also subjects from public and private life, its productions became so numerous that even hamlets and villages had their collections. The most distinguished masters in sculpture were, Phidias, who executed in gold and ivory the statues of Zeus at Olympia, and of Athēnē in the Parthĕnon at Athens, and the colossal image of Athene in the acropolis of Athens, in brass—Polyclētus, Myron, Scopas, Praxitĕles, and Lysippus.

c. Painting was for a long time confined to the deli- 331
neation of figures on earthenware, and was consequently B
considered subordinate to sculpture, until the age of Pericles, and especially the fourth century B. C., when it was raised to the rank of an independent art by Polygnōtus, Zeuxis, and Parrhasius, and attained the highest degree of perfection under Apelles, in the reign of Alexander the Great. His works consisted partly of frescoes, and partly of painted tablets.

5. TRADE.

The trade of the Greeks in the heroic age was merely 332
passive. They permitted the commerce of the Phœni- C
cians, who brought them not only the products of their own manufacturing industry, but also those of Ethiopia, Arabia, India, and other foreign countries (electron,[1] for instance). At a very early period, however, the Cretans and Phæacians were notorious for their sea-voyages and acts of piracy. The Phœnicians being gradually sup- D
planted, and piracy in a great measure suppressed, the trade became *active*, and was carried on principally by Corinth, Sicyon, Ægīna, Athens, the Cyclădes, and the Ionian colonies, and promoted by the establishment of colonies and by commercial leagues and religious unions.

Principal branches of Greek commerce :— 333

1. Between the Grecian states themselves.
2. Between the mother country and its colonies.
3. To foreign countries—*a. Eastward* to the coasts of Asia Minor, and thence into the interior as far as Cappadocia and Pontus.

[1] Acording to Hüllman, the term "electron" signifies, in Homer and Hesiod, not amber, but precious stones in general.

(333) b. *North-eastward* to Thrace, the Propontis, the Bospŏrus, the Pontus
A Euxīnus, and from the cities on its northern shore (Dioscurias and Olbia) to the interior of Sarmatia. c. *Southwards* to Cyprus, Egypt (the Hellenion, originally a merely religious but afterwards a commercial union, founded by Naucratis as an emporium), Cyrēne, and thence into the interior of Africa. d. *Northwards* to the Ionic and Adriatic sea, and from Epidaurus into the interior of Illyria. e. *Westward* to Italy, Spain, and Gaul.

Principal articles.—1. Of import:—Grain from the colonies on the Cimmerian Bospŏrus in Egypt and Sicily—timber from Thrace and Macedonia—ivory from Africa—slaves from Phrygia, Thrace, and the countries of Scythia and the Caucasus—linen and papyrus from Egypt. 2. Of export:—Wine, oil, honey, wax, works in metal, &c

II. The Macedonians.

Sources of Information.

334 Diodōrus, in seventeen books.—Arrian (see § 50).—Plutarch, in
B his Biographies of Demosthenes and Alexander the Great.—Curtius de rebus gestis Alexandri Magni, 3—10, B.—Some of the orations of Demosthenes and Æschines.—A few notices in Herodotus, Thucydides, and Justin.

Modern Authorities.

The settlements, origin, and early history of the Macedonian people, by K. O. Müller, Berlin, 1825.—Flathe; History of Macedonia, and of the empire ruled by the Macedonian Kings; Leipzic, 1832—34, two parts.—Mannert; History of the immediate successors of Alexander the Great; Leipzic, 1787.

§ 73. *Geography of Macedonia.*

335 Boundaries.—Macedonia, as the term was originally
C understood, or Emathia, extended from Mount Olympus to the mouth of the Lydias; consequently that portion of it which bordered on the Thermaïc gulf was a mere narrow strip of land. But as the power of the Macedonian kings increased, the term obtained a wider signification; and in the days of Alexander the Great was taken to indicate the whole country, bounded on the west by the lake Lychnītis, on the north by the Scardian mountains, on the east by the Nestus, and on the south by the Macedonian or Olympian chain, and the Ægean sea. As a Roman province, Macedonia comprised also Thessaly and a part of Illyria.

336 Mountains.—In the south the Macedonian, or Olympian range (also Cambunii Montes); in the west, north, and

east, several branches of the Scardus. Mount Athos, on the peninsula of Acte.

WATERS.—The Thracian sea, with the Strymonic and 337
Thermaïc gulfs, inclosing the peninsula of Chalcidĭce, A
which is again divided into three smaller peninsulas, formed by the Singitic and Toronaïc gulfs. The names of these peninsulas were Acte, Sithonia, and Pallēnē.—The lake Lychnītis.

RIVERS.—*a.* Flowing into the Strymonic gulf, the Nes- 338
tus, and Strymon; *b.* into the Thermaic gulf, the Axius, and Haliacmon.

CITIES.—1. Pydna (battle in 168). 2. Pella, the ca- 339
pital, and residence of the sovereign. 3. Thessalonīca B
(formerly Therma—now Salonichi—the place of Cicero's exile), built by Cassander. 4. Potidæa, on the isthmus of Pallĕne. 5. Olynthus, destroyed by Philip II. 6. Amphipŏlis, on the Strymon, an Athenian colony (battle in 422). 7. Philippi, formerly Crenĭdes (battle in 42).

§ 74. *History of Macedonia to the Reign of Philip II.*

There exist two traditions respecting the establishment 340
of the Macedonian monarchy; neither of which, however, C
asserts more than the fact that the kings of Macedonia were descended from Hercules. 1. The Temenide (and consequently Heraclide) Carānus of Argos conquered Edessa in Emathia, and named it Ægæ. 2. Perdiccas, also a Temenide from Argos, in conjunction with his two brothers, made himself master of Emathia.

By degrees the whole of the sea-coast, from the frontiers of Thessaly to the Axius, fell into the hands of the Heraclide kings, who exercised also a certain authority over the petty barbarian sovereigns in the interior. The first continuous notices of Macedonian history commence with the subjection of the country to the Persians by Mardonius, B. C. 490.[1]

The Macedonian king Alexander, who was compelled D
to take a part in the expedition of Xerxes against Greece,

[1] King Amyntas I. had already given earth and water, the emblems of submission, to Megabazus, the Persian satrap of Thrace; but Macedonia remained free from Persian dominion until the year 490.

(340) was employed ineffectually by Mardonius as an ambassa-
A dor to the Athenians, to whom he betrayed the barbarians'
plan of operations before the battle of Platææ. The retreat of Mardonius in 479 liberated Macedonia, as well
as Greece. The next king, Perdiccas II., at the commencement of his reign, was an ally of the Athenians;
but when they supported his rebellious brother Philip, and
the Thracian king Sitalces, in their opposition to his government, he went over to their enemies, promoted the rising of the Chalcidians (Potidæa) in the Peloponnesian war,
B and formed an alliance with Brasidas. His son Archelāus improved the condition of the country by his promotion of agriculture, the encouragement which he gave
to literary and scientific Greeks (Euripides lived at his
court), the construction of public highways, fortification of
the cities, discipline of the army, &c. His death was succeeded by a gloomy period of confusion and revolution,
which lasted until the time of Philip II.; who availed
himself of his influence, as guardian of his nephew,
Amyntas III., to assume the reins of government in the
year 359.

341 Constitution of Macedonia during this period.—The king was
C commander-in-chief, high priest, and chief justice; but in all questions
which concerned the general welfare he was bound by the votes of
his nobles, and was also obliged to share the judicial authority with
his people. Under Alexander the Great this power was exercised
by the army.

§ 75. *Philip II.*

(359—336.)

342 The Thebans (Pelopidas) having settled the disputed succession in Macedonia by the partition of the kingdom between two claimants, Philip[1] (son of Amyntas II.) was

[1] Amyntas II. †370.

Alexander II. †368.	Perdiccas III. †359.	Philip II. †336.
	Amyntas III.	Alexander the Great. †323.

sent as a hostage for the observance of the treaty to (342)
Thebes; where, during a residence of three years in the A
house of Epaminondas, he not only received a *Greek* education, but acquired a thorough knowledge of the Theban tactics, and of the fearful jealousies which existed between the different states of Greece. After the dissolution of this compact by the assassination of one of the claimants to the throne, Philip returned to Macedonia, where he was invested with a petty principality. On the succession, however, of Amyntas III., the infant son of Perdiccas III., the empire being threatened by the neighboring barbarians (Illyrians, Pæonians, and Thracians), and two other pretenders to the crown having raised the standard of rebellion, Philip assumed the office of protector, overthrew both the pretenders, beat back the barbarians, and himself ascended the throne. We have no minute account of these occurrences.

Thenceforward the grand object of Philip seems to have B
been the subjugation of the Persian empire. With this view, he not only increased the efficiency of the army by the introduction of the Macedonian phalanx—the terrific power of which consisted in its close ranks, the heavy armor of the men, and their long spears—but also endeavored to make himself master of the coasts of Thrace (that they might serve as means of communication with the countries which he intended to conquer), and to acquire over the Grecian states a Hegemony, which should place their forces at his disposal. For an account of the manner in which this object was gradually attained see 312, sqq.

Scarcely, however, had this Hegemony been acquired, C
and the advanced guard of the army commenced its march into Asia, when the king was assassinated, on coming out of the theatre at Ægæ, by one Pausanias, whose complaint of having received ill-treatment from a member of the royal family had been contemptuously dismissed by Philip.

§ 76. *Alexander the Great.*

(336—323.)

Alexander, born in the year B. C. 356, on the same night in 343
which Herostrătus set fire to the temple of Artĕmis [*Di-* D
ana], at Ephesus, was scarcely 20 years old, when he ascended the throne. His education had been superintended by

(343) Aristotle (cf. 328, c), from whom he had acquired a taste for
A poetry, especially for the compositions of Homer. The first acts of his reign were to punish the murderers of his father; and remove certain pretenders to the throne, who disputed the legitimacy of his birth. On receiving information that the Greeks, at the instigation of Demosthenes, had refused to recognize his Hegemony, Alexander suddenly appeared in Greece, at the head of an army, and at the συνέδριον, at Corinth, was chosen commander-in-chief of the forces destined to act against the Persians, all the states, except Lacædemon being thoroughly humbled, and concurring in the election.

B Lest however his plans should be disconcerted by the breaking out of fresh disturbances, he compelled the Greeks to conclude a general peace with each other, and with the Macedonians; the settlement of their disputes being referred to a Synedrion, which seems to have sat at Corinth during the whole of Alexander's reign.

344 An expedition was now undertaken against the Thracians, Triballi, and Getæ, who had manifested symptoms of a desire to regain their independence; and Alexander, having advanced beyond the Ister and accomplished his object, was returning, having, in his march homewards, subdued the Illyrians and Taulantians, when intelligence reached him, that fresh disturbances had broken out in Greece, in
C consequence of a false report of his death. Thebes, which, in spite of the freedom and independence guaranteed by her ally, was still occupied by a Macedonian garrison, had revolted. Within twelve days Alexander appeared before the place, overthrew the Thebans in a pitched battle, and having obtained a decree of the Synedrion at Corinth, demolished the city, with the exception of the Cadmēa, the temples, and the house of Pindar, and sold the surviving inhabitants (30,000) into slavery.

345 His campaign against the Persians. Having left
D Antipăter as regent in Macedonia, Alexander undertook the *conquest of the Persian empire*, which intestine weakness had already brought to the verge of dissolution. In the spring of 334, a Macedonian force of 30,000 infantry, and 5000 cavalry, crossed the Hellespont, and overthrew the satraps of Darius and the Greek mercenaries under Memnon, a Rhodian, on the banks of the Granīcus, where Clitus saved the life of Alexander. As he advanced along the western coast of Asia Minor, he was hailed as

their deliverer from Persian tyranny by the inhabitants of (345)
the Greek towns, to whom he granted independence, on A
condition of their closing their ports against the Persian fleet. The only resistance offered was by the Persian governor of Milētus, and by Memnon, the Rhodian, at Halicarnassus; but both cities were carried by storm. Alexander then divided his army, himself proceeding along the southern coast of Asia Minor, as far as the frontiers of Cilicia, whilst his general, Parmenio, made himself master of Phrygia. The further advance of Alexander along the southern coast being barred by the rocky B
mountains of Cilicia, he marched northwards into the interior of Asia Minor, with the intention of wintering in the fruitful district of Phrygia. In order to render the superstitious belief of the people of Asia subservient to his purpose, he *cut* the famous knot at Gordium.

In the year 333 Alexander, in conjunction with his general Parmenio, entered Cilicia, and falling sick at Tarsus, after bathing in the Cydnus, was cured by his calumniated physician, Philip. At Issus, on the borders of Syria, Darius himself was overthrown by Alexander, in a battle in which 100,000 Persians fell, and their king escaped with difficulty. The rich camp of the Persians, with the C
magnificent royal tent, the mother, wife, two daughters, and a son of Darius, fell into the hands of the conqueror, who treated the prisoners with his accustomed clemency. Damascus, with the royal treasury, was taken by Parmenio. Meanwhile Darius had escaped to the other side of the Euphrates, and was in vain endeavoring to purchase a peace by the resignation of all his dominions as far as that river.

In the year 332 Alexander conquered Syria, Cyprus, 346
and Phœnicia, where the insular city of Tyre alone D
refused to admit a Macedonian garrison, and after a siege of seven months was stormed by means of a dam thrown across from the mainland to the island. In Palestine, Gaza, (the only city that offered any opposition) was taken after a siege of two months. In Egypt, where Alexander was welcomed as a deliverer from the Persian yoke, he endeavored to perpetuate his power by founding at the western embouchure of the Nile the port and (almost entirely *Greek*) city of Alexandria.

347 From this place, Alexander, at the head of a considerable
A portion of his army, marched through the Libyan desert to
the temple of Zeus Ammon (by whose priest he was pronounced to be the son of the god), probably for the purpose
of offering, in the sight of the Egyptians, a solemn act of
homage to their supreme deity. By the conquest of Phœnicia and Cyprus, he had also acquired a powerful fleet,
consisting of ships which at an earlier period had composed
the main strength of the Persian marine. Returning to
Asia, he overthrew Darius at Gaugamēla near Arbēla
B (1 Oct.), 331. The defeated monarch fled for refuge to
the inaccessible north-eastern regions of his kingdom,
whilst the conqueror promptly took possession of the more
important and wealthy provinces of the southeast, viz.,
Babylonia, Susiana, and Persis. Retracing his steps
through Media, in the hope of discovering the fugitive,
Alexander, on his arrival in Parthia, found that Darius
had already fallen by the hands of the satraps of Bactria
(Bessus), and Arachosia.

348 The death of Darius removed the last barrier which
C withheld the principal Persians from throwing themselves
into the arms of the conqueror, whose crafty policy, even
more than his brilliant victories, enabled him to found a
Persico-Macedonian kingdom. The rapid subjugation of the eastern portion of the empire was effected
principally by the adoption of three measures: 1. The
satraps, who were willing to recognize him as sovereign of
the east, were permitted to retain their satrapies. This
secured the eastern portion. 2. The dress, manners and
court ceremonial of the earlier Persian kings were adopted
by Alexander, that he might appear as little as possible in
D the light of a foreign conqueror. 3. In accordance with
a system which had hitherto worked well, he governed
with more mildness than the Persian monarchs, and with
more respect for the principle of *nationality*.

349 After traversing the eastern provinces, Alexander proceeded to Sogdiana, in pursuit of the satrap Bessus (the murderer of Darius, who had assumed the title of Artaxerxes III.), and having taken him prisoner, ordered his immediate execution. The north-eastern limits of the Persian empire having been reached, and the country completely subjugated, Alexander conceived the design of

making himself king of all Asia, the extreme boundaries of (349)
which were, as he supposed, at no great distance. With A
this view he undertook an expedition against the Scythians and Indians, and crossed the Juxartes; but finding that the nomadic hordes avoided a battle, and that as he advanced the country became more inhospitable, he retraced his steps, contenting himself with posting garrisons along the line of frontier formed by the river.

Meanwhile discontent had manifested itself in two quarters. 1. 350
Among the Macedonian nobles, who had followed him to Asia, and B
could neither brook the appointment of the Persian nobility to satrapies, nor readily accord to their sovereign the divine honors which he now claimed as king of Persia. Some of the most distinguished among them, as Parmenio, and his son Philotas, Clitus, and Callisthenes, lost their lives in consequence of their refusal to render this unworthy homage. 2. *In Greece,* where the severities of Alexander and his lieutenant, Antipăter, became every day more intolerable, the Spartan king, Agis II., availing himself of the opportunity afforded by the absence of Antipater in Thrace (whither he had gone for the purpose of chastising his revolted officer Memnon), raised the standard of patriotic warfare. None however supported him, except the Achæans, Eleans, and Arcadians; and a single victory (near Ægæ, in Arcadia) put an end to the insurrection (330).

Campaign of Alexander in western India, 327 351
and 326.

With an army, of which the nucleus alone was composed C
of Macedonians and Greeks, the main body consisting of the most promising barbarians, Alexander, in the spring of 327, crossed the Indian frontier, and in the expectation of soon reaching the eastern coast of Asia, fought his way to the Hyphăsis, the brave savages of the Punjâb offering the most determined resistance to his progress. For his success he was, in a great measure, indebted to dissensions among the chieftains of northern India, and to the alliance of the most powerful sovereigns, such as Taxila and Porus, who were induced, by the promise of important benefits, to acknowledge the supremacy of the Macedonians, permit the establishment of fortresses within their dominions (e. g. Nicæa, and Bucephala, at the two most important
fords of the Ganges), and receive Macedonian satraps as D
commanders of the garrisons, or themselves become satraps. As Alexander's knowledge of the extent of India became more accurate, and his army melted away in repeated and

(351) obstinate combats with the barbarians, whilst at the same
A time distressing intelligence reached him of the misconduct of his satraps, the idea of subduing India was gradually abandoned. On the Hyphăsis he was compelled (it is said, by the discontent of his soldiers [?]), to give his line of march a southerly, instead of an easterly, direction. Embarking, with a part of his army, on board a fleet of 1800 to 2000 vessels built on the Hydaspes, and commanded by Nearchus, he sailed down the Hydaspes and the Acesines, and thence (after the overthrow of the brave Malli and Oxythracians) down the Indus (the mouths of which were accurately surveyed and fortified, in anticipa-
B tion of a future enterprise) into the Indian ocean. Nearchus piloted the fleet through the Erythræan sea into the Persian gulf, and discovered the mouths of the Euphrates and the Tigris; but Alexander, with the larger division of his army, returned overland to Persia. Taxila and Porus seem to have been the only Indian sovereigns who continued in a sort of dependent state until the death of Alexander.

352 His return to Babylon, 326—324.

C Alexander, with that portion of his forces which had not embarked on board the ships, continued his march from the mouth of the Ganges, along the sea shore, for the purpose of keeping his fleet in sight and supplying it with provisions. When this line of march became no longer practicable, he proceeded through Gedrosia, Carmania, Persis, and Susa, to Babylon, where he punished the arrogant satraps with great severity. The last years of his life were spent (with the exception of a short campaign against the wild Cossæis) in making arrangements for the internal regulation of his dominions, and in preparing for a future expedition, probably against India.

353 *Internal arrangements.* The barbarian satraps, who oppressed the
D people, were removed, and their places supplied by Macedonians. In order still further to conciliate the barbarians, Alexander married Barsine, the eldest daughter of Darius Codomannus, and Parysatis, the youngest sister of King Artaxerxes III., and, at the same time, compelled the most distinguished of his suite, as well as 10,000 other Macedonians, to take Persian wives. The discontent of the Macedonians at finding that the ranks of the army, and even of the king's body-guard were filled with barbarians, whilst the services of his own veteran soldiers were forgotten, occasioned a mutiny, which was suppressed by the energy and firmness of the king.

In the year 323, Alexander, in consequence of his ex- 354
traordinary exertions, and his undue indulgence in the A
pleasures of the table, died at Babylon [of a fever] at
the early age of thirty-two.

§ 77. *Partition of the Persico-Macedonian empire.*

After Alexander's death, his most distinguished generals 355
and friends, Perdiccas, Leonatus, and Ptolemæus, the son
of Lagus, in conjunction with the leaders of the army, determined to proclaim as king the child to which his widow,
Roxane,[1] expected shortly to give birth, in the hope that it
would prove a male. Perdiccas (at first in conjunction B
with Leonatus) was to govern as regent (ἐπιμελητής) in Asia,
Antipater and Cratĕrus in Europe; and the most distinguished Macedonians were to be advanced to satrapies.
The army, however, compelled them to recognize Arrhidæus, the weak-minded half-brother of the late king, together with his posthumous son, Alexander.

The eastern portion of the kingdom was entirely unaffected by this *partition of satrapies;* but in the west Ptolemæus Lagi obtained the satrapy of Egypt, Leonātus of the Hellespontine Phrygia; Cassander of Caria; Antigŏnus of Pamphylia, Phrygia, and Lycia; Eumĕnes (Alexander's private secretary) of the still unconquered districts of Paphlagonia and Cappadocia; and Lysimăchus of Thrace and the western coasts of Pontus.

Perdiccas, who had accepted the regency in the 356
hope of being able to set aside the two royal puppets C
Arrhidæus and Alexander, and himself ascend the
throne, pursued his plans so incautiously as to raise up against him a confederacy of satraps: and when he appealed to arms, he was slain by his own troops during a campaign in Egypt in the year 321. The vacant regency was now conferred by the army on Antipăter, who, at his death in 318, bequeathed the guardianship of the two young kings, not to his own son, Cassander, who was a bitter enemy of the royal family of Macedonia, but to his former lieutenant-general Polysperchŏn. This

[1] Alexander the Great
by Roxane — Alexander.
by Barsine — Hercules.

(356) arrangement occasioned a war between Cassander and
A Polysperchon, the former allying himself with Antigŏnus, the governor of Western Asia, the latter with Eumĕnes. Antigonus was victorious in Asia, and Cassander in Europe; whilst the ruin of Eumenes in Asia, through the treachery of his partisans, occasioned also the fall of Polysperchon in Europe. The ambitious designs of Antigonus, who had portioned out the satrapies of eastern Asia according to his own caprice, and every where taken possession of the royal treasures, had now become so apparent, that a confederacy was formed against him by the satraps of the west, Cassander of Macedonia, Ptolemæus Lag:, Lysimachus, and Seleucus, who had been expelled from Babylon. This occasioned, at two different periods (314, 301),
B war between Antigonus and those satraps. For a long time Antigonus, assisted by his son, Demetrius Poliorcētes, made head against his enemies, but in the year 301 he was defeated and slain in a battle fought at Ipsus, against Lysimachus and Seleucus. His dominions were divided among themselves by the conquerors, so that on the ruins of the Persico-Macedonian empire there now arose four new monarchies. Meanwhile the two royal puppets were murdered.

357 First War (314—311). Antigonus endeavored by his activity
C and cunning to divide his opponents, whose plans of operation were different. Whilst he was preparing for an invasion of Egypt, and commencing a war with Ptolemy, by making himself master of Phœnicia, he caused it to be proclaimed to the Greeks (by the Macedonians in his army,) that they were emancipated from the Macedonian yoke. This was done for the purpose of weakening Cassander of Macedonia. Then he subdued the south-western part of Asia Minor, and had already reached the Hellespont, intending to cross into Europe, when his son Demetrius, whom he had left behind in Phœnicia, was totally defeated by Ptolemæus, near Gaza (in 312.) Seleucus then regained the satrapy of Babylon (312), of which he had been deprived, and united with it Media and Susiana. In order to reconquer the east, Antigonus abandoned his European campaign, and concluded a peace with Cassander, Lysimachus, and Ptolemæus, reserving for himself the sovereignty over the whole of Asia, and stipulating that his promise of independence to the Greeks should be confirmed.

358 Second War (309—301). As neither party observed the conditions of this peace (for the garrisons of Cassander as well as the
D lieutenants of Antigonus still remained in Greece; and Alexander had moreover procured the assassination of Hercules, the last scion of the ancient royal house), the war broke out afresh. Demetrius,

who was now commissioned by his father Antigonus to effect the (358)
liberation of Greece, drove the troops of Cassander out of Athens, A
and for this service was rewarded with the most extraordinary
marks of respect; two new tribes, Antigonias and Demetrias, being
named after his father and himself. He then, in obedience to his
father's commands, returned into Asia, and after a splendid victory
over the Egyptian fleet, wrested Cyprus from Ptolemæus Lagi. In
their joy at having obtained this advantage, both Antigonus and
Demetrius assumed the title of king, an example which was followed
by Ptolemæus, Lysimachus, and Seleucus. After an unsuccessful
attempt on Egypt, Demetrius tried to avenge himself on the flourishing
and powerful republic of Rhodes, which had refused to assist
him against Ptolemæus; but notwithstanding the most tremendous
exertions, and the construction of an engine termed Helepŏlis, which
consisted of nine stories, and was worked by 3400 men, he was
compelled to raise the siege, and gladly accepted the invitation of the
Greeks to aid them in opposing the ambitious designs of Lysander.
The rapid and successful progress of Demetrius (who had been
nominated commander-in-chief of the Grecian forces at the Synedrion
at Corinth), compelled Lysander to enter into a fresh alliance
with Lysimachus, Seleucus, and Ptolemæus. Lysimachus having in B
consequence of this arrangement marched into Asia Minor, whilst
Seleucus at the same time advanced from the east, Antigonus, who
was now in his eighty-first year, recalled his son from Greece, but
fell in the battle of Ipsus, 301. His territories were divided among
the conquerors, Lysimachus receiving the whole of Asia Minor on
this side the Taurus, and Seleucus the rest of that district together
with Syria, including Phœnicia and Palestine. Demetrius, who still
retained possession of Cyprus, Tyre, and Sidon, and had the largest
fleet at his disposal, proceeded towards Greece.

III. The Kingdoms which arose out of the Macedonian Monarchy.[1]

§ 78. *Macedonia and Greece.*

(323—146.)

The Lamian War, 323—322. 359
On receiving the intelligence of Alexander's death, the C
Greeks, who even during his lifetime had made an attempt
to recover their freedom (see § 76), united, at the summons
of the Athenians, for a last struggle. Leosthĕnes, com-

[1] Succession of kings: a) *Of various families:* 1. Philip Arrhidæus and Alexander. 2. Cassander. 3. Philip. 4. Antipater and Alexander. 5. Demetrius Poliorcĕtes. 6. Pyrrhus. 7. Lysimachus. 8. Seleucus Nicator. 9. Ptolemæus Ceraunus. 10. Meleăger. 11. Antipater. 12. Sosthĕnes. b.) *Of the family of Demetrius Poliorcetes.* 1. Antigonus Gonatas. 2. Demetrius II. 3. Antigonus II. Doson. 4. Philip III. 5. Perseus. 6. Andriscus.

(359) mander-in-chief of the allied army, transferred the theatre
A of war to Thessaly, where Antipater, after sustaining *a*
defeat, threw himself into Lamia, with the intention of
awaiting the arrival of his allies Cratĕrus and Leonatus.
Leonatus came first, and fell in a *second battle;* but
Craterus having now joined Antipater, and obtained a
considerable advantage in a *third engagement* (near Cranon),
most of the Greek states endeavored to make terms
for themselves, leaving the Athenians and Ætolians to
B carry on the war. Even Athens, when the Macedonian
army advanced to her walls, was compelled to sue for
peace, which was granted on condition of her paying the
expenses of the war, together with a heavy fine, receiving
a Macedonian garrison into Munychia, delivering up the
orators Demosthenes and Hyperides, and accepting such a
constitution as Antipater thought fit to offer. The two
orators had fled from Athens, but were overtaken; Hyperides
was conveyed to Macedonia, where his tongue was
cut out—Demosthenes swallowed poison in the island of
Calauria.

360 The kings of the new Macedonian empire, being fully
C aware that any attempt to recover Asia would be fruitless,
contented themselves with endeavoring to render Greece
(which as yet was but loosely connected with Macedonia)
a province of that country. Notwithstanding, however,
the pertinacity with which they kept this object in view,
their plans were continually rendered abortive even when
they seemed on the eve of being accomplished, partly by
repeated disputes respecting the succession to
the throne, partly by quarrels with the barbarians
of the north, especially the Gauls, and at a later period
D by the invasion of the Romans. Another obstacle
to the complete subjugation of Greece existed in the
mutual jealousies of those who were at the head of the
three greater monarchies, and in the formation of the
Ætolian, and revival of the Achæan confederacy
(280). Thessaly alone remained a Macedonian province,
most of the other states being merely allies of Macedonia,
and bearing each a different relation to the king, as the
head of the Græco-Macedonian Symmachy.

361 Macedonia and Grece invaded by the Gauls
in 280. A detachment, consisting of three hordes, of

those Gallic tribes, whose immigration a hundred years (361)
before had convulsed the south-western portion of western A
Europe, appeared in Macedonia in the year 280. The
first horde overthrew king Ptolemæus Ceraunus, who was
slain in the engagement; but the invaders were subsequently driven out of the country by Sosthĕnes. A
second horde under Brennus advanced as far as Delphi,
laying waste the country with fire and sword; but the
attacks of the allied Grecian force (now strengthened by
the addition of Macedonians and Syrians), and the suffer-
ings which they endured through earthquakes (?), cold, and
hunger, reduced their army to a mere skeleton. Brennus, B
their king, being grievously wounded, fell by his own
hand; and the few who escaped, joining their countrymen,
who had remained in Thrace, formed a Gallic settlement
in that country, which since the death of Lysimachus had
been united with Macedonia. A part of them crossed
over into Asia Minor, and settled in Galatia.

The establishment of the Ætolian and re- 362
newal of the Achæan confederacy (280) had for C
its object the restoration and maintenance of Grecian independence. The *Ætolian confederacy*, at the head of
which was placed a stratēgos, held an annual meeting
(Panætolion) at Thermus, at which questions affecting the
general interests of the confederacy were discussed.
They had also the great council of the Apoclētæ. The
ancient insignificant union of the *Achæan cities* (see
§ 58) was revived, at first by four and subsequently by all
the rest; but this confederacy, which held its session twice
a year at Ægium, and subsequently at Corinth, under the
presidency of a strategos, did not acquire any considerable
influence until the time of Arātus, who, as the soul of the
whole union, gained over to the cause his own native city
of Sicyon, together with Corinth, and all the principal
cities of Peloponnesus (Sparta excepted). Even the D
Athenians were persuaded to join the confederacy through
the policy of Arātus, who bribed the Macedonian governor
to withdraw his garrison from their city (229).

These successes of the Achæans excited the jealousy of 363
the Ætolians, who endeavored to establish a confederacy
of the whole of Greece with themselves at its head. The
pursuit of this object among the Peloponnesian states, the

(363) union of which was also the great end of the Achæan
A league, produced a struggle for the Hegemony of Greece between the two confederacies. The Achæans being at first unsuccessful, abandoned the principle on which their confederacy had been formed, and applied for aid to the king of Macedonia.

364 In the *Cleomenian war,* as it was called (228—222), the Ætolians formed an alliance with Sparta, each party perhaps promising the other that they would divide the Hegemony of Greece between them. The Achæans after sustaining many defeats, were on the point of submitting themselves to the Hegemony of Sparta, when the ambitious Arātus, in order to prevent the decline of his personal
B influence, called in the Macedonians. Cleomĕnes, king of Sparta, wearied out by the long war, which had exhausted all his resources, was vanquished, in attempting to make good the pass of Sellasia between Arcadia and Laconia, by the numerical superiority and greater warlike skill of the Macedonians. The subjugation of the Ætolians, who were not comprehended in the great Græco-Macedonian Symmachy, was left by Antigonus as a legacy to his son Philip III. The opportunity for effecting this seemed to have arrived, when the brave Ætolians came forward to resist the further extension of the great Græco Macedonian Symmachy, and hence arose the *war of the confederates,* between the Ætolians and a portion of the Symmachy. This war was carried on almost single-handed by Philip with such success, that at the end of two years peace was concluded, the intelligence of Hannibal's victories in Italy having drawn his attention to the feasibility of attacking Rome. Ætolia and Elis retained their independence.

For the relations of Macedonia and Greece with Rome see § 123—126.

Civilization of the Greeks from 338 to 146.

365 Literature: 1. In poetry the most remarkable phe-
C nomenon was the *New Comedy* (without a chorus), the chief aim of which was to present a characteristic picture of ordinary life, and to assail with the weapons of ridicule those irregularities, which were inaccessible to the attacks of graver moralists. The most successful writer of this description of comedy was Menander, the model of
D Plautus and Terence. 2. Eloquence lost more and more its political character, and was merely cultivated as an art in the schools of the rhetoricians, chiefly at Rhodes. 3. The cultivation of philosophy as a distinct science occupied the attention of five recently established schools.

366 a. The *Peripatetic,* that of Aristotle and his disciple Theophrastus (his Ethics.) b. The *Epicurean,* founded by Epicurus, which repre-

sented pleasure (ἡδονή) as the chief end of man. c. The *Stoic*, (366)
founded by Zenon (Zeno), which recognized real good only in virtue, A
and enjoined a life in accordance with nature. d. The *Skeptic* (founded by Pyrrhon [Pyrrho]), which denied certainty of notions received through the *senses*, or formed from sensible impressions by *reflection*. e. The *New Academy* (founded by Carneades), which combated the Stoics with its skeptical eloquence.

b. Commerce. The principal commercial places, after 367
the decline of Grecian freedom, were Corinth, Rhodes, and Byzantium. Articles of Asiatic luxury, which had become better known by means of Alexander's expedition, were soon eagerly sought after by Europeans.

§ 79. *Egypt under the Ptolemies.*

(B. C. 323—30.)

Flourishing condition of the empire under the 368
three first Ptolemies, 323—221. B

Of the three greater empires into which the Macedonian monarchy was divided after the death of Alexander, the smallest, but for that very reason, the most easily tenable, fell to the lot of the Ptolemies. They enjoyed the advantage of being able to dispense with the satraps, and of governing an unwarlike people, who, having been long accustomed to a foreign and often oppressive dynasty, were little disposed to take offence at the accession of a foreign race, or the presence of Greek and Macedonian officers in the army and at court; especially as the new rulers treated their subjects kindly, and respected their religion, constitution, and customs. Notwith- C
standing, however, the sagacity displayed by the three first kings, Ptolemy Soter,[2] Ptolemy Philadelphus,[1] and Ptolemy Euergĕtes,[3] in their endeavors to render Egypt, and particularly their Græco-Macedonian capital, Alexandria, *a grand emporium for the commerce of the whole world, as well as the central school of Grecian science and art*, their foreign policy was singularly injudicious and unfortunate. As a proof of this, we may

[1] A surname bestowed on him by the Rhodians, whom he had assisted against Demetrius Poliorcetes.

[2] So named, because he married his own sister Arsinoe.

[3] *Euergĕtes* [= the benefactor] was a surname given to Ptolemy by the priests, for having brought back the images of the Egyptian gods from Asia.

(368) mention the stupid obstinacy with which they persisted in
A their endeavors to add the desirable, but by no means indispensable, neighboring districts of Cœle-Syria, Phœnicia, Palestine, and even Asia Minor, to Egypt, Cyrēne, and Cyprus, which they possessed, the first by right of conquest, the last in virtue of a treaty. Their perseverance in this line of policy not only involved them in frequent quarrels with the Seleucidæ, but rendered the revival of the satrapy-system indispensable in the conquered districts.

369 In order to facilitate the commerce between India and the
B Mediterranean, Ptolemy Philadelphus completed a canal from the Red Sea to the Nile, which had been commenced by Necho (see § 92), and continued by Darius Hystaspes. It would seem, however, that little use was made of this mode of communication, until the time of the Arabian Caliphs, it being considered safer on account of the numerous reefs at the upper end of the Arabian gulf to ship only as far as the ports of Berenīce and Myos Hormos (both founded by the above-mentioned king), where the cargoes were discharged and conveyed on camels to Coptus, and thence forwarded by canal to the Nile. Thus Egypt became a principal emporium for the Indian and Arabian trade, an advantage which it in a great measure retained until the discovery of a passage to India by the Cape of Good Hope.

370 B. Decline and fall of the Empire, B. C. 221—
C 30.

The decline of the Egyptian empire dates its commencement from the reign of the luxurious tyrant Ptolemy IV. Philopător. From this time portion after portion of the foreign possessions acquired by the swords of their ancestors was wrested from the feeble hands of successive sovereigns, who gave themselves up to effeminacy and debauchery, leaving the administration of public affairs to their favorites; whilst the people, goaded to madness by the oppressive government, made repeated attempts to shake off the yoke of a foreign dynasty, and a disputed succession furnished the Romans with an excuse for intervention, and finally for the dismemberment of the kingdom (comp. § 125). Cæsar's Alexandrian war against Ptolemy
D XIII. Dionȳsus, at the instigation of Cleopatra (see § 148, 1). War of Augustus against Cleopatra and Mark Antony (see § 154). Egypt a Roman province, B. C. 30.

371 C. Alexandrian Literature.

From the time of Alexander the Great, or rather from

the establishment of the Alexandrian Museum by (371)
Ptolemy Philadelphus, the new capital of Egypt took the A
place of Athens as the seat of Grecian learning, the object and character of which were however materially altered by its transplantation to a different quarter of the globe. The creative arts, as well as poetry and rhetoric, manifestly declined, whilst scientific subjects were treated more profoundly and systematically.

1. *Poetry.* The Alexandrian poets are deficient in 372
poetic genius, imagination, and not unfrequently taste in B
the choice and treatment of their subject. In tragedy, we have the "seven stars," as they are called, in lyric poetry Callimăchus (elegies), in epic Apollonius Rhodius (the Argonautica), in didactic poetry Arātus, and in Bucolic (which now first developed itself) Theocrĭtus (thirty of his Idylls are extant), Bion, and Moschus.

2. Grammar, in conjunction with criticism and the 373
interpretation of the ancient writers (*philology* in short), was first raised in this century to the position of a substantive science by the Alexandrian grammarians, who selected the best productions of Grecian literature, formed them into a canon, and corrected the text, which they illustrated with grammatical, historical, and æsthetical comments. The most celebrated grammarians were Zenodŏtus of Ephesus (about 280), and his disciple Aristophănes of Byzantium (about 240), who arranged the first
canon of classic writers. His pupil Aristarchus (about C
180) was considered the most distinguished critic of antiquity. His "Recension" of Homer's poems (the division of which into twenty-four cantos is ascribed to him) forms the ground-work of the text which we now possess.

Mathematics also, which had hitherto been considered only a 374
branch of philosophy, first began to be treated systematically during this period, principally by Euclid (his "Elements"), Ctesibius (inventor of the water-organ), Apollonius of Perga (Conic Sections), a pupil of Archimēdes of Syracuse, the founder of *Statics*.

The first scientific systems of *astronomy* and *geography* were established at Alexandria by Eratosthĕnes (γεωγραφικά in three books).

Philosophy was eagerly cultivated here in the second century by the Eclectics, who selected from different systems whatever they considered most worthy of their attention.

§ 80. *The Syrian Empire under the Seleucidæ.*[1]

(312—64).

375 Seleucus, satrap of Babylon, being summoned by
A Antigonus to give an account of his administration, had
fled into Egypt; but in the year 312 returned at the head
of an army of Egyptian auxiliaries to Babylon, which he
defended successfully against Demetrius, the son of Antigonus, and remained in undisturbed possession of Babylonia, Media, Susiana, and some of the neighboring districts.
By his victory at Ipsus (p. 182) he became master of the
principal countries governed by Antigonus, and, after the
defeat and death of that monarch (282), of his Asiatic
B dominions also. Thus the Syrian empire comprised all
the Asiatic countries which had belonged to the monarchy
of Alexander the Great (Cœle-Syria, Palestine, and
Phœnicia, were soon lost to the Egyptians), with more
natural boundaries than that monarchy had ever possessed.
Instead of availing themselves of such a favorable position
of affairs, the Selucidæ endeavored to restore the unnatural connection with Europe, and to establish a Græco-Macedonian dominion in newly-built cities[2] on the western
frontier, instead of rendering the inhabitants of Asia their
friends, by the establishment of a purely oriental system
of government in the capital of their empire (Susa, Baby-
C lon, Ecbatana), and thence throughout the provinces. In
consequence of this policy the people of the west were
estranged, the more distant north-eastern provinces (Parthia and Bactria) soon revolted, the chieftains of northern
Asia Minor, whom Alexander had been unable to subdue,
not only retained their independence, but extended their
dominions, and even Grecian satraps, renouncing their
allegiance to the effeminate and debauched successors of
Seleucus, made themselves masters of those portions of

[1] Succession of the kings: Seleucus Nicator, Antiochus I. Soter, Antiochus II. Theos, Seleucus II. Callinicus, Seleucus III. Ceraunus, Antiochus III. the Great, Seleucus Philopator, Antiochus IV. Epiphanes, Antiochus V. Eupator, Demetrius I., &c., &c.

[2] Among these were seventeen Antiochs, so named after the father of Seleucus.

Asia Minor, which had not already fallen into the hands of the Egyptians.

The ruin of the declining empire was for a time averted 376
by Antiochus III., surnamed the Great (224—187), who A
even endeavored to re-establish it in all its integrity.
His first attempt was to wrest their Asiatic conquests from
the Ptolemies, and when this failed, he undertook the
reconquest of Parthia and Bactria. The Parthians, who
had spread as far as Media, and perhaps to the other side
of the Tigris, were again confined to Parthia and Hyrcania; but Antiochus was compelled to recognize their
independence as well as that of the Bactrians, and return
to the west with the conviction, that so far from there being
an opening for fresh conquests in the north-western portion
of the Persian empire, it would be difficult to retain even
the territory which he already possessed in that quarter. B
The war against the weak Ptolemy Epiphanes was now
renewed with better success, almost all the cities of Cœle-
Syria, Phœnicia, and Palestine becoming Syrian. Scarcely
however had Antiochus re-established his authority over
the countries on the southern and western coasts of Asia
Minor (which had revolted, partly to the Ptolemies and
partly to the kings of Pergamus), and well-nigh completed
their subjugation, when the Romans, who ever since the humiliation of Philip of Macedonia had been seeking a pretext
for war with Syria, issued a proclamation, in which they
declared that all the Greeks of Asia were free and independent. Antiochus, deceived as he was, and at a later C
period annoyed and insulted, by the Romans, still strove
by every means in his power to avoid a war; but finding
all his endeavors unavailing, he allowed himself to be
persuaded by the Ætolians to visit Greece, for the purpose
of forming a Symmachy between Syria, Macedonia, and
all the Grecian states, and thus checking the aggressive
movements of Rome in the east. Even here, however, he
found himself miserably deceived; for Philip of Mace- D
donia was soon seduced by the fair promises of the
Romans, and the Greeks, partly through fear, partly
because they had persuaded themselves that the Romans
were the real protectors of their liberties, were slow in
joining the confederacy, whilst the Achæans replied to his

(376) proposals by a declaration of war, which was soon fol-
A lowed by a similar proceeding on the part of the Romans. Under these unfavorable circumstances Antiochus, instead of returning at once into Asia and there joining the forces assembled in the interior of his kingdom, still lingered in Greece in a state of miserable indecision, until a defeat at Thermópylæ compelled him to seek safety in flight. The Romans followed him into Asia, and having gained a second battle at Magnesia on the Sipylus, compelled him to pay 15,000 talents, deliver up his fleet and elephants, and renounce all claim to the portion of Asia Minor within
B the Taurus; a district which they divided provisionally between their allies, Eumenes, king of Pergamus, and the republic of Rhodes. The satraps of the Greater and Lesser Armenia availed themselves of this crisis to refuse the further payment of tribute, and renounce their allegiance to the Seleucidæ.

377 After the death of Antiochus III., two causes slowly
C but surely undermined the empire of the Seleucidæ:—1. The increasing prevalence of the eastern spirit over the Grecism of the Seleucidæ, aided as it was by the advance of the Parthians westwards, and of the Bactrians towards the south-east. 2. The policy of the Romans, who fostered the mutual disgust of the Ptolemies, Seleucidæ, and the kings of Asia Minor, and thus not only withheld them from uniting for the purpose of resisting the aggressions of Rome, but reduced them to such a miserable state of weakness, as rendered the conquest of their country a
D work of little difficulty. King Antiochus IV. Epiphanes so little understood his position, that when the Romans attacked Perseus of Macedonia, instead of uniting with that monarch to oppose Rome as the common enemy, he availed himself of the opportunity to reconquer the provinces of Cœle-Syria, Palestine, and Phœnicia, which had again revolted, and even to make himself master of the whole of Egypt except the capital. The Ptolemies appealed to the Romans, who compelled Antiochus to disgorge his Egyptian conquest. In Palestine he found, besides the Israelites, who jealously observed the law and supported the Ptolemies, an innovating Grecizing party, by whom he was persuaded to persecute those who

adhered to the ancient faith. This treatment occasioned (377)
their defection from the Syrian monarchy.[1] Compare A
§ 81, 6.

Under his feeble successors, most of whom bore the name of Antiochus, and were continually subject to humiliation and annoyance from the Romans, the kingdom, which no longer extended eastwards over Babylonia and Mesopotamia, was shaken to its foundation by disputes respecting the succession to the throne, which were kept alive by the Romans. At length, in the year sixty-four, the Syrian empire, already limited to Syria Proper by the conquests of the Parthians, was reduced by Cn. Pompeius to the condition of a Roman province.

§ 81. *Kingdoms which revolted from the Syrian dominion.*

1. Pergamus (Pergamos) (283—180), Philetærus, 378
lieutenant of Lysimachus in Pergamus, revolted to Seleu- B
cus Nicator, and during the disturbances which followed his assassination, made himself independent by the aid of a band of mercenaries. His successors assumed the title of king, and extended their dominions. Eumenes II. supported the Romans in their war against Antiochus III. of Syria, and on the conclusion of peace received the greater portion of that monarch's possessions in Asia Minor. He was the founder of the celebrated library of Pergamus (which was afterwards presented to Cleopatra by M. Antony), and the first who patronized the manufacture of parchment (perga-
mena charta). His next successor but one, Attalus III., C
a prince of weak intellect, bequeathed his kingdom to the Romans, who converted it into a Roman province under the name of Asia Propria. One Aristonīcus, who had set up a claim to the throne, was overthrown by the consul Perperna. Compare § 132.

2. In Galatia, three Gallic tribes, who had migrated 379
to Asia Minor, were presented by Nicomēdes, king of D
Bithynia and Paphlagonia, with allotments of land, on which they lived, under the government of four tetrarchs, of whom Deiotărus was the first who assumed the title of king, and was invested by Cæsar with the sovereignty of

[1] [*Antiochus Epiphanes*, as the fiercest persecutor of God's people, is the great type of the *Antichrist*.]

the whole country. It was made a Roman province by Augustus (25 B. C.).

380 3. Parthia. *a.* Under the *Arsacidæ* 256 (?) B. C. to
A A. D. 226. Agathŏcles, the universally unpopular Syrian satrap, was assassinated by Arsăces, who founded an independent kingdom, which was extended by his successors over all the countries between the Euphrātes, Indus, and Oxus. Residences: Ctesiphon and Seleucia on the Tigris. The victory of Arsaces XIV. over the Roman Triumvir Crassus was followed by frequent wars with the Romans, occasioned principally by disputed successions in Armenia. Arsaces XXX. (called also Artabanus IV.) was deposed in the year of our Lord 226 by a Persian named
B Artaxerxes, son of Sassan. With this Artaxerxes begins *b.* the dynasty of the *Sassanidæ* or *new Persian empire*, 226—651. Narses (297) was deprived by the Roman emperor Galerius, of Mesopotamia, five provinces on the other side the Tigris, and the sovereignty of Armenia and Iberia—but the five provinces were restored by the emperor Jovian.

381 4. Bactria, which revolted from the Syrian monarchy
C at the same time as Parthia, formed an independent kingdom, until Arsaces VI. united the province of Bactria with that of Parthia, whilst other conquerors made themselves masters of the other component parts of the Bactrian kingdom.

382 5. Armenia. After the unfortunate wars of Antiochus the Great, both the governors of Armenia revolted (189), and assuming the royal title divided the country between them. *a.* The *Greater Armenia.* Among the kings the most worthy of notice is Tigrānes I., who ruled at the same time over Syria, the Lesser Armenia, and Cappadocia; but having formed an alliance with his father-in-law Mithridātes VI., king of Pontus, he was attacked by the Romans, and his sovereignty restricted to the Greater
D Armenia. At a later period, the succession to the throne furnished a subject for contention between the Romans and Parthians. Trajan conquered Armenia in 106, and reduced it to the condition of a Roman province, but the government was again vested in native princes (subject to the supremacy of Rome), by the emperor Hadrian in 117. Finally, Armenia became a part of the new Persian

empire (412). *b.* The *Lesser Armenia*, ruled by its own (382
kings until the conquest of the country by Tigranes I. It A
fell subsequently into the hands of the Romans, by whom it was alternately conferred on some neighboring king, or merged in the Roman province of Cappadocia.

6. Palæstīna. 383

a. Dependent on the *Ptolemies* and *Seleucidæ* 323—167. At the division of the kingdom after the death of Alexander the Great, Palestine fell to the lot of the governor of Syria, but was soon conquered by Ptolemy I., who transported a colony of Jews to Alexandria, where the Seventy translated the Old Testament into Greek [the
Septuagint]. In the war of Antiochus the Great against the B
Egyptians, the Jews, weary of Egyptian rule, attached themselves to the king of Syria, and remained subject to the Seleucidæ from the year 203 to the reign of Antiochus IV. Epiphanes; when the people, enraged at the sale of their high priesthood to the Grecizing party, and the attempts of the king to enforce attendance on the idolatrous worship of Greece, took up arms under the command of Mattathias, a priest of the race of the Asmoneans, and his five sons, of whom Judas Maccabæus was the most renowned.

b. Under the *Asmoneans* or *Maccabees*, 167—39. The 384
Jews, whose success was promoted by the family quarrels C
of the Seleucidæ, maintained their independence during a period of nearly forty years, 167—130. At length, Simon Thassi, the son of Mattathias, was recognized by Demetrius as high-priest and independent prince of Judæa, and his grandson Aristobūlus assumed the title of king (in 107). Under his successors the struggles of the two sects of Pharisees and Sadducees prepared the way for the dependence of their country on Rome; Hyrcānus, the leader of the Pharisaic party having called in Pompey, who wrested Jerusalem out of the hands of the Sadducees, and promoted Hyrcanus to the high-priesthood, but at the same time compelled the little state of Judæa to pay a tribute to the Roman exchequer.

The *Pharisees*, in addition to the written law of Moses, recognized 385
the authority of tradition, and believed in predestination. They also D
held the [true] doctrines of the immortality of the soul and the existence of angels. The *Sadducees* on the contrary rejected all these doctrines. A sect of the Pharisees, the *Essenes*, were distinguished by the ascetic severity of their discipline.

(385) As the new high-priest troubled himself very little
A about the administration of public affairs, the supreme authority fell into the hands of a favorite of the emperor's named Antipater, a native of Idumæa, who placed his son, a lad of fifteen, over the province of Galilee. This son, whose name was Herod, being supported by the Romans, was enabled to bid defiance to the enmity of the Pharisees, and in the year B. C. 39, was proclaimed by the Triumviri king of Judæa.

386 *c.* Under the Herodians from B. C. 39 to A. D. 70. The government of Herod the Great (!), imposed as it was on the country by the swords of a foreign power, was
B of course hateful to every Jewish patriot. His policy, therefore, during a tyrannical reign of thirty-seven years, was to ally himself closely to the Romans, and endeavor by every means in his power to root out the ancient Jewish customs and institutions.

In the last year but one of his reign, four years before the commencement of our epoch,[1] JESUS CHRIST was born at Bethlehem. After the three sons of Herod had reigned a short time, Judæa was included in the Roman province of Syria, retaining however its own procurators or governors. Of these, the most notorious was Pontius Pilate [Pontius Pilatus], under whom our blessed Lord suffered in the year 30.

387 Under Herod Agrippa I., a grandson of Herod the Great, who
C had rendered important services to the emperor Claudius, Palestine was again a kingdom for three years; but after his death it became as before a Roman province, administered by procurators. At a later period (A. D. 53) a small portion of the country was ruled by the last of the Herodians, king Agrippa II., a son of Herod Agrippa I.

An insurrection, occasioned by the severity of these governors (A. D. 66), ended in the destruction of the city by Titus [as the instrument by which the righteous judgment of the Almighty was executed] in the year 70; 1,100,000 Jews, who had come up to the feast of the Passover, losing their lives by famine, pestilence, and the sword. The Roman governor now transferred the seat of government to Samaria. The settlement of a colony on the site of Jerusalem, and erection of a temple of Jupiter Capito-

[1] [Mr. Browne places it in B. C. 5. *Ordo Sæclorum*, p. 36.]

līnus by the emperor Hadrian, occasioned another general (387)
insurrection of the Jews (A. D. 133), of whom more than A
half a million lost their lives; but in spite of this opposition, the new city of Ælia Capitolina rose on the ruins of Jerusalem. Dispersion of the Jews.

§ 82. *The Kingdom of Pontus.*

Pontus, which had been a Persian satrapy from the time 388
of Darius I., became independent in the general insurrection of the satraps against Artaxerxes II. The Pontic king, Mithridātes II., submitted to Alexander the Great; but expelled Antigonus, to whom Pontus had been assigned in the partition of the kingdom. The last king, Mithrida- B
tes VI., or "the Great," a man of learning and an author, subdued Colchis, extended his empire as far as Armenia, and was thrice involved in war with the Romans in consequence of his conquests in Asia Minor (87—84; 83—81; 74—64), see §§ **138** and **143**. His own son Pharnăces, to whom he was at last compelled to fly for protection, having seduced his troops, Mithridates laid violent hands on himself. The central portion of Pontus was incorporated into the Roman province of Bithynia, but at a later period conferred, together with the eastern district, on a grandson of Mithridates (Polemo). Finally, both C
countries became Roman provinces in the reign of Nero; the western portion, which bordered on Galatia, being conferred on the Galatian prince Deiotărus.

§ 83. *Bithynia and Cappadocia.*

In both provinces the Persian satraps assumed the title 389
of king, and maintained their independence against the Macedonians. Among the Bithynian kings, the best known are Prusias II., at whose court Hannibal sought an asylum; and Nicomēdes III., who was expelled by Mithridates VI., but restored by the Romans, to whom he bequeathed his kingdom (B. C. 75).

Cappadocia, after the death of her last king (Archelāus), I
who was inveigled to Rome by the emperor Tiberius (A. D. 18), became a distinct province of the Roman empire. The manner of his death is not known.

IV. The Romans.

Sources of Information.

390 *a. The most ancient authorities.* Roman history commences with a
A few detached and meagre records; among which the most important are, 1. The *Annales Maximi* or *Pontificum*, which originated in the yearly registration of magistrates, with a short notice of the most important events of each year, inscribed at the end of the year on a white tablet, by the Pontifex Maximus, in whose house it was hung up for public inspection. This practice continued from the earliest times to the days of the Gracchi. It seems probable, however, that the annals of events antecedent to the storming of Rome by the Gauls, were partially destroyed when the city was burnt, and perhaps replaced by others at a later period. 2. The *Fasti Capitolini*, or Consular Fasti, a list of the Consuls to the time of Augustus, in whose reign this record was compiled from ancient authorities. It was found at Rome in 1547, and has very recently been augmented
B by fresh discoveries. 3. The *Laudes funebres*, or funeral orations, in which triumphs, consulates, &c., often imaginary, were ascribed to the ancient Romans, and thence transferred to history.

391 *b. The Annalists,* whose numerous works are lost, with the exception of a few passages cited by more recent authors. The most ancient are *Q. Fabius Pictor* and *L. Cincius Alimentus;* both of whom served in the second Punic war, and wrote a history of their own times, with an introductory essay on the earlier history of Rome. A few years later we have a metrical history, in eighteen books, under the title of "Annales," by *Q. Ennius,* who brings down the narrative to his own times; and a treatise (Origines) on the same subject, in seven books, brought down to the year 151, with profound criticisms, by *M. Porcius Cato* Censorius. The most shameless falsifier of history, especially of numbers, was *Valerius Antias.*

392 *c. Historians.*

C *aa.* In the Greek language, the chief authority for the more important events of Roman history, between the years 220 and 157, is *Polybius.* The fragments which we possess of *Diodōrus Siculus* are mere detached notices, reaching only to the year 302, and often unworthy of credit. *Dionysius,* in his Ἀρχαιολογία Ῥωμαϊκή (in twenty books, of which one to eleven are extant), gives an account of the earliest history and constitution of Rome. *Appian* (Appianus), a principal authority for the times immediately following the second Punic war, and for the civil wars. *Dio Cassius,* of whose works fragments are extant, comprehending the period between B. C. 87 and 8. *Herodian* (*Herodianus*)—History of his own times from A. D. 180 to 238. *Zonăras,* in the twelfth century, wrote a χρονικόν of events from the beginning of things to the year 1118. *Plutarch's* βιοὶ παραλληλοί contain the lives of twenty-two celebrated Romans.

393 *bb.* In Latin.—*a.* Writers who bring down the Roman
D history from the commencement to their own times.—1. *Titus Livius* [called by *us, Livy*] (born at Padua B. C. 58, died there A. D. 19). Of his "Annales" (in 142 books) we possess unmutilated only books 1—10 (authorities for the period between 753—293), and

21—45 (218—167). 2. *C. Velleius Paterculus* (in the first century (393)
of the Christian æra). In his Historiæ Romanæ libri ii., we have a A
brief outline of universal history, with especial reference to the Romans (to A. D. 30). 3. *L. Annæus Florus* (probably in the reign of Trajan). His Rerum Romanarum libri iv., bring down the history from the building of Rome to the reign of Augustus (B. C. 29). 4. *Eutropius* (in the fourth century) wrote a Breviarium Histor. Rom. from the building of Rome to the reign of Valens. We find also short notices of Roman affairs, down to the reign of Augustus, in the Historiæ Philippicæ (forty-four books) of *Trogus Pompeius*, of which there exist merely a few extracts in the works of *Justin* [Justinus].

β. Writers who treat of particular portions of Roman 394
history.—1. *C. Julius Cæsar* (99—44) describes his campaigns in B
Gaul in his Commentarii de Bello Gallico (eight books), and his war with Pompey and his party in the Commentarii de Bello Civili (three books). 2. *C. Sallustius Crispus* (86—35). His Bellum Catilinarium and Bellum Jugurthinum are entire; but we possess only a few fragments of the Histor., lib. vi. [79—67). 3. *C. Cornelius Tacitus* (somewhere between A. D. 152—130?). Portions only are extant of his Historiarum Libri (68—96) and Annales, in sixteen books (14—68). *Ammianus Marcellinus* (about A. D. 400). Of his Rerum Gestarum libri xxxi. (A. D. 91—378), we possess only eighteen (352—378), the last and the most important.

γ. Biographers.—1. *Cornelius Nepos* (in the first century of 395
the Christian æra), whose lives of Hannibal, Cato, and Atticus C
(from his "Vitæ Excellentium Imperatorum"), belong to Roman history. 2. *C. Cornelius Tacitus*—Vita Agricolæ. 3. *C. Suetonius Tranquillus* (about A. D. 100), Vitæ XII. Imperatorum (Cæsar to Domitian). 4. *Scriptores Historiæ Augustæ;* a collection of thirty-four biographies of Roman emperors (from Hadrian to Carus and his sons, or from 117 to 285), by six different authors. 5. *S. Aurelius Victor* (in the fourth century), De Viris Illustribus Romæ and de Cæsaribus. We have a collection of interesting traits of character and anecdotes in the "Factorum Dictorumque Memorabilium" libri ix., of *Valerius Maximus* (in the reign of Tiberius). Besides the historians, we may consult *Cicero's* books, De Republicâ (only two of the six remain, and those in an imperfect state), and the three books, De Legibus, for the history of the earlier constitution; and his letters for that of his own times. Among the geographers, the first place must be assigned to *Strabo* (5 and 6 books).

Modern Authorities.

The Roman histories of the early modern writers are mere com- 396
pilations from the works of ancient historians, without any attempt D
at testing the credibility and value of their testimony. After this fashion, *Freinshemius* (Supplementa Livii, 1654) tried to replace the lost books of Livy. The first writer who applied the rules of criticism to Roman history was *Jac. Perizonius,* whose masterly investigations (Animadversiones Historicæ, 1685) soon fell into unmerited oblivion; whilst, on the other hand, the skepticism of *L. de Beaufort* (sur l'Incertitude des cinq premiers Siècles de l'Histoire

(396) Romaine, 1750), though it is here and there carried too far, enjoyed
A in its day considerable reputation and influence. In the same spirit of mere negation, *Levesque* wrote his Histoire critique de la République Romaine (1807). *Edward Gibbon's* "History of the Decline and Fall of the Roman Empire," from the second century of the Christian æra to the downfall of the Byzantine empire, is a work distinguished by critical acuteness and the surpassing beauty of the narrative.[1] An entirely new epoch, as regards the treatment of Roman history, began with the publication of *B. G. Niebuhr's* "Roman History" (two parts, 1811 and 12; a second edition, carefully revised and corrected, was published in 1827 and 1830, followed in 1832 by a third part, bringing down the history to the end of the first Punic war; fourth edit., one
B vol., in 1834 [translated into English by Hare and Thirlwall, vol. iii. by Dr. Schmitz]). In this work, the historian not only proves the untenable character of those statements which formerly passed for Roman history, but also selects, with great critical acuteness, from the mass of legends, conjectures, and forgeries, all that deserves the name of unfalsified fact; and on this foundation essays to build a critical history of Rome. Niebuhr's Rome has been very well abridged by Twiss (Oxford, 1845). A full course of Roman history down to Constantine will be found in Niebuhr's lectures (3 vols. 8vo.). Arnold's Rome gives Niebuhr's views of the early history with great beauty, and with the posthumous volume and early work (v. Appleton's ed.) brings you down through the Republic. v. also Eliot's Liberty of Rome, Schmitz's Roman History, Greene's Historical Series, vol. 2, Ferguson's Roman Republic, Sismondi's Roman Empire.

A. Geography of Italy.

§ 84. *Names and Boundaries of Italy.*

397 The name of Italia originally belonged only to the ex-
C treme southern portion (called at a later period Bruttium, and extending northwards as far as the isthmus on the gulf of Scylla), nor had the peninsula in ancient times (any more than Asia Minor) a general name, each district being merely designated after the people by whom it was inhabited; e. g. Œnotria (the south-western peninsula from the Laüs), Ausonia, or Opica (northwards from the Laüs to the Tiber), Tyrrhenia (from the Tiber to the Apennines), Umbrica (the north-eastern part of the penin-
D sula), Iapygia (its south-eastern part). It was not until the Romans had united the whole peninsula under one government (in 266) that Italia became a general name

[1] In Milman's edition all the objectionable parts and doubtful questions are carefully discussed in the notes.

for the entire country, extending northwards to that branch (397)
of the Apennines which stretches from the maritime Alps A
nearly to the Adriatic, and as far as the river Rubicon. Gallia Cisalpīna, which had been subdued in the year 221, was called in Cæsar's time (49) Liguria; but together with the territory of the Carni, Istri, and Venĕti, was considered from the time of Augustus a part of Italy; the western boundary of which towards Gaul was now the river Varus [the *Var*], and the eastern, the river Arsia [*Arsa*].

We find, however, even at a later period, many of the ancient B
names employed by both Greek and Latin poets to designate sometimes the whole peninsula, sometimes particular portions. Italy is also called by them Hesperia (literally the land of the West) and Saturnia (perhaps the name given by the ancient Latins to a portion of central Italy.)

§ 85. *The Mountains of Italy.*

A. The Alps, which inclose Italy in a direction from 398
south-west to north-east, are divided into three principal ranges, each of which consists of three chains.

1. The Western Alps, consisting of the *Alpes Maritĭmæ*, (from the sea to Viso), the *Alpes Cottiæ*, or Alps of Dauphiné (as far as Mont Cenis), and the *Alpes Graiæ*, or Alps of Savoy (as far as Mont Blanc).

2. The Central Alps, subdivided into the *Alpes Pennīnæ*, or Valaisian Alps (from Mont Blanc to Monte Rosa), the *Alpes Lepontiæ*, or Alps of the Grisons (the St. Gothard), and the *Alpes Rhæticæ*, or Tyrolese Alps (as far as Grossglockner).

3. The Eastern Alps, consisting of the *Alpes Noricæ*, or Alps C
of Salzburg and Styria (as far as the Danube at Vienna), the *Alpes Carnicæ*, or Carinthian Alps (as far as Terglu), and the *Alpes Juliæ*, or Alps of Carniola (to the Adriatic sea).

B. The Apennīnus, a single chain, with short branches 399
on each side, running from the maritime Alps through the peninsula (of which it occupies the entire centre from north to south), and extending into Sicily, interrupted only by the strait of Messina.

The Apennines, like the Alps, are divided into three sections. D
1. The *northern* Apenninus, which stretches from the maritime Alps east and south-east, running nearly parallel with the Alps, and separating the plain of the Po from the sea and the Arno. 2. The *central* Apenninus, beginning at the sources of the Arno, forms the peninsula, properly so called (406), and attains its greatest height on the frontier of the kingdom of Naples (in the Abruzzi 7000—9000 feet), and its greatest breadth (from the Tyrrhenian sea to the Adriatic,

(399) where it terminates in the promontory of Gargānus). 3. The *southern*
A Apenninus consists of two arms, of which the eastern is the higher and the western the lower; the two together forming a peninsula. The granite mountains of Sardinia and Corsica belong neither to the Alpine nor Apennine system.

§ 86. *The Waters of Italy.*

400 Seas.—Mare Tuscum (Tuscan sea), or Tyrrhēnum, or Infĕrum—Mare Hadriaticum, or Superum—Mare internum (Mediterranean).

401 Gulfs.—Sinus Ligusticus (gulf of Genoa), Sinus Tarentīnus (gulf of Taranto), Sinus Tergestĭnus (gulf of Trieste).

402 Lakes.—*a.* In *Upper Italy*—Lacus Verbānus (Lago
B Maggiore), L. Larius (Lago di Como), L. Benācus (Lago di Garda). *b.* In *Central Italy*—L. Trasimēnus (Hannibal's third victory, 217, now Lago di Perugia), L. Albānus (Lago di Castello), L. Regillus (battle in 496, now Lago di Regillo), L. Fucĭnus (Lago di Celano).

403 Rivers.

a. Running into the Adriatic.—The two greater Alpine streams, viz., the Athĕsis (the Adige) and Padus (Ἠρίδανος? now Po), and the small rivers in the narrow eastern strip of land between the Apennines and the sea; viz., the Rubicon (now ?) the Metaurus (Metauro—Hasdrubal's defeat in 207), and the Aufĭdus (Ofanto).

C The Po rises in the Vesŭlus (Monte Viso), and after receiving the waters of thirty tributary streams from the Alps and Apennines, is raised, by means of the alluvial soil deposited in its bed, thirty feet above the level of the surrounding country, which is protected by dams; and, finally, forms with its seven mouths a swampy Delta. The most important tributary streams are—*a.* Rising in the Alps—the Ticīnus (now Tessino, Hannibal's first victory in 248), the Addua (now Adda), and the Mincius (Mincio), which precipitate themselves together from the mountains into one of the greater lakes of Upper Italy, and thence run with clearer water into the Po. *b.* Rising in the Alps—the Trebia (Hannibal's second victory in 218).

404 *b. Running into the Tyrrhenian sea.*—From the broader
D space on the western side of the Apennines—1. The Arnus (Arno), and, 2, the Tibĕris (Tevere); the course of which is lengthened by their running at first through valleys, nearly parallel to the coast, and then passing into others at right angles with the former, until they discharge themselves by swampy embouchures into the sea. 3. The

Liris (Garigliano). 4. Vulturnus (Volturno), Silărus (404)
(Silaro, victory of Crassus, 71).

The tributary streams of the Tiber are—on the left the Allia (victory of the Gauls, 389), and the Anio (Teverone); and on the right the Cremĕra (the 300 Fabii).

§ 87. *Soil, Climate, and Products of Italy.*

1. The Italian Lowlands, or plain of the Po, are 405
inclosed on the north-west by the Alps, the summits of A
which are covered with eternal snow, and on the south by the lower and less precipitous Apennines; but on the east they are open to a much-frequented inland sea, and are watered by a navigable river, with its numerous tributaries and canals, as well as by four beautiful lakes; and whether we consider the mildness of their climate, the luxuriant vegetation (maize, rice, the vine, fruit and mulberry trees, ever verdant meadows, pastures, &c.), or the industrious and productive habits of the inhabitants, may fairly be ranked among the most highly-favored countries of Europe.

2. The Italian peninsula, lying westward, south- 406
ward, and south-eastward of the Apennines, is broken up B
by an uniform mountain-chain into a number of small valleys, watered by forest streams, and of plains abutting on the coast; and contains, in consequence, a series of districts separated from one another by peculiarities of situation and character. The ridge of this mountain-chain affords merely pasturage; but its sides are covered with chestnut forests of immense extent, and its foot with vineyards, plantations of olives, and orange orchards. Calabria and Sicily have almost an African climate, which permits the cultivation of the palm-tree, the cotton-shrub, and the sugar-cane.

The country westward of the Apennines is of a volcanic nature, of 407
which we have distinct indications, *a.* (as far *northward* as Terracina,
especially on the Campagna di Roma) in the lakes which occupy C
craters of extinct volcanoes, and in the sulphureous vapors which rise out of holes and clefts in the ground. In southern Tuscany and the Pontine marshes, luxuriant districts are rendered so pestilential by this malaria as to be uninhabitable in summer, and used only for the pasturage of cattle in winter. *b.* In the *southern* portion of the western side of the peninsula the existence of volcanic matter is still more plainly indicated by the eruptions of Mount Vesuvius (3700 feet), the Phlegræan fields, and Mount Ætna (10,280 feet), by frequent earthquakes, and by the breaking out of fresh volcanoes.

§ 88. *Divisions of Italy.*

408 A. Upper Italy contains those districts which were
A not reckoned among the Italian states by the Romans until the time of Cæsar and Augustus. 1. Liguria; 2. Gallia Cisalpina, or Togata; 3. the country of the Venĕti, with that of the Carni and Istri.

409 B. Central Italy contains—

a. On the *western side,* Etruria, Latium, and Campania.

b. On the *eastern side,* Umbria, Picenum, and Samnium.

410 C. Lower Italy—

a. On the *western side,* Lucania and Bruttium.

b. On the *eastern side,* Apulia and Calabria.

411 D. The Islands—

Sicilia [Sicily], Sardinia, Corsica, the smaller islands.

§ 89. *The ancient Inhabitants of Italy.*

A. The most ancient races.

412 1. The Pelasgi inhabited not only the entire western
B coast from the Arnus to the southernmost point of Italy (where the northern portion of them were called *Tyrrhēni,* and the southern *Œnotrii*), but also parts of the eastern coast; the *Venĕti* in the north, and the *Daunii* and *Peucetii* in the south, belonging probably to the Pelasgian race.

413 2. The Opici, Osci, and Ausŏnes, inhabited the western branch of the Apennine chain. To this race belonged the *Æqui* and *Volsci,* in Latium the *Casci* (or *Prisci*), who dwelt at first round the lake Fucĭnus, and at a later period were driven out by the Sabines, and migrated to Latium, and probably the *Apŭli* (westward of the Gargānus), who subdued the Pelasgian Daunii.

414 3. The Sabelli, an offset of the ancient *Sabini.* The
C original seat of the Sabines was among the highest mountains of the Abruzzi about Amiternum, whence the superfluous population migrated in various directions—the *Picentes* to Picenum, the *Hernĭci* to Latium, the *Samnĭtes* to Campania, and the *Lucani* to Lucania. In the ancient seats there remained the Marsi, Peligni, Vessini, and Marucini, who composed a confederacy.

415 4. The Umbri, an aboriginal people of Italy, who,

before the immigration of the Etrusci, had spread from the Padus into the country of the Sabines, and probably also into southern Etruria.

5. The Ligŭres, whose origin is unknown. At an 416
early period they had considerably transgressed the boun- A
dary assigned to Liguria by Augustus (perhaps from the Pyrenees to the Tiber, and in the north as far as the Sevenine and across the Po), but were afterwards driven back by the Ibēres on one side, and the Celtæ on the other.

B. Foreign Settlers.

1. The Etrusci, or Tuscans (Rasĕni in their own lan- 417
guage), came from Rhætia, being probably driven out by the Celtæ, and entering Upper Italy, drove back the Venetians and Umbrians, and founded in Gallia Cisalpīna (of which the Ligurians retained the western part) a confederate state of twelve sovereign cities. At a later period they crossed the Apennines and the Arnus, and founded in Tuscany a second confederate state of twelve cities; having first subdued or expelled the Umbrians and Tyrrhenians, who dwelt
between the Arno and the Tiber. At length (about the B
year 470) they forced their way into Campania, where they founded colonies (probably a third confederate state of twelve cities), such as Capua and Nola; of which, however, they were soon deprived by the Samnites.

Religion, &c. of the Etrusci.

a. Religion. Their gods (in Tuscan Æsar) were divided by the 418
Etrusci into two classes. 1. The *higher* or *veiled* divinities, dark, C
mysterious powers, working in secret, whose number was unknown; and, 2, the twelve inferior gods. Jupiter (in Tuscan Tina, or Tinia), occupying probably a middle position between the two classes, and believed to be the centre of the divine world. He consults the higher divinities on matters of importance, whilst those of the lower class compose his ordinary council. Different parts of the creation, e. g. the heavens, water, the infernal regions, &c., were also supposed to be under the protection of Dæmons (Lares, Penates, and Manes). A distinguishing characteristic of the Etruscan religion was the prominent position occupied by divination, or the discovery of the divine will by means of auguries. This art, or "discipline," which, according to the legend, was revealed by Tages, the grandson of Jupiter, and at first propagated by tradition in the families of the nobles, was subsequently imparted to all classes in schools set apart for that purpose, and rules for its acquisition, accurately laid down in books (Etruscæ Disciplinæ Volumina). This "discipline" assumed that the gods were wont to declare their will to mankind by D
lightning, the flight and cry of birds, the entrails of victims, and

other signs, which it was the business of the Haruspices to interpret.

419 *b.* The Constitution. The whole of Etruria formed *a confederacy*
A *of twelve independent cities;* but which of these were members of the league cannot be satisfactorily ascertained, as there seems to have been more than twelve, equally independent. Probably some of the twelve nations (πόλεις) of Etruria were not restricted to *one capital*, but inhabited several cities, independent of each other, but having only one vote in the confederacy. The members of the league had regularly every year *religious meetings* in the temple of Voltumna (the situation of which cannot be distinctly ascertained). On these occasions public fairs were held, expeditions agreed on by the "principes" of the confederacy, and commanders of the allied forces elected. Each of the allied states had, at least in the earliest times, a *king* elected for life, and a hereditary *nobility*, named by the Romans "principes" (= Lucumones?), who alone could aspire to the highest offices in the state. There was also a commonalty personally independent of the nobles, and a crowd of *clients*, who were probably descendants of the vanquished aborigines (Tyrrheni and Umbri).

420 *c.* Arts and Sciences. All the religious celebrations of the
B Etruscans, particularly their solemn processions, were accompanied with *music* (flutes, trumpets, horns, &c.). Scenic art was confined to the *dance*, in which the performers, without employing words, represented the plot by means of gestures. Their architectural works, city-walls, of the Pelasgian order, indicating the transition from the Cyclopian style to that in which hewn stones are employed, vaulted gateways, monuments, temples, theatres, and amphitheatres, are of colossal dimensions, and were probably raised by feudal labor; as were also their *aqueducts*, sewers, dams, and canals, by means of which the Delta of the Po was regulated, and the marshes drained
C on the banks of the Arnus. From their famous manufacture of vases, relievos, and statues, in *terra cotta*, they gradually learnt the art of casting in bronze such articles as ornamental arms, candelabra, patĕræ, &c.; in the production of which they attained a high degree of excellence. *Painting* was employed partly for the coloring of statues and relievos in stone and clay, and partly, as an independent art, for frescoes on the walls of tombs. In the absence of any legends of native heroism, the Etruscan artists borrowed for the most part their subjects from the Greek mythology, which they were wont to combine, in a modified form, with their local traditions. In Etruscan *literature*, we find, besides their books of "discipline," a few religious hymns, the Fescennine verses (ribaldrous songs, in alternate verse), and historical notices. From them the Romans borrowed most of their knowledge respecting the interpretation of signs, the designation of numbers by figures, and the division of the month into calends, nones, and ides, as well as the dress and insignia of their magistrates.

421 *d.* Commerce. The Tuscans seem at an early period (perhaps
D even in Homer's time) to have carried on a considerable *land-traffic* in their settlements on the Po; and also to have brought overland from the coasts of the Baltic the amber which they obtained from Germanic tribes, and subsequently transported by sea into Greece. Their *maritime traffic* began with piracy in the western Mediterra-

nean, accompanied by the establishment, through commercial leagues, (421)
of friendly relations with particular nations, especially with the A
Carthaginians and Greeks of Lower Italy. The articles of export were partly the natural and artistic productions of those districts of Italy which were in the hands of the Etruscans (grain, iron from Ilva, wine, earthenware, works in bronze, &c.), partly those which they had obtained by traffic with foreigners; amber, for instance. Their imports were the products of the east. A third branch was their *domestic trade,* which was closely connected with the religious festivals, each of them being at the same time a fair; the business of which must have been considerable, since the Etruscan monetary system was adopted by the whole of central Italy.

2. For the Grecian settlements, see § 62. 422

3. The Gauls, a rude offset of the great tribe of the Celtæ, which had spread itself over western Europe, migrated (about B. C. 400) in great numbers (300,000) into Italy; a portion of them overrunning Upper Italy and marching upon Rome; whilst the remainder directed their course towards Pannonia.

§ 90. *Topography of Italy.*

A. Upper Italy.

1. Liguria, in the time of Augustus, comprehended 423
the line of coast between the rivers Varus and Macra, B
northwards as far as the Padus. Genua (Genova), chief commercial city of the Ligurians.

2. Gallia Cisalpina, or Togata. 424

This vast plain, which was occupied by the Gauls, is divided by the Po into two parts.

A. Gallia Cispadana (inhabited by the Boii, Senŏnes, 425
and Lingŏnes). Cities.—1. Placentia (Piacenza), at the confluence of the Trebia with the Padus; founded by the Romans in 219. 2. Mutĭna (Modĕna; defeat of M. Anthony in 43). 3. Bononia (Bologna). 4. Ravenna, formerly on the sea-coast, now an inland town; imperial residence from the time of Honorius.

B. Gallia Transpadana (inhabited by the Taurini, Insŭ- 426
bres, and Cenomani). Cities.—1. Augusta Taurino- C
rum (Taurino, Turin), on the Padus (originally the capital of the Taurini, under the name of Taurasia). 2. Vercellæ (Vercelli), defeat of the Cimbrii in the Campi Raudii (101). 3. Ticīnum (Pavia), on the Ticinus. 4. Mediolanum (Milano, Milan), under the emperors the seat of the arts and sciences (hence Novæ Athenæ), and frequently the imperial residence. 5. Cremōna on the Padus, founded

by the Romans in 219. 6. Mantua, in a lake formed by the river Mincius; near it was the village of Andes, in which Virgil was born.

427 3. The country of the Venĕti.

A Cities.—1. Verōna, on both sides of the Athĕsis; amphitheatre for 22,000 spectators. 2. Patavium (Padova, Padua), founded, according to the legend, by Trojan exiles, under the command of Antēnor. Birth-place of Livy (hence his "Patavinitas," or provincialism).

From the time of Augustus the following districts were also included in the country of the Venĕti:—1. The country of the Carni, with the city of Aquilēia, demolished by Attila (A. D. 452). 2. Istria, with the city of Tergeste (Trieste).

B. Central Italy.

428 1. Etruria, or Tyrrhenia; at a later period also
B Tuscia.

Boundaries.—On the north, the Macra; east and south, the Tiber; west, the sea. Aboriginal inhabitants—Tyrrhenian Pelasgians; settlers—the Etrusci from Rhætia. The most remarkable of its *twelve sovereign cities*, which were for the most part situated on eminences, were—1. Cære, where Mezentius ruled, and where the Romans concealed their sacred images during the Gallic war. 2. Veii, the largest and most powerful city of Etruria (100,000 inhabitants), which carried on seven wars against Rome, and after its capture by Camillus (395) remained
C uninhabited. 3. Tarquinii. 4. Clusium (Chiusi), Porsenna. 5. Perusia (Perugia), defeat of the Etrusci (309); it was destroyed in the Perusian civil war (40). 6. Arretium (Arezzo), the birth-place of Mæcēnas.

Non-sovereign places—1. Luca (Lucca). 2. Pisæ (Pisa), on the Arnus, with the Portus Pisanus (where now stands Livorno, or Leghorn). 3. Florentia (Firenze, Florence), on the Arnus.

429 2. Latium, was divided into *Latium vetus*, from the Tiber to the promontory of Circeii, and *Latium adjectum*, or *novum*, to the Liris. Latium vetus was originally inhabited by the Siculi (Tyrrhenian Pelasgians), of whom a considerable number fled into Sicily, when the Casci, retiring before the Sabines, took possession of their country; whilst the remainder, submitting to the invaders, formed

in conjunction with them the nation of the Latini. In (429)
contradistinction to the nation thus established by conquest, A
the Siculi, as the earlier inhabitants of Latium, were also styled aborigines. By degrees there arose thirty small independent states, forming a confederacy, which annually celebrated the feriæ Latinæ on the Alban mount, and held a diet, in a grove near the fountain of Ferentīna, for the discussion of questions affecting the general interests of the league. Southward and eastward of Latium vetus dwelt the Æqui, Hernici, Volsci, and Ausŏnes; whose territories, after the last Latin war (337), were added to Latium, under the title of Latium novum.

Cities of the Latini.—1. Roma, which originally stood 430
on the left bank of the Tiber, on seven hills, Palatinus, B
Capitolinus, Quirinalis, Viminalis, Esquilinus, Cælius, and Aventinus, to which was added in the time of Aurelian, the collis Hortulorum (Monte Pincio), the Janiculum and Vaticanus (on the other side of the Tiber), and at a later period the Mons testaceus.

The ancient city of Romulus was confined to the Palatine. On the 431
opposite hill (the Quirinalis), was a Sabine colony, the citizens of which were named Quirites. After the Sabine war these two districts united, forming a single city protected by a fortress on the Capitoline, which they occupied as a common citadel. An addition was made to the city by Tullus Hostilius, who settled the Albans on the Cælian hill, after the demolition of their own city, and by Ancus Martius, who established the vanquished Latins on the Aventine. Tarquinius Priscus drained the swampy flats (particularly the Velābrum between the Palatine and Aventine), by means of cloācæ. Servius Tullius surrounded the seven hills with a wall, which extended on the other side the Tiber to the summit of the Janiculum. C
On the eastern side alone, from the porta Collina to the Esquilina, the city was protected merely by a mound of earth (agger), with fosses. Servius divided the city into four regions. (Suburana, Esquilina, Collina, and Palatina). When Rome was burnt by the Gauls, the whole city was destroyed as far as the Capitoline hill, and subsequently rebuilt without any regular plan. From the time of the Punic war, and still more from the reign of Augustus (who divided the city into fourteen regions), there were considerable additions and embellishments. After the conflagration in Nero's reign, the three districts which had been laid in ashes were rebuilt and presented a uniform appearance. Aurelian entirely surrounded the city with a new wall (with towers, battlements, and breastworks), and under Diocletian Rome had attained her highest pitch of beauty and splendor: but with the transfer of the imperial residence to Byzantium, the prosperity of the ancient capital began rapidly to decline,

[1] In this sketch, Niebuhr's views are followed. Nardini, Nibby, and Canino differ from him on many points.

and several quarters were gradually deserted, especially after the sack and pillage of the city by the Goths (410), and Vandals (455).

432 The *mons Capitolinus,* originally Saturnius, consisted of two portions separated by the "intermontium." The southernmost of these
A rocky peaks was the rupes Tarpeia (approached by the centum gradus), the northern, which was fortified, was named arx. On the southwestern side (according to Niebuhr), stood the temple of Jupiter Capitolinus, built by Tarquinius Superbus, which was thrice burnt (B. C. 84, A. D. 69 and 80). Between the Capitoline and Palatine was the *forum Romanum,* anciently the velabrum (now campo vaccino), divided by the rostra, (so named from the beaks of the Antian ships, anciently "templum," or stage from which orators addressed the people,) into the comitium (place of meeting for the patricians), and
B the forum properly so called (where the plebeians assembled). Near the comitium stood the curia Hostilia, originally the citadel of king Tullus Hostilius, which was granted by that monarch to the senate for their sittings. The building was destroyed by a fire, which broke out during the burning of the dead body of Clodius, and was subsequently restored by Cæsar, who gave it the name of curia Julia. Between the Palatine and Aventine was the *Circus Maximus* (which held, at the lowest estimate, 150,000 persons; according to A. Victor, 385,000). The handsomest streets were the *Via Sacra* (leading from
C the Colosseum to the forum), and the *Carīnæ,* between the Esquiline and Cælian. The most considerable place of public resort was the *Campus Martius,* which was used for gymnastic exercises, reviews of the army, and the comitia centuriata. At a later period it was surrounded by public buildings.

433 The most important buildings were, among the *temples* (of which there were more than 400), that of Jupiter Capitolinus, and the Pantheon of Agrippa (now Santa Maria della Rotonda); among the *palaces,* the golden house of Nero, which not only covered the whole of the Palatine, but even extended as far as the Esquiline, and comprehended within its walls temples, baths, groves, race-courses, &c. Among the *theatres,* the three built by Pompey (for 40,000 spectators), that of Marcellus (with 30,000 seats); among the *amphitheatres* the Amphitheatrum Flavium, (afterwards the Colosseum [Coliseo], begun by Vespasian, and completed by Titus. It contained 100,000 persons. Among the baths, or *Thermæ,* those of Titus (in which the group of the Laocoon was discovered), of Caracalla and Diocletian; among the *columns,* the columna rostrata Duilii, in the forum Romanum, and
D the pillar of Trajan in the Forum Ulpium. Among the *monuments,* the mausoleum of Augustus, the moles Hadriani (now the castle of St. Angelo), and the Septizonium of Septimius Severus; and among the *triumphal arches,* those of Titus, Septimius Severus, and Constantine. Besides these buildings there were several porticos (ten), basilicæ (thirty-seven), gates (eighteen), fora (ten), circuses, naumachiæ, obelisks, statues (the bronze colossal statue of Nero, and that of M. Aurelius, which has been preserved), odēa (twenty), aqueducts, cloācæ, &c., &c.

The environs of the city (especially on the sixteen scientifically constructed roads leading to all parts of Italy), were crowded with innumerable villas, sepulchral monuments, and ornamental buildings of every description. Underneath the city and the via Appia were catacombs. On the Alban mount was a temple to Latial Jove, where consuls went to offer sacrifice before setting out for the army. A

2. Ostia; founded at the mouth of the Tiber by Ancus Martius, as the port of Rome. 3. Laurentum, also on the coast, where Latinus was king when Æneas landed in Italy. 4. Lavinium, built, according to the legend, by Æneas, and—5. Alba Longa, on the slope of the Alban hill (where the feriæ Latinæ were held), and on the border of the Alban lake, (the mother city of Rome, if we may believe tradition). It was destroyed by Tullus Hostilius. 6. Tusculum (near the modern Frascati), surrounded by numerous villas (Cicero's Tusculanum). 7. Præneste (now Palestrina), built on the slope of a hill in the form of terraces, and strongly fortified. It was demolished in the civil wars of Sulla (82). 8. Gabii, said to have been taken by stratagem, by S. Tarquinius. 9. Tibur (now Tivoli), on the Anio, a favorite residence of the Roman nobles, and consequently surrounded by villas (those of Mæcenas and others). 10. Collatia, the residence of Tarquinius Collatinus, the husband of Lucretia. 434 B

Other nations in Latium. 1. The *Rutŭli*, with the city of Ardĕa, which was besieged by Tarquinius Superbus. 2. The *Hernĭci* (with the city Anagnia). 3. The *Volsci* and *Æqui*, with the cities of Antium (taken and deprived of its fleet in 338). Terracīna (or Anxur), Suessa Pometia (stormed by Tarquin the Proud), Fregellæ, Arpīnum, the birth-place of Marius and Cicero, Coriŏli (see § 106). 4. Some of the *Ausŏnes*, or *Aurunci*, with the city of Minturnæ on the Liris (Marius). 435

3. Campania (from the Liris to Silarus). 436

Inhabitants: Tyrrhenian Pelasgians, then Opicii (Ausonians), Greek settlements on the coast, and immigrations of the Etruscans, whose dominion was speedily crushed by an invasion of the Samnites. From the amalgamation of the Samnite invaders with the earlier inhabitants of the country, the Opici, Greeks, and Etruscans, sprang the Campanians. Mountains: the Gaurus on the Gulf of Puteŏli (first defeat of the Samnites, 342), Vesuvius (defeat of the Latins, 339), Falernian and Massic wines. *Cities.*—a. *On the coast.* 1. Cumæ, the most ancient C D

(436) Greek colony in Italy, founded by emigrants from Chalcis
A in Eubœa (B. C. 1030?), with its port Dicæarchia (the modern Puteoli). In the vicinity was the lake Avernus (Ἄορνος), near which was a cavern, believed to be the entrance to the infernal regions. 2. Misenum, a sea-port. 3. Baiæ, a bathing-place; near it was the lacus Lucrīnus, out of which arose, in the year 1538, the monte nuovo. 4. Neapŏlis (Napoli, Naples), near it was Parthenŏpe, or Palaiopolis, a colony of Cumæ. 5. Herculaneum (over which now stand the cities of Portici and Resina), Pompeii, and Stabiæ, at the foot of Vesuvius, (by an eruption of which they were destroyed, A. D. 79). The two first were again brought to light in the eighteenth century, and afforded
B a rich harvest to the antiquarian. b. *Cities in the interior.* 1. Capua; at first a Tyrrhenian settlement under the name of Vulturnum, then Etruscan, afterwards Samnite, and lastly, a Roman municipium, and the second city of Italy, until it espoused the cause of Hannibal, when it was a second time captured, and suffered the vengeance of the conqueror; it continued, however, to be an important city until the middle ages. 2. Nola (second defeat of Hannibal); Augustus died there A. D. 14.

C The *Picentini* were transplanted by the Romans from Picenum into southern Campania, for the purpose of cutting off the Samnites from the lower sea. Principal sea-port, Salernum.

437 4. Umbria (from the Rubicon to the Æsis and Nar). *Cities.*—a. *On the coast.* 1. Arimīnum (Rimini). 2. Sena (Sinigaglia, Hannibal defeated in 207). b. *In the interior*, Sentīnum (defeat of the Samnites, 295).

438 5. Picenum.

Inhabitants—originally Pelasgians, afterwards Picentians, a Sabine people. *Cities.*—1. Ancona (Ἀγκών). 2. Asculum Picenum (Ascoli), sacked in the war of the confederates.

439 6. Samnium.

D Inhabitants—the Sabines, and their offspring the Sabelli. A. The *Sabines* with the cities, 1. Cures (-ium), capital of the Sabines (where T. Tatius reigned, and Numa Pompilius was born). 2. Fidēnæ. 3. Crustumerium, in the territory of which stood the mons sacer. 4. Amiternum (birth-place of Sallust). B. The *Sabelli:* a. the *Samnites*

(Σαυνῖται), whose dominions, previously to their wars with (439)
the Romans, extended from the Hadriatic sea to the A
Tyrrhenian, with the cities—1. Beneventum (Benevento), originally Maleventum (defeat of Pyrrhus in 275). 2. Bovianum (battle in 305). Caudium, with the pass called the furculæ Caudīnæ (victory of Pontius, the Samnite general in 321). b. The confederacy of the *Marsi*, *Peligni* with the cities, Corfinium, capital of the Italian confederacy, and Sulmo, the birth-place of Ovid), *Marrucini* and *Vestini*. c. The *Hirpini* and *Frentani*.

C. Lower Italy, or Magna Græcia.

1. Lucania and Bruttium (separated by the river 440
Laus).

Inhabitants.—The Œnotrii, who were Grecized by B
Grecian settlements on the coast, were subdued by the Lucanians (Sabelli), and reduced to the condition of serfs. At a later period, however, they rose against their oppressors, and, with the assistance of the Osci, wrested from them the southern half of the district, hence their name Bruttii, i. e. revolted serfs. To these we may add the Greek settlements on the coast, viz., *Cities in Lucania*—
1. Sybăris (510, destroyed by the Crotoniates—its luxury). [Posidonia, or Pæstum (of which magnificent ruins C
still remain), was founded by settlers from this city.] 2. Thurii, founded by the Athenians (446), in the vicinity of the demolished Sybăris. 3. Helia (also Velia and Eleă), seat of the Eleatic school of philosophy. 4. Heraclēa (victory of Pyrrhus, 280). *Cities in Bruttium*—(now Calabria), Croton, near the promontory of Lacinium (its inhabitants destroy Sybăris; school of Pythagoras, the Athletes, Milo). 2. Rhegium (Reggio). 3. Locri Epizephyrii (the law-giver Zaleucus). 4. Consentia, capital of the Bruttii. Alaric died here, and was buried in the bed of the Busentinus.

2. Apulia and Calabria, named by the Greeks 441
Iapygia. D

Inhabitants.—Messapians, Peucetians, and Daunians; hence, Apulia was divided by the Aufidus into Apulia Peucetia and Ap. Daunia. The Byzantines, after losing

(441) the south-eastern peninsula, transferred the name of Cala-
A bria to the south-western. *Cities in Apulia.*—1. Luceria (§ 114). 2. Asculum Apulum (victory of Pyrrhus in 279). 3. Cannæ (fourth victory of Hannibal in 216). 4. Venusia (a Roman colony established after the Samnite wars; birth-place of Horace). *Cities in Calabria.*—1. Brundusium (Brindisi), usual port of embarkation for Greece (to Dyrrhachium). 2. Tarentum (*Τάρας*; now Tarento), founded by the Parthenii from Sparta; the most flourishing commercial and manufacturing Grecian city in Italy (with 300,000 inhabitants), Archytas; ten years' war with the Romans.

D. The Islands.

442 1. Sicilia (*Σικελία, Σικανία, Τρινακρία*).
B This island, the granary of Italy, studded in ancient times with magnificent cities, and possessing an unusually numerous population, was separated from the Italian peninsula by the Sicilian strait (now str. of Messina), in which the currents of the Hadriatic and Tyrrhenian seas met, and formed the whirlpools known by the names of Scylla and Charybdis. A continuation of the Apennines, which extends along the northern coast, and sends out a branch towards the south-east, gives the island its form, which is triangular, terminating in three promontories (Pelōrum,
C Pachȳnum, and Lilybæum). The most fertile part of the island is the volcanic formation on the eastern coast, where Mount Ætna (Mongibello), rises to the height of 10,000 feet.

443 Inhabitants.—The Sicani (probably immigrants from Iberia), were driven back in the south and west part of the island, by the Siculi, who came from Latium; Phœnician and Greek settlements, the former on the north-western coast (they afterwards joined the Carthaginians), the latter
D on the southern and western coasts. *Cities.*—a. *In the east*, 1. Messāna (anciently Zancle, now Messina), where the Messenians, and, at a later period, the Mamertines, formed settlements. 2. Tauromenium (with a theatre, which still remains, capable of holding from 30,000 to 40,000 spectators). 3. Catăna (Catania), at the foot of Mount Ætna. 4. Syracusæ (Siragossa), a fourfold city

(Ortygia, Archradina, Tycha, Neapolis), a Corinthian (443)
colony founded in 735. At the period of its greatest pros- A
perity it contained probably a million of inhabitants. b. *In the south*—1. Gela (a Rhodian colony), and its daughter cities. 2. Agrigentum (Girgenti, with its magnificent remains of Greek temples, one of which, the temple of Zeus Olympios, is described by Diodorus as the largest in the world). 3. Selinus. c. *In the west and north*—1. Lilybæum (the Phœnician Motye). 2. Drepăna. 3. Segeste, or Egesta. 4. Panormus (Palermo). 5. Himĕra (Gelon's victory in 480). d. *In the interior*—Henna (Enna). (Rape of Proserpine; outbreak of the first servile war.)

2. Sardinia (Σαρδώ and Σαρδών).

The two neighboring islands of Sardinia and Corsica 444
are essentially distinguished from the mainland of Italy by B
the granite formation of their mountains, as well as by the rugged character of their inhabitants. The Sardinians lived in caves, and were clothed in the skins of wild beasts. The only parts of Sardinia which enjoyed the blessings of civilization were a few Phœnician, and, at a later period, Carthaginian, settlements on the coast. Capital, Carălis (Cagliari), on the southern coast.

3. Corsica (Κύρνος). 445

Inhabitants.—Ligurians and Iberians, Phocæans (see § C
21), Carthaginians. The Phocæans founded on the eastern coast the city of Alalia, which afterwards, as a Roman colony, bore the name of Aleria.

4. The smaller Islands.

1. Ilva (Αἰθαλία, now Elba), on the Etruscan coast. 446
It abounds in iron. 2. Capreæ (now Capri), opposite D
Naples; the favorite residence of Tiberius. 3. The (eleven) insulæ Æoliæ or Vulcaniæ (now the Lipari islands), the largest was called Lipăra. 4. The Ægătes (-ădes, now the Ægadian islands). Naval victory of Lutatius Catulus over the Carthaginians (242). 5. Melĭte (Malta), with its capital of the same name, a Phœnician colony. Under the rule of Carthage its trade and manufactures were exceedingly flourishing.

B. History of events antecedent to the building of Rome.

§ 91. *Legend concerning the immigration of the Trojans into Latium.*

447 It would seem that previously to the Trojan immigra-
A tion, Latium had been visited by an Arcadian prince, named Evander, who built the city of Palatium, on the hill of the same name, and introduced arts and civilization into Italy. With the aid of Hercules, who came from Iberia, Evander is reported to have vanquished and slain a giant named Cacus, who dwelt on the Aventine (?). At a later period, so runs the tale, Æneas, accompanied by a few Trojans, and bearing with him the statues of his country's gods, landed in the dominions of the Laurentian king, LATINUS, and married his daughter LAVINIA. The first settlement in Italy was named by the Trojans, Troja. Afterwards they founded Lavinium (on the spot to which a sow had fled from the knife of the sacrificer).

B Turnus, king of the Rutuli (at Ardea), to whom Lavinia had been previously betrothed, declares war against Æneas and Latinus, and is vanquished in a battle in which Latinus loses his life. Turnus then, in conjunction with Mezentius, king of Cære, renews the war, and is also slain. The Latins nevertheless are driven from the field, and Æneas throws himself into the river Numicius, and thenceforward receives divine honors under the name of Jupiter Indiges. Iulus (Ascanius), the son of Æneas, slays Mezentius, and becomes sovereign of Latium.

448 Thirty years after the building of Lavinium, Ascanius led the Latins from the pestilential Maremna to the slope of the Alban Mount, where he founded the city of Alba Longa.

C The catalogue of fourteen kings, from Ascanius to Amulius, is of very doubtful authenticity, whether we regard the suspicious character of the names (which are sometimes repetitions of those which occur in previous or subsequent history, sometimes mere adaptations of geographical names, set down at random without any connecting narrative), or the exact agreement of the dates with the canon of Eratosthenes, and not with the usual Roman chronology.

C. History of Rome.

§ 92. *Legend concerning the building of Rome.*

449 This myth is known to us under two principal forms:
1. Ilia, the daughter of Æneas, was the mother of

Romulus. 2. Procas, king of Alba, left two sons, Numi- (449)
tor and Amulius; the latter of whom wrested the sove- A
reignty from his elder brother, killed his nephew, and enrolled his niece Silvia among the vestal virgins. The maiden became pregnant by Mars, and brought forth twin sons, Romulus and Remus, who were exposed, by command of Amulius, at the foot of the Palatine, on a spot flooded by the Tiber, which in after times was indicated by the ficus Ruminalis. The children, however, escaped death, being suckled by a she-wolf and fed by a woodpecker, until they were discovered by the herdsman of Faustinus, who placed them under the care of his wife,
Acca Larentia. As soon as they were grown up, the B
brothers slew Amulius, and replaced Numitor on the throne. A dispute respecting the building of their new city is decided in favor of Romulus by the flight of twelve vultures—Remus slain by his brother. Commemoration of the building of Rome, 21st April (festival of the Palilia).

First Period.

Rome under Kings.

(B. C. 753—510.)

§ 93. *Romulus.*

Reigned thirty-seven years (from B. C. 753 to 716).

The new city was soon peopled by the opening of an 450
asylum for malefactors of every description; and the C
overtures of Romulus for matrimonial alliances with the neighboring nations having been contemptuously rejected, thirty Latin and Sabine maidens, who had been invited with their parents to the festival of the Consualia, were forcibly carried off by the Roman soldiers. Hence war with *three Latin cities* (Cænīna, Antemnæ, and Crustumerium), which were subdued one after the other; and with the *Sabines*, whose king, Titus Tatius, was admitted into the capitol by the treachery of Tarpeia. A peace being concluded through the intervention of the captive maidens themselves, the Romans and Sabines (Quirites) formed a united commonwealth, which was governed, until

(450) the death of Tatius, by the two kings conjointly—100
A Sabines were also admitted into the senate founded by Romulus, which had previously consisted of 100 Roman members. War with Fidenæ, (related in almost the same terms as that which happened in 424), and with Veii (Romulus slays 8000 Etruscans!). During an eclipse of the sun Romulus is carried up into heaven in a chariot of fire by his father Mars, and appearing to Proculus Julius, enjoins the people, through him, to pay divine honors to their late monarch as the god Quirinus.

Interregnum for a year.

§ 94. *Numa Pompilius.*

Reigned thirty-nine years [according to Livy forty-three years], from 715 to 672.

451 Numa Pompilius, of Cures, son-in-law of T. Tatius,
B was chosen *out of* the Sabines *by* the Romans. He divided the conquered lands among the people, and under the instruction of the Camena Egeria, commenced the establishment of a regular system of religious worship, appointing 1, the Pontifices; 2, the Augures; 3, the Flamīnes, or priests of the temples; 4, the Vestales; 5, the Salii Palatini, and probably also (6) the Fetiales (see § 165). To him also is ascribed the division of the year into twelve months, as well as the building of the temple of Janus, which remained closed during the whole of his peaceful reign.

§ 95. *Niebuhr's view of the origin and earliest inhabitants of Rome.*

452 The inhabitants of Rome (a Siculian, and subsequently
C a Latin settlement on the Palatine, founded at an unknown period), having formed matrimonial alliances (represented in the myth by the rape of the Sabine virgins), and political engagements with the Quirites, who inhabited the opposite hills of Capitolinus and Quirinalis; the two nations soon became *one* state, with *one* senate, *one* general assembly of the people, and *one* king, chosen *by* one of the two nations *out of* the other. Hence the term Populus Romanus (et) Quirītes.

Before the formation of the plebs,[1] the Roman people 453
consisted of Patrons and Clients (dependents, from A
the verb *cluere*, *κλύω*), a distinction almost universally recognized by the Italian nations, although no historical record exists of its origin. No doubt the victorious Casci brought many clients with them, and this number was augmented by the admission of foreigners and emancipated serfs, and even by the voluntary assumption (by the plebeians) of a status which afforded many important advantages.

The patron was bound to protect his client, plead his cause before the tribunals, and, if he were poor, assign him a portion of land for his support—in return for these benefits the client was expected to contribute towards the portions of his patron's daughters, release him from arrest for debt, assist him in the payment of taxes, &c.

To these *Romans* and *Quirites* (who enjoyed equal 454
rights), was added at a very early period a third com- B
ponent part of the Roman people—the *Lucĕres* (of uncertain origin), who possessed inferior privileges, and thence were styled gentes minores. Thus the most ancient division of the Roman people was into three tribes—*Ramnes* (Romans), *Tities* (Sabines), and *Lucĕres*. The three tribes were subdivided into thirty curiæ, and these into 300 gentes—consequently, each tribe comprised 100
gentes, and thence was also termed a centuria. Each tribe C
was presided over by a tribunus, each curia by a curio, and each gens by a decurio, who were their magistrates in peace, and leaders in war. The family of a gens were not necessarily allied by blood, but merely formed a

[1] According to *Niebuhr's* latest views (I. 452, 3rd edit.) the Roman plebs was composed of the most heterogeneous elements. The community of which the nucleus had been formed in the three original cities, owed almost all its importance to the subsequent accession of Latins from the places conquered by the early kings of Rome, especially by Ancus Martius. These Latins were sometimes permitted to reside in their own country, and sometimes transferred to Rome—but in either case they enjoyed all the privileges of Roman citizens. According to *Walter* (Geschichte des Röm Rechts, S. 11), the origin of the patricians may be traced to the Casci, who took possession of the greater part of the land on the conquest of Latium, and that of the plebeians to the vanquished Siculi, who were permitted to retain a portion of the soil.

(454) corporation the members of which were connected by a
A common sacra, the obligation imposed on them to assist one another, and the right of inheritance. They all bore the same *nomen gentile*. Each gens sent its president (decurio) as a deputy to the senate, which consequently contained 300 members.

§ 96. *The earliest constitution of Rome under Servius Tullius.*

455 The supreme authority was divided between the king,
B the senate, and the comitia of the curiæ.

The King was chosen for life by the curiæ (at first by those of *one* tribe), on the nomination of the senate; and after the election had been ratified by a favorable augury from the gods, was invested with the sovereign authority (according to the provisions of the lex curiata de imperio) by the curiæ of all the tribes. This authority was threefold—*priestly*, *judicial*, and *military*. The first was exercised when the king offered sacrifice for all his people; as judge, he sat every nine days to hear complaints, and either decided disputes himself, or commissioned judges to
C perform that duty. From this sentence the patricians, however, enjoyed the right of a *provocatio* to the citizens. Lastly, as commander-in-chief he possessed *unlimited* power in time of war, and during his absence in the field was represented at home by a senator nominated by himself, with the title of custos urbis. A certain portion of the ager publicus was set apart for his support.

456 The Senate, which at first consisted of 100 members, after the union of the Romans and Quirites of 200, and from the time of Tarquinius Priscus of 300, and was divided into thirty decuriæ, was called together by the king for the dispatch of public business.

457 The Comitia Curiata, in which the patricians alone,
D and not their clients, took part, decided questions of war and peace, the adoption of new laws, and the choice of the king and other officers, but were always restricted to the consideration of subjects proposed by the senate.

During the interval beween the death of a king and the election of his successor, the ten chief members of the

senate (*i. e.* the presidents of the ten decuriæ of the (457)
Ramnes) acted as Interrēges, each of them being in- A
vested with sovereign authority and bearing the insignia of royalty for five days. If at the expiration of fifty days a new king were not chosen, the cycle began afresh.

§ 97. *Tullus Hostilius.*

Reigned thirty-two years (672—640.)

A war with Alba Longa, the head of the Latin con- 458
federacy, which had broken out in consequence of mutual B
depredations, was decided favorably for the Romans, by a victory gained, according to the legend, by the three Horatii (Romans ?) over the three Curiatii (Albans ?), in a combat proposed by the Alban dictator, Mettius Fuffetius. The surviving Horatius murders his sister; but the sentence of death passed on him is remitted at the intercession of his father.

Second war with Veii and Fidenæ, at the instigation of Mettius Fuffetius, whose attempted desertion to
the enemy in the midst of a battle is punished by the C
tearing of his body into four quarters. Alba is levelled with the ground, and its inhabitants transported to the Cælian mount. During a successful war with the Sabines, a pestilence breaks out at Rome. Tullus himself sickens, and is slain by lightning as he stands before the altar.

§ 98. *Ancus Marcius.*

Reigned twenty-three years (according to Cicero; according to Livy twenty-four years, 640—616).

Ancus, the son of Numa's daughter, caused the laws 459
respecting religion to be written out, and exposed to view D
in a public place.

A war with four Latin cities (Politorium, Tellēnæ, Ficana, and Medullia), occasioned by depredations in the Roman territories, was speedily terminated, and the inhabitants transferred to the Aventine. Ancus founded Ostia, the first Roman colony, built the carcer, erected the pons Sublicius, and fortified the Janiculum.

§ 99. *L. Tarquinius Priscus.*

Reigned thirty-eight years (616—578.)

Damaratus

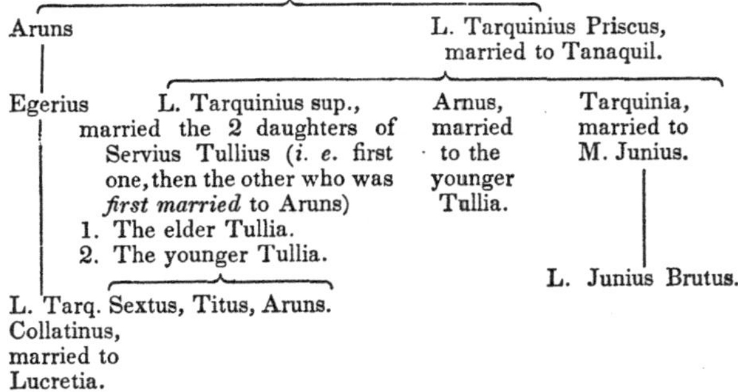

460 Tarquinius, a son, according to the legend, of the
A Bacchiad Damaratus, who took refuge at Tarquinii from the tyranny of Cypsĕlus of Corinth, came to Rome with his wife Tanaquil, and was appointed guardian of the sons of Ancus, but, after the death of that prince, was himself chosen king, and thus put an end to the alternate choice of Roman and Quiritic kings. His victories (over the Latini, Sabini, and Æqui, and according to Dionysius the overthrow of twelve Etruscan cities), are less memorable than his architectural labors and the changes which he effected
B in the constitution. He began the wall round the city, which was completed by Servius, built the cloacæ, and in the valleys thus drained laid the foundations of the Forum, and of the Circus Maximus for the celebration of the ludi Romani or magni. At the same time he increased the number of senators to 300 by the admission of the Lucĕres, and that of the vestals to six; and was inclined to form three new tribes out of the plebeians, whom his various conquests had rendered exceedingly numerous; but the opposition of the ruling order (the Augur Attus Navius) compelled him to content himself with *merely doubling the number of the gentes* by a selection from the plebeians. These new gentes were enrolled (with inferior privileges) among the ancient gentes, with the title of Ramnes, Tities, and Luceres *secundi*. In the same manner

the three ancient knightly tribes were retained, but the (460)
number of knights was doubled, so as to form six centuries. A
Tarquin died by the hand of an assassin, at the instigation of the sons of Ancus.

§ 100. *Servius Tullius.*

Reigned forty-four years (578—534).

According to the legend, Servius was the offspring of 461
some god by Ocrisia, a female slave of Queen Tanaquil (hence his name of Servius). In consequence of a luminous appearance on his head, Servius is educated as the king's son, whose daughter he marries, and after his death becomes viceroy, and subsequently king (successful
war against Veii). He obtained for Rome admission into B
the Latin confederacy, and built a second confederate temple (that of Diana) on the Aventine, where the Roman king offered sacrifice for Romans and Latins, as the head of the Latin confederacy did at the feriæ Latinæ on the Alban Mount. For the wall of Servius Tullius, see § 90. He was murdered by his son-in-law L. Tarquinius Superbus, who, after the assassination of his brother Aruns, had married his widow Tullia, the murderess of her own sister, and placed himself at the head of those senators who were discontented with the institutions of Servius (see § 101).

§ 101. *The Constitution of Servius Tullius.*

The chief object of the constitution of Servius Tullius 462
was the organization of the Plebs, a new and im- C
portant order, which had been created, principally since the reign of Ancus Martius, by the naturalization of the inhabitants of conquered places, and possessed no inconsiderable influence, in consequence of its numbers and property. It consisted exclusively of free agriculturists,[1] dwelling in the city and suburbs, but chiefly in the country towns and hamlets. Servius was well aware that the only security for the maintenance of peace at home, and for the prosperity of the republic, was the admission of these

[1] The names of persons engaging in trade or mechanical employments, or convicted of gross offences, were erased from the register of their Tribus, and placed among the ærarii.

(462) supplemental citizens to political privileges, and to a par-
A ticipation in the distinctions enjoyed by others. He therefore commenced his reforms with the partition of the Roman territories into thirty "regiones;" viz., the city into four urbanæ (Suburana, Esquilina, Collina, Palatina), and the country into twenty-six rusticæ. The plebeians settled in each region formed a community, which, like the patrician tribes, was denominated Tribus, and had a tribune as its president. Thus the plebeians in the thirty tribes corresponded to the patricians in the thirty curiæ.

463 With the view of extending the enjoyment of civil
B rights to the plebeians (especially as regarded the privilege of voting), and of defining, at the same time, the extent of their liability to taxation and the performance of military service, Servius introduced (with reference to the assemblies of the people and the muster of the army) a new division of the inhabitants into Centuriæ, in which the patricians (and their clients?) were comprehended, together with the plebeians. According to this division, the nation consisted of three grand component parts, viz.—

C *A*. Eighteen centuries of knights (or cavalry soldiers), six patrician and twelve plebeian.

B. The infantry, divided into five classes, or 170 centuries.

1. Those who possessed at least		100,000	asses =	80 centuries.
2.	"	75,000	each 20 =	60 centuries.
3.	"	50,000		
4.	"	25,500		
5.	"	12,000	"	30 centuries.

D *C*. Those not comprehended in the classes, seven (or five) centuries, viz.—

1. Fabri, one century.
2. Liticines and cornicines, two centuries.
3. Accensi and velati (with 1500—12,500 asses), two centuries(?).
4. Proletarii (with 375—1500 asses), one century.
5. Capite censi (with less than 375 asses), one century.[1]

[1] This representation of the Centuriæ (as collected by Niebuhr from ancient testimonies, especially Cic. de Rep. ii. 22) differs but little from the accounts given by Dionysius and Livy; and that only in the case of the centuries which were not comprehended in the

Each century had a voice in the assembly of the people; 464
the votes of the knights and the first class deciding the A
question, provided they voted on the same side. They formed also, in war, divisions, of course of very unequal strength. Thus there existed a very intimate connection between the military and civil constitutions of the kingdom; the same men (the cavalry and heavy-armed) who led the charge in the field deciding the questions proposed in the assembly of the people. In each of the five classes, half the number of centuries assigned to the class belonged to the juniors, and the other half to the seniors, in order that the latter, although inferior in numbers, might possess their full share of influence. Tradesmen and artisans who B
possessed no landed property formed a distinct class; the members of which were exempt from military service, but were liable to taxation, and thence called ærarii.

The property qualification was settled by the Census, which was 465
held in each lustrum (every five years[1]), at first by the king, then by the consuls, and at a later period by the censors. It comprehended houses, lands, slaves, cattle, brass, and the precious metals. Each Roman was compelled, under heavy penalties, to give in an account of all these items, as well as of the births and deaths in his family, the attainment of the age of puberty by any of its members, and all changes of residence or transfers of property. The administration of the public exchequer was intrusted to two quæstores classici.

The comitia centuriata, *i. e.* the general assembly 466
of the people, convoked by the king on the Campus Mar- C
tius, was invested by Servius with the threefold privilege hitherto enjoyed by the comitia curiata, viz.—1, The right of adopting new laws; 2, the election of kings; and, 3, the decision of questions relating to peace and war. In elections and legislation, however, they possessed merely the right of accepting or rejecting candidates, or

---

classes. These writers make no distinction between the *proletarii* and the *capite censi* (a distinction expressly stated by Gell. xvi. 10): both also make two centuries of *fabri*, &c. Cic. (l. c.) knew of but one. Moreover, Dionysius makes no mention of the *accensi* and *velati*, and consequently reckons 193 centuries. Livy makes 194 centuries, one consisting of the *accensi*. In recent investigations the number 193 is generally retained, as being mentioned in three distinct passages of Dionysius.

[1] This was decidedly the older signification of the word *lustrum*, but it never acquired the *fixed* meaning that belonged to the Greek *Olympiad*.

(466) measures proposed to them by the senate; and even this
A signification of their acquiescence in any proposal had not the force of law until it was confirmed by the curiæ. By the laws of the twelve tables, the judicia capitis (decisions respecting offences punishable by death or banishment) were committed to the comitia centuriate.

467 The Military Constitution.

1. The *knights* (equites) served on horseback. The state granted them 10,000 asses for their outfit, and an annual allowance of 2000 asses (the payment of which was charged on rich virgins, widows, and orphans) for the support of a war-horse, and the maintenance of a mounted yeoman with his horse. The census equester—one million of asses—belongs to a later period. See § 131.

B 2. The classes, and only they [cf. 463 D], were equally divided into centuries of juniores and seniores; the former, which comprehended all males between the ages of sixteen and forty-five, being destined for service in the field, the latter (from forty-six to sixty) for the defence of the city. The Roman legion consisted originally of 1200 men. The three first classes were heavily armed, and the fourth lightly. The fifth served as slingers in front of the line.

3. The *accensi* and *velati* stood apart from the legion: "but one by one they filled up the gaps that were made, and received arms for that purpose." Niebuhr i. 441.

4. The *Proletarii* were armed by the state only in extraordinary cases,—the *capite censi* and *ærarii* never.

§ 102. *L. Tarquinius Superbus.*

Reigned twenty-five years (534—510).

468 Without any election on the part of the people, or con-
C firmation by the curiæ, Tarquin ascended the throne of his murdered father-in-law, and commenced his cruel and oppressive reign under the protection of a body-guard, which enabled him to bid defiance to the resentment of his subjects. The senate, reduced by murders and banishments, was no longer convoked; heavy taxes were imposed on the plebeians, who were not only deprived of the privileges conferred on them by Servius, but compelled to perform feudal service: the Latins and Hernicans were subjugated, and Tarquin presided as head of the Latin confederacy at the feriæ Latinæ on the Alban Mount.

469 His Wars.

D 1. He is said to have carried *Suessa Pometia* by storm, sold its inhabitants (the city nevertheless was recaptured in 503), and employed the booty in building the Capitoline temple of Jupiter, and those of Juno and Minerva, where the three Sibylline books, purchased from an unknown old (469) woman, were preserved in a subterraneous cell by two A (afterwards by ten, and from the time of Sulla fifteen) guardians.

2. *Gabii*, which had refused to join the Roman alliance, 470 was taken by stratagem and treachery.

The narrative of the self-mutilation of Sextus, and of the advice conveyed by the act of cutting off the poppy heads, seem to be adaptations to Roman history of the story of Zopyrus (83 B), and the answer of Thrasybûlus to Periander; both recorded by Herodotus. Mission of Titus and Aruns to Delphi, accompanied by their cousin, L. Junius Brutus (whose life had been saved by his feigning madness).

3. During the siege of *Ardea*, the wealthy capital of 471 the Rutuli, a dispute arose between the sons of the king B and their cousin, L. Tarquinius of Collatia, respecting the virtue of their respective wives. Lucretia is dishonored by Sextus, and dies by her own hand. Brutus, as Tribunus Celerum, assembles the people, who banish the Tarquins, abolish the sovereignty, and lodge the supreme power in the hands of two prætors (afterwards named consuls), who hold their office for a year. The two first are L. Junius Brutus and L. Tarquinius Collatinus. The constitution of Servius is restored, and remains unchanged in all essential particulars.

The flight of the king (regifugium or fugalia) was commemorated C yearly on the 24th of February. An armistice for fifteen years seems to have been concluded with Ardea; but in the commercial treaty between Rome and Carthage (in 509), Ardea is mentioned as a city subject to Rome. There are several inconsistencies in the chronology of this period. Tanaquil must have lived to the age of 115 years, and Brutus is called a child (at the beginning of Tarquin's reign), and twenty-five years later is mentioned as the father of grown-up sons.

Second Period.

Rome as a free State.

(B. C. 509—30.)

a. Aristocracy.

(509—366.)

§ 103. *The Consuls.*

The consuls (a term probably equivalent to collega), 472 who were named prætores until the time of the decem-

(472) virate, were at first exclusively patricians, but from the
A year 365 plebeians were also eligible to the office. By the lex annalis (180), none could be consuls who had not attained their forty-third year, and already discharged the offices of quæstor, ædile, and prætor.

The election by the centuries was always succeeded by the confirmation (or approbation of the gods, declared by an augurium) and by investiture, on the part of the curiæ. The day of their entering on office was different at different periods. From the year 154 it was on the first of January.

473 At first the consuls possessed an authority almost equiv-
B alent to that of the kings (the priestly duties alone being committed to a separate functionary termed rex sacrorum), but this power was gradually circumscribed, at first by the provocatio, afterwards by the intercession of the tribunes of the people, and the separation of the censorship and prætorship from the consulship. Under extraordinary circumstances of danger, the consuls were invested by the senate with unlimited powers. They might be impeached at the expiration of their year of office. Under the emperors, the consulship continued nominally to exist until the reign of Justinian (A. D. 541). The year was named after them.

§ 104. *Consequences of the expulsion of the Tarquins.*

474 Tarquin retired to Cære, and thence to Tarquinii. A
C conspiracy against the new constitution organized by his emissaries at Rome was betrayed; the sons of Brutus slain, by command of their own father, for participation in the plot, and the whole gens Tarquinia banished, including even Tarquinius Collatinus, whose place as consul was filled by P. Valerius (as consul suffectus). The royal demesnes were consecrated to the god Mars, and named the Campus Martius. The number of senators, which had been diminished by proscriptions and murders in the reign of Tarquin, was again raised to 300 by the admission of plebeian knights (conscripti).

475 War with Veii (and Tarquinii? 500). The leaders of the
D cavalry on both sides, Aruns, the son of Tarquin, and Brutus, having fallen each by the other's hand, the combat remained undecided, until the voice of the forest dæmon proclaimed at midnight that victory belonged to the Romans, because the Etruscans had lost one man more than their enemies! The Roman matrons mourn a whole year for Brutus.

P. Valerius (Publicŏla) obtains for the plebeians, by the lex de (475)
provocatione, the right of appealing (within the distance of one mile A
from the city) from the sentence of a consul to the assembly of the people; that is, to the comitia centuriata. First commercial treaty with Carthage, by which the Romans were prohibited from navigating the seas southward of the Hermæan promontory (509). Dedication of the Capitoline temple by the consul suffectus, M. Horatius, the first who drove the clavus as a mark for reckoning time (508 ?).

The war with Porsenna of Clusium (508 ? insti- 476
gated, it is said, by the Tarquins) was rich, if we may believe the legend, in heroic deeds, such as the defence of the bridge over the Tiber by Horatius Cocles, the unsuccessful attempt of Mutius Scævŏla to assassinate Porsenna, the escape of Clœlia, &c.; but there seems to be much embellishment and improbability in the narrative, in the account especially of one fact—the unresisted occupation of the Janiculum by the Etruscan army, and the consequent famine. After carrying on this war for some time, B
the Romans were compelled to conclude an ignominious peace. The city was given up to the enemy, its inhabitants disarmed, a third of their territory taken from them (the number of the tribes reduced to twenty), and the remainder probably held by the Romans as tributaries; the royal insignia were sent to Clusium in token of subjection, and twenty hostages (among whom was Clodia) were placed at the disposal of the conqueror.

Under the name of a dictatorship (an office of Latin 477
origin), the royal authority was revived (without provo- C
catio) for a period not exceeding six months, in times of extraordinary embarrassment and danger. The first dictator was appointed in 501, when Rome was threatened with a Latin war. By the establishment of such an office, the government hoped to obtain that unity and promptitude of action which can only be secured by the delegation of absolute power to an individual.

The dictator, taken at first exclusively from the patricians and consulares, but at a later period (355) from the plebeians also, was elected in the same manner as the kings.

War with the Latins, who had thrown off their al- 478
legiance to Rome during the Etruscan war, and were in D
arms, probably at the instigation of the Tarquins. The Romans claim the victory in a battle on the banks of the lake Regillus (496 ?), the account of which has a very

(478) poetical character; but a few years later they concede to
A the Latins, and subsequently to the Hernĭcans, the right of sharing the command of the allied army, and an equal portion of the booty and conquered territories.

King Tarquin, now in his ninetieth year, is wounded in a single combat with the Roman dictator Postumius, who is perhaps mentioned as commander in this battle merely on account of his family name Regillensis. The Dioscūri are also reported to have appeared during the engagement.

§ 105. *Secession of the Plebs*, 494.

479 Their condition before the Secession.
B After the expulsion of the kings, the plebeians had been favored by the restoration of the constitution granted by Servius Tullius, the Valerian laws, &c.; but no sooner was the Etruscan war terminated, and all fear of disturbance from the Tarquins at an end, than the patrician party began to press heavily on them. The dictatorship was created with the view of curtailing their privileges, and all participation in the lands, won by their own swords, refused to those who were the sole payers of the tribūtum,
C and composed the flower of the army. In addition to these wrongs, the plebeians, who had been ruined by repeated predatory wars, and were deeply indebted to patrician usurers, were subjected to a severe law of debtor and creditor. Any one who had given personal security for the repayment of money borrowed was termed *nexus*. If he failed to redeem his pledge within a given time, he was assigned (*addictus*) to his creditor as a serf, and lost his civil rights (capite deminutus).
480 The Secession.
D The people, roused by the sight of an old soldier who had been imprisoned for debt and escaped from his dungeon, demanded the abolition of arrest, and refused to serve in the army (495 and 494), but were persuaded to take the field by the arguments of the consul, P. Servilius, and the dictator, M. Valerius, and returned victorious (over the Sabines, Volscians, and Æquians). Finding, however, the promises of their commanders unfulfilled by the senate, the plebeians crossed the Anio, and occupied the mons sacer in the territory of Crustumerium. After a few days (not four months, as asserted by Dionysius), the patricians, through the intervention of Menenius Agrippa (his alle-

gory of the belly and the members), concluded a formal (480)
peace with the plebeians; the engagements of those who A
were unable to pay being declared void, whilst the right of arrest remained as before. At the same time, the plebeians were placed under the protection of magistrates of their own (the five, afterwards ten, Tribunes), who were chosen by the centuries out of the five classes, subject to the confirmation of the curies (curiæ); until the passing of a law, proposed by Volero Publilius (471), by which it was enacted that they should be chosen by the tribes, without any such confirmation. The persons of these tribunes
were sacred and inviolable (sacrosancti). *Object and* B
powers. Protection of the people against the patrician authorities (within the distance of one mile from the city), in order to secure the right of appeal; together with the power of calling the magistrates to account before the tribes at the expiration of their year of office. In the college of Tribunes all questions were decided by a majority of votes; but at a later period (about 400) the veto of an individual was sufficient to neutralize a proposal or resolution
(intercedere). They summoned the people (without consult- C
ing the auspices) to the comitia tributa, in the forum, where resolutions (plebiscīta) were adopted, affecting at first only the interests of the plebs, but, after the passing of the law of Volero Publilius, comprehending all questions of state policy. At a still later period (by the lex Valeria, see 490, 4) these plebiscita were declared equally authoritative with the decrees of the comitia centuriata.

The ædīles plebeii (an office which perhaps existed 481
at an earlier period), were charged with the superintendence of religious festivals, and the guardianship of the plebeian archives. They seem also to have been intrusted with the administration of the communal exchequer, and the execution of all police regulations affecting the plebs.

The attempt to obtain for the plebs a share of the ager publicus 482
completely miscarried. The consul, Sp. Cassius, by whom the law D
was proposed, was impeached at the close of his year of office, by the populus (not the plebs, whose benefactor he had been, but the curiæ), and being pronounced guilty of aiming at absolute power, was beheaded, and his house levelled with the ground. His law although in all probability adopted, was never carried into execution; and when, at a later period, one T. Genucius, a tribune, ventured to charge all the consuls who had been elected since the time of Cassius with having neglected its provisions, he was silenced by the dagger of an assassin.

§ 106. *Wars to the period of the Decemvirate.*

483 1. The war with the Volsci.

A The war with the Volscians continued after the conclusion of peace with the plebs. In the year 493 (?) Cn. Marcius is said to have taken Coriŏli, and thence obtained the surname of Coriolanus, but as Corioli was one of the thirty Latin cities, it could not have been attacked by the Romans. Having been condemned by the comitia tributa for proposing, during a season of scarcity, that corn (imported from Sicily?) should be distributed among the people on condition of their renouncing the tribunate, Marcius at once went over to the Volscians, with all his adherents; and taking the command of their forces, captured several
B Latin cities; among the rest Corioli. Advancing to Rome, he summoned the city to surrender unconditionally, demanding, at the same time, the restoration of all the districts which had been forcibly taken from the Volscians, and the recall of the Roman settlers; but being overcome, it is said, by the entreaties of his mother and wife, he raised the siege and returned into the country of the Volscians, where he lived in peace to extreme old age.[1]

484 2. War of the Fabii against Veii (482—474).

With the view of recovering the territory which had been wrested from them by the Etruscans, as well as of finding employment for the plebeians, the patricians, chiefly at the instance of the gens Fabia, renewed the war with Veii, which was terminated by a peace for forty years.

485 The plebeians having refused to serve in the army, 306 Fabii, with
C their families and clients, established themselves in a fortress on the river Cremĕra, where they were all (with the exception of one boy,) cut to pieces by the Veientines; having been allured, according to the commonly received story, to a distance from their stronghold by the prospect of booty, or, as another legend relates, having set out unarmed for Rome, with the intention of offering sacrifice. Like Porsenna in days of yore, the Veientines appeared on the Janiculum, but after a few skirmishes, they were driven back, and having sustained another defeat close to the gate of their own city, were glad to accept conditions of peace.

[1] There is nothing surprising in this, after the benefits conferred on the Volscian state by Coriolanus; nor was it until a much later period, that Roman vanity invented the myth of the surrender of all his conquests at the instance of his mother and wife. To make the story consistent, it was necessary to add, that Coriolanus was murdered by the enraged Volscians.

Wars with the Æqui and Volsci, to 458. 486
Both these Ausonian tribes had extended their authority A over Latium as far as the sea, and taken possession of Antium, which was wrested from them by the Romans (who colonized it in 468); and again restored at the Volscian peace in 459. The war with the Æquians still continued. A Roman army was beaten on the Algidus and surrounded by the enemy, but was rescued by the dictator, L. Quinctius Cincinnatus (458).

The narrative of his campaign on the Algidus is full of improbabilities.

§ 107. *Struggle of the Plebeians with the Patricians for equality of Civil Rights.*

1. The rogation of the tribune C. Terentilius 487
Harsa (462). B

The want of any written code of laws for the plebeians, and the caprice with which patrician consuls decided all disputes between patricians and plebeians, not by any fixed rules, but according to precedents, which might be interpreted to signify whatever the judge desired, induced the tribune C. Terentilius Harsa, to propose the formation of a code by five or ten persons chosen from the classes. All the obligations of plebeians towards the state were to be accurately defined, and a rule to be established by which their disputes should thenceforth be decided. On the other C hand, the patricians, who were well aware of the advantages afforded to their order by the uncertain state of the law, endeavored by every means in their power, even by forcibly obstructing the proceedings of the comitia tributa, to render this "rogatio" ineffective. After a succession of fierce and bloody struggles, certain advantages were conceded to the plebeians, such as the doubling the number of tribunes and placing the Aventine in the hands of the commons; and in the end a general measure of legislation, embracing the interests of both classes, obtained the assent of the curiæ.

The mission of three senators to Athens, for the purpose of making D themselves acquainted with the laws of Solon and those of the other Grecian states, may perhaps be a historical fact, without necessarily leading us to the inference that the Roman code was derived immediately from that of Athens.

488 2. The first decemvirate, 451.

A After a long delay on the part of the patricians, and the modification by the plebeians of their original proposition into the appointment of a mixed commission, selected equally from both orders, the functions of all magistrates were suspended, and ten senators appointed, as interrēges, with irresponsible authority, and instructions to frame a code of written laws. In accordance with these instructions, the commissioners produced a series of legal provisions, divided into ten sections, which were engraved on ten tables of brass, and hung up in a conspicuous place, after they had received the assent of the senate, the centu-
B ries (consequently of the plebs), and of the curies. Of these laws, which formed the groundwork of Roman legislation down to the time of the emperors, nothing now remains but a few insignificant fragments. One of the most important changes consequent on the formation of this code was the admission of patricians into the plebeian tribes, which thus became a national division, and the comitia tributa a national assembly.

489 3. The second decemvirate (450) added two new
C tables of laws; but instead of laying down their authority, or making arrangements at the end of their year for the election of consuls or other magistrates, the decemvĭri continued to exercise a despotic power, which gave great offence to the people (murder of the veteran L. Siccius Dentatus, who had counselled an insurrection of the commons). At length the discontent, which had long been smouldering, was blown into a flame, by an act of wanton cruelty on the part of one of the decemviri. In the midst of a war with the Sabines and Æquians, a young maiden named Virginia (the daughter of L. Virginius, an officer in the army), who had been assigned, during her father's absence, to one of his clients as a slave by Appius Claudius, the chief of the decemviri, was stabbed to the heart by her own father, as the only mode of saving her from dishonor.
D On receiving intelligence of this event, all the plebeians in the army returned to Rome and encamped on the Aventine. The abolition of the decemvirate being obstinately refused by the patricians, the plebeians again retired to the mons sacer, whither they were followed by L. Valerius and M. Horatius, by whose intervention peace was restored on the following terms:—the decemviri were required to lay

down their office, the tribunate was re-established, and Valerius and Horatius were elected prætors, or, as they were thenceforth called, consuls. The decemviri were impeached by Virginius before the plebs, two of their number (Appius Claudius and the plebeian Sp. Oppius), died in prison, probably by their own act, and the rest escaped punishment by voluntary exile. Their property was confiscated to the use of the state. (489) A

4. The laws of the consuls Valerius and Horatius (448). 490

The first endeavor of the newly-elected consuls was to establish on a firm basis the freedom thus restored to the people. With this view the following laws were enacted—1. The plebiscīta were declared to be of equal authority with the resolutions of the centuries, and had the force of law, when they emanated from, or were sanctioned by, the senate, and confirmed by the curies. 2. The right of provocation against the consuls, and all future magistrates, was secured. 3. The inviolability of the tribunes and ædiles plebeii was re-established and extended to the judges. B

We find also, about the same time, a seat reserved for the tribunes in front of the open doors of the senate-house, that they might hear the debates.

An essential change in the constitution was effected by

5. The rogations of the tribune C. Canuleius and his colleagues, 444. 491 C

The "rogatio" of the tribune C. Canuleius for the legalization of marriages (connubium), between patricians and plebeians, was adopted after a severe struggle; but when his colleagues proposed that one consul should be chosen from each of the orders, it was settled, that instead of thus dividing the office between the patricians and plebeians, the supreme authority should be vested in tribūni militum consulari potestate, an office to which plebeians were declared admissible; the functions of the censorship being at the same time separated from those of the consular tribunate, and reserved for patricians. The number of these military tribunes varied at different periods (three, four, six, eight). Among the six was always a prætor urbanus (patrician); and among the eight, were two censors. Every year a law was passed, declaring D whether consuls or military tribunes should be elected for the succeeding year.

492 At first the two Censors were taken exclusively from
A the patricians (generally from *consulares*), but after the passing of the law of Publius Philo (338), they were chosen, one from each order. At the first institution of the office, they were elected in each lustrum (for five years; afterwards for eighteen months, and at a still later period for thirty-two), originally by the curies, and afterwards by the centuries. Their functions were twofold: 1. Registration of the citizens according to their rank (senators, knights, burgesses), coupled with the right of admitting individuals into, or removing them from, the senate, the
B knightly order, and the tribes. The right of expulsion was exercised, either in accordance with the sentence of a tribunal, or (in the case of offences not strictly cognizable by the courts) on the individual responsibility of the censor (notatio censoria). 2. Administration of the exchequer. It was a part of their office to farm out the duties and similar sources of revenue, contract for public works, and apportion the payment of the tributum according to the census.

493 During a famine, in the year 439, a distribution of corn having been made to the people, by Sp. Mælius, the richest of the plebeian knights, a cry was immediately raised that secret meetings were held in his house, and arms deposited there, which it was his intention to use for the purpose of raising himself to absolute power.
C L. Cincinnatus was nominated dictator, and the unarmed, and probably innocent, Mælius, was slain in the forum, by his master of the horse. The assassin escaped impeachment by voluntary exile.

The number of questores classici was increased from two to four, chosen without distinction from all ranks (420), and thenceforth the senate was recruited from the list of persons who had filled the office of quæstor.

494 Hitherto all questions had been decided in the college of tribunes of the people by a majority of votes, but about this time (between 415 and 394), it was enacted that the "veto" of any one tribune should be sufficient to arrest a proposed decree; an arrangement which proved, in the end, advantageous to the patricians.

D The practice was introduced of giving *regular* pay (stipendium) to the infantry (probably then for the first time to each legionary), for which purpose a tenth part of the ager publicus was set aside (305).

§ 108. *The last war against Veii.*

(404—395.)

After the termination of the Sabine wars by the decisive victory 495
of M. Horatius, repeated wars were carried on by the Romans (for A
the most part successfully), against the Æquians and Volscians. Fidĕnæ, which had expelled some Roman colonists, was taken, and afterwards, in consequence of the assassination of the Roman ambassadors, was levelled to the ground. Then followed the last war against Veii, which had formed an alliance with Fidenæ.

The Romans having in vain demanded satisfaction for 496
the murder of their ambassadors, which had been perpetrated at the instigation of the king of Veii, declare war
against that state. After a blockade of ten years, effected B
by means of a line of works drawn at some distance round the city, Veii is taken by the dictator M. Furius Camillus. The account of this capture belongs rather to poetry than history.

The Alban lake having, in the driest season of the year, overflowed 497
its banks, it was declared by a captive Etruscan aruspex (in accordance with the oracle of Delphi), that until the waters of the lake were confined to their proper limits Veii could not be taken. In consequence of this intimation, the drawing off of the waters was undertaken by means of a tunnel, six feet deep, three and a half broad and 6000 in length. Then the city was taken, it is said, by means of a
mine carried as far as the temple of Juno. It would seem, however, C
that neither this gallery, nor the tunnel, was completed during the dictatorship of Camillus; still less could the temple have been reached with any certainty; if such a gallery, therefore, were formed at all, it was probably for the purpose of opening a breach in the wall. Similarity of this war to that of Troy.

A body of the plebeians having determined to quit Rome 498
and settle in the beautifully situated and well-built city of Veii, a portion of the Veientine territory was assigned to them in lots of seven jugera each. Camillus, after his triumph, was accused of appropriating to his own use a portion of the booty, and being condemned to pay a "multa," went into exile.

§ 109. *War with the Gauls*, 389.

During the last war against Veii, the Gauls, a Celtic 499
tribe, had crossed the Alps and entered Italy, where a D
portion of them remained, whilst the rest continued their march towards Pannonia. Having overthrown the Etruscans and Umbrians, the Italian division, under the com-

(499) mand of Brennus, appeared before Clusium (whither,
A according to the legend, they had been invited by a burgher of the city, who had failed to obtain redress for the violation of his wife). The Clusinians applied to the Romans for help, and three ambassadors (Fabii) were sent to treat with the Gauls—but these men took part in the battle, and slew one of the Gallic leaders. The Romans having refused to deliver up their ambassadors, an army of 70,000 Gauls advanced towards Rome, and on their march encountered on the banks of the Aleia a Roman army 40,000 strong, commanded by Q. Sulpicius, which they utterly routed, the Romans flying in confusion, some to Rome and others to Veii. This battle was fought on the 16th July, 389. On the 18th of the same month Rome was taken, sacked, and laid in ashes—eighty aged
B patricians were slain in the forum. An attempt to scale the capitol (which was defended by Manlius[1] with 1000 armed followers), was discovered by the cry of some geese, consecrated to Juno. On receiving intelligence that the Venetians had invaded their country, the Gauls consented to withdraw their forces from Rome, on condition of receiving 1000 pounds' weight of gold. The legend however declares, that at this critical moment, Camillus, the Dictator, appeared at the head of the Roman soldiers who had taken refuge at Veii, prevented the payment of the gold, twice overthrew the Gauls, took Brennus prisoner, and put him to death.

C A second plan of the plebeians for withdrawing to Veii was happily rendered abortive by Camillus (thence surnamed the second founder of the city), and the place dismantled; but within a year it was restored and peopled by Capenatians, Faliscans, and Veientines, who formed four new tribes (22d—25th.)

500 M. Manlius. Many persons having been reduced to insolvency by the expenses incurred in the restoration of their houses and replacement of the cattle and furniture which they had lost in these wars, M. Manlius, the preserver of the capitol, advanced money without interest to 400 ruined citizens, demanding at the same time that all debts should be liquidated, either by the sale of the public

---

[1] Manlius was surnamed Capitolinus, not because he had saved the capitol, but because he dwelt there. The name, according to Niebuhr, already existed in his family.

lands, or out of the Gallic gold, which the patricians had unfairly (500)
appropriated to their own use. Manlius was immediately thrown A
into prison by the indignant patricians; but was soon afterwards
liberated in consequence of an insurrection of the plebs, and acquitted by the centuries. As however he still occupied the capitol,
sentence was passed against him by the curiæ in the fourth dictatorship of Camillus, and he was treacherously thrown from the Tarpeian rock in the year B. C. 308. At the same time a law was passed that thenceforth no person should inhabit the capitol.

§ 110. *Termination of the struggle between the Patricians and Plebeians by the Licinian Rogations.*

(376—366.)

An attempt to relieve the continued embarrassment of 501
the plebeians was made by the tribunes C. Licinius B
Stolo, and L. Sextius, who proposed the three following laws: 1. That the office of military tribune should be abolished, and two consuls be nominated, one of whom should always be a plebeian. 2. Every Roman citizen (consequently every plebeian) should enjoy a share of the ager publicus, but none should hold more than 500 jugera, with a correspondent number of heads of cattle in the common pasture. The rent paid for the use of this pasture to be farmed out from lustrum to lustrum by the censors, and the proceeds employed for the payment of
the soldiers. Land occupied by individuals to be given C
up, and divided among the plebeians in lots of seven jugera each. 3. Debts to be liquidated by three yearly instalments, after deducting the amount of interest already paid. The reading of these rogations was stopped by eight of the tribunes, who had been gained over by the senators; but for ten years the same two men were regularly re-elected to the tribunate, and at last, in the year 366, their rogations were adopted, subject to this condition, that the prætura urbana (an office established chiefly for the administration of justice within the city, and hitherto held by a patrician military tribune), should be separated from the consulate, and, as well as the
censorship, be reserved for patricians. On the other hand, D
it was settled that the curule ædileship (an office created at this time in the room of the quæstores parricidii), should be held alternately by patricians and plebeians.

L. Sextius was nominated the first plebeian consul in 365.

502 The Prætorship. The prætor urbanus was in some
A sort a third consul, elected in the same manner as the consuls, styled their colleague, exercising during their absence the functions of their office, and enjoying probably the distinction of the six fasces. At first the office was open only to patricians, but subsequently (probably after the law of Q. Publilius Philo in 336), it was held by a patrician and plebeian alternately. His principal duty was the administration of justice, both in criminal proceedings, inasmuch as he presided over the assemblies of the people, before which offenders against the state were tried, and in civil more especially, it being his business to publish the decisions of judges nominated by himself, and
B see that they were carried into effect. His authority was indicated by three words—dare (judicem), dicere (sententiam), addicere (rem). When he entered on his office, the prætor published an edictum (or formula), which served as a guide for his decisions in cases to which the law did not extend. He sat on the Nundĭnæ (dies fasti). The settlement of disputes between citizens and foreigners continued for a long time to be one of the duties of the consulate; but the increase of litigation consequent on the extension of the Roman territories, and the frequent absence of the consuls, at length rendered it necessary to appoint a special officer (in 242), named prætor inter
C peregrīnos et cives. The number of prætors was increased, for the administration of the provinces, to four and afterwards to six; but after the introduction of the quæstiones perpetuæ (144), these functionaries remained at Rome until the expiration of their year of office, when they entered on the government of their province with the title of proprætor. Sulla increased the number to eight, and Cæsar to sixteen.

503 The Curule Ædiles (ædīles curūles). Number,
D two; alternately two patricians and two plebeians. They presided at the ludi Romani, of which at a later period (after the first Punic war), they generally bore the expense; and were charged with the inspection of public and private buildings, streets, markets, and provisions, as well as the investigation and prosecution of certain offences.

It was only after the expiration of twenty-five years (503)
that the plebeians were peaceably established in the A
possession of their newly acquired rights. The election of consuls was often interrupted by the nomination of a dictator—and within a space of thirteen years (354—342), we find seven illegal consulates.

b. Democracy.

(B. C. 366—30.)

aa. To the subjugation of Italy in 266.

§ 111. *Their wars—to the Samnite wars.*

(361—346.)

Four wars with the Gauls (361—346), a succes- 504
sion probably of fresh swarms. The first was decided B
by the single combat of T. Manlius (Torquatus) with a Gallic giant, the second and third by victories obtained by the Roman armies, and the fourth by the single combat of M. Valerius (Corvus) with a Gallic warrior, and the victory of L. Furius Camillus (son of M. Camillus).

The Hernicans were also subjugated after repeated defeats; but a 505
war with the Tarquinians and Faliscans (in which C. Marcius C
Rutilus, the first plebeian dictator, stormed the Etruscan camp, and triumphed without the consent of the senate), terminated ingloriously in an armistice for forty years.

§ 112. *First war with the Samnites.*

(342—340.)

The Samnites, a nation whose dominions, extending 506
from the Hadriatic to the Tyrrhenian sea, contained a D
population exceeding in number the Romans with their allies, having attacked the Sidicini (whose capital was Teānum), that people called in the Campanians; and they, after sustaining two defeats, applied for assistance to the Romans. The consul, M. Valerius Corvus, marched into Campania, and obtained a victory at Mount Gaurus, near Cumæ (342), whilst the other consul (A. Cornelius Cossus), who had penetrated into Samnium, was surrounded near Caudium, but afterwards rescued by the military tribune P. Decius, in conjunction with whom he

506) stormed the Samnite encampment. A rich booty (40,000
A shields) fell into the hands of the Romans after a second great victory gained by Valerius (perhaps with both the Roman armies) at Suessŭla. In the year 341, fresh advantages were perhaps obtained, but by the Latins ['for Rome was paralyzed by the insurrection of the army.' *Niebuhr*]. A separate peace and separate alliance was concluded between Rome (without Latium) and the Samnites, one of the conditions being, that the subjugation of the Sidicini should be permitted by the Romans.

§ 113. *War with the Latins*, 339—337.

507 The alliance between Rome and Latium, which had
B been dissolved after the capture of the city by the Gauls, was renewed in 357, when the Romans were threatened with fresh danger from the same quarter; but the Latin confederation refused to recognize the supremacy of the Romans; insisting that Rome and Latium should be united into one nation, and that the senate and consulate should be shared between them. The Romans having rejected this demand, a Latin war broke out, which ended in the
C complete subjugation of the Latins. Two consular armies marched through Samnium into Campania (where the legions of the Latins were still stationed near Capua), and, under the command of T. Manlius, obtained, with the assistance of the Samnites, a victory near Mount Vesuvius, for which they were chiefly indebted to the self-sacrifice of P. Decius Mus. Manlius inflicted capital punishment on his son, who, in defiance of his father's prohibition, had slain a Latin general in single combat. A second victory gained by T. Manlius at Trifanum broke up the Latin confederacy, the cities surrendering one by one, and receiving Roman garrisons.

508 Of these cities some were admitted to the full rights of Roman
D citizenship, and from one of them two new tribes were formed; whilst the inhabitants of others were regarded as mere vassals, without the right of voting; and some Latin as well as Campanian places were considered allies of Rome, as the whole of Latium had formerly been. Antium lost its ships of war (the rostra were carried to Rome), and became a Roman colony; the Latins were forbidden to hold diets, and connubium and commercium were permitted only between inhabitants of the same city.

§ 114. *Second War with the Samnites.*

(325—304.)

Causes.—The Romans having established a colony in the Volscian 509
city of Fregellæ, which had been taken and sacked by the Samnites, A
its withdrawal was required by the original conquerors, and refused. About the same time, the Romans demanded satisfaction from Palæopŏlis and Neapŏlis for certain acts of plunder committed in Campania; and this being refused by both cities (by advice of the Tarentines and Samnites), they were invested by Q. Publilius Philo, whose term of consular authority was extended. As proconsul (the first who ever bore that title) Philo obtained possession of Palæopolis by treachery.

In order to divide the forces of the Samnites, the 510
Romans concluded an alliance with the Apulians, and sent B
an army into their country. At the very commencement of this war the Samnites were four times defeated with considerable loss (by Q. Fabius Maximus and L. Papirius Cursor), and sued for peace; but being unable to obtain any reasonable terms from the Romans, they continued the war, and laid siege to Luceria (which had been stormed by Fabius, and was now occupied by a Roman garrison). A Roman force, sent to the relief of the place (under the consuls, T. Veterius and Sp. Postumius), was intercepted and beaten by the Samnite general C. Pontius, in the
narrow passes near Caudium (furcŭlæ Caudīnæ). The C
survivors, unable to extricate themselves from the defile, capitulated on terms, which, considering their helpless position, were not unreasonable, and, having passed under the yoke, withdrew to Capua (321). The Roman senate having refused to ratify this capitulation, the war still continued, at first with various success, but latterly with decided advantage to the Romans.

After the battle of Caudium, Luceria was taken by the Samnites, and subsequently (probably in 315) recaptured by the Romans, and colonized. The war was carried on with various success (victory of the Romans near Saticula, defeat of their army under Q. Fabius Maximus at Lautŭlæ) until the year 314, from which period the advantage was decidedly on the side of the Romans.

Contemporaneous War against the Etruscans, Samnites, 511
Umbrians, and Hernicans.—The Etruscans, who had main- D
tained friendly relations with Rome as long as the Gauls were in their neighborhood, endeavored, now that the

(511) Romans were occupied with the Samnite war, to re-establish
A their ancient boundaries. In pursuance of this plan, they laid siege to the frontier fortress of Sutrium, where they were defeated by Q. Fabius Maximus, who then forced his way through the Ciminian forest, and again defeated the enemy near Perusia (309). For this victory Fabius was not only rewarded with a triumph, but was also, as an especial honor, re-elected consul for the following year. Meanwhile, L. Papirius Cursor (whom Q. Fabius, suppressing his personal dislike, had proclaimed dictator) obtained a victory over the Samnites, near Longula. Fabius then took the command in Samnium (except for a short period, during which he marched against the Umbrians, who were speedily subdued), and overcame (as proconsul)
B the Samnites and Hernicans near Allīfæ (307). Fresh victories were gained by the consuls of the ensuing year —one over the Hernici, and two over the Samnites. It required, however, two more defeats at Bovianum and Tifernum, 305) to convince the Samnites that their only chance of safety consisted in their recognizing the supremacy of Rome. A peace was concluded in 304; the Samnites being permitted to retain their own dominions, but losing their sovereignty over Lucania.

512 The armistice was renewed with the Etruscans (from 309) every
C year. The revolted cities of the Hernicans became municipia [cf. 523, A], without the right of voting, and were deprived of connubium and commercium with the rest of the Hernicans; and the Volscians and Æquians, who had afforded assistance to the Samnites, were compelled to accept the privilege of Roman citizenship, subject to the same degrading conditions.

§ 115. *Third War with the Samnites.*

(298—290.)

513 The Lucanians having applied for aid against the Sam-
D nites, who had invaded their country for the purpose of re-establishing their ancient supremacy, the Romans demanded the immediate evacuation of Lucania; and this being refused, war broke out afresh. The two first campaigns proved disastrous to the Samnites, who then sent an army into Etruria, and formed an alliance with the Etruscans, Umbrians, and Gauls; but in the year 295 they were totally defeated near Sentīnum by Q. Fabius

Maximus (in his fifth consulate), whilst P. Decius Mus (513)
(for the fourth time consul) checked the advance of the A
Gauls by the sacrifice of his life. The war still continued in Samnium : at first the Romans were victorious in three engagements (at Luceria, Aquilonia, and Cominium), but, on the other hand, Q. Fabius Gurges (son of Fabius Maximus) was defeated by C. Pontius. This loss, however, was repaired by the elder Fabius, who, as his son's lieutenant, was once more victorious (it is not known where). The brave C. Pontius was taken prisoner, conveyed in triumph to Rome, and executed! Colonies were B
sent to Venucia to check the alliance between Tarentum and Samnium. The war with the Samnites (290) was terminated by M'. Curius Dentatus; but we are not acquainted with the conditions on which peace was concluded.[1]

The Sabines were attacked by M'. Curius Dentatus (probably because they had assisted the Samnites in the Etruscan campaign), and being speedily subdued, were admitted to the privilege of citizenship without the right of voting. The sovereignty of Rome now extended to the shores of the Adriatic sea.

§ 116. *War with Tarentum and with Pyrrhus of Epirus.*

(282—272.)

Soon after the termination of the Samnite wars, the 514
Romans, interfering in the affairs of Lower Italy, com- C
pelled the Lucanians and Bruttians to raise the siege of Thurii and placed a Roman garrison in the town. A fleet of ten triremes being sent at the same time into the bay of Tarentum to protect Thurii by sea (in contravention of a treaty with the Tarentines, by which the Romans were prohibited from passing the promontory of Lacinium), five vessels were taken by the Tarentines, Thurii stormed, and the garrison expelled. An embassy, sent by the Romans to demand satisfaction, having been insulted by the Tarentines, war was immediately proclaimed.

Being disappointed in their expectation of a general 515
rising of the Italian states, the Tarentines applied for assistance to Pyrrhus, king of Epirus, who entered the

[1] The only notice on this subject is found in Livy, Epitome xi. *Cum Samnitibus pacem petentibus fœdus quarto renovatum est.*

(515) country (by the invitation of most of the Greek cities in
A Lower Italy) with a considerable force, including twenty elephants, to which he was chiefly indebted for a victory on the banks of the Siris, near Heraclēa. Pyrrhus now sent his friend, the orator Cineas, to offer peace to the Romans, provided they were willing to restore to his allies (the Samnites, Lucanians, Apulians, and Bruttians) all the places which they had lost in the war. This proposal having been rejected, by the advice of the blind Appius Claudius, Pyrrhus advanced to Præneste, for the purpose of joining the Etruscans; but finding that they had already concluded a peace with Rome, he retreated to Tarentum, and went into winter quarters.

B The upright C. Fabricius was sent with two other Romans to treat with Pyrrhus for the liberation of his prisoners, who were permitted to visit Rome for the purpose of celebrating the Saturnalia; but being unable to persuade the senate to conclude a peace, they were obliged to return into captivity.

516 The following year, Pyrrhus attacked the places in Apulia, which were garrisoned by Roman soldiers, and compelled the consuls (P. Sulpicius and P. Decius) to retreat, after sustaining considerable loss in a battle fought near Asculum Apulum, 279. In this battle, P. Decius, the grandson, is said to have offered himself as a victim to
C the infernal gods. The victory, however, had been dearly purchased; and this circumstance, joined to the intelligence of an alliance between Rome and Carthage, and the invasion of Macedonia by the Gauls, induced Pyrrhus to conclude an armistice with Rome. An invitation, which he soon afterwards received from the Syracusans, to pass over into Sicily, and protect them from the Carthaginians, was willingly accepted, as affording him an opportunity of evacuating Italy without loss of honor (comp. § 40, II.).

517 At the expiration of three years he was compelled to
D abandon Sicily, taking with him the treasures which he had acquired there, and returned into Italy, for the purpose of protecting the Samnites, Lucanians, and Bruttians, against the attacks of the Romans. In the year 275, his mercenaries having been defeated by M'. Curius Dentatus, near Beneventum, Pyrrhus, leaving a garrison in Tarentum under the command of Milo, set out on his return to Epirus, and soon afterwards was slain at Argos. In the year 272.

Tarentum was treacherously delivered up to the Romans by Milo.

§ 117. *Complete Subjugation of Italy.*

After the termination of the Samnite wars, the Galli Senŏnes, in northern Umbria, who had been persuaded by the Etruscans and Umbrians to assist them in prosecuting the war against the Romans, encountered and utterly defeated a Roman army. But this insult was speedily avenged by the consul, P. Dolabella, who laid waste the whole territory of the Senŏnes, and overthrew (at the lake Vadimon) the Boii, who were hastening to their assistance (283). Peace was granted to the Boii, but the Senŏnes were almost exterminated; the Etruscan cities were subdued one after another; and those which held out the longest, obtained from the Romans (in consequence of the advance of Pyrrhus on Rome) peace on very favorable terms (280). 518 A

The Samnites, Lucanians, and Bruttians, having recognized the supremacy of Rome, after the death of Pyrrhus (272), were compelled to cede a portion of their territory and receive Roman colonists. 519 B

The Picentians were subdued after a battle in 268, and a portion of them transplanted into southern Campania, for the purpose of cutting off the Samnites from the Tyrrhenian sea. 520

The subjugation of the Sallentinians, in Calabria (266), completed the conquest of Italy as far as the rivers Rubicon and Macra. 521

Connection of the conquered States with Rome. 522 C

A. As regards their connection with Rome, the Italian *states* may be divided into three classes.

1. Those nations which had been admitted to the privilege of Roman citizenship, either in an inferior degree without, or to its full extent with, the right of voting. In the latter case, they were incorporated into the Roman tribus.

2. Those which nominally retained their independence, as allies of Rome, being either Latins or confederates in other parts of Italy. Both classes retained their own territorial rights, but were bound to furnish contingents of troops, money, ships, corn, &c. The Italian confederates were those nations which, although subdued, had kept or received back from the conqueror their own codes of laws.

3. The subject States, whose position, as regarded their connection with Rome, varied exceedingly; some (revolted allies, for

example) being deprived of their personal freedom and the honor of serving in war, whilst others were personally free, but in other respects subject to many severe restrictions.

523 B. The circumstances *of single cities* were also of a threefold
A character.

1. Municipia, i. e. cities, the inhabitants of which enjoyed, to a certain extent, the rights of Roman citizenship (either with or without the suffragium).

2. Coloniæ; partly Roman, partly Latin. For the purpose of retaining a conquered people in a state of dependence, the Romans, agreeably to an Italian usage, were accustomed to transplant a certain number of Roman families (at first exclusively patrician, but afterwards plebeian also) into some of the cities, where they formed a standing garrison. To these colonists were assigned the reserved lands, which were generally a third, and sometimes, but very rarely,
B the whole of the conquered territory. A city colonized in this manner had a double population; viz. the original inhabitants, now vassals of Rome, and occupiers of a portion only of the estates which had formerly been their own; and the new colonists, in whom the entire administration of public affairs was vested. This plan at once secured a provision for the poorer Roman families, and relieved Rome of her discontented citizens. After the union of Rome with the Latin confederacy, colonies were sent out by the two nations conjointly. Hence the distinction between Roman and Latin colonies; the former being those which were established previously, and the latter subsequently, to the Latin alliance. The sending out of a colony was consequent on a Senatûs consultum [or, as one word, senatusconsultum], and at a later period on a plebiscītum, and was managed by curatores. The colonists were, as far as possible, volunteers; but if the number of these was insufficient, others were chosen by lot.

C 3. Præfecturæ were municipia to which a præfect, or magistrate charged with the administration of the laws, was sent out every year from Rome, for the purpose of maintaining the supremacy of the Roman code.

§ 118. *Domestic History of Rome during this period.*

524 From the time that the consulate became accessible to plebeians, and the most distinguished men of that class were admitted into the senate, or connected themselves by marriage with patrician families, the offices which had formerly been reserved for patricians gradually fell into plebeian hands, and the importance of the patrician order declined.

525 The first decided step towards a complete equalization
D of the two orders was taken by the plebeian dictator, Q. Publilius Philo (338), who proposed three laws—1. That plebiscīta, emanating from or approved by the senate, should thenceforth have the force of law, even

without the confirmation of the curies. 2. That the curies (525)
should beforehand promise their assent to any law about A
to be passed by the centuries. 3. That one of the censors should always be a plebeian, as had once already been the case under extraordinary circumstances in the year 350. As this legislator was the first plebeian prætor (in 336), it seems probable that the alternate appointment of a patrician and plebeian to that office was secured by one of his laws. The dictatorship had already (soon after the passing of the Licinian laws in 355) been held by a plebeian (compare § 111). By the lex Ogulnia (300), the plebeians were declared admissible to a number of offices under the pontifices and augures. The lex Mænia (286?) ex- B
tended the second Publilian law to the *election* of magistrates, and the curies, whose right of confirmation had become a mere form, ceased to assemble for that purpose. Finally, the dictator, Q. Hortensius (after the secession of the plebs to Mount Janiculum, in consequence of the cruelties practised by their creditors), declared the plebiscīta binding on all classes, even without the assent of the senate (?). Thus the democracy was completely established.

In the year 312 Appius Claudius Cæcus admitted, as censor, the 526
whole body of libertīni into the plebs, to fill up the number of per- C
sons qualified to bear arms, which had been diminished by the war. This arrangement, however, was set aside by his successors (after eight years) in the censorship, L. Fabius and P. Decius, who confined the libertīni (304) to the city tribes As the chief agitator on this occasion, Fabius received the surname of Maximus.

The increased amount of the revenue rendered it necessary to appoint *three* censors, whose discharge of this office qualified them for admission into the senate.

bb. From the subjugation of Italy to the Gracchi.

(266—133.)

Foreign wars.

§ 119. *The first Punic war.*

(264—241.)

1. Campaign in Sicily.

Causes.—1. In order to secure their Sicilian possessions, 527
the Carthaginians had supported the Tarentines in their

(527) struggles against Rome, and thus violated the treaty which
A had been renewed with the Romans in 347. 2. War having been proclaimed by Hiero II., king of Syracuse, against the marauding Mamertines (Sabellian mercenary troops), who had made themselves masters of Messana and the surrounding territory, those freebooters separated into two parties, one of which admitted a Carthaginian garrison into the citadel of Messana, whilst the other applied for assistance to the Romans. Although these disputes had been settled previously to the arrival of the Romans, by a compromise between Hiero and the Mamertines, they landed nevertheless, and were admitted into Messana, where they were blockaded by the Carthaginians and
B Syracusans. The place was, however, soon relieved by Appius Claudius Caudex, who overcame both the blockading armies, and proceeded to lay siege to Syracuse. Most of the cities (sixty-seven), in the interior of Sicily having, in the following year (263), submitted to the Romans, Hiero concluded a peace with the invaders, who were enabled, with this reinforcement, to blockade the Carthaginians (under Hannibal, the son of Gisgon), for seven months in Agrigentum. An army which had marched, under the command of Hanno, to the relief of the place, having been utterly routed, Agrigentum was stormed and sacked, and 25,000 of its inhabitants sold into slavery (262).

528 2. *Sicily the theatre of war by sea and land*
C (260—257).

In order to obtain possession of the maritime towns, which were still in the hands of the Carthaginians, the Romans now determined to create a naval force ; and taking a stranded Carthaginian galley for their model, built and equipped within sixty days a fleet of 130 ships, the command of which was given to C. *Duilius*, who gained the *first naval victory off Mylæ*, in the year 260. For this success, which was obtained by boarding the enemy (on bridges invented by the commander), and thus giving to a naval engagement the character of a battle on land,
D Duilius was honored with a columna rostrata. The Romans now ventured to attack the Carthaginian settlements in Sardinia and Corsica, and to establish themselves in those islands, whilst their land forces subdued one city

after another in Sicily. An attempt was even made, by (528)
M. Atilius Regulus, to transfer the war to Africa itself, A
and thus bring the struggle to a speedy issue. Steering for that coast with a fleet of 330 sail, Regulus fell in with a Carthaginian fleet of 350, off cape Ecnŏmus, on the southern coast of Sicily, and having dispersed them, landed, without opposition, near Clupea in Africa.

3. Campaign in Africa (256—254). 529

Regulus sent back the greater part of his fleet and army, and, with the remainder, subdued almost the whole of the Carthaginian territory, and made preparations for laying
siege to the capital. In their distress, the Carthaginians B
sued for peace, but, being dissatisfied with the unreasonable conditions required by the Romans, they placed their army under the command of the Spartan general Xanthippus, who had recently landed with a body of Greek mercenaries. The Roman soldiers, although superior in numbers, were unable to withstand the assaults of 100 elephants, and fled in confusion, leaving their commander, Regulus, a prisoner in the hands of the Carthaginians. A fresh fleet, dispatched to Africa by the Romans in the same year, annihilated the naval force of the Carthaginians off the Hermæan promontory, and effected a landing
near Clupea. Again the Romans were victorious by land, C
but want of provisions soon compelled them to re-embark on board their ships, most of which were lost in a terrible storm off the coast of Sicily.

4. Sicily a second time the theatre of war by 530
sea and land (254—242).

Another Roman fleet captured Panormus and several other Carthaginian settlements on the coast of Sicily, and plundered the rich coast of Africa, bordering on the lesser Syrtes; but on the homeward voyage it was overtaken by a storm (off the promontory of Palinūrus), and nearly
annihilated. On receiving intelligence of this new calam- D
ity, the Roman senate determined to renounce naval warfare. Meanwhile the war was prosecuted vigorously by land. In the year 250, L. Cæcilius Metellus gained a splendid victory near Panormus, and carried off 104 elephants to adorn his triumph. In consequence of this disaster, the Carthaginians were obliged to abandon the whole of the island except Lilybæum and Drepănum.

(530) Regulus was sent to Rome with proposals of peace, which
A were rejected.[1] On the other hand, the endeavors of the Romans to obtain possession of Lilybæum and Drepănum were rendered abortive by the obstinacy of the besieged; and an attempt to renew the war by sea, ended in the destruction of a Roman fleet commanded by that P. Claudius Pulcher (son of Appius Cæcus), who had ordered the sacred chickens to be thrown into the sea. This loss, the third which they had sustained by sea, induced the Romans
B again to abandon naval warfare. The Carthaginians maintained themselves in Sicily seven years longer, under the command of Hamilcar Barcas (father of the renowned Hannibal), who principally occupied the fortress of Eryx. At length, in the year 242, the war was terminated by a decisive victory gained by a Roman fleet (which had been fitted out by private enterprise, and placed under the command of the consul, C. Lutatius Catulus), over the Carthaginian fleet commanded by Hanno, near the Ægatian islands. The exhausted condition of both nations now rendered them desirous of peace, which was concluded on the following terms:—the Carthaginians renounced all authority over Sicily and the adjacent islands, delivered up the Roman prisoners without ransom, and engaged to pay
C a sum of 3200 talents (241). The whole of Sicily, with the exception of the Syracusan possessions, became the first Roman province.

531 A few years later (238), the Romans, availing themselves of the confusion occasioned by the war of the Carthaginian mercenaries (see § 40, iii.), took possession of Sardinia and Corsica, which, in all probability, they had never entirely abandoned since their first settlement in those islands.

§ 120. *War with the Illyrians.*

(230—228.)

532 Having in vain demanded satisfaction from the Illyrian queen, Teuta, for acts of piracy committed in the Ionian

[1] The death of Regulus, by torture, after his return to Carthage, is not mentioned by Polybius, and is pronounced by Dion Cassius to be a mere legend.

sea, the Romans, after the murder of one of their ambassadors, declared war against the Illyrians. After the loss of several cities, which soon yielded to the combined forces of the Romans, and the Illyrian traitor, Demetrius, the queen concluded a peace with the invaders, pledging herself to pay a considerable tribute, to resign the greater part of her dominions, and to confine the navigation of her fleets within very narrow limits. (532) A

533 B In gratitude for their deliverance from Illyrian piracy, the Greeks conferred on the Romans the privilege of taking part in the Isthmian games, and the Eleusinian mysteries, together with the freedom of the city of Athens.

§ 121. *Conquest of Cisalpine Gaul.*

534 The distribution among the plebeians (in consequence of the agrarian law of the tribune, C. Flaminius), of the ager Picenus, which had been forcibly taken from the Senones, occasioned a general rising of the Boii, Insŭbres, and transalpine Gæsatæ (226). The insurgents penetrated into Etruria, where they defeated a prætorian army (near Fæsŭlæ?), but were soon afterwards attacked near Telamon by both the consuls, and utterly routed. C After the defeat of the Boii, the Romans prosecuted the war on the other side of the Padus, in the territory of the Insŭbres, where they gained fresh victories (Flaminius, on the river Addua; Cl. Marcellus near Clastidium, on the Padus), took the most important cities of the Insŭbres (Mediolanum, Comum), and subdued the whole of Gallia Cisalpina (221). For the security of this newly-acquried territory colonies were established in Placentia and Cremona.

535 From the year 238 to 230 the Romans were engaged in wars with the Ligurians, but their campaigns, although repeated almost annually during the whole of that period, produced as yet no decided advantage.

§ 122. *Second Punic War.*

(218—201.)

Pedigree of the Scipios.

A L. Cornelius Scipio

Cn. Cornelius Scipio Calvus. — P. Cornelius Scipio.

Cn. Cornelius Scipio Calvus: His grandson P. Cornelius Scipio Nasīca — his son P. Corn. Sc. Nasica Serapio.

P. Cornelius Scipio: P. Corn. Scipio Afric. Major — L. Corn. Scipio Asiaticus

P. Cornelius Scipio Nasīca married the daughter of P. Corn. Scipio Afric. Major.

P. Corn. Scipio Afric. Major: a son; who adopted P. Corn. Scipio, son of Paulus Æmilius (thence surnamed Æmilianus), Africanus Minor, Numantinus. — Cornelia, the mother of the two Gracchi.

536 Causes.—With the view of indemnifying his native
B city for the loss of her best provinces, Sicily and Sardinia, Hamilcar Barcas had commenced the subjugation of Spain, which was carried on by his son-in-law, Hasdrŭbal, until his progress was stopped by the conclusion of a treaty with the Romans, in which he pledged himself not to pass the Iberus, and to respect Saguntum as an ally of Rome. After the assassination of Hasdrubal, the command of the army devolved on Hannibal, son of Hamilcar Barcas, who took Saguntum, after a siege of eight months. The
C result of this act of aggression was a war, which Hannibal at once resolved to carry into Italy; and leaving his brother, Hasdrubal, in Spain, he crossed the Pyrenees (after subduing all the nations between the Iberus and those mountains), traversed southern Gaul, forced a passage through the Rhodănus [*Rhone*], crossed the Alps in fifteen days (by the Little S. Bernard), and, in the month of October, 218, appeared in Italy with 20,000 infantry, 6000 cavalry, and a few elephants.

537 The Romans had resolved, after the capture of Saguntum, to attack
D the Carthaginians both in Spain and Africa. In pursuance of this plan, one of the consuls, Tib. Sempronius, was dispatched into Sicily (in the year 218), with orders to effect a landing on the African coast, whilst the other, P. Cornelius Scipio, marched into Spain. Learning, however, on his arrival at Massilia, that Hannibal had

already advanced as far as Gaul, Scipio sent his brother, Cneius Scipio, into Spain, and himself returned to Italy, to await the arrival of Hannibal.

A. The war in Italy (218—203). 538

In the year 218, Hannibal overthrew both the consuls; A
P. Cornelius Scipio on the banks of the Ticīnus, and afterwards (with the aid of a Gallic reinforcement), Tib. Sempronius Longus, on the Trebia. The latter of these generals had been recalled from Sicily, and had effected a junction with the remnant of Scipio's beaten army. In the year 217 Hannibal traversed the marshes on the banks of the Arnus, and gained a third victory near the lake Trasimēnus, over the raw legions of the consul Flaminius, who was slain with most of his soldiers. Instead of ad- B
vancing at once on Rome, Hannibal now marched into Apulia and thence into Campania, in the hope of inducing the allies of Rome to revolt. These movements were closely watched by the dictator, Q. Fabius, who hoped, by avoiding an engagement, to weary out the enemy (hence his surname of Cunctator [*the Delayer*]). In the year 216 Hannibal forced the consuls, C. Terentinus Varro, and L, Æmilius Paulus, to give him battle near Cannæ, and obtained a decisive victory through the superiority of his cavalry. Æmilius Paulus with 40,000 Romans and allies C
lay dead on the field. The most important result of this victory was the accession to the Carthaginian cause of the nations and cities of central and lower Italy, together with the Campanians and Samnites, none remaining faithful to the Romans except the Latins and a few insulated cities of central and lower Italy. The Romans nevertheless strained every nerve to equip a fresh army, with which Q. Fabius Maximus and M. Claudius Marcellus checked the advance of Hannibal in Campania, defeated him twice near Nola, forced him to retreat still further southwards, and endeavored to bring back the revolted states to their allegiance.

Whilst Hannibal was occupied in besieging Tarentum (which 539
surrendered, with the exception of the citadel), the city of Capua,
where he had established his head quarters,[1] was closely invested D

[1] Livy's account of the enervation of Hannibal's army by the luxuries of Capua is worthy of little credit; for the troops, although

(539) by a Roman army. On receiving this intelligence, Hannibal, who
A had failed in his attempts to reduce the citadel of Tarentum, returned into Campania, attacked the blockading army, and spread universal consternation by advancing almost to the gates of Rome[2] (Hannibal ante portas!). Finding however that no relief could be afforded to Capua, the Carthaginian leader fell back on Bruttium, and the Romans, storming Capua, avenged themselves by putting to death seventy of her senators. Meanwhile, the war was prosecuted with various success in the south of Italy, where Marcellus was three times victorious in one year (209), but in the following he was drawn into an ambuscade by Hannibal, and lost his life. Tarentum was retaken by Fabius.

540 Being unsupported by the government at home through
B the intrigues of his adversary Hanno, Hannibal endeavored to obtain the assistance of foreign powers. But Philip III., king of Macedonia, with whom he had concluded an alliance immediately after the battle of Cannæ, was prevented from landing in Italy by a Roman fleet which cruised in the Ionian sea; and at the same time Syracuse, where the Carthaginian party had obtained the ascendency, was blockaded by sea and land by M. Claudius Marcellus, and after an obstinate defence, which lasted two years, was taken (212) by means of the engines invented by Archimēdēs, among which, if we may
C believe tradition, were several burning glasses. Agrigentum having also been betrayed into the hands of the Romans, the remaining cities surrendered voluntarily, and in the year 210 the whole of Sicily became a Roman province. It was at length resolved by Hannibal to recall the Carthaginian troops from Spain, where they were stationed under the command of his brothers, Hasdrubal
D and Mago. The former of these generals crossed the Alps, but, before he could join his brother, he was attacked on the banks of the Metaurus by both the consuls of the year 210 (M. Livius Salinator and C. Claudius Nero, the latter of whom had misled Hannibal by the abandonment of his camp near Canusium), his army completely routed, and himself slain. Mago, who had landed in Liguria from the Balearic islands, after struggling for three years

---

unsupported by the Carthaginian government, remained in Italy fourteen years after the capture of that city.—*Niebuhr*.

[2] The story of a battle before the gates of Rome being twice prevented by a storm is a mere poetical fiction.—*Niebuhr*.

against the Romans without any important result, was (540)
recalled by the Carthaginian government, together with A
Hannibal, whose operations since the battle of the Metaurus had been restricted to Bruttium. Mago died on the passage of wounds received in his Italian campaign.

B. Contemporaneous war in Spain (218—206). 541
Cn. Scipio, supported by several Spanish tribes, which were struggling to liberate themselves from the Punic yoke, opened the campaign with the conquest of the whole line of coast between the Pyrenees and the Ebro. In the second year of the war, Publius Scipio arrived in Spain; and for six years the two brothers fought with uniform success against Hasdrubal and his brother Mago (who had been sent from Carthage to his assistance). At B
this period, nearly the whole of Spain was in the hands of the Romans, but the brothers having imprudently divided their forces (in 211), with the view of ending the war at once by a simultaneous attack on the two hostile armies, both were surrounded by the Carthaginians and Numidians (under Masinissa), themselves slain, and their armies almost annihilated. The Carthaginians now commenced the re-conquest of the revolted Spanish provinces, but the arrival of P. Cornelius Scipio the younger (afterwards Africanus), gave another direction to the war. After C
storming New Carthage, the head-quarters of the Carthaginian army, Scipio, who had made himself exceedingly popular among the Spanish tribes, overthrew Hasdrubal (near Bæcula, to the north of the Bætis [*Guadalquiver*]), and after the departure of that general gained a victory on the same spot over Mago, who retreated to Cades, and eventually followed his colleague into Italy. Spain was D
now (206) divided by the Romans into two provinces, which they named Hispania Citerior and Hispania Ulterior. Scipio, who, on his return to Rome, had been elected consul, instead of receiving Africa as his province (the opposition of the veteran generals rendering such an arrangement impossible), was nominated governor of Sicily, permission being at the same time granted him to transport an army of volunteers into Africa.

C. Conclusion of the war in Africa (204—202). 542
With this force and the ships of his allies, Scipio (in

(542) 204) effected a landing in Africa, where he was joined by
A Masinissa, king of the eastern Numidians, who had been
deprived of his kingdom by Syphax, king of western
Numidia. As the husband of Sophonisba, daughter of
Hasdrubal, Syphax allied himself to the Carthaginians,
and in conjunction with his father-in-law planned an attack
on the Roman camp. But their design was anticipated by
Scipio and Masinissa, who burnt the enemy's camp, and
annihilated the combined Punic and Numidian forces.
Syphax then retreated, but was pursued into his own
B dominions and taken prisoner. Several cities having
fallen, and the capital itself being threatened by the united
forces of Scipio and Masinissa, the Carthaginian government deemed it advisable to recall Hannibal and Mago from Italy. The latter of these generals died, as we have already mentioned, on the voyage. Hannibal, after fruitless endeavors to negotiate a peace, sustained a signal defeat near Zama, on the 19th October, 202. Carthage, being now blockaded by sea and land, was compelled to accept peace on the following terms:—All her ships of war (except ten triremes) and elephants were to be delivered up to the Romans, 10,000 talents to be paid within fifty years, and no war to be undertaken without the consent of Rome.

543 Masinissa was rewarded with the sovereignty of the two Numi-
dias. Scipio obtained a triumph which was conducted on a scale
C of unprecedented magnificence, Syphax, the captive monarch walking in the procession. He was also honored with the surname of Africanus (the first instance of such a name being bestowed in commemoration of a victory). The states of Lower Italy, which had revolted to Hannibal, were reduced for the most part to the condition of vassalage.

§ 123. *The Two Wars against Philip III., king of Macedonia.*

544 Having thus established on a firm basis their supremacy
D in the west, the Romans commenced a struggle for preponderance in the east, for which the protection of the Greeks furnished them with a convenient pretext. The foresight with which these plans of conquest were laid,

and the patience displayed in the execution of them, were the best security for the durability of their triumphs.

First Macedonian war (214—204). 545

A Philip of Macedonia having formed an alliance with Hannibal [cf. 540, B], the Romans endeavored to defeat his ambitious projects in Illyria; but being unable to attain this object, they courted the friendship of Philip's enemies, the warlike Ætolians, with their allies, the Eleans and Lacedæmonians, Attalus of Pergamus, and the Messenians, who had been ill-treated by the Macedonian king. By thus creating a diversion, they hoped to find sufficient employment for Philip at home, and thus to prevent his passing over into Italy. A protracted war between Philip and the Ætolians with their respective allies (in which the Romans latterly took hardly any part), ended in a general peace (204), which contained the seeds of fresh hostilities, in the provision that neither party should make war on the allies of the other.

Second Macedonian war (200—197). 546

B Notwithstanding this agreement with the Romans, Philip continued to persecute their allies, the Illyrians, and sent to the assistance of the Carthaginians a body of auxiliaries, who fought against Scipio in the battle of Zama. After the conclusion of the second Punic war, the Romans availed themselves of an opportunity of punishing Philip, afforded by the applications made to them by Attalus, king of Pergamus, and the republic of Rhodes, for protection against his tyranny. The war nevertheless was prosecuted with little vigor or success, until the time of T. Quinctius Flaminius (son of that Flaminius who was slain in the battle of the Trasimene lake). This C general soon made himself master of the whole of Epirus, compelled the Achæan league to form an alliance with the Romans, and, being supported by the most important Grecian states, put an end to the war (in 197), by the victory of Cynoscephălē, in Thessaly. Philip was compelled to renounce the Hegemony of Greece, and to evacuate all the Greek districts and towns of which he had taken possession. These places were proclaimed free by Flaminius at the Isthmian games in 196.

547 D Before he quitted Greece, Flaminius compelled the tyrant Nabis to deliver up the maritime cities of Laconia and his possessions in Crete; but he was still allowed to exercise some authority, as a counterpoise to the influence of the Achæans.

§ 124. *War with Antiochus III. of Syria.*

(192—190.)

For the Syrian war, see § 80.

548 During the war in Asia, the Ætolians, encouraged by a false
A report of the total defeat of L. Scipio, had violated the armistice and renewed the war with the Romans. They were however speedily subdued (by the consul M. Fulvius Nobilior), and compelled to recognize the supremacy of Rome.

The two Scipios were charged by the tribunes of the people (at the instance of M. Porcius Cato Censorius), with having received bribes from Antiochus during the negotiations for peace. Publius retired to his estate near Linternum, where he died in the year 185. Lucius was condemned to pay a multa, for the discharge of which his property was sold.

B The Romans having called on Antiochus to deliver up Hannibal, that general fled to Prusias, king of Bithynia, and being apprehensive of treachery on the part of his new protector, he swallowed poison in the year 183.

§ 125. *Third Macedonian war.*

(171—168.)

549 Philip III., who had been greatly irritated by the
C vexatious tyranny of the Romans, was engaged in preparations for a new war, for the purpose of recovering the dominions of which he had been despoiled, when death put an end to his projects. The preparations were continued by his son and successor Perseus, a man of undecided character, who endeavored to strengthen his cause by alliances with various nations in Greece, Illyria, Rhodes, Syria, &c., but was often impeded by his own avarice and cruelty. The breaking out of war was precipitated by the conduct of a crafty and contemptible prince, named Euměnes, of Pergamus, who, fearing for his Thracian possessions, went to Rome and disclosed the
D proceedings of Perseus to the senate. The first three campaigns were indecisive; but discipline having been restored by the appointment to the command-in-chief of L. Æmilius Paulus (son of the general who fell at Cannæ), a battle was fought at Pydna, which lasted only one hour, and decided the fate of the Macedonian monarchy. Perseus, who had fled to Samothrace at the

commencement of the engagement, was compelled to sur- (549)
render, and died in captivity at Alba. With a show of A
generosity the Romans declared Macedonia a free state, but in order to prepare the country for submission to their sovereign rule, they divided it into four districts, which were precluded from connubium and commercium with one another, and required to pay the half of the tribute hitherto exacted. The booty brought by Æmilius to Rome was so enormous, that from that time until the reign of Augustus no direct taxes were paid by the Roman citizens; but the effect of this apparent indulgence was to deprive the people of the means of resistance which they had hitherto possessed in refusing the tribute, and thus to throw the whole management of foreign affairs into the hands of the senate.

Illyria (after the defeat of king Genthius) was divided, 550
as a punishment for its alliance with Perseus, into three B
districts; whilst in Epirus, which had yielded to the Romans almost without striking a blow, seventy cities were sacked in *one* day, and 150,000 inhabitants sold into slavery. About 1000 of the principal Achæans (among whom was Polybius), being falsely accused by a party of traitors (headed by Callicrătes) of attachment to the cause of Perseus, were summoned to Rome (ostensibly that they might purge themselves from the charge) and detained there, without being allowed a hearing, for seventeen years, at the end of which time (in 151), the 300 who still survived were permitted to return to their own country.

Thenceforward there existed a predominant Roman C
party in each of the Grecian cities; and the disputes of these states with one another were fostered by the Romans, that they might have a pretence for acting the part of arbitrators, as they had lately done in Syria and Egypt.

Antiochus IV. Epiphanes was compelled by the Romans to 551
abandon his warlike designs on Egypt. After his death, Demetrius, the rightful heir to the throne, was detained at Rome as a hostage, and Antiochus V., a boy of nine years old, appointed king in his room, that the Romans might be enabled to act as his guardians. Demetrius, however, escaped and regained possession of his throne. With the view of weakening Egypt, the Romans divided the sovereignty of that country between two brothers, Philomētor and Physcon.

§ 126. *The last Wars with Macedonia and Greece.*

552 Relying on the discontent occasioned by the abolition of
A the royal authority in Macedonia and the measures generally adopted by the Romans, one Andriscus (who gave himself out as Philip, the brother and adopted son of Perseus, and thence is commonly named Pseudo-Philippus), made an attempt to re-establish the Macedonian monarchy. After taking possession of the whole of Macedonia, and making two inroads into Thessaly, the impostor was defeated in two battles by the Roman prætor, Q. Cæcilius Metellus, and taken prisoner. As a punishment for its revolt, Macedonia was made a Roman province in the year **148**.

553 Of the thousand Achæans who had been sent to Rome,
B three hundred at length returned to their country after a captivity of seventeen years; amongst them were Critolaus and Diæus, who endeavored to persuade their countrymen to resist the Romans; upon this the latter, availing themselves of a dispute between the Achæan league and Sparta (for the territory of Belmina), declared the league dissolved. Critolaus now came forward in the character of demagogue, and proclaimed war against Sparta; but was utterly defeated near Scarphea in Locris, by Metellus (who had arrived in that country after the destruction of the Mace-
C donian monarchy). Critolaus himself disappeared during the engagement. The more sensible among the Achæans now sued for peace, but the party of Critolaus, headed by Diæus, persisted in carrying on the war. Metellus was superseded by the barbarian L. Mummius, who, after gaining a victory at Leucopĕtra on the isthmus, sacked and burnt the city of Corinth, partly plundered and partly destroyed the other towns, which had taken part against Rome, and carried off the fairest works of Grecian art to adorn his triumph. In the year **146**, Hellas, with the Peloponnesus, was proclaimed a Roman province, under the name of Achaia, by ten commissioners sent from Rome for that purpose.

§ 127. *The Third Punic war.*

(150—146.)

554 The Carthaginians having made war on Masinissa without the permission of the Romans, it was resolved by the

Roman senate, on the motion of M. Porcius Cato (whose mediation had been rejected by the Carthaginians), in opposition to the opinion of P. Corn. Scipio Nasīca, to declare the peace at an end. The Roman consuls then compelled the Carthaginians to give up all their ships and weapons; and having thus disarmed them, required them to abandon their city and build another, two miles from the sea. In their despair the Carthaginians offered a furious resistance, which continued for two years. At the end of that time P. Corn. Scipio Africanus (147) being appointed commander-in-chief, cut off all communication by land with the besieged city by establishing an intrenched camp on the isthmus, and at the same time blockaded the harbor by means of a dam. In the follow- B
ing year the inhabitants, worn out by famine, surrendered after bravely fighting from street to street for six days. The city was then plundered and destroyed; and the whole of the Carthaginian empire, except that portion which belonged to Numidia, became a Roman province, under the name of Africa, with Utīca for its capital.

§ 128. *Further Wars in Spain.*

(200—133.)

Although the Romans had been accustomed since the 555
year 206 to consider Spain as one of their provinces, it C
was full 200 years from the first invasion before they obtained quiet possession of the peninsula, the last Cantabrians having yielded to Augustus B. C. 19. Until 133 they were perpetually occupied in putting down revolts of the Spanish tribes. A brilliant victory over the Celtibēri (195) placed the whole of Spain on this side the Ibērus at the disposal of the consul M. Porcius Cato, who commanded the inhabitants of all the towns to demolish their walls on the same day. The war nevertheless continued, D
not only with the Lusitani in further Spain, but with the Celtiberi on this side the river—and from 153 to 133 without intermission. The most determined opposition was offered by the Lusitani until the death of their leader Viriāthus, a brave herdsman, who was assassinated during sleep by his faithless comrades. The war which was still carried on successfully by the Celtiberians, and

(555) especially by the Numantians, was at last terminated by P.
A Cornelius Scipio Æmilius Africanus Minor, who destroyed the fortress of Numantia on the Durius after a siege of fifteen months (133). Hence his surname of Numantīnus. From that time the whole of Spain, with the exception of the northern highlands, became subject to the dominion of the Romans.

§ 129. *Wars against the Gauls, Ligurians, Carnians, and Istrians.*

556 During the progress of these events in Spain the
B Romans were constantly engaged in struggles with the Cisalpine Gauls, who had been subdued previously to the second Punic war, and with the Ligurians. The result of these disputes was the subjugation of the district termed "Provincia" in Transalpine Gaul.

557 During the second Punic war the Gauls had attached themselves to Hannibal. After the conclusion of that war, the Gallic and Ligurian campaigns were repeated almost annually; the former for eighteen (200—182), and the latter for forty years (193—154). The aid given by the Romans to the city of Massilia against the neighboring Gallic tribes afforded them an opportunity of making conquests also in Transalpine Gaul, where the first Roman colonies,
C Aquæ Sextiæ and Narbo, were established in 123. Fresh conquests speedily followed their interference in the disputes of the Gallic tribes—the Arverni became dependent on Rome under the name of allies, and the Allobrŏges Roman subjects. The territories thus acquired formed a Roman province, which in later times was denominated pre-eminently "Provincia" (hence the modern name of Provence).

The Carnians, Istrians, and Dalmatians, were also subjugated (colony of Aquileia founded), as well as the Balearic islands.

§ 130. *First Insurrection of the Slaves in Sicily.*

(136—131.)

558 The cruelties to which they were subjected in Sicily
D occasioned a general insurrection of the slaves, who invited the Syrian Eunus to become their king (Antiochus). At the head of 70,000 men, this leader made head for a while against the Roman armies; but the reduction of their principal fortresses, Tauromenium and Enna (by Rupilius),

and the capture of Eunus himself at length put an end to the insurrection.

§ 131. *Domestic History during this period.*

During this period the republic reached its highest state 559
of development. The distinction between patricians and A
plebeians had become obsolete (hence since the year 174 both consuls had frequently been plebeians), and the struggles between the hereditary nobility and commons were at an end. The term "Populus" now comprehended the entire population (the comitia centuriata), including of course the plebs. On the other hand, there arose a new order of nobility, consisting of persons whose ancestors had filled curule offices (the consulate, prætorship, ædileship). In contradistinction to these *nobiles* or *optimates*, B
the families which had never produced any magistrates of the higher order were termed *ignobiles* or *obscuri*, and their members *homines novi*. The nobles not only endeavored, like the patricians at an earlier period, to retain as far as possible all the higher offices among themselves, but were anxious also to give them more importance and a more extensive sphere of action (the censorship and auspices).

The exclusion of all but the richest families from this order was 560
the necessary consequence of a practice, which prevailed from the C
time of the first Punic war, of defraying the expenses of the public games, not out of the exchequer, but from the private resources of the ædiles. Thus none but wealthy men were admissible to the ædileship, which was the first step to the higher offices of state. The equestrian dignity was also in the hands of the rich, the rank having no longer any connection with actual military service in the cavalry, but belonging to all who possessed a certain census equester (1 mill. asses). Thus there arose eventually a distinction between equites and ordo equester. The knights, on account of their pecuniary transactions and the farming of the public revenues, were in a variety of ways dependent on the senate and the censors, and were obliged in consequence to take part with the optimates; as were also the allies, whose affairs were administered by the senate.

Increase in the number of Prætors.—In addition 561
to the prætor urbanus, a second prætor was appointed in D
242, for the settlement of disputes between foreigners resident at Rome and between foreigners and Roman citizens. Four prætors were soon added for the administration of

(561) the provinces—viz. two for Sicily and Sardinia (in 227),
A and two for the two Spains (199). But latterly all these magistrates remained at Rome, during their year of office, as presidents of the four *standing* criminal tribunals (quæstiones perpetuæ), which had been established for the trial of the more common offences, in the room of the comitia centuriata. At the commencement of their second year the whole body of prætors, who then assumed the title of proprætors, set out for the provinces assigned to them by lot, accompanied by legates and quæstors.

The four quæstiones perpetuæ (from 144) were—1. De repetundis—concerning extortion; 2, de ambitu—obtaining office by undue means; 3, de majestate—treason; 4, de peculatu—peculation of public moneys.

562 Administration of the Provinces.

B a. *Meaning of the term "province."*—A province comprehended, strictly speaking, only those cities of a conquered country which had been reduced to the condition of subject and tributary states; consequently, the imperium of the prætor did not extend to those which had either always retained their independence and been admitted into the rank of allies, or which, after their subjugation, had been restored to freedom, or had received extraordinary privileges, such as exemption from taxes and other burdens. Colonies were also gradually established in the provinces; and these, whether Roman or Latin, were exempted from the imperium of the prætor.

C b. *Constitution of the provincial government.*—As a general rule, the provinces received, immediately after their subjugation, a form of constitution (forma) from the hands of the conqueror, or through a commission of ten senators. The duty of the provincial governor was threefold. 1. The executive government; 2, police and the administration of justice; 3, command-in-chief of the garrisons established in the country.

c. *Taxation in the provinces.*—The provincial imposts were different in different provinces, but consisted generally of a poll-tax and property-tax; the latter being paid partly in coin and partly by a tithe of the produce. This tax was not collected immediately by the government, but farmed out to private speculators. To these may be added money paid for the use of the public pastures, duties, taxes on mines, and salt works, &c. The provincials were never required to serve in the army, except in cases of extraordinary emergency. The garrisons were always sent out from Rome.

563 Relations of Rome with other free States.

D These relations were based on treaties, concluded either on equal terms (æquo fœdere) with nations previously unconnected with the Romans, or which had made a successful stand against them, or on unequal terms (fœdere iniquo) with weaker states; for instance, with Carthage, after the first and second Punic wars. Alliances were also concluded, on equal or unequal terms, with foreign sovereigns, who were styled the friends and allies of the Roman people.

Attempts were made to check the progress of luxury 564
and the increasing adoption of foreign manners, by the A
enactment of laws (respecting female ornament, the expenditure at feasts, the senatus consultum de Bacchanalibus), and by severe censors; among whom M. Portius Cato Censorius was the most conspicuous.

(For the lex annalis, see § 103.) The tribes were increased to thirty-five.

cc. From the Gracchi to the autocracy of Augustus, 133—30. Decline and Fall of the Republic.

Civil and Foreign Wars.

§ 132. *The two Gracchi.*

(133—121.)

The population of Rome consisted at this period of the 565
nobiles (who had enriched themselves by holding lucrative B
offices at home and in the provinces), and an indolent and poverty-stricken commonalty. The former were tenants of the whole ager publicus; and the free peasantry, ground down by military service and compelled by absolute want to sell their birthright, were gradually disappearing. Under these circumstances, a tribune of the people, named Tiberius Sempronius Gracchus, revived in the year 133 an obsolete agrarian law of Licinius, by which it was enacted that no individual should hold more than 500 jugera of ager publicus. Half the quantity was allowed in addition
for each non-emancipated son. The remainder was to be C
restored to the state (a reasonable compensation being made for buildings erected thereon), and to be divided as a fief among the poorer classes. One of the tribunes (M. Octavius), who had been persuaded by the senate to interpose his veto, having been removed from office, the project of law was adopted by the tribus, and three commissioners appointed to carry out its provisions. Attalus III., king of Pergamus, who had bequeathed his kingdom to the Roman people, dying about the same time, Tiberius proposed that his treasures, instead of being intrusted to the senate for distribution, should be divided among the people, for the purpose of forming agricultural establishments on the farms about to be assigned to them.

(565) In the following year, Tiberius, whose re-election was
A eagerly desired by the people, was assassinated, with 300 of his adherents, by the senators, at the instigation of P. Corn. Scipio Nasīca Serapio. Under color of an embassy, Scipio Nasica was banished into Asia, where Aristonīcus, a pretended son of Eumĕnes, who was endeavoring to establish his claims to the throne of Pergamus, was overthrown by the consul Perperna. Asia Propria a Roman province.

566 The commissioners for carrying out the agrarian law of Gracchus, succeeded at length in effecting a partial distribution of the land. Scipio Africanus Minor, the leader of the Optimates, who had successfully resisted the proposal of Papirius Carbo, that the same individual should be permitted to hold the office of tribune for several successive years, was soon afterwards found dead in his bed[1] (129).

567 Caius Sempronius Gracchus (who had been em-
B ployed by the senate for three years as quæstor in Sicily) revived, as tribune, the agrarian law of his brother, with the addition, that a certain number of estates belonging to the republic should be annually divided among the poor. By this and similar proposals, Gracchus secured the favor of the people, and, being a second time elected tribune, obtained the passing of a lex judiciaria, by which the judicial authority was transferred from the senate to the knights; the former being deemed unfit for the office on account of the partiality which they had displayed towards
C their own order. Another candidate for popular favor was brought forward by the senate in the person of the tribune, M. Livius Drusus, whose efforts to outbid his rival were aided by the circumstance of C. Gracchus being sent to Carthage to establish a colony. After his return, Gracchus brought forward a lex de suffragiis sociorum, by which it was proposed to grant the full privileges of Roman citizenship to the Latins, and perhaps the right of suffrage to all the Italian allies; but the passing of this law was arrested by the veto of Livius Drusus. In the year 122, Gracchus and 3000 of his adherents lost their lives in a brawl with the aristocrats, occasioned by the assassination of a lictor. (His head weighed against gold —a temple of Concordia built!)

---

[1] F. D. Gerlach, "*Historical Studies*" [p. 201—254], shows that Scipio was murdered, the assassin being probaby C. Papirius Carbo.

The Optimates availed themselves of this victory over the com- 568
mons to neutralize the agrarian law of Gracchus, by allowing the A
poor to sell the portions of land allotted to them ; and when by these means the rich had obtained possession of all the landed property, the lex Thoria was passed, prohibiting any further distribution of the ager publicus. The pauper citizens, whose numbers were greatly increased by this measure, were now supported principally by bribes received from the rich, who exercised unlimited control over the votes given by their dependents at the comitia. This influence was restricted by a law proposed by C. Marius, a homo novus [cf. 559, B], who had been elected tribune ; but the bribery still continued.

§ 133. *The War with Jugurtha.*

(112—106.)

Micipsa, the son of Masinissa, had divided his kingdom 569
of Numidia between his sons Hiempsal and Adherbal, and B
his adopted son Jugurtha. In the year 116, Jugurtha put Hiempsal to death, and made war on Adherbal, who appealed to the Romans. A partition of the kingdom between Jugurtha and Adherbal was proposed by those members of the senate who had been bribed by the former; but Jugurtha, in defiance of this intervention, attacked Adherbal, blockaded him in his capital, Cirta, took him prisoner, and put him to death. The Romans now declared war against Jugurtha, at the instance of C. Memmius; but the African prince purchased terms of peace from the consul L. Calpurnius Piso (111), which Memmius refused
to ratify. Jugurtha was now summoned to appear at C
Rome, where he assassinated a grandson of Masinissa (named Massiva), who laid claim to the Numidian empire as heir of his grandfather. This daring act produced a renewal of the war, in which the Romans were at first unsuccessful, until the appointment to the chief command of Q. Cæcilius Metellus, who took C. Marius with him as his lieutenant; and, rejecting all the overtures of Jugurtha, overthrew him in a battle, ravaged his dominions, and compelled him to fly for refuge to his father-in-law
Bocchus, king of Mauritania. Meanwhile, the intrigues of D
Marius at Rome had obtained for him the consulate and chief command of the army in Numidia. He overthrew the two kings near Cirta (capite censi in the legions), and his quæstor, L. Cornelius Sulla, induced Bocchus to deliver up Jugurtha (106), who was exhibited in chains in the triumphal procession of Marius, and then starved to

A death in prison. Numidia was divided between Bocchus and the descendants of Masinissa.

§ 134. *War with the Cimbri and Teutŏnēs.*

(113—101.)

570 A short time before the Jugurthine war, the Cimbri, a German race, had wandered from their home (on the shores of the Baltic ?) as far as Styria, and overthrown a Roman army (under Cn. Papirius Carbo) near Noreia. Thence they directed their march westwards, and skirting the northern edge of the Alps reached the Rhine, where they united their forces with those of the Teutŏnes (Tigurīni and Ambrōnes) and demanded from the Romans a grant
B of territory in Gaul. This being refused, they attacked and routed three Roman armies in Gaul, the last of which is reported to have lost 120,000 men. They then separated, and were cut off in detail by C. Marius, who held the consulate for four successive years (104—101). The Teutŏnes (and Ambrōnes) were defeated near Aquæ Sextiæ in 102, and their leader Teutoboch taken; and the Cimbri, who had entered Italy from Rhætia, and defeated the consul Catulus on the Athesis, were overthrown
C near Vercellæ (in campis Raudiis) in the year 101. The number of slain and prisoners amounted in each of the battles to 100,000. Marius was rewarded with a triumph, elected consul for the sixth time (100), and honored with the title of third founder of the city.

§ 135. *Second Insurrection of the Slaves in Sicily.*

(103—99.)

571 The Roman prætor in Sicily having only partially car-
D ried into effect a decree of the senate, by which freedom was granted to those persons who were unjustly detained in slavery, a new servile war broke out, which seems to have cost a million of slaves their lives, and was terminated, after several skirmishes, by a decisive battle.

§ 136. *To the Social War.*

(100—91.)

572 From the time of his sixth consulate, Marius had been steadily endeavoring by every means in his power to

undermine the influence of the senate and place himself (572)
at the head of affairs. His first step was to persuade L. A
Apuleius Saturninus, a wretch who had obtained the tribunate by murder, to propose a distribution of land among his veterans (chiefly Italian allies); the senators being, at the same time, warned of the consequences which would follow the rejection of his plan. Q. Metellus Numidicus, who stood alone as an opponent of this proposal, was banished to Rhodes. The assassination of the consul elect (for the year 99), C. Memmius (to make way for Glaucia, a friend of Saturninus), occasioned an insurrection, in which both lost their lives.

There was now a cessation of domestic feuds, until the B
breaking out of a civil war occasioned by the jealousy between Marius and Sulla, which had gone on increasing since the conclusion of the Jugurthine war. The commencement of actual hostilities was, however, deferred in consequence of an unexpected quarrel with the Italian confederates.

Metellus having been recalled in 99, Marius, as the only means of 573
sustaining his declining influence, travelled into Asia, and persuaded Mithridates, king of Pontus, to make war on the Romans. Mithridates commenced his conquests in Asia Minor with the occupation of Cappadocia, from which he was expelled by Sulla, at that time proprætor in Asia, who thus became unintentionally a rival of Marius.

§ 137. *The Marsic or Social War.*

(91—88.)

Most of the Italian nations, although compelled to serve 574
in the Roman armies and pay taxes, were excluded from C
any participation in the government; the admission of the Latins to the full rights of citizenship and of the other Italians to the privilege of voting, as proposed by C. Gracchus, having been negatived by the veto of M. Livius Drusus. His son and namesake, M. Livius Drusus, having lost his life in a fresh attempt to obtain these concessions, the Italian confederates resolved to deliver themselves from the Roman yoke.

Immediate causes of the War.—The gross acts of injustice 575
perpetrated in the provinces by the knights, as farmers of the public

(575) revenue, remaining unpunished, because the offenders themselves
A were the judges, an attempt was made by M. Livius Drusus to deprive them of their jurisdiction, at least in part, by admitting 300 knights into the senate, and then choosing the judges from the whole body of senators. In order to carry out this plan, Drusus urged the Italian allies to exercise their influence over the citizens of Rome, for the purpose of securing their votes in favor of his "rogatio," promising to procure for them in return the political rights which they were so anxious to obtain. The project of Drusus became law; but when he went on to propose the admission of the allies to the rights of citizenship, he was assassinated, and his law repealed.

576 All the Italian nations, with the exception of the Latins,
B Etruscans, and Umbrians, now formed themselves into a confederacy against Rome. Their plan was to establish a republic, under the name of Italica, with the city of Corfinium for its capital—the government to be in the hands of a senate (consisting of 500 deputies from all the states), two consuls, and twelve prætors. The Latins and some tribes of the Etruscans were propitiated by a grant of Roman citizenship, made to them at the commencement of the war by the lex Julia (a law of L. Julius Cæsar). The theatres of war were three. 1. Northwards in Picenum, where the city of Asculum (the inhabitants of which had commenced hostilites with the murder of a prætor) was
C taken by Cn. Pompeius Strabo. 2. In central Italy, in the territories of the four united cantons, where the Romans were for the most part unsuccessful, except against the Marsians (under the command of Marius). Here also the war was terminated by Pompeius. 3. In the south, in Samnium and Campania, where Sulla (libertini in the legions) fought with distinguished success. As the war with Mithridates threatened Rome at the same time, the rest of the Italians, as fast as they submitted, were invested (in accordance with the lex Plautia Papiria) with the privileges of Roman citizenship, which were soon afterwards
D conferred on all the municipia. Lest, however, the great numbers of the new citizens should give them a preponderance over the old, they were formed into eight new tribes, instead of being incorporated into the thirty-five which already existed.

§ 138. *Civil War between Marius and Sulla,* 88—82; *and first War against Mithridates,* 87—84.

1. The civil War to the death of Marius (88—86). 577

A Sulla, after his glorious campaign against the Italian confederates, was elected consul, and received Asia as his province, with the command-in-chief of the army destined to act against Mithridates. On the other hand, Marius, through the instrumentality of the tribune P. Sulpicius, who was supported by a number of young knights (anti-senatus) and gladiators, obtained the distribution of the freedmen (who had hitherto been confined to the four tribus urbanæ) amongst the ancient thirty-five tribes, and by means of their votes procured the removal of Sulla, and his own appointment to the command-in-chief. B Marius, on receiving intelligence of these proceedings, at once returned to Rome, which (after a skirmish at the Esquiline gate) was stormed for the first time by Roman legions. The Sulpician laws were immediately repealed, and Sulpicius himself put to death. Marius, after various adventures, reached Minturnæ (attempt to assassinate him), and thence passed over into Africa. Whilst, however, Sulla was carrying on the war against Mithridates, one Cinna, a consul of the popular party, whose election Sulla had been unable to prevent, was endeavoring to compel the re-enactment of the Sulpician law, and procure the recall of Marius, through the votes of the new citizens. C He was, it is true, expelled from the city by the Optimates, but succeeded in gaining over the army, which was still kept on foot in Campania to oppose the Italian confederates, and in joining Marius, who had returned from Africa. The two leaders then invested Rome, which was compelled by famine to open its gates; and this success was followed by the proscription and murder of Sulla's friends, not only at Rome, but throughout Italy. Cinna and Marius nominated themselves as consuls for the year 86; but Marius died at the commencement of his seventh consulate, and was succeeded by L. Valerius Flaccus.

2. First War against Mithridates, 87—84. 578

Mithridates, availing himself of the confusion occasioned

(578) by the Social war, proceeded to carry out his plans for
A checking the progress of the Roman arms in Asia, by the establishment of a union among all the nations of the east. His first step towards the accomplishment of this mighty project, was the subjugation of Asia Minor, for which an occasion was furnished by disputes respecting the possession of Paphlagonia, Galatia, and Cappadocia. Mithridates then sent his general Archelaus with an army and a fleet into Greece, where he was joined by most of the inhabitants. In order, however, to prevent his arrival in Italy and junction with the Italian confederates, the Romans put an end to the war at home by various conces-
B sions, and then dispatched Sulla into Greece. After storming Athens, which made an obstinate resistance, Sulla quitted the exhausted territory of Attica, and entering Bœotia gained two brilliant victories at Chæronēa and Orchomĕnus. The Marian party at Rome now assigned the province of Asia and the conduct of the Mithridatic war to the consul, L. Valerius Flaccus, who was murdered by his own lieutenant, Fimbria. The war was carried on by this new leader with such success, that an Asiatic peace was soon afterwards concluded at Dardanus, on the following terms—

579 Mithridates was required to withdraw his garrisons from the pro-
C vince of Asia and Paphlagonia, to evacuate Bithynia and Cappadocia in favor of Nicomēdes and Ariobarzānes, to deliver up seventy (or eighty?) ships of war, and pay 2000 talents as an indemnity for the expenses incurred by the Romans in carrying on the war. Sulla then demanded that Fimbria should resign the command of the legions to him as the legitimate governor of Asia, whereupon Fimbria committed suicide; and Sulla, after extorting a fine of 20,000 talents from the revolted cities of Asia Minor, returned to Rome. Cinna, who was embarking troops at Ancona, in order to dispute his landing, was slain by his own soldiers.

580 3. Termination of the civil War.

D In the year 83, Sulla, at the head of his victorious army (40,000 strong), landed at Brundusium, and having received a reinforcement of troops, raised for his service by the younger Pompey and other Optimates, advanced by slow marches as far as Campania, where he was met by the united armies of the two consuls. Whole squadrons of the consular force, including the entire army of Scipio, were induced by bribery and fair promises to go over to

the enemy. The other consul (Norbanus) was left dead (580
on the field. In the following year (82) Sulla overcame A
C. Marius (consul of that year, and probably a son of the Marius who had been seven times consul), and having left one of his lieutenants to blockade him in his strong-hold of Præneste, proceeded to Rome, and thence into Etruria, where the other consul (Cn. Papirius Carbo) still offered considerable resistance, which the continual subdivision of his forces compelled him at last to abandon, and escape into Africa. The Samnites (who had never laid down their arms since the Social war, and in consequence had not been admitted to the privileges of Roman citizenship), after an unsuccessful attempt to relieve Præneste, advanced to Rome with the intention of storming and sacking the city, but were completely routed before the gates, and many thousands of them captured and put to
death. Præneste was also taken and plundered, the Sam- B
nites and Prænestines proscribed *en masse* without any investigation, and Marius himself slain by a slave at his own request.

The numerous proscriptions at Rome as well as through- 581
out the whole of Italy, of persons who had supported Marius, afforded Sulla an opportunity, not merely of avenging himself on his enemies, but of rewarding also his soldiers and supporters, and utterly destroying the sovereignty of the people. In pursuance of this plan, he caused himself to be nominated Dictator for an unlimited period, and, with unrestricted authority, assumed the surname of Felix, and celebrated a triumph over Mithridates,
which lasted two days. At the end of two years he so- C
lemnly laid down the dictatorship, and died at his country house near Puteŏli. His funeral rites were celebrated with great pomp by his adherents.

Cn. Pompeius, after the conclusion of the war in Italy, 582
in which he had taken an active part, undertook the annihilation of the Marian party in Sicily, Africa, and Spain.

He captured and put to death the consul Carbo, who had returned into Sicily, and overthrew Cn. Domitius Ahenobarbus (Cinna's son-in-law), with his ally Hiarbas, king of Numidia. On his return he received, probably from Sulla himself, the surname of Magnus, and celebrated his first triumph against the wishes of his patron. (For his war in Spain, see § 140.)

§ 139. *Changes effected in the Constitution by Sulla.*

(82—79.)

583 Instead of rendering his victory and the sovereign au-
A thority with which he was invested available for any plans
of personal ambition, Sulla directed all his efforts towards
the re-establishment of the aristocracy. 1. In pursuance
of this object, he, in the first place, *deprived all the cities*
belonging to the opposite party (especially in Samnium,
Lucania, and Etruria) *of the rights of citizenship, and con-*
fiscated their lands, which he bestowed on his own soldiers,
with the view of securing their support to the new constitution. Thus military colonies were created with the
B full rights of citizenship. At the same time, in order to
secure a popular party, he granted liberty and political
privileges to 10,000 slaves belonging to the proscribed
families. These new citizens were named after their patron
Cornelii. 2. The *tribunitial power*, which had degenerated
into licentiousness, was restrained within its original
bounds; the tribunes being deprived of the right of proposing laws and addressing the people, as well as of becoming candidates for the higher offices. It would seem
that the "intercessio" was the only privilege which they
C were allowed to retain. 3. On the other hand, Sulla
endeavored to raise the *senate*, by filling up the number
of its members principally from the equestrian order
(though not always with discretion), and restoring to it the
judicial authority, the right of assigning provinces, and
conferring commands-in-chief, as well as of previous de-
liberation on questions about to be proposed to the general
assembly of the people. The quæstors were declared ex
officio members of the senate; and, in order to render the
filling up of the senatorial list a less difficult task in future,
D their number was augmented to twenty. 4. Another plan
adopted by Sulla for strengthening the aristocracy, and
especially his own party, was by increasing the number
of pontifices, augurs, and guardians of the Sibylline books
(which had been restored after the burning of the Capitol)
to fifteen, who were no longer to be chosen by the people, but
elected by the members of their respective colleges. 5. In
order to diminish the influence of the people in the courts

of justice, and at the same time to increase the power of (583)
the judges, who were now exclusively men of senatorial A
dignity, Sulla added two new courts to the four which already existed,—an arrangement which rendered it necessary to increase the number of prætors from six to eight; but it is not distinctly known what sort of questions were decided by the new magistrates.

584 The order in which the higher offices might be held, as settled by the lex annalis (see § 103), was again defined, and the acceptance of the same office a second time within ten years prohibited as before. Several criminal laws were also re-enacted by Sulla, and rendered more stringent (lex de sicariis, a law against assassinations; de falso, against fraud; de majestate, defining more accurately the crime of high treason; lex repetundarum, lex de injuriis, &c.).

585 Immediately after the death of Sulla, the repeal of all
his laws was proposed by the consul Æmilius Lepidus; B
but this could only be effected gradually, on account of the opposition which the aristocracy (under Catulus and Pompey [Pompeius]) offered to such a measure. The first step was to render the tribunes eligible to the higher offices of state. Then Pompey, who on his return from Spain (see § 140) had abandoned the senatorial party, effected the restoration of the tribunitial power in its fullest extent, and procured the enactment of a law (the lex Aurelia), by which the knights were declared admissible to judicial offices. Thus he became the man of the people.

§ 140. *The War against Sertorius.*

(80—72.)

586 Q. Sertorius, who at the breaking out of the civil
war had joined the party opposed to the nobles, and been C
rewarded with the proprætorship of further Spain, having been proscribed by Sulla and deprived of his province, fled to Africa (where he conquered Mauritania). The Lusitani, who at that great distance scarcely recognized the authority of Rome, recalled him from his banishment, and chose him as their leader against the governors appointed by Sulla (81). Thus supported by the Lusitani and the remnant of the Marian party, Sertorius made head not only against the feeble Q. Metellus Pius (son of Numidius), but against Pompey himself. Mithridates,

(586) who observed with delight that the Romans were becoming
A more and more occupied with the civil war, and with their enemies on the shores of the Atlantic, now concluded an alliance with Sertorius, who was soon afterwards assassinated at a banquet at the instigation of his own lieutenant Perperna. The command of the army was then assumed by Perperna, who was defeated by Pompey and executed. This victory put an end to the war; but the dominion of the Romans over Spain was not yet completely re-established.

§ 141. *The Servile War; or War of the Gladiators and Slaves.*

(73—71.)

587 Some gladiators, principally Thracians and Gauls, who
B had escaped from a school at Capua, placed themselves under the command of a Thracian named Spartăcus, and collected an enormous band of gladiators and slaves, with which they defeated four Roman armies. Spartăcus would have quitted Italy, but his comrades, who thirsted for booty and revenge, determined to attack Rome itself. The Romans, panic-stricken, as they had been at the approach of Hannibal, conferred the supreme command, during the absence of Pompey, on the prætor M. Licinius Crassus, who put an end to the war by two decisive battles; in the second of which, on the Silarus, Spartăcus lost his life. A remnant of the defeated army (5000 men) having crossed the Alps, fell in with Pompey, on his march homewards from Spain, and was utterly annihilated.

588 On his return to Rome, Pompey, who boasted that he had de-
C stroyed every vestige of the servile war, obtained a triumph (together with Metellus Pius), on account of his victories in Spain, and was chosen consul, with Crassus for his colleague. In this office he conciliated the favor of the people by restoring the tribunitial power, and abrogating the law of Sulla concerning the administration of justice. (See § 139, ad finem.) After his consulship he did not accept the command of a *province*, but remained at Rome till the chief command against the pirates was conferred upon him.

§ 142. *War against the Pirates.*

(75—67.)

589 Causes of their power in Cilicia and Isauria.—1. The oppression of the inhabitants of Asia Minor through the

avarice of the Roman governors, farmers of the revenue, (589)
and usurers. 2. Neglect of maritime affairs by the A
Romans since the destruction of Carthage. During his three years' government in Asia, P. Servilius had wrested from them several towns on the southern coast of Asia Minor, subdued Isaura (hence his surname of Isauricus), and settled Cilicia as a Roman province (75). But these losses, so far from weakening the freebooters, merely served to augment the ferocity with which they carried on their system of robbery and murder. From Cilicia and Crete they swept the whole of the Mediterranean with more than 1000 vessels, landed on the coasts, especially of Italy, plundered the cities and country houses, carried off the inhabitants (Cæsar himself fell into their hands at sea), and intercepted the remittances of money and cargoes
of grain. The famine which in consequence prevailed at B
Rome induced the people (on the motion of the tribune Gabinius) to confer on Cn. Pompeius for three years the uncontrolled command of the Mediterranean and its coasts (67). Pompey surprised the pirates, whom he chased from one haunt to another; and in two short campaigns (of forty and forty-nine days) cleared first the western and then the eastern Mediterranean almost without a battle, demolished their strongholds, and granted to those who surrendered cities and lands in Cilicia (Pompæopolis, anciently Soloë). Crete, one of the principal stations of the C
pirates, after a three years' war, surrendered to Q. Cæcilius Metellus (thence surnamed Creticus), and became a Roman Province.

§ 143. *The two last Wars against Mithridates.*

590 The second War (83—81). As Mithridates, after the conclusion of peace, still continued his preparations, and refused to withdraw his forces entirely from Cappadocia, Muræna, proprætor of Asia, established garrisons in that country, and made predatory excursions into the Pontic territory; but being overthrown at the river Halys, he was compelled to abandon Cappadocia.

591 The third War (74—64), began when Nicomēdēs III.,
king of Bithynia, and brother-in-law of Mithridates, be- D
queathed his dominions to the Romans, who formed them into a new province. Mithridates now concluded an alliance with Sertorius, and sent a force into Bithynia, which

(591) overthrew the consul Aurelius Cotta by water as well as
A by land near Chalcēdon, and laid siege to the city of Cyzicum, on the island Cyzicus, which had remained faithful to the Romans. The place was relieved by the other consul L. Licinius Lucullus, who advanced in pursuit of the king as far as Pontus, and after a succession of fresh victories compelled him to fly for refuge to his son-in-law Tigranes, king of Armenia. This monarch having refused to deliver up his father-in-law, Lucullus crossed the Euphrates and Tigris, and overthrew the army of Tigranes, which was 20 (?) times as numerous as his own, near Tigranocerta (69), and both the sovereigns at Artaxata
B (68). The refusal however of his soldiers (who were seldom allowed to pillage) to advance any further into those inhospitable regions, prevented him from profiting by his victories, and Mithridates with little labor reconquered his dominions. Heavy charges being at the same time brought against Lucullus by the Roman knights in Asia, whose avarice he had endeavored to repress, the entire direction of the war against the two kings was committed by the people to Cn. Pompeius Magnus (who had unexpectedly put an end to the piratical war and was still in Asia) agreeably to the lex Manilia, which was
C supported by the eloquence of Cicero. After a battle by night, in which he was defeated, Mithridates fled to Colchis, and Tigranes, who had surrendered without striking a blow, was allowed by Pompey to retain a portion of his dominions as a barrier against the Parthians, surrendering Syria, Phœnicia, the Lesser Armenia, and parts of Cilicia, Galatia, and Cappadocia. After following Mithridates as far as the river Phasis, Pompey gave up the pursuit, and turned his arms against the nations on the eastern coast of the Mediterranean and the Arabian and Persian gulfs.

D On his return he introduced the Roman provincial administration into Pontus, marched into Syria, which he proclaimed a Roman province, and in Palestine restored the high priest Hyrcanus (who had been deposed by his brother Aristobūlus), and compelled the inhabitants to pay tribute to the Roman government.

592 Having received intelligence that Mithridates had destroyed himself (at Panticapæum on the Tauric Chersonēsus) in a fit of despair

occasioned by the treason of his son Pharnăces, Pompey re-entered (592)
Pontus, and having confirmed Pharnaces in the sovereignty of A
Bosporus, and re-arranged the constitution of the Asiatic provinces, returned to Rome, where his second triumph, which lasted two days, was celebrated with unprecedented magnificence (61).

§ 144. *Catiline's Conspiracy.*

(66—62.)

A conspiracy to assassinate the consuls elect was set on 593
foot by L. Sergius Catilina (an accomplice of Sulla in his murderous proscription), who had been rejected as a candidate for the consulship on account of certain charges brought against him of extortion practised during his pro-prætorship in Africa. His project having miscarried through the indecision of the conspirators (young and ambitious Romans, and bad characters of every description), Catiline was brought to trial, and being acquitted, became a candidate for the consulship, which however was conferred (in 63) on M. Tullius Cicero[1] and C. Antonius (a friend of Catiline). In consequence of this dis- B
appointment Catiline renewed his conspiracy, and endeavored to increase the number of his adherents, in order to secure his election for the year 62. Cicero, to whom Catiline's intention of assassinating him during the election, and then seizing on the consulship, had been communicated by one of the conspirators (Curius), through the intervention of Fulvia, appeared at the comitia with such an escort, as rendered an attack impossible (Silanus and Murena were chosen consuls for 62). All further attempts of the conspirators were rendered fruitless by the vigilance of Cicero, whose eloquent denunciations drove Catiline from the city. He then joined one of his fellow- C
conspirators, Manlius, who had raised an army in Etruria. Both were immediately proscribed, and five of the conspirators at Rome (who had been discovered through their correspondence with the ambassadors of the Allobrŏges) were executed in prison (speeches of Cicero and Cato in opposition to Cæsar; Cicero pater patriæ). The army of

[1] Born at Arpīnum in 106, fought under Sulla in the war of the confederates, travelled to Athens and Asia Minor. Quæstor in Sicily in 76, impeached Verres in 70, ædilis curulis in 69, prætor urbanus 66, declined the administration of a province as proprætor.

Etruria was routed by M. Petreius, lieutenant of C. Antonius, near Pistoria (62), where Catiline himself fell.

§ 145. *The First Triumvirate*, 60.

594 C. Julius Cæsar,[1] whose acute mind had long since dis-
A covered that the republic was in its dotage, resolved to overthrow the power of the nobility through the people and their idol Pompey, and then reign triumphantly over both parties.

595 This plan he followed out with unwearied perseverance, but with such moderation and prudence, that for a long time his object was not suspected. He became a supporter of all measures calculated to undermine the influence of the nobility (such as the restoration of the tribunitial power, and the partition of the judicial functions), attached himself to Pompey, as soon as that general abandoned the party of the senate, and endeavored by every means in his power to render himself popular and the nobility odious. This systematic resistance to the dominant party subjected him to the suspicion of being concerned in Catiline's conspiracy, especially as he spoke against the infliction of capital punishment on the conspirators.

596 On his return to Rome, Pompey demanded the con-
B firmation of all the measures which he had adopted in Asia, and a distribution of lands among his veterans: but both these proposals were vehemently resisted in the senate. About the same time Cæsar returned from further Spain, which he had governed as proprætor, and notwithstanding the opposition of the Optimates, was chosen consul for the year 59, but with Bibulus, a violent aristocrat, for his colleague. A reconciliation having been effected between Pompey and Crassus, through the intervention of Cæsar, the three entered into a compact to op-
C pose the aristocracy. This "union of talent with reputation and wealth, by means of which the one party hoped to rise, the other to retain, and the third to win," is called the first Triumvirate. Cæsar now, in defiance of all

[1] Born on the 12 Quinctilis 100; as son-in-law of Cinna, an opponent of Sulla, by whom he was proscribed but afterwards pardoned. He served in Asia and was taken prisoner by the pirates; was quæstor in Spain, pontifex maximus in 63, prætor 62, proprætor in Lusitania in 61, after Crassus had become security for his debts (830 talents).

opposition from the senate, obtained from the people the (596)
assignment of lands in Campania to 20,000 citizens, prin- A
cipally veterans of Pompey's army, gave his only daughter Julia in marriage to Pompey, and procured his own nomination to the proprætorship for five years of Cisalpine Gaul and Illyricum. This last usurpation of their rights by the people occasioned such alarm to the senate, that they resolved to anticipate further encroachments by assigning to Cæsar in addition the still more important province of Transalpine Gaul. Before he set out for his province, Cæsar contrived (by means of the tribune P. Clodius) to withdraw from Rome the two leaders of the senate, M. Porcius Cato and Cicero. The former was B
sent to Cyprus, with a commission to reduce the island, without a show of justice, to the condition of a Roman province. Cicero, after an unsuccessful attempt to gain over Cæsar, was banished to Thessalonīca (58), in consequence of a charge brought against him by Clodius of having occasioned the execution of Catiline's conspirators. From this exile, however, he was recalled at the end of sixteen months (on the motion of the tribune, T. Annius Milo), to support Pompey and the senate against Clodius.

In the year 56 the triumvĭri held a meeting in Cæsar's winter 597
quarters at Luca, at which it was agreed that Pompey and Crassus C
should be the consuls of the following year, and be appointed to provinces and the command of armies, Cæsar not only consenting to such an arrangement, but pledging himself to use all his influence with the people that it might be carried into effect. In return for these concessions, Cæsar's colleagues insured him the prolongation of his government for five years; and Pompey, who anticipated important advantages from his own residence at Rome, continued to supply him with fresh legions.

§ 146. *Cæsar's War in Gaul.*

(58—51.)

The object of Cæsar in carrying on the Gallic war, was 598
not merely the extension of the Roman dominions, but the D
more important advantage of keeping together a body of veterans, attached to his person, and ready at all times to render him unconditional obedience. With this view he formed a regular standing army.

599 Gaul, like Spain, was peopled by a multitude of small clans,
A which, instead of uniting against Rome, continued to prosecute their own petty feuds. This circumstance, joined to their superiority in the art of war, rendered the struggle comparatively easy for the Romans; but at the same time prolonged the war, which, instead of being terminated, as in the east, by one or two decisive engagements, could only be decided by the subjugation of the tribes *one after another* and *by means of each other*, and by the *suppression of repeated insurrections*.

600 In the year 58 the Helvetii, who had migrated from
B eastern Gaul in search of a better settlement, threatened the Roman province and plundered the territories of the Ædui. These applied for assistance to Cæsar, who overthrew the Helvetians, cutting some to pieces and driving the rest back into their own country. At an earlier period the Arverni in a war with the Ædui had taken into their pay a German army commanded by Ariovistus. The Æduans applied to Cæsar for protection; and the Germans, after sustaining a defeat at Vesontio (Besançon), were compelled to recross the Rhine.

C In 57 the Belgians, who had the reputation of being the bravest nation between the Rhine and the Pyrenees, prepared to resist the advance of the Romans, by a *levée en masse* of 300,000 men. This force was separated by Cæsar, who pursued the different divisions and overcame them in detail. The most obstinate combat was with the warlike Nervii (between the Schelde and Sambre), and their neighbors; but even here the superiority of their discipline insured victory to the Romans.

601 In the year 56 the Venĕti on the north-western coast were
D vanquished by a sudden attack (by Decimus Brutus), their chief men executed, and the rest sold as slaves, whilst the Aquitani, in south-western Gaul, were subjugated by the younger Crassus (son of the triumvir). Thus the conquest of Gaul was accomplished, with the exception of a few tribes on the Belgic coast and at the foot of the Pyrenees.

602 In 55 the Usipĕtes and Tenchtēri, who had been driven by the Suevi across the Lower Rhine into Belgium, were compelled to return by Cæsar, who now, in order to find employment for his legions, not only crossed the Rhine into the territory of the Sicambri, but even visited Britain, without however making any conquest in either of those countries. His second expedition to Britain (in 54),

with 800 ships, and a second campaign in Germany (in 53), had no better results.

In the years 54—51 the Gauls, who, in addition to the 603
loss of their freedom, were grievously oppressed by taxa- A
tion, the winter quartering of troops, and pillage of their estates, made repeated attempts to throw off the Roman yoke. A combined insurrection of the Trevĕri and Eburōnes, under the crafty Ambiŏrix, having failed, the whole nation of the Gauls rose as one man, under the command of Vercingetŏrix (an Arvernian), by whom the war was carried on with great circumspection and patience. Their leader being besieged by Cæsar in the fortress of Alesia, the united army of the Gauls (about 250,000 strong) appeared before the place, but were utterly defeated; whereupon Vercingetorix surrendered to
the Romans. A few Gallic tribes still resisted, but were B
overcome in the year 51. As the conclusion of his five years' government drew near, Cæsar, by means of gentle treatment, conferring honors on their chiefs, and maintaining their laws and constitutions, succeeded in tranquillizing the Gauls, and thus securing his conquest.

§ 147. *The Civil War between Cæsar and Pompey.*

(49—48.)

Pompey and Crassus had been a second time elected to 604
the consulship (55), and obtained the provinces which they C
desired, viz. Crassus Syria, where he was slain in a campaign against the Parthians, and Pompey the two Spains, the government of which he intrusted to a lieutenant, and remained at Rome in the expectation that the disturbed times would require his appointment to the dictatorship. With this object in view, he caused the election of consuls for the year 52 to be deferred, under the pretext that the auspices were unfavorable, and by fostering intestine disturbances (assassination of Clodius by Milo), succeeded in obtaining his own appointment to the consulship (without a colleague), for the purpose of suppressing them. The Optimates were so besotted as to suppose that it would be possible to disarm Cæsar by an act of the senate, or at all events by means of Pompey's army.

605 Their first step was to withdraw from him two legions under pre-
A tence of their being required for the Parthian war; but they were still retained in Italy under the command of his rival. Then he was required, before the expiration of his second five years, to resign his command and retire from the provinces. Cæsar having offered to do this, if Pompey would follow his example, the senate pronounced him contumacious, and notwithstanding the veto of two tribunes, resolved to proscribe him as an enemy of the republic, unless he consented to resign the command of his army, which consisted of eleven legions.

606 Irritated by these and similar insults, Cæsar determined
B to cross the Rubicon (the boundary of his Cisalpine province), before the forces of Pompey could be brought into the field. Pompey, accompanied by the two consuls and a majority of the senate, fled to Brundusium, and being closely pursued by Cæsar, crossed over into Greece. Meanwhile, Cæsar, who, within two months had become almost without opposition master of Italy, Sicily, and Sardinia, employed the time which must elapse before a fleet could be built for the transport of his troops to Greece, in visiting Spain, where the lieutenants of Pompey
C submitted without a battle. Returning to Rome, he was appointed dictator by a senate composed of his own friends, and having laid down this dignity at the end of eleven days, was a second time chosen consul; whilst on the other hand the senators who had fled with Pompey re-elected the officers of the past year.

During these proceedings, Cæsar's lieutenant, Curio, had subdued Sicily, but lost his life in an engagement with Juba, king of Numidia, who supported the party of Pompey, because Curio, as tribune, had proposed the annexation of Numidia to the Roman dominions.

607 In the beginning of the year 48, Cæsar landed in southern
D Illyria, and cut Pompey off from Dyrrachium, his chief arsenal, but was repulsed in the first encounter. Instead, however, of pursuing and cutting to pieces the scattered forces of his enemy, Pompey persisted in his plan of starving him into surrender; until at length, on the ninth of August, 48, Cæsar, by a feigned flight, brought on the decisive battle of Pharsălus, in which his admirable tactics gained him a complete victory over the Optimates, whose army consisted of 52,000 men, whilst his own numbered only 23,000. By the advice of one of his favorites,

Pompey sought an asylum at the court of Ptolemæus (607)
Dionȳsus, king of Egypt, whose father had been indebted A
to him for the restoration of his crown; but the intrigues of the Egyptian courtiers soon occasioned his assassination. A few days after his death Cæsar appeared before Alexandria, and bewailed the fate of his son-in-law.

When Cæsar quitted Greece, in pursuit of Pompey, he had de- 608
spatched M. Antonius with a portion of his army into Italy, to secure that country, and obtain for his patron the sovereign power, under a title recognized by the constitution. So well did Antony discharge the duty intrusted to him, that Cæsar was not only elected dictator for a year, but also invested with the tribunitial authority for life, and the power of making war and concluding peace, and of nominating the provincial governors.

§ 148. *Cæsar's Wars in the East.*

(48—47.)

1. The Alexandrian War, 48 and 47. 609
On his arrival in Egypt, Cæsar found the country dis- B
tracted by disputes between Ptolemæus Dionȳsus and his sister Cleopatra, who were required by their father's will to marry one another, and reign conjointly. Cleopatra, being expelled by her brother, applied for aid to Cæsar, who was so captivated by her charms that he at once proposed to act as arbitrator. A general insurrection in Alexandria was the consequence of this interference. Cæsar intrenched himself in Bruchium (the quarter adjoining the port), burnt the Egyptian fleet in harbor (destruction of the largest of the three Alexandrian libraries), with the aid of a reinforcement from Asia overthrew Ptolemy (who was drowned in the Nile in attempting to escape), and placed the crown on the heads of Cleopatra and her younger brother.

2. The War against Pharnăces, 47. 610
Pharnăces, the son of Mithridates, availed himself of the C
disruption of the Roman republic to extend the limits of his little empire on the Cimmerian Bosporus. He had already occupied the lesser Armenia and Cappadocia (countries which at an earlier period had been governed by the Romans), overthrown Cæsar's lieutenant, Domitius Calvinus, whose defeat enabled him to take possession of the whole northern coast of Asia Minor), and was on the

(610) point of returning to quell an insurrection of his lieutenant
A on the Bosporus, when he was overtaken by Cæsar, who after a campaign of only five days (hence "veni, vidi, vici") compelled him to retreat in disorder to the Bosporus, where he was defeated and slain by his lieutenant.

§ 149. *Cæsar's last Wars against the Partisans of Pompey.*

(46—45.)

611 1. The War in Africa, 46.

B Towards the end of the year 47, Cæsar landed in Africa, where Pompey's son Sextus, his father-in-law Metellus Scipio, Cato, Petreius, and other Optimates, had assembled after the death of their leader, and formed a league with Juba, king of Numidia. Cæsar overthrew the united army of the republicans and Numidians at Thapsus (where the allies lost 50,000 men and Cæsar only fifty), took Utĭca, the chief residence of the Optimates, and made Numidia a Roman province. Cato died by his own hand; and his example was followed by Juba, Scipio, and Petreus: the rest (S. Pompeius, Labienus, &c.) escaped into Spain, and joined Cn. Pompeius.

612 After the conclusion of the African war, new and unprecedented
C honors were heaped on Cœsar. A solemn thanksgiviug was ordered for forty days, and a statue erected of the conqueror, who was invested with the dictatorship for ten years, and the censorship, without colleagues, for three, with the modest title of præfectus moribus. Triumphs were celebrated on three several days for his victories in Gaul, Egypt, Pontus, and Africa: the people were feasted at 22,000 triclinia, presented with doles of money, corn, and oil, and gratified with public spectacles; whilst the soldiers were rewarded with grants of money and land. Cæsar then took measures for the restoration of order, by means of sumptuary laws and enactments, against violence and treason; limited the duration of provincial governments, and increased the number of the senators. As pontifex maximus, he undertook a reformation of the calendar, in which he was assisted by the Alexandrian mathematician Sosigĕnes (see § 4.) Great offence was caused by the arrival of Cleopatra at Rome, and by her haughty behavior.

613 2. The War against the sons of Pompey in
D Spain, 45.

The last campaign of Cæsar was against the sons of Pompey (Cnæus and Sextus), who, after the battle of Thapsus, had collected a considerable force in Spain. By

the most extraordinary exertions, he was enabled to win (613)
the battle of Munda in Bætica, where 33,000 of Pom- A
pey's adherents were slain. Cn. Pompey, who attempted to fly, was betrayed into the hands of the conqueror and put to death: Sextus escaped into north-eastern Spain. On his return to Rome, Cæsar celebrated his fifth triumph, and was honored with a festival of thanksgiving, which lasted fifty days.

§ 150. *Death of Cæsar.*

The senate, dazzled by the brilliancy of Cæsar's exploits, 614
and eagerly flattering him from motives of fear or self- B
interest, outstripped the dictator himself in the revolutionary race. In addition to the other honors, some of them almost divine, which were heaped upon him, they voted him the dictatorship, the præfectura morum, and title of Imperator for life, invested him with the consulship for ten years, gave him the entire control over the army and the exchequer, named him father of his country, altered the title of the month in which he was born from Quintilis to Julius, and proclaimed their recognition of his supremacy by granting him authority to coin money with his own
effigy. During the last months of his life, the giant mind C
of Julius Cæsar was occupied with plans for erecting public buildings, framing a code of laws, and establishing public libraries; and, more than all, with preparations for an invasion of Parthia to avenge the fall of Crassus. His intention was first to subdue the Dacians on the banks of the Danube, and the Getæ; and then marching onwards into Asia, and conquering the Parthians, to traverse the countries on the Caspian and Black seas, and return to Rome through Germany and Gaul; thus extending his dominions on all sides, as men believed, to the very shores
of the ocean. No important steps had, however, yet been D
taken for the permanent organization of this absolute power. His friends had made several ineffectual attempts to present him publicly with a diadem, which he was compelled on each occasion to refuse, because the offer was unconfirmed by the people. At length, they discovered in the Sibylline books (which had been burnt in Sulla's time, and replaced in part by forged documents) a prophecy to

(614) this effect—" that Parthia could only be subdued by the
A Romans under a KING"—and immediately demanded that their leader should be invested with sovereign authority beyond the limits of Italy. Meanwhile a conspiracy to assassinate Cæsar was organized by sixty Optimates, partly adherents of Pompey, and partly disappointed followers of the Dictator; with the prætors C. Cassius and M. Brutus at their head. At a meeting of the senate (in the curia of Pompey), on the 15th of March, 44, Cæsar received twenty-three dagger wounds, and fell lifeless at the base of Pompey's statue.

§ 151. *Consequences of Cæsar's Assassination.*

615 The murderers, having perpetrated their bloody deed,
B were content to leave all further proceedings to the senate, who endeavored to conciliate both parties by confirming the laws and ordinances of Cæsar (on the motion of the Consul, Marcus Antonius [Mark Antony]), and at the same time passing an act of indemnity for his assassination. Antony alone refused to sanction this amnesty, and delivered over the body of Cæsar a funeral oration, which excited the people to fury, and drove the assassins from the city into the provinces assigned them by Cæsar; Decimus Brutus into Gallia Cisalpīna, M. Brutus into
C Macedonia, C. Cassius into Syria. No sooner were they departed, than Antony, who had obtained possession of the late dictator's papers immediately after his death, contrived by the most unscrupulous falsification of his ordinances to dispose, as he thought fit, of offices, provinces, estates, privileges, and civil rights. These proceedings were soon resisted by **Octavianus**, a youth of nineteen, great nephew and adopted son of Julius Cæsar, who availed himself at first of the assistance of the aristocracy, then annihilated them by the aid of Antony, and finally destroyed Antony himself.

D Desiring, like Cæsar, to have an army and a province in the neighborhood of Rome, Antony persuaded the people to pass a resolution, calling on D. Brutus to exchange Gaul for Macedonia. The refusal of Brutus to recognize this decree, unsanctioned as it was by the senate, occasioned

616 **The civil war of Mutĭna**, 44—43, between M.

Antony and D. Brutus. Antony blockaded his adversary (616)
in Mutĭna [now, *Modena*], and was denounced by the senate A
(on the motion of Cicero; his Philippic orations), as an enemy of the republic. The two consuls of the year 43, Pansa and Hirtius, then marched to the assistance of Brūtus, accompanied by Octavian (as proprætor); Pansa fell in the first engagement, and Hirtius in the battle of Mutĭna, where Antony was defeated. Octavian now took the command, as the only surviving general; but finding himself at present too weak to encounter both Antony and the conspirators, he determined, in the first place, to destroy the murderers of Cæsar, and in order to effect this, abandoned his pursuit of Antony, who escaped into Gaul. This change of plan was the more easy, as the senate had intrusted the duty not to himself, but to Brutus.

§ 152. *The Second Triumvirate.*

Octavian, on his return to Rome, obtained the consul- 617
ship by means of his troops, and persuaded the people to B
institute proceedings against the murderers of Cæsar, notwithstanding the amnesty. Then he marched nominally against Antony (with whom he had already entered into negotiations through M. Lepidus, proprætor of Gaul), compelled the senate to recall its decree against him, and *established a union* on an island near Bononia [now *Bologna*] (in the Lavinius?), *with Lepidus and Antony, for the administration of the government during a period of five years, and the annihilation of the party of Brutus and Cassius.* This was called the second triumvirate. The people, on their part, were required to confirm the triumviri in their office for five years.

Before, however, they commenced the war against the 618
assassins of Cæsar, it was desirable to remove the most C
influential of their enemies at Rome, lest, during their absence, S. Pompeius, who still maintained his position in Sicily, should be invited to return. With this view they revived the proscription, and under pretence of avenging the murder of Cæsar and restoring peace to the state, denounced more than 100 senators and 2000 knights, the confiscation of whose estates would supply funds for a fresh war. Among these victims was Cicero. Antony and

(618) Octavian now marched into Macedonia and took the field
A against Brutus and Cassius. Two battles were fought at Philippi. In the first, Brutus routed the army of Octavian, and Antony that of Cassius, who compelled one of his slaves to put him to death; in the second, Brutus also was defeated by Antony, and fell on his own sword.

After the battle the victors separated; Antony undertaking to raise the money promised to the troops in the countries which they had wrested from the murderers of Cæsar, whilst Octavian returned to Italy for the purpose
B of allotting lands to his veteran soldiers. Cleopatra had been summoned to Tarsus by Antony, to answer for her conduct in supporting Cassius, but the charms of the Egyptian queen so captivated the conqueror, that he followed her into Egypt. Meanwhile, the attempts of his wife, Fulvia, to compel his return by stirring up insurrections at home occasioned the

619 Perusian civil war, 41—40.
Octavian had experienced considerable difficulty in arranging the distribution of lands among his veterans, the original proprietors requiring indemnification, and the soldiers themselves being dissatisfied with their allotments. At the instigation of Fulvia, L. Antonius, brother of the triumvir, came forward as the champion of these discontented spirits, but was compelled to surrender (at Perusia), at the beginning of the next year (41).

620 M. Antony had returned to Italy, and was in the act of
C negotiating an alliance against Octavian with S. Pompeius, who had subdued Sicily, Sardinia, and Corsica, when the death of Fulvia smoothed the way for a reconciliation. The triumviri having met at Brundusium, a final division of the empire was arranged, Octavian receiving the western provinces, Antony the eastern, and Lepidus Africa. To cement their friendship, Antony married Octavia, the sister of Octavian. The blockade of Italy by S. Pompeius having occasioned a famine in the city, the triumviri concluded an armistice (at Misenum), by which the province of Achaia and the consulate were guaranteed to him, together with an indemnification for the loss of his property, Pompey, on his part, pledging himself to supply Italy with
D grain. The imperfect fulfilment of these conditions by both parties occasioned

621 A renewal of the war between Octavian and S. Pompeius. The war was carried on at first with indif-

ferent success by Octavian, who received very little assist- (621)
ance from his colleagues. A considerable naval force A
having however been assembled by M. Vipsanius Agrippa, and reinforced by a squadron from the fleet of Antony, a battle was fought off M y l æ, in which Pompey was defeated. He fled to Asia Minor and was assassinated at Miletus. Lepidus had also landed in Sicily, and claimed the sovereignty of the island; but his troops being gained over by Octavian, he was compelled to resign his provinces and the office of triumvir, and retired to Circeii (where he lived as pontifex maximus until B. C. 13). Having thus set aside two of his rivals, Octavian prepared for a decisive struggle with the third.

§ 153. *Foreign Wars of Antony and Octavian.*

War of Antony with the Parthians. In the year 622
39 the Parthians, who in the preceding year had overrun B
Syria, Palestine, Phœnicia, and Asia Minor, were driven across the Euphrates by Ventidius, the lieutenant of Antony. A considerable portion of the Roman possessions in Asia (Phœnicia, Cœlesyria, and parts of Cilicia and Judæa), was presented to Cleopatra by Antony, who had entered Asia for the purpose of putting an end to the war, and now (in 36) undertook an expedition against the Parthians, in conjunction with Artavasdes, king of Armenia. In a very short space of time he had penetrated, by forced marches, as far as Media; but the constant alternation of flight and attack, with which he was harassed by the enemy, the scarcity of provisions, the advanced season of the year, and the defection of the Armenians, compelled him
to retreat. At a later period (in 34) the faithless king C
of Armenia was taken prisoner, and conveyed in triumph to Alexandria. The Roman provinces in Asia were presented by Antony to Cleopatra, her children, and Cæsarion (whom the triumvir declared to be the legitimate son of Cæsar, in order to invalidate the claims of Octavian), and soon afterwards (32) letters of divorce were forwarded to his wife Octavia.

Wars of Octavian. 623

In order to find employment for his legions, and replen- D
ish his military chest, Octavian undertook several expedi-

A tions against the imperfectly reduced tribes among the Julian Alps and on the shores of Illyria. The Iapўdæ, Pannonians, and Dalmatians were now subjected to the authority of Rome.

§ 154. *The War between Octavian and Antony.*

(31 and 30.)

624 The term of the triumviral league, which, although twice
B confirmed for five years by the people, had for a long time been little more than a name, expired at the end of the year 33. War was declared by the senate against Cleopatra, who now exercised unbounded influence over Antony, and hoped, through him, to become mistress of the Roman empire. The immediate cause of hostilities was a demand on the part of the Egyptian queen, that the extravagant grant of Antony should be confirmed by the senate.

625 Antony, instead of crushing his enemies (as he might easily have
C done in their unprepared condition), by a sudden descent on the shores of Italy, wasted his time in dalliance with Cleopatra; and on the appearance of Octavian in the Ionian sea, with a fleet under the command of Agrippa, determined, in obedience to the will of his mistress, to risk a naval engagement.

626 On the 2d of September, 31, a brilliant victory was gained by M. Agrippa off the promontory of Actium. Cleopatra and Antony fled, before the fortune of the day was decided, and sought refuge in Egypt; their fleet was burnt, and the land forces surrendered to the victor. Octavian proceeded into Syria, and thence invaded Egypt, where he urged Cleopatra to rid him of his adversary. Egypt became a Roman province.

D Antony, who had been abandoned by his fleet and cavalry, was now informed, by command of Cleopatra herself, that she had committed suicide; and fell on his own sword. Finding her efforts to captivate Octavian utterly fruitless, and having learnt that she was destined to adorn his triumph, Cleopatra also destroyed herself (probably by taking poison), and was buried by the side of Antony.

Third Period.

C. Rome under Emperors.

(B. C. 30.—A. D. 476.)

§ 155. *C. Julias Cæsar Octavianus Augustus.*

(B. C. 30.—A. D. 14.)

In the month of Sextīlis (named from him Augustus), 627
B. C. 39, Octavian returned to Rome, where he distributed A
largesses among the citizens, and celebrated a triple triumph for his victories in Dalmatia (and the neighboring countries), at Actium and in Egypt. The temple of Janus was now closed for the third time. Perceiving the impossibility of establishing his authority on a permanent footing by acts of violence, Octavian determined to obtain from the senate, as free concessions (at least in appearance), the recognition of those privileges which he had already virtually conferred on himself. With this view he persuaded B
them to invest him with all the highest offices of state, and, at a later period, to commit to him the legislative authority and emancipate him from the control of the laws. At the same time most of the magistracies were retained in name, but were entirely dependent on the will of the emperor; a form of constitution which lasted for more than 300 years. The title of Augustus, conferred on him in the year 27, was also borne by his successors.

The constitution under the emperors to the reign 628
of Diocletian. C

1 The imperial prerogative comprehended the levy of the army, the imposition of taxes (the right of deciding questions of war and peace), the command-in-chief of all the legions, and the power of life and death. The princeps exercised, at the same time, the censorial and tribunitial authority, was pontifex maximus and a member of the other sacerdotal colleges, and his edicts and ordinances had the force of laws and decrees of the senate. The election of his successor was, it is true, pronounced by a decree of the senate and a resolution of the curiæ (lex regia), but for the first two centuries the choice regularly fell on the person whom his predecessor thought fit to indicate by adopting him as his son, or by conferring on him the title of Cæsar, or admitting him, as his colleague, to a share in the government.

2. The senate was limited by Octavian [Augustus] to 600 mem- 629
bers, all of whom were devoted to his person. At a later period Italians and other provincials as well as Romans, were nominated by the

(629) princeps, provided they possessed a census of 1,200,000 sesterces and
A were twenty-five years of age. Instead of the senate, the advisers of the Imperator were generally the members of his privy council (concilium, or consistorium principis). From the time of Tiberius the people ceased to have any share in legislation, their decisions being superseded by senatûs consulta and edicts of the emperors, which latter soon became the chief sources of law.

630 3. The magistracies.

a. *The ancient magistrates.*—The Consuls were generally elected every two months, and retained merely the privilege of presiding in the senate, and a share in the jurisdiction; the Prætors, Ædiles, and Tribunes, continued to exercise their functions with certain alterations; the Censors (of whom the Princeps was always one), were suppressed in the second century; the Quæstors (from the time of Claudius), were charged also with the superintendence of the gladiatorial combats.

B b. *New officers.* *α.*—The Præfectus urbi, who was intrusted with authority sufficient for the preservation of public order, and with the jurisdiction in criminal cases (at first in conjunction with the quæstiones). *β.* The Præfecti prætorio, originally only the commandants of the body-guard (of ten prætorian cohorts), raised by Octavian, but employed, soon after the institution of the office, in the administration of justice and other duties. They took precedence immediately after the emperor. *γ.* The Præfectus annonæ, who superintended the supply of corn.

The Emperor always exercised considerable influence over these appointments, which after the third century were entirely in his own hands.

631 4. Rome and Italy.—After the admission of all Italians to the
C rights of citizenship, Rome, instead of being itself the state, became merely the capital of a more extended empire. Octavian divided the city (which had been considerably embellished by his exertions), into fourteen, and Italy, as far as the Alps, into eleven regiones. The other cities were distinguished by the titles of municipia, coloniæ, and præfecturæ, but their internal constitution was the same in all essential particulars. The population of these cities was presided over by magistrates elected annually, and by a senate or ordo decurionum.

632 5. The provinces were divided by Octavian into—*a. provinciæ principis,* the more important provinces, which were always occupied by a considerable military force, and regarded the emperor himself as their governor. Consequently the administration was always committed to imperial lieutenants with prætorian authority (termed,
D at a later period, præsides and correctores). *b. Provinciæ senatûs,* comprehending all the others, which required only a small force, and were administered by proconsuls with the assistance of lieutenants and quæstors.

633 6. Taxation.—In addition to the public exchequer, Octavian established from taxes, and other sources, a *military ærarium,* for the remuneration and maintenance of his soldiers; and a *fiscus,* or privy purse.

For the protection of the frontiers, standing armies were quartered in castra stativa on the Rhine, the Danube, and the Euphrates.

The wars of Augustus. 634

The object of these wars was not so much the acquisition of fresh territory as the security of that which Rome already possessed. Thus, for the purpose of tranquillizing Spain, the hitherto unconquered Cantabrians and Asturians were completely subjugated by Agrippa (19). The eastern frontier of the empire was secured by a campaign against the Parthians, whose king (Phraātes) no sooner heard of the arrival of Augustus in Syria (20), than he restored the standards and prisoners captured from the army of Crassus. To protect Italy and Gaul against the invasion of the Germanic tribes, Drusus and Tiberius, step-sons of Augustus, first subdued the Alpine clans in Rhætia, Vindelicia, and Norĭcum, as far as the Danube (15). Then expeditions were undertaken, by Drusus, and after his death by Tiberius, from Gaul into the interior of Germany (comp. B. ii. § 3). Although the people of lower Germany were rather won by fair promises and alliances than subdued by the sword, the Romans nevertheless treated the whole country from the Rhine to the Elbe as their province, built fortresses, and introduced the Roman language, laws, and system of taxation. The oppressive administration of the governor L. Quinctilius Varus at length occasioned an insurrection of the tribes of Lower Germany (Cherusci, Bructĕres, and Marsi), under Herman or Armĭnius, the son of a prince of the Cherusci. Varus, misled by a false report of the revolt of some remote German tribe (the Amsivarii [*al.* Ampsivarii], or Sigambri ?), allowed himself to be drawn into the trackless waste of the Teutoburgian forest, where he was attacked by Herman, and three of the best Roman legions were cut to pieces, A. D. 9.

For the golden age of arts and sciences (under Augustus), see § 165.

635 The remaining days of Augustus were rendered miserable by the excesses of his daughter, Julia, and his granddaughter, and by the unscrupulous perseverance with which his third wife, Livia, labored to secure the succession of her son, Tiberius, whom Augustus was at last persuaded to adopt and nominate as co-regent. The emperor died at Nola in the seventy-sixth year of his age.

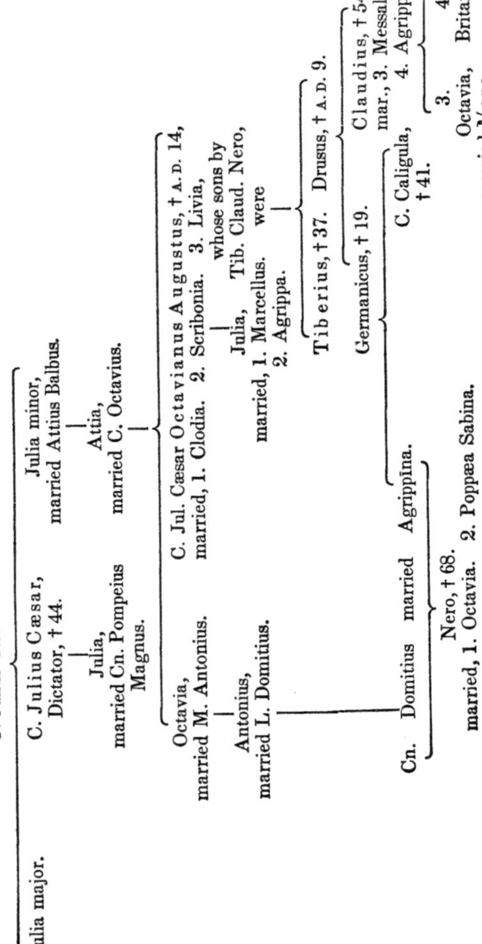
C. Julius Cæsar.
Julia major.
C. Julius Cæsar, Dictator, † 44.
Julia minor, married Attius Balbus.
Julia, married Cn. Pompeius Magnus.
Attia, married C. Octavius.
Octavia, married M. Antonius.
C. Jul. Cæsar Octavianus Augustus, † A.D. 14, married, 1. Clodia. 2. Scribonia. 3. Livia, whose sons by Tib. Claud. Nero, were
Antonius, married L. Domitius.
Julia, married, 1. Marcellus. 2. Agrippa.
Tiberius, † 37.
Drusus, † A.D. 9.
Germanicus, † 19.
Claudius, † 54, mar., 3. Messalina. 4. Agrippina.
Cn. Domitius married Agrippina.
C. Caligula, † 41.
Nero, † 68. married, 1. Octavia. 2. Poppæa Sabina.
3. Octavia, married Nero.
4. Britannicus.

§ 156. *Four Emperors of the House of Livia.*

(14—68.)

1. Tiberius, 14—37, the chief traits in whose character 636
were envy, dissimulation, and cruelty,[1] had been persuaded A
by his mother Livia, to adopt his nephew Germanĭcus,
whom he was now eagerly striving to set aside. With this
intention he recalled him from Germany, (where he had
made three campaigns, (especially against the Chatti and
Cherusci), and overthrown Arminius (at Idistavisus), and
was in the very act of wiping out by fresh victories the
disgrace which the Roman arms had sustained in that
country,) and sent him into the east, where he reduced
Cappadocia and Commagēnē to the condition of Roman
provinces, and soon afterwards died of poison. For the B
security of his person, Tiberius assembled the guards,
who were scattered throughout Italy, and quartered them
in a camp near Rome. Their commander Sejanus was
also allowed to exercise considerable influence over the
government, which had now assumed an entirely despotic
character. The anxiety of Tiberius was so effectually
fostered by Sejanus, that after a little time he quitted the
Capitol, and retired to the luxurious island of Capreæ,
leaving Sejanus as his lieutenant at Rome. After nine C
years of tyranny at Rome and throughout Italy, Sejanus
fell a victim to his own ambitious project of raising himself
to the imperial throne. Tiberius, in the seventy-seventh
year of his age, was smothered with pillows, near Misenum.

2. His successor, C. Caligŭla, in the very first year of 637
his reign squandered the enormous treasure of Tiberius in
public entertainments, magnificent spectacles of every
description, useless buildings, &c. A severe illness gradually deprived him of his understanding, and after a reign of D
four years, rendered infamous by the most atrocious cruelties, he was hurled from his throne by a conspiracy. The
senate now wished to re-establish the republic; but this
proposal was resisted by the guards, who raised to the
throne the weak-minded uncle of the murdered emperor.

---

[1] [He possessed, however, "a strong intellect, great wit, unwearied industry, a body of the happiest organization, and a beautiful and majestic figure."—*Niebuhr.*]

638 3. Claudius, 41—54, who resigned the reins of go-
A vernment into the hands of his profligate wives Messalina and Agrippīna, and a gang of abandoned freedmen, among whom Polybius, Narcissus, and Pallus were the most conspicuous. In this reign began the Roman conquests in Britain, to which country Claudius himself undertook an expedition; Mauretania, Lycia, and Thrace became Roman provinces, and Judæa (after the death of Herod Agrippa) was again ruled by Roman governors.

After the execution of Messalina, Claudius married his niece Agrippina, who at once persuaded him to adopt her son Nero) in the place of his own (Britannicus). Then she poisoned her husband, in the hope of exercising more uncontrolled power in the name of her son.

639 4. Nero, 54—68, reigned at first with wisdom and
B moderation, under the direction of his præfectus prætorio Burrus, and the philosopher Seneca, both of whom opposed the ambitious designs of Agrippina. The murder of his step-brother (Britannicus) was however deemed necessary for his security, and was speedily followed by that of his mother, and the execution of his wife Octavia at the instigation of his mistress Poppæa Sabina. After the perpetration of these acts of cruelty, and the death of Burrus, Nero gave the reins to his naturally capricious and ferocious disposition, appeared in public, both in Italy and Greece, as a charioteer and stage-player, and incurred the suspicion of having occasioned the great conflagration at Rome, by which fourteen regions of the city were destroyed, only
C three remaining uninjured. The blame of this atrocity was thrown by Nero on the Christians, whom he persecuted with unrelenting severity. When the city was rebuilt, Nero erected a palace called his golden house, which occupied the whole of the Palatine hill, and a considerable space beyond. Repeated conspiracies furnished a pretence for a great number of executions; but the excesses and cruelties of Nero having at length occasioned a general insurrection throughout the empire, Sulpicius Galba, governor of Hither Spain, a veteran of seventy-three years of age, was proclaimed emperor by his legions. On receiving intelligence of this revolution, Nero fled from Rome, and caused himself to be put to death by one of his freedmen.

§ 157. *Three Emperors proclaimed by the Legions.*

(68, 69.)

Sulpicius Galba (June, 68—Jan. 69), on his arrival at 640
Rome, rendered himself odious by the cruelty of his A
punishments (some of which were however necessary), his avarice, and the partiality which he displayed towards his favorites. He was put to death by a conspiracy headed by

Otho (Jan.—April, 69), a former favorite of Nero's, 641
who had purchased the adherence of the guards. The B
legions on the Rhine had, however, already chosen (at Cologne), their own commander Vitellius, who was speedily recognized by the entire western portion of the empire. His generals entered Italy, and defeated the army of Otho, who died by his own hand.

Vitellius (April—December, 69) returned to Rome, 642
where he expended enormous sums on the luxuries of the table. The legions employed against the Jews in Palestine having proclaimed their commander Vespasian, almost the whole army and all the provinces abandoned Vitellius, who was murdered before the arrival of Vespasian at Rome.

§ 158. *The Three Flavii.*

Vespasianus (69—79) endeavored, by every means 643
in his power, to repair the injuries inflicted on the empire C
by his tyrannical predecessors. He restored discipline in the army, and order in the finances; completed the rebuilding of the city; reinstated the senate in its ancient privileges, after he had improved its character by increasing the number of members, and removing those who were unworthy of the office; countenanced every useful undertaking, patronized the arts and sciences, and supported at his own
expense professors of eloquence. He himself afforded an D
example of severe morality, and practised a frugality which sometimes degenerated into parsimony. *Wars.*—1. He committed to his son Titus the task of crushing a revolt of the Jews which had broken out in the reign of Nero, and which was terminated by the storming of Jerusalem, A. D. 70 (see § 81, 6). 2. An insurrection of the

(643) Batāvi, who were soon joined by other German and Gallic
A tribes, was suppressed by Vespasian's general, after a bloody engagement near [Augusta Treverorum] Trèves. 3. The war in Britain was commenced afresh by Agricŏla, whose mild and just administration reconciled the Britons to the Roman yoke. His eldest son

644 Titus (79—81), surnamed amor et deliciæ generis humani, on account of his distinguished qualities, was the wisest and noblest of all the Roman emperors. During his short reign occurred the unexpected and terrible eruption of Mount Vesuvius (which destroyed the cities of Herculaneum, Pompeii, and Stabiæ), a conflagration which lasted three days, and the pestilence at Rome. His younger brother

645 Domitian (81—96) commenced his reign auspiciously,
B but soon brought back the abuses of Nero's time. With a vanity utterly ridiculous in one whose chief amusement was the slaughter of flies, he assumed the titles of "Lord" and "God;" combining with this childish folly a disposition to extravagance, which led him to commit acts of gross oppression and cruelty. Agricola had already reduced England and Scotland, as far north as Edinburgh, to the condition of a Roman province, when the suspicious jea-
C lousy of Domitian occasioned his recall. The tyrant himself undertook an expedition into Germany, during which he probably made Swabia a province of Rome, and carried on an unsuccessful war against the Dacians, whose turbulence he appeased by the promise of an annual tribute; and then celebrated his triumph as if a victory had been gained. Domitian was murdered at the instigation of his wife (whom he had destined to the same fate), and his name erased from the records of the Roman Empire.

§ 159. *The most flourishing period of the Empire.*

(96—180.)

646 (M. Cocceius) Nerva (96—98), an aged senator, was
D called to the imperial throne after the assassination of Domitian. His parsimony occasioned discontent among the people, and disgusted the Prætorians, whose vengeance he avoided by adopting their favorite general Ulpius Trajanus.

Trajanus [Trajan] (98—117), a Spaniard (the first 647
foreign emperor), whilst he exhibited the most commenda- A
ble anxiety for the improvement of every branch of the administration, more especially directed his attention to the aggrandizement of the empire. The Dacians, on his refusal to continue the tribute granted to them by Domitian, resumed their predatory incursions, and were *finally subdued after two campaigns;* the events of which are represented in relief on Trajan's column. *In two (?) campaigns against the Parthians* (who had placed a vassal on the throne of Armenia), Trajan reduced Armenia, Mesopotamia, and Assyria to the condition of Roman provinces, stormed Ctesiphon the Parthian capital, and advanced towards Arabia as far as the Persian Gulf. Some advantages were also gained by
the governor of Syria in Arabia Petræa. The revolt of B
some nations and cities in his rear, especially of the Jews, compelled the emperor to commence a retreat, during which he died, leaving his throne to his learned, but vain and pedantic, countryman and kinsman,

(P. Ælius) Hadrianus (117—138), who concluded a 648
peace with the Parthians, to whom he restored the almost untenable conquests of his predecessor on the other side of the Euphrates (Armenia also received back her kings, as vassals of Rome). *The attention of the new emperor was directed exclusively to the improvement of the internal
administration of his empire.* To promote this object, he C
travelled through all the provinces, generally on foot, embellished the capitals—Athens by the addition of "Hadrian's town"—erected monuments (in Rome the moles Hadriani) and frontier fortresses (in Britain a rampart of earth against the Picts, in Germany a line of palisades from the Main to the Danube); commanded Salvius Julianus to compile from the edicts of the prætors a code of civil law, which was termed edictum perpetuum; selected the members of his consistorium principis chiefly from the college of jurists, and introduced a new arrangement of the offices of state, which continued to the latest period of the
empire (officia palatina, publica and militaria). The D
establishment of a Roman colony (Ælia Capitolina), with a temple of Jupiter Capitolinus on the ruins of Jerusalem, occasioned a *terrible insurrection,* which was only sup-

A pressed after an obstinate struggle of three years (131—133). Hadrian was succeeded by his adopted son,

649 Antonīnus Pius (138—161), of whose peaceful and mild reign we possess only a few detached notices, relating chiefly to his private life, and anxiety for the internal welfare of his empire. A small portion of his time seems to have been occupied in unimportant wars with the Germans and Dacians, and the suppression of revolts in some of the provinces. Antoninus had already, at the desire of Hadrian, adopted the stoic philosopher,

650 M. Aurelius Antoninus (161—180), and the weak and
B profligate L. Verus, who ascended the throne together. At the request of M. Aurelius, Verus undertook the conduct of a war against the Parthians, who had invaded the eastern provinces. The management of the campaign was, nevertheless, intrusted by Verus to his lieutenants, who brought the war to a satisfactory conclusion; whilst their general, both in the east, and after his return, seemed only to live for his dissolute pleasures. During the Parthian war, the southern provinces of the Roman empire, already devastated by a pestilence brought into them from the east, were ravaged by the Marcomanni, Quadi, and other German tribes, who extended their
C conquests to Italy itself. Their audacity occasioned the great war of the Marcomanni, which was carried on by Marcus Aurelius in person (166—180). Thrice he crossed the Alps, and remained several years in the countries on the other side of those mountains. The two first wars were terminated by treaties; but these attempts to conciliate the barbarians proving ineffectual, Aurelius again attacked them, and gained an important victory, but died before he could bring the war to a conclusion.

§ 160. *Decline of the Empire under the Prætorians.*

(180—284.)

651 Commŏdus (180—192), the feeble-minded son of
D Marcus Aurelius, granted peace to the Marcomanni and Quadi, on condition of their furnishing a yearly contingent. The flatterers of the young emperor availed themselves of

his weakness to lead him into the most scandalous excesses, (651)
and of the mistrust occasioned by the discovery of several A
conspiracies, to counsel acts of ferocious cruelty. The government was intrusted to the præfect of his guard for the time being, whilst the emperor exhibited himself as Hercules Romanus in gladiatorial shows (735 times) and combats with wild beasts. His insane pranks at last so terrified even his favorite courtiers, that, in order to save their own lives, they put him to death, and raised to the throne Pertinax, the præfectus urbi, who enjoyed the confidence of the senate.

Pertĭnax (193) was murdered by the guards (whose 652
excesses he endeavored to restrain), after a reign of three B
months. The imperial throne was now offered to the highest bidder, and purchased by

Didius Julianus. In three provinces, however, the 653
legions declared against him, and proclaimed their own generals, one of whom, the commander of the Illyrian legion,

Septimius Severus, being the first to appear in Italy, 654
was recognized by the senate, after the assassination of Pertinax, and enabled to bid defiance to his rivals. All the leisure allowed him by his constant wars, was devoted by this emperor to the correction of various abuses, which had crept into the administration, and to the amendment of the legal code, a task in which he was assisted by the
jurists Papinianus, Paulus, and Ulpianus. In extreme old C
age, Severus, in conjunction with his sons Geta and Caracalla, undertook an expedition into Britain, for the purpose of chastising the Scottish Highlanders, who had broken through the rampart of Hadrian. After penetrating the most remote recesses of the Highlands, and strengthening the former mound (probably that of Hadrian) by a wall, Severus died at York, partly of grief occasioned by the ingratitude of his sons, who succeeded him on the imperial throne.

Caracalla (211—217), in the first year of his reign, murdered 655
his brother, and soon afterwards put to death 20,000 men, women, D
and children, under pretence of their being his adherents. Among these victims was the advocate Papinianus, who had refused to defend the fratricide. In order to satisfy the greediness of his soldiers, and at the same time procure sufficient funds for his own prodigal

(655) expenditure, Caracalla, after exhausting the treasures accumulated
A by his father, put to death a number of the richer citizens, granted the full privileges of Roman citizenship to the inhabitants of all the provinces (constitutio Antoniniana de civitate), that he might subject them to the payment of heavier taxes, and visited the provinces in person for the purpose of extorting money. On these excursions he appeared in Macedonia as Alexander, and in Asia as Achilles. At Alexandria he put to death a great number of persons in revenge for some insult offered to him by the citizens. After invading and ravaging Media, he was murdered at the instigation of the præf. præt.

656 Macrinus (217), who succeeded him on the throne. This em-
B peror purchased peace from the Parthians, who had entered the Roman dominions with the intention of making reprisals for the invasion of Media by Caracalla. The withdrawal of several privileges hitherto enjoyed by the army in Syria, so disgusted the soldiers, that they raised to the imperial throne a priest of the sun, named Bassianus Heliogabalus, a youth of fourteen, the son, as they pretended, of the late emperor, Caracalla. Macrinus was defeated near Antiochia, and lost his life in attempting to escape from his pursuers.

657 Heliogabalus (217—222) gave himself up to every sort of sensual enjoyment; whilst his mother and grandmother administered the affairs of his empire, and even attended the meetings of the senate. He was persuaded to adopt his cousin Alexander Severus, whom he afterwards wished to destroy, and lost his own life in endeavoring to carry his murderous intentions into effect.

658 Alexander Severus (222—235), under the direction
C of his excellent mother Mammæa, and a council of sixteen senators (among whom was Ulpianus), reigned with as much credit as was possible, considering the military tyranny to which the empire was now subjected; but the severity with which he treated the soldiers occasioned several mutinies in the legions. In the year 226 the Parthian empire was dissolved, and the new Persian, founded by a Persian, named by the Greeks Artaxerxes, who boasted of being a descendant from the ancient Persian
D kings. The new sovereign having, in his eagerness to extend his empire, passed the Roman frontier, and proceeded as far as Cappadocia, the emperor undertook an expedition into the east, where he gained many important advantages. At a later period of his reign an irruption of the Germans into Gaul rendered his presence necessary on the banks of the Rhine, where his severity occasioned a mutiny among the Gallic legionaries, which ended in the murder of himself and his mother, by whom he had been accompanied in all his expeditions.

Under his successors, until the reign of Aurelian, the 659
empire continued to decline, partly through the incessant A
incursions of neighboring nations (particularly the Germans), and partly through intestine divisions, which occasioned the elevation of rival emperors (nineteen against Gallienus, the so-called thirty tyrants). The nine emperors, who reigned during this period of thirty-five years, as well as the anti-Cæsars, obtained and lost the throne, generally speaking, through assassination.

In opposition to Maximinus (235—238), a Thracian herdsman, 660
of gigantic size and strength, two rival emperors were proclaimed in B
Africa—Gordian I., and his son, Gordian II. The son was slain in an engagement with the governor of Mauretania; the father died by his own hand. The senate now nominated to the imperial dignity two members of their own body, Maximus and Balbinus; to whom, at the request of the people, they added Gordian III., grandson of Gordian I. Maximinus, on his return from Germany, was murdered by his own soldiers during the siege of Aquileia; the two senators were slain by the Prætorians.

Gordianus (238—244), who governed well during the lifetime 661
of his father-in-law Misitheus, was assassinated, after the death of his adviser, by the Arabian

Philippus (244—249), who celebrated with great magnificence 662
the thousandth anniversary of the building of Rome. The Pan- C
nonian Decius, having been sent into Mœsia for the suppression of a revolt, was proclaimed emperor by the legions quartered in that country, and overcame Philip, who lost his life in the engagement.

Decius (249—251) [the persecutor of the Christians] was slain 663
in battle against the Goths, who had invaded Thrace. The legions now proclaimed their commander

Gallus (251—253), who consented to pay a yearly tribute to the 664
Goths; and on that account was deposed and murdered by Æmilianus, governor of Mœsia, by whom the Goths had been attacked and compelled to relinquish their booty.

Æmilianus (253) was put to death by his soldiers after a reign 665
of four months, and succeeded by

Valerianus (253—260), who had entered Italy with the inten- 666
tion of avenging the murder of Gallus. During the reign of this D
emperor, the Roman dominions were invaded on all sides by the Franks, Alemanni, Goths, and Persians, who were feebly resisted by Valerian and his son Gallienus. The emperor himself was taken prisoner in a war against the Persians.

Gallienus (260—268) was opposed by about nineteen rival em- 667
perors (the so-called thirty tyrants), whose conflicting claims occasioned the most hopeless confusion. Most of them, it is true, were soon set aside; but Tetricus maintained his position in Gaul and Spain, whilst Odenathus of Palmyra, after his victory over the Persians, obtained, as co-regent with Gallienus, the sovereignty of the east, which after his assassination (267) was assumed by his widow Zenobia. Under these two sovereigns, Palmyra became one of the

A most flourishing cities of the east. Gallienus, whilst besieging his rival Aureolus in Milan, fell by the hand of an assassin, and was succeeded by the bravest of his generals,

668 Claudius II. (268—270), who took Milan, and put Aureolus to death. This emperor materially weakened the power of the barbarians by a victory over the Alemanni who had invaded Italy, and by thrice defeating the Goths and their allies. He died of the plague, after recommending the ablest of his generals, Aurelian, as his successor.

669 Aurelianus (270—275), on his accession, found the empire divided; Tetricus reigning in the west, and Zenobia being mistress of the whole Syrian empire, and most of the provinces of Asia Minor and Egypt. His successful endeavors to restore the integrity of the empire obtained B him the surname of restitutor patriæ. Before, however, this object could be accomplished, he was compelled to sustain several invasions of the German tribes. The province of Daria, which it was almost impossible to protect, was abandoned to the Goths, the Roman inhabitants being transplanted to Mœsia (Dacia Aureliani); but on the other hand, the Marcomanni and Alemanni (the latter of whom had penetrated as far as Umbria) were driven back into their own country. A new wall was also erected for the security of Rome against the barbarians. Aurelian then marched against Zenobia, who was in the act of subduing the rest of Asia Minor. After two defeats (at Antiochia and Emĕsa) she retreated to her capital, which C was besieged by Aurelian. Zenobia escaped from the city, but was afterwards taken prisoner and conveyed to Rome, to adorn the triumph of her conqueror. Palmyra, which had opened its gates after the capture of the queen, was at first spared; but the citizens having, after the emperor's departure, murdered the Roman garrison, Aurelian returned, butchered most of the inhabitants, and destroyed the city, with its magnificent temples and palaces. Having subdued Egypt also, he marched into Gaul, where Tetricus weary of sovereignty, suffered himself to be taken pri soner in a battle near Châlons. The emperor, whose severity had rendered him odious, was assassinated, during an expedition against the Persians, at the instigation of his secretary.

670 Tacitus (who was nominated to the imperial dignity by the senate), and his brother Florianus, reigned only a few months.

Probus (276—282) strained every nerve to restore (670)
the ancient military discipline, and resisted with great zeal A
and success the numerous inroads of German tribes (Burgundians, Alemanni, Vandals, and Franks) into the Roman provinces. He advanced into Germany as far as the Elbe, compelled nine princes to pay tribute, strengthened the frontier lines from the Rhine to the Danube, and enlisted a number of Germans into the Roman legions (Return of the Franks from the Black sea to the Rhine?). After a campaign in the east, followed by a magnificent triumph, the emperor put in execution a plan for re-peopling the deserted provinces with German settlers. The discontent B
of his soldiers (who were compelled to plant vineyards, dig canals, make roads, drain swamps, &c., for the new colonists) having occasioned the assassination of Probus, the army chose as his successor the præfectus prætorio

Carus (282, 283), who appointed his sons Carinus and Numerianus to be his co-regents, defeated the Sarmatæ (who had invaded Illyria), and lost his life (probably by assassination) during a campaign against the Persians. 671

Carinus and Numerianus (284). Numerianus, on his march 672
back from Persia, was murdered by his own father-in-law. The C
soldiers, who were disgusted at the extravagant luxury in which Carinus lived at Rome, having raised to the imperial throne Diocletian, commander of the household troops, Carinus took the field against his rival, and lost his life in Mœsia.

§ 161. *Period occupied by partitions of the Empire, until the reign of Constantine.*

(284—324.)

Diocletianus (284—305) appointed as co-regent his 673
comrade in arms Maximianus, to whom he committed the administration of the western district. Diocletian himself established his residence in Nicomedia, where he introduced the oriental court ceremonies, whilst his colleague resided alternately at Trèves, Arles, and Milan. The in- D
creasing audacity of the Germanic tribes on the banks of the Rhine and Danube, soon compelled each of the two emperors to appoint a colleague (Constantius Chlorus and Galerius). The four sovereigns now apportioned among themselves the administration of the provinces and the defence of the frontiers; but, in spite of this arrangement, rival emperors established themselves in the provinces (Carausius in Britain, and afterwards Allectus and Achil-

(673) leus in Egypt), where they continued to reign for many
A years. On the other hand, the inroads of the neighboring tribes were repressed; and Galerius, in a war with the Persians (which he had undertaken for the purpose of settling the succession to the throne of Armenia), obtained possession of five provinces on the other side of the Tigris, and compelled the Persians to renounce their claims on Mesopotamia. At the instigation of Galerius, Diocletian prohibited the celebration of Christian worship, and commenced a cruel persecution of the Christians throughout
B the empire. Finding himself, after a severe illness, too feeble to transact the business of government, Diocletian abdicated (contemporaneously with Maximian), and passed the rest of his life at Salōna in Dalmatia, where he amused himself with the cultivation of a garden.

674 The practice of apportioning the government among four sovereigns still continued; Constantius and Galerius being proclaimed Augusti, and nominating each a colleague. Ater the death of Constantius (306), which happened during an expedition into Britain, his son Constantīnus was proclaimed emperor in that country. He deposed all the coadjutors, the number of whom now amounted to five, and became in the year 324 sole occupant of the imperial throne.

675 After the death of Constantius, his son Constantinus was pro-
C claimed emperor by the troops in Britain, and Maxentius, the feeble son of Maximian, by those at Rome; Galerius nominated his friend Licinius as his coadjutor; Maximian again appeared in the character of emperor, and Maximin also assumed the title of Augustus. Thus in the year 308 there were six emperors.

Constantius caused his father-in-law Maximian (who had attempted his life) to be secretly strangled; and defeated his son Maxentius in three engagements (at Turin, Verona, and Saxa rubra on the Tiber). In the last of these battles Maxentius was drowned in the Tiber. Galerius died in consequence of his excesses—Maximinus was defeated by Licinius, and took poison.

676 Constantinus, and his brother-in-law Licinius (313—324).
D Constantine soon quarrelled with his brother-in-law (who had become too powerful since his victory over Maximin), and after two defeats forced him to content himself with the Asiatic provinces, Thrace and eastern Mœsia. In a second war, Licinius was again defeated in two engagements (at Adrianople and Chalcĕdon). Being shut up in Nicomedia, he consented to abdicate on condition of being permitted to depart unmolested; but this compact was violated by Constantine, who put him to death at Thessalonica, and thus became monarch of the entire Roman empire.

§ 162. *Constantine the Great, sole Emperor.*

(324—337.)

Constantine, who from the commencement of his reign had permitted the free exercise of their religion to the Christians, himself embraced Christianity, in consequence of a miraculous appearance in the heavens, immediately before his third victory over Maxentius, and proclaimed it as the religion of the state, but deferred his baptism until the close of his life. He assembled the first œcumenical council at Nicæa (325), where the doctrine of Arius (that the SON of GOD is inferior to GOD the FATHER [even 'as touching his Godhead']) was condemned, and the doctrine of the SON's essential equality with the FATHER[1] asserted in the Symbŏlum Nicænum ['*the Nicene Creed*'], in which it is expressed by the term ὁμοούσιος (consubstantialis). 677 A

2. New organization of the Empire. 678

Constantine laid the foundation of a future division of the empire in the establishment of a new capital at Byzantium, which was restored on a scale of great magnificence, and repeopled, but not without the commission of many acts of violence and oppression. At its dedication in 330 or 334, this city was called Nova Roma, but at a later period it received the name of Constantinopolis. The two capitals were placed on an equal footing, each having its own senate and præfect of the city. The remainder of the empire was divided into thirteen dioceses, which were subdivided into 116 provinces. At the head of the state was the emperor, who in most cases received the title of Cæsar and Augustus from the armies, or was admitted to that dignity by his predecessor. His lieutenants were, as before, the præfecti prætorio, whose influence Constantine weakened by increasing the number to four (1, for the East with Thrace; 2, for Illyria, with Macedonia and Greece; 3, for Italy and Africa; 4, for the B C

[1] This question fills an important place in the history of the invasion and the revolutions which followed it. Many of the Barbarians embraced Arianism, and their subsequent hostility to the Romans, or to other barbarian tribes, may often be traced to this circumstance. Gibbon's 21st ch. contains a masterly exposition of the whole subject, to be used always with due precaution.

(678) West). He also transferred the military command from
A those officers to a magister peditum and magister equitum. The dioceses were administered by vicars (deputies of the præfects), and the provinces by rectors. The commanders of the troops in the provinces were termed duces, and sometimes also comites.

679 The seven chief court offices were—1. The præpositus sacri cubiculi (grand chamberlain), who superintended the internal arrangements of the imperial palace. 2. The magister officiorum (imperial chancellor), who was charged with the care of the solemn representations at the imperial court, and exercised a jurisdiction over all the other officers. 3. The quæstor sacri palatii (secretary of state), through whom all new laws and the decisions of the emperor on petitions were made known to the public. He also countersigned the cabinet orders. 4 The comes sacrarum largitionum (minister of finance). 5. The comes rei privatæ (privy-purse). 6
B and 7. The two comites domesticorum, commanders of the household troops, which occupied the place of the disbanded prætorians. These seven officers, with the præfectus præt., the præf. urbi, and the counsellors of state properly so called (comites consistoriani), composed the council (consistorium) of the emperor, by whom they were especially consulted on questions of legislation. Many of the institutions of former days were also retained—a senate, for instance, in each of the capitals, which were sometimes consulted respecting the laws, or commissioned to decide the more important criminal cases—two consuls, prætors and quæstors, dignities from which a heavy expenditure was inseparable. The highest civil and military officers down to the comes rei privatæ were designated "illustres;" next to them were the "spectabiles," then the "clarissimi," "perfectissimi," and last of all the "egregii."

680 The Taxes.—1. An annual land and poll-tax, levied by an im-
C perial edict termed indictio. This tax, which was paid partly in cash and partly in agricultural produce, was founded on a census, renewed every fifteen years. 2. A tax on manufactures and trade. 3 Revenue derived from harbor dues and duties on articles brought overland, mines, coinage of money, and imperial manufactures. 4. Golden crowns (aurum coronarium), presented to the emperor on solemn occasions as marks of honor.

681 Towards the end of his reign, Constantine assisted the Sarmătæ and Vandals in a war against the Goths; and when the latter entered Mœsia with the intention of avenging themselves, they were driven back into their own
D country. A great number of the Sarmatæ (300,000) were settled by Constantine in the Roman provinces on the Danube. His eldest son Crispus having been put to death on the accusation of his wife Fausta (who was herself stifled in a bath), his three younger sons divided the empire among themselves.

§ 163. *The successors of Constantine the Great to the permanent division of the Empire.*

(337—395.)

682 Of Constantine's three sons, Constantius (337—364) became at last sole emperor, through the death of both his A brothers; one of whom was murdered by the other, and the assassin himself destroyed by a conspiracy. The rival emperors were also all set aside.

683 Constantine II. inherited the west, Constantius the east with Constantinople, and Constans the country lying between the dominions of his two brothers. Whilst Constantius was engaged in a long war with the Persians, by which great injury was inflicted on both nations, Constantine lost his life in an attempt to depose his brother Constans; who rendered himself contemptible by his excesses, and fell a victim to a conspiracy. Thus Constantius (after also expelling two usurpers) became sole occupant of the throne.

684 The Alemanni and Franks having invaded Gaul, Constantius intrusted the defence of that province to his ne- B phew Julian, who compelled the Alemanni and a portion of the Franks to recross the Rhine, and assigned settlements in Belgium to the Salian Franks, who were vassals of Rome. The military reputation of his nephew, and his admirable administration of Gaul, excited the envy of the emperor, who was engaged in an unsuccessful war against the Persians, which he made a pretence for withdrawing several legions from Julian. Instead, however, of marching eastwards, the Gallic legions proclaimed Julian emperor at Paris, and Constantine died in Cilicia on his march homewards to oppose the nomination.

685 Julianus Apostăta (361—363), who had been educated in the Christian faith, was perverted to paganism by C the study of heathen literature and initiation into the Greek mysteries. He endeavored to re-establish the ancient idolatrous worship, wrote against Christianity, and manifested his hatred of the religion from which he had apostatized by protecting the Jews; but his attempts to restore the temple at Jerusalem were rendered abortive by the bursting forth of flames out of the ground. In an expedition against the Persians, whose proposals of peace he had rejected, Julian crossed the Tigris, and gained a

A decisive victory near Ctesiphon; but was mortally wounded on his return. He was succeeded by a Christian emperor,

686 Jovianus (363—364), who accepted the conditions of peace offered by the Persians (for thirty years), ceded the five provinces on the other side the Tigris, which had been conquered by Diocletian, and left Armenia to its fate. After his death, which happened on the homeward march from Persia, the army chose the commander of the household troops,

687 Valentinianus I. (364—375), who appointed his
B brother Valens (364—378) co-regent, and assigned him the eastern half of the empire, the frontiers of which were at that period invaded in almost every direction by the barbarians. Thenceforward the empire continued to be divided into eastern and western, except in the last year of Theodosius, when the two portions were re-united.

688 Valentinian I. was occupied during the whole of his reign with war against the *Alemanni,* who had ravaged Gallia and Rhætia. The enemy were compelled to re-cross the Rhine, and for several years maintained the conflict in their own country. A chain of fortresses was established on the Rhine from Bâsle to Mainz (Mayence), and another on the Neckar. Finally, Valentinian drove the *Quadi* and *Sarmătæ,* who had invaded Illyricum, across the Danube, and died of hæmorrhage, occasioned by the excitement of an angry discussion with the ambassadors of the Quadi. *Britain,* which had been overrun by the Picts and Scots, was re-conquered in some sort by Theodosius, father of the next emperor, who extended the frontier as far as the rampart of Antoninus, and formed a new province, named Valentia, out of the territory thus acquired.

C Valens, as an Arian, persecuted the orthodox party, and at the same time ill-treated the pagan favorites of Julian. His incapacity and worthlessness favored the elevation to the throne of Procopius, a relation of Julian, who owed his election to the bought votes of the soldiers at Constantinople. After maintaining his position for nearly a year, Procopius was delivered up to his rival by his own soldiers. Wars of Valens. 1. The *West Goths* or Thervingians (under their "Judge" Athanaric) were kept at bay for three years, and prevented from crossing the frontier by an irregular army collected from all parts of the Roman provinces and sent across the Danube. 2. A war with the *Persians* respecting the right of nomination to the throne of Armenia and Iberia was not yet concluded, when fresh outbreaks rendered the emperor's presence necessary on the banks of the Danube.

Commencement of the immigrations. The
689 Huns having entered Europe from Eastern Asia and

joined the Alāni (between the Caspian and Black sea), (689)
attacked the Goths, a partially christianized people, dwel- A
ling between the Don and the Danube. A portion of the West Goths were permitted by Valens to settle in Mœsia; but the severity of the Roman governor having driven them to revolt, they in company with the Ostro-Goths forced their way into Thrace, traversed Macedonia as far as Thessaly and defeated Valens near Adrianople (378), where the emperor and two-thirds of his soldiers were slain. His successor in the east,

Theodosius (379—395), terminated the war with the 690
Goths by assigning to whole tribes of that nation tracts of B
waste land in Mœsia, Thrace, Phrygia, and Lydia. In the last year of his reign, Theodosius re-united the eastern and western empires, which he again divided between his two sons, Arcadius receiving the east, and Honorius the west, 395.

In the west, Valentinian I. was succeeded by his sons Gra- 691
tianus, and Valentinianus II. a child of seven years old. C
Gratian defeated the Alemanni near Colmar, and having received intelligence of the death of his uncle (Valens), dispatched the younger Theodosius into the east, and after he had delivered the empire from the Goths, rewarded him with the eastern portion. Gratian having rendered himself odious by favoring the barbarians, the legions quartered in Britain called Maximus to the throne, and Gratian lost his life in attempting to escape from his rival. Maximus reigned many years in Gaul, but having entered Italy, he was defeated and put to death by Theodosius, to whom Valentinian II. had fled for safety. Thus Valentinian became sole emperor, but the management of public affairs was intrusted to Arbogastes, a Frank, who had conquered Gaul for Theodosius. An attempt on the part of the emperor to circumscribe the power of this favorite
occasioned his own assassination. The murderer did not however D
himself assume the imperial crown, but proclaimed Eugenius, the magister officiorum, who was defeated and executed by Theodosius, upon which Arbogastes slew himself. Thus Theodosius became sole emperor in the year 394.

§ 164. *The Western Roman Empire—to its Fall.*

(395—476.)

Honorius (395—423), under the guardianship of the 692
Vandal Stilĭcho. Imperial residence at Ravenna (since 404).

693 The two first wars with the West Goths [Visi-
A goths]. Alaric, king of the West Goths, having invaded Macedonia and Greece, and threatened Italy itself, under pretence that the subsidy granted by Theodosius to his countrymen had not been paid, Stilicho unexpectedly appeared with a small fleet off Peloponnesus, whereupon Alaric withdrew to Illyria. Having recruited his army the Gothic prince entered Upper Italy with his whole force but was defeated by Stilicho at Pollentia and Verona, and again retired into Illyria.

694 Several German tribes who had also invaded Italy under
B the command of Radagais, were permitted by Stilicho to advance as far as Florence, where he blockaded them with the assistance of other barbarians, and compelled the greater part of them to surrender at discretion.

695 Stilicho having recalled the legions quartered in Britain and on the Rhine for the protection of Italy, the German tribes overran the western provinces without opposition, the Alemanni settling in Alsace and Lorraine, the Franks in north-western Gaul, the Burgundians in the districts bordering on the Jura, and the Vandals, Alans, and Suevi in Spain, whilst the tracts of country on the banks of the Danube, which the invader had quitted, were occupied by the Gepidæ, Sarmatæ, and especially by the Huns, who took possession of Pannonia.

696 The third war with the West Goths. Stilicho
C having persuaded the senate to grant Alaric an indemnification for sums expended in abortive preparations for a common expedition (against Constantinople ?), was accused by Olympius (a favorite of the emperor) of trafficking with the barbarian, and suffered death. Alaric, who probably had never received the subsidy voted to him, now advanced into Italy, and blockaded Rome ; but consented to raise the siege on payment of a large sum of money by the inhabitants. The court at Ravenna having refused his claim to rank as the first general in the service of Honorius, Alaric persuaded the præf. urbi Attalus to accept the imperial dignity ; but soon deposed him, and
D resumed his negotiations with Honorius. An ambuscade near Ravenna occasioned another siege of Rome, which was taken and given up to plunder during six (?) days in the year 410. Alaric died at Consentia, on an expedition

into Lower Italy. His brother-in-law and successor (696)
Ataulphus, concluded a peace with Honorius (whose sister A
Placidia he married), and led the West Goths into Gaul (in 412), and Spain (414).

The western empire was now tottering to its fall—for not only 697
were Gaul and Spain almost entirely in the hands of barbarian invaders, but several rival emperors were striving with each other and with Honorius for possession of the remaining portion. An attempt was also made by the governor of Africa to depose Honorius by landing in Umbria, but his whole army was cut to pieces in a single engagement. Constantius, an Illyrian, who had subdued the usurpers in Gaul, held the reins of government during the last years of Honorius, married Placidia, the emperor's sister, and was invested with the imperial dignity; but died a short time before the decease of Honorius.

Honorius (after the short usurpation of his secretary Johannes B
(423—425), who was never recognized by the court of Constantinople) was succeeded by his son

Valentinianus III. (425—455), a child of six years 698
old, under the guardianship of his mother Placidia, who conferred on Aëtius the command-in-chief of the army and the presidency of her council of state. The intrigues of this minister involved his mistres in a dispute with Bonifacius, governor of Africa, whom he advised the empress to recall in order to test his fidelity, warning the governor at the same time not to obey the command. On C
receiving this intelligence, Bonifacius, whose province was infested by marauding African hordes, called in Genseric, the fierce and cruel king of the Vandals. The barbarians who landed in Africa in consequence of this invitation soon forgot the distinction between friend and foe; and after ravaging the whole northern coast, established a Vandalic pirate state, of which Carthage was the capital. Mauretania and Numidia remained faithful to the Roman empire, but the rest of the province was entirely subject to the barbarians, whose fleets rendezvoused in the African ports, and rendered the navigation of the Mediterranean exceedingly insecure. Britain, since the departure of the D
Roman legions, had been torn by intestine divisions and harassed by the repeated incursions of hostile tribes. In his distress one of the British princes called in some bands of Saxons, Angles, and Jutes, who landed under Hengist and Horsa in the year 445 (?), expelled the Picts

(698) and Scots, and settled in Britain, where they gradually
A established the seven Anglo-Saxon kingdoms. Genseric, king of the Vandals, formed an alliance against the West Goths and Latins with Attila, king of the Huns, who invaded Gaul with an enormous force, composed of all the nations subjected to his dominion from the Volga to the Rhine. This army was defeated by Aetius, in conjunction with the West Goths (under Theodoric I.), the Burgundians, and a portion of the Franks (under Merovæus), in the Catalaunian Fields (near Châlons-sur-Marne), in the year 451. Attila then invaded Italy, where he sacked Aquileia, and ravaged the plains of Lombardy northwards from the Po, driving a part of the inhabitants to the lagunes of the Adriatic sea, where they founded the city
B of Venice. An attack on the capital was averted by the intercession of a Roman deputation, headed by Bishop Leo. The sudden death of Attila in the following year (453) was succeeded by the dissolution of the Hunnish empire (compare B. II. § 6). Valentinian murdered Aetius (who seems to have manifested a desire to secure the imperial throne to his family by the marriage of his son with the emperor's daughter), and was himself openly assassinated on the Campus Martius by two senators, friends of Aetius, at the instigation of the senator Procopius Maximus, whose wife he had debauched.

699 Maximus (455) was called to the throne by the
C soldiers, whose support he had in all probability secured previously to the death of the late emperor. The widowed empress, Eudoxia, indignant at being compelled to marry Maximus, avenged herself by calling in Genseric, king of the Vandals, who entered the Tiber with his fleet, plundered Rome, ravaged the whole line of coast from the Tiber to Naples, and carried off the principal Romans to Africa, in the hope of obtaining large sums for their ransom. Maximus in attempting to fly was slain by his own soldiers.

700 After his death the empire, which now comprehended
D little more than Italy itself, was ruled by eight emperors, who followed one another in rapid succession. Of this number, the six first were entirely dependent on the Gothic chief, Ricimer, commandant of the foreign troops in the service of Rome; nor was the authority of any one

of them respected beyond the limits of the district in which A
he actually resided.

1. The immediate successor of Maximus was Avitus (455, 456), 701
commander-in-chief of the Roman troops in Gaul, who rendered himself contemptible by his excesses, and lost his throne and life in consequence of a conspiracy. After an interregnum of seven months, during which the Greek emperor (Marcianus) was regarded as regent, the imperial title was assumed by

2. Majorianus, commander-in-chief in the west, who seems to have recovered the eastern coast of Spain in a war with the West Goths. During his reign a Roman fleet fitted out against the Vandals was burnt by Genseric, but, on the other hand, the almost yearly invasions of those barbarians were terminated by the conclusion of a peace with their leader. In consequence of an attempt on the part of Majorian to circumscribe the influence of Ricimer, he was deposed and murdered by that general, who now exercised sovereign power in the name of his puppet

3. Livius Severus (461—465), but only in Italy, Marcellinus B
refusing to recognize his authority in Dalmatia, and Ægidius (father of Syagrius) in Gaul. After the death of Severus, the western empire was governed by Ricimer, in the name of the Greek emperor Leo, who at last, with the consent of Ricimer, nominated

4. Anthemius (467—472). A large fleet fitted out by this emperor, in conjunction with Leo, for the re-conquest of Africa, was utterly destroyed by Genseric. Anthemius having quarrelled with Ricimer, the latter caused

5. Anicius Olybrius to be proclaimed emperor, took possession of Rome in his name, and put Anthemius to death; but soon afterwards himself died, together with Olybrius, of a pestilential disease.

6. Glycerius, who had assumed the imperial dignity without C
the sanction of the Greek emperor, was soon compelled to resign his throne to

7. Julius Nepos, and he to his general Orestes, who proclaimed his son

8. Romulus Augustulus.

Since the death of Ricimer, Italy, instead of being 702
ruled by one sovereign, had been divided between Odoacer and Orestes, each of whom exercised supreme authority in the district occupied by his army. Scarcely had Orestes placed his son Romulus Augustulus on the imperial throne, when he was besieged in Pavia by an army composed of Heruli, Rugii, and other German tribes under the command of Odoacer, who carried the city by storm, and having put Orestes to death, deposed his son Romulus, and caused himself to be proclaimed *king of Italy* in the year 476.

§ 165. *Religion, &c. of the Romans.*

703 1. Religion.

A The Romans were accustomed to ascribe the establishment of their religion to their king, Numa Pompilius, to whom they also attributed the formation of the sacerdotal colleges, and the publication of the most ancient religious records. To the original Sabino-Latin element of the Roman national religion was soon added a Tuscan, and under the later kings the influence of Greece was also manifested in the adaptation of her representations of the gods and religious ceremonies to the peculiarities of the Roman faith, which they served to develope rather than
B to destroy. Thus men believed concerning Jupiter, Juno, and Minerva, all that was related by the Greeks of Zeus, and Hērē, and Athēnē, as far as that belief was consistent with the Roman character and history. The decline of the Roman religion at the commencement of the first century, before Christ, may be attributed to the introduction of the mystic worships of Egypt and of Asia, with their dark superstitions, and to the distinction established between the popular religion and that of the philosophers and poets. In the last years of the republic there seems to have been a complete dissolution of all religions as well
C as political relations. Notwithstanding the efforts of the earlier emperors to check the propagation of strange doctrines, idolatry and irreligion continued to increase, whilst on the other hand Christianity, in spite of ten fearful persecutions, steadily extended its sphere of action, until its establishment as the state religion by Constantine the Great.

704 The chief Deities of the Romans.

a *The three Capitoline divinities.* 1. Jupiter, as prince of the air, is the author of all changes in the atmosphere; rain and storm,
D thunder and lightning. He is supreme among the gods, and the most powerful agent in the direction of human affairs (optimus maximus), the protector of probity and virtue, the guardian of oaths, landmarks, and all obligations which are based on fidelity and credit. Among the many festivals celebrated in his honor, the most remarkable were the Capitoline, or great Roman Games, in the circus maximus, and the Feriæ Latinæ on the Alban mount. 2. Juno, the queen of heaven, afforded the same protection to the female sex as Jupiter to the male, and was the especial patroness of all relations

founded on marriage; she accompanied the woman from the cradle (704)
to the tomb, and befriended her in all the important occurrences of A
life. 3. Minerva was the patroness of arts and manufactures. She bestowed on the housewife the dexterity requisite for her handiwork, inspired the warrior with cunning, prudence, and courage, and imparted creative energy to the artist and the poet.

b. *Of the planets* only the two most important, the sun (sol) and 705
moon (luna) were invoked as deities. The *earth* was personified under the name of Tellus.

c. *Deities of the lower world.*—The infernal empire (like its ruling 706
divinity, was termed Orcus, Dis (*i. e.* dives). To him belongs in all probability the name Consus, and the festival Consualia. His consort, the queen of this shadowy realm, was called Libitīna.

d. *Deities of the elements.*—1. Of water: Neptunus. 2. Of fire: 707
Vulcanus, the god of furnaces and forges; and Vesta, or the fire B
of the hearth, who was honored by the women in every private house at each meal, as well as publicly in her temple, under the direction of the Vestal virgins (see 712, 5).

e. *Deities presiding over agriculture and the rearing of cattle.*— 708
The introduction of agriculture was ascribed by the Latins to their ancient king Saturnus; to whom they also attributed the first establishment of civilization (hence the golden age). His wife Ops (*i. e.* wealth) was worshipped on earth under the title of Dēmētēr. The Saturnalia, or feast in honor of Saturn, as guardian of all fruits in gardens and fields, was the general harvest festival especially designed for the recreation of slaves. To these Latin rural deities were added, about B.C. 500, three Grecian, viz. Ceres, Liber, and Libera, who had their temples and feasts (Cerealia) in common.
The protectress of the flocks was Pales, whose feast, the Palilia, C
was held on the anniversary of the building of Rome, probably because Romulus established her worship when he founded the city. Mars, also, their highest divinity next to Jupiter, and the father of their founder by a vestal virgin, was honored by the ancient Latins, not only as the god of war, but as the patron of agriculture and all other industrial pursuits of the male sex. On the Campus Martius, which was dedicated to him, were held races twice a year, and every four years a census of the Roman citizens. (For the Salii, see 712, 6.)

f. The *oracular deities* of the Latins were—1. Their deified king 709
Faunus, whose responses were given in dreams, or by mysterious voices in forests. 2. Fauna, a daughter, sister, or wife of Faunus. D
This deity, who was known among mortals as the "good goddess," communicated her oracles exclusively to females, as Faunus to males. 3. Carmentis and the Camenæ, prophetic nymphs, among whom the most renowned was Egeria, the instructress of king Numa. The worship of Apollo was introduced at a later period, but that of Diana seems to have been established contemporaneously with the settlement of the Sabines and Latins as plebeians at Rome.

g. *Deities presiding over physical and moral events.*—1. Janus, 710
who directs the commencement of every undertaking, opens and closes all things; and at the beginning of every year, month, and day, beholds with his double countenance both the past and future. His

(710) principal festival was on New Year's day. At the commencement of
A a war the temple of Janus, founded by Numa (strictly speaking, a mere gate), which was kept closed in time of peace, was solemnly opened by the consul. 2. The Parcæ, or goddesses of fate, who indicate the unchangeable destiny of man, as settled at his birth, in contradistinction to — 3. Fortuna, or chance, the directress of variable events, to whom men addressed themselves at every important crisis of their lives. 4. The worship of Venus, an ancient national divinity of the Latins, derived its importance from the identification of that goddess with the Greek Aphrodītē. 5. Divine honors were also paid to personifications of abstract ideas; such as Salus, Pax, Concordia, Libertas, Felicitas, Faustitas, Bonus Eventus, Juventus, Victoria, Terminus, and especially to moral qualities; as Mens,
B Pietas, Pudicitia, Virtus, Honos, Spes, and, above all, Fides. Amor, Cupīdo, and Voluptas, were known only through the Greeks and the poets. 6. Among the deities of trade and gain the most important was Mercurius (from mercari). 7. Bellona was the goddess of war. 8. A temple was first erected to Roma in the reign of Augustus.

711 h. *Life, death, and existence after death* are severally represented in the Roman religion by—1. The Genii, or guardian spirits, who attend men as constant companions from their birth to the hour of their death. 2. The Manes, or souls of the dead in general. 3. The Lares, a sort of saints, who either protected the commonwealth, like the great Greek heroes (such as Romulus, Remus, Quirinus, Numa, Tatius, &c.), or were worshipped as the guardians of private families. The Lares were also distinguished according to the places in which they were supposed to exercise their power; and in this point of view the most important were the House-Lares, or Penates.

712 The principal priesthoods.

C a. *The priestly colleges.*—1. The Pontifices, four, eight, fifteen, sixteen, chosen for life by the college, were charged with the superintendence of public and private worship, as well as the management of the entire priesthood and the administration of ecclesiastical law. The president of this college, the pontifex maximus, who was chosen by the people, regulated the calendar, announced the festivals, and wrote the Annales Maximi. 2. The Augures, three, four, nine, fifteen, chosen also for life by co-optatio, ascertained the will of the gods on all public questions by means of—*a.* Atmospheric phenomena, as thunder, lightning, the shooting of stars, &c.; *b.* the flight and cry of birds; *c.* the manner in which certain sacred animals
D devoured their food. The inspection of victims was conducted by the Haruspĭces (foreigners hired for that purpose). Auspicia are those signs which present themselves unsought; auguria those which are vouchsafed in answer to prayer. 3. The inspectors of the Sibylline books, two, ten, fifteen, who, on important occasions and in times of great difficulty, were empowered by the senate to consult (in presence of the chief magistrates) the books purchased, according to tradition, by Tarquinius Superbus. 4. The twenty Fetiales, appointed by Numa, or Ancus Martius, for the purpose of proclaiming war, and concluding treaties of peace and alliance in the

name of the Roman people. 5. The Vestal Virgins (four; from (712)
the time of Tarq. Priscus six), subject to the Pontifex Maximus, by A
whom they were chosen between the ages of six and ten. They were required to continue in the service of the temple thirty years; of which the first ten were employed in learning their duty, the next ten in discharging it, and the last in instructing others. Their most important duties were the keeping watch over the Palladium, and maintaining the sacred fire. 6. The Salii Palatini, established by Numa, as guardians of the shield of Mars (ancīle), which fell down from heaven, and of the eleven made in imitation of it.

b. *The priests of particular deities* were termed Flamĭnes, and 713
their wives Flaminicæ. They were distinguished as Flamines majores and minores. To this order belonged the priests of the three principal guardian deities of Rome, Jupiter, Mars, and Quirinus
(Flamen Dialis, Martialis, Quirinalis). After the expulsion of the B
Tarquins, the duty of offering public sacrifices, which had previously been discharged by the kings, was intrusted to a rex sacrorum, or rex sacrificulus.

Modes of worship. 714

The holy places were either mere consecrated inclosures (fana, delubra) or temples (templa, ædes,), with two altars; one of which (ara) was intended for libations and incense, and the other (generally termed altare) for burnt sacrifices. The sacred usages consisted of prayers, vows, consecrations, purifications, sacrifices, feasts, and public games.

2. The art of war was more successfully cultivated 715
by the Romans than by any other nation of antiquity.

a. *Land force.*—Every Roman citizen, from his six- C
teenth to his forty-fifth year, was *bound*, or, in the language of the best days of the republic, *privileged* to perform military duty in the field; the capite censi and freedmen alone being exempt, until the time of Marius. In the arrangement of the legions, they adopted, until the time of the Punic wars, the principle of the centurial constitution of Servius Tullius.

The legion consisted originally of three divisions of 1200 men, of 716
which the two first were heavily and the third lightly armed. At a D
later period (from the time of Camillus) there were five divisions, or cohorts (hastati, principes, triarii, rorarii, accensi); each cohort consisting of fifteen maniples, each maniple of two centuries, a Roman and Latin, and each century of thirty men, besides the centurion; in all 4500 men (at a later period 6000). To each legion was attached a body of cavalry, generally 300 strong. Two legions composed, in most instances, a consular army. The wings of the main army were covered by the auxiliaries, who were organized in the same manner, but with a much greater proportion of cavalry.

Towards the end of the republic, the citizens, and at a 717
later period the allies, were excused from military service,

(717) which was performed by mercenary troops from various
A countries. The emperors organized a standing body-guard (the ten cohortes prætorianæ). The army was commanded at different periods by the kings, consuls, dictators, prætors, and emperors, to whom a quæstor and a certain number of legati were assigned as lieutenants. At the head of each legion were the tribuni militum, and under them the centuriones. Constantine the Great placed in command of his entire force a magister perditum and magister equitum. Some sort of remuneration seems to have been granted under the kings, but the practice of giving regular pay to each legionary was not introduced until a short time before the Veientine war (compare page 236, D).
B Rewards were also given in the shape of participation in the booty, crowns of different descriptions, weapons of honor, and after the civil wars allotments of land, the title of imperator for the commander-in-chief, solemn thanksgivings, and, above all, the triumph (or at least the ovatio).

718 b. *The maritime force.*—(For its origin, see page 250, C.) The Roman fleets consisted of vessels of burden, light transports, and from 100 to 300 ships of war, with three or five banks of oars, manned with citizens of the lowest class, freedmen, and foreigners, who served either as seamen or marines.

719 3. Literature.

C The history of Roman literature may be divided into four periods; of which the first begins with Livius Andronīcus, about 240 years before Christ. Of the period antecedent to that date we possess nothing beyond a few religious hymns, oracular responses, table songs, a kind of popular drama (the Atellanæ), some meagre chronicles, and fragments of laws and inscriptions. The foundation of Roman literature, properly so called, was laid in the year 240 in the adaptation of some Greek poetical works, which were soon followed by similar attempts in prose.
D The second period, from the death of Sulla to that of Augustus, was the *golden age* of Roman literature, which flourished under the influence of Greek civilization and learning. Eloquence especially developed itself as an independent study, and pervaded every department of literature, which assumed in consequence a decidedly rhe-

torical character. The different kinds of poetry (with the (719)
exception of satire) were formed on Greek models, the A
subjects being borrowed from the Greek mythology, and the lack of invention supplied by elaborate diction.

The *silver age*, from the death of Augustus to the reign of Hadrian, was distinguished by an attempt to surpass the elegance and sublimity of the classical period by means of exaggeration, refinement, and rhetorical bombast. This depraved taste was not merely displayed in poetry, which had now lost its simplicity and natural character, and in eloquence, the chief employment of the Romans, and the groundwork of all scientific instruction; but pervaded all their studies, and gave to the works of this period a declamatory character.

In the last, or *brazen age*, from A. D. 410 to 476, the B
belles lettres [rejected almost all extraneous support, and] daily became more worthless and insignificant: subtle refinement, exaggeration, and the most ridiculous bombast in language and expression, now reigned in every department of literature, and drove good taste entirely from the field.

A. Poetry. 720

a. The *Epos.* The first attempts of the Romans in Epic poetry consisted partly of translations from Greek poems, especially those of Homer, and partly versified narratives of the wars and heroic deeds of the republic. Thus Ennius wrote an epic history of Rome from the most ancient times to those in which he lived (Annales, eighteen books), introducing at the same time the Hexameter metre into Roman literature. A more intimate C
acquaintance with the correct and polished productions of the Alexandrian school directed epic poetry into two principal channels, viz. the historical and didactic epos. Both these departments were represented by P. Virgilius Maro (B. C. † 19), and the didactic by Ovidius Naso (A. D. † 17), in his Ars amandi, Remedia amoris, Metamorphoseôn libri, and Fastorum libri.

b. The *drama.*—In tragedy the Roman writers (Livius 721
Andronicus, Cn. Nævius, Ennius, Pacuvius, Attius, and D
in Nero's time L. Annæus Seneca) distinguished themselves merely as polished translators or imitators of Greek models. In comedy, also, they confined themselves at first to the imitation or free translation of the so-called

(721) New Comedy of the Greeks; as we find in the instances
A of M. Attius Plautus († 184) and P. Terentius Afer (Terence: † 154).

That they had, however, also a Roman drama, strictly so called, is evident from the distinction between comœdia togata and palliata; the former being the national drama, the latter an imitation of the Greek models. One form of the comœdia togata was the *Mimes*, which represented, like the Atellan farces, only scenes of Roman life, but in more polished language, and with more of dramatic unity. By degrees language ceased to be essential to these Mimes, which degenerated into a mere exhibition of gesticulation, with dancing and music, termed *Pantomīmus*.

722 *c. Lyric poetry*, which developed itself at the period when Greek influence was predominant, always retained in some degree its character of being a mere imitation. The most remarkable performances in this department are the elegiac poems of Catullus, Tibullus, Propertius, Ovid, and the Odes and Epodes of Horace (B. C. † 8).

723 *d. Satire* is a species of poetry, purely Roman, origi-
B nating in an ancient popular theatrical representation, termed Satura, which was raised by C. Lucilius to the rank of a literary production. A more severe as well as polished character was given to satirical poetry by Q. Horatius Flaccus [Horace], who good humoredly exposes the perversities and absurdities of vice; whilst his graver successors (in the first century after Christ), Persius and Juvenalis [Juvenal], lash with extreme severity the gross immoralities of their time.

724 *e.* The *epigram* was introduced in the reign of Augustus, but the
C only complete collection which we possess of such poems is that of Martialis [Martial].

725 *f.* The *fable* and *Idyl* found few admirers. Phædrus published a Latin imitation of the Greek fables of Æsop, and Virgil of the Idyls of Theocritus.

726 B. Prose.

a. History (see page 198).

D *b. Oratory* was the most distinguished and influential branch of Roman literature. At an early period Roman generals and statesmen, such as Brutus, Camillus, the elder Cato (in more than 150 speeches), the younger Scipio Africanus, and the younger Gracchus, were wont to influence their contemporaries by the force of natural eloquence, long before the introduction (in defiance of repeated decrees of

the senate) of a regular system of instruction in oratory, (726
by Greek rhetoricians. From this period a rhetorical and A
philosophical education was the surest road to honor and influence. Among the distinguished orators who displayed their talents in the forum were Crassus, Antonius Orator, Hortensius, and above all M. Tullius Cicero (106—43), the great master of Roman eloquence.

With the decline of the republic, oratory lost its influence over the 727
government, and gradually confined its exhibitions to the courts of B
justice, and schools of rhetoric. The orations pronounced in honor of the later emperors, in imitation of the panegyricus of Pliny on Trajan, display it in its most debased character. Besides the practice, the theory and history of eloquence were also taught (the former, in some measure, according to Greek systems), principally by Cicero and Quinctilian.

c. The *letters* of Cicero and of his imitator, the younger Pliny, furnish us with much valuable information concerning the domestic life of the Romans, and the character of their contemporaries.

d. In *philosophy* the Romans confined themselves to the C
study of the various Greek systems (especially those of the Academy, of Epicurus, and of the Stoa), and their eclectic application to practical life, especially as regarded oratory, without attempting the formation of any independent system. The philosophical writings of Cicero entitle him to the highest praise as the introducer and disseminator of the Greek philosophy at Rome.

In the earlier days of the monarchy, the most attractive system 728
seems to have been that of the stoa [or the *Stoic* Philosophy], to which Seneca, the tutor and counsellor of Nero, manifests a decided inclination in his numerous writings. In the second century, stoicism, which still found a worthy admirer in the emperor Marcus Aurelius, was compelled to give place to Neoplatonism.

e. Under this head we may also class *natural philosophy.* A most D
valuable attempt to add to the results of Alexandrian learning by discoveries of his own, was made by the elder Pliny in his great encyclopædia, to which he gave the title of Historia naturalis. In the other *practical sciences* Rome possesses few writers of reputation.

f. Jurisprudence. At a very early period the Roman jurists (jure consulti), began to frame a system of legal science by examining the existing laws, reducing them to first principles, collecting precedents and authoritative legal maxims, &c., but it was not until the second and third centuries, that jurisprudence attained its highest degree of excellence under Gaius, Papinianus, Ulpianus, and Paulus, whose authority as jurists was confirmed by imperial edicts. Their writings were the groundwork of later compilations, especially of the corpus juris civilis, published by Justinian.

729 4. Arts.

A *a. Architecture.* Under the kings, and for a considerable time after the establishment of the republic, the temples and other public works (circus, capitol, cloacæ, water-courses, military roads), were completed with the assistance of the Etruscans. After the subjugation of Sicily and Greece, and especially since the time of Sulla, the columns and statues brought from conquered countries served to adorn the Roman edifices; Greek artists also visited Rome, and the massive Etruscan masonry was partly superseded, and partly amalgamated with the columnar architecture of
B Greece. In the latter days of the republic, and under the first emperors, the glory of Grecian art was revived at Rome, but its grand and majestic character was soon destroyed, especially after the time of the Antonines, by a load of meretricious ornament. In opposition to this superfluity of decoration, the Roman architects, about the time of Constantine the Great, fell into the contrary extreme of excessive, and almost rude, simplicity. For an account of the principal public buildings, see 433 (p. 210).

C *b. Sculpture.* The earliest specimens of Roman art are of the coarsest material, generally wood or terra cotta. Bronze seems to have been employed from the year of the city 300, at first for statues of celebrated men, and soon afterwards for representations of the gods. The translation to Rome of the best specimens of Grecian art, from the conquered cities of Sicily, Macedonia, and Greece, succeeded, as it shortly was, by the arrival of a crowd of Grecian sculptors, improved in the highest degree the taste of the Roman artist. Notwithstanding, however, the eagerness with which he copied these Grecian models, enough of peculiarity still remained to give a decidedly Roman character to his productions.

730 The demand for works of art gained ground with the increasing
D taste for magnificence in public and private buildings. The decoration of the numerous edifices erected by Augustus and his friends, as well as by succeeding emperors until the reign of Commodus, employed a number of artists, whose names for the most part are unknown. After the time of the Antonines, works of art abounded, in the shape of statues of the emperors and their relatives, sarcophagi and urns in marble, alabaster, and other materials; but in all these productions there was a want of vigor, study, and system; nor has the name of a single artist of that date been handed down to posterity.

c. Painting. Until the reign of Augustus, the professors (730)
of this art at Rome were almost exclusively Greeks, whose A
pictures represented the triumphs of Roman generals, and mythological subjects. The fresco paintings so common in the time of the empire, were, for the most part, mere mechanical copies from ancient masters.

Trade and manufactures. 731

The Romans, like the Greeks, abandoned trade and manufactures to foreigners, freedmen, and slaves, as being employments unworthy the attention of free citizens. In the latter days of the republic, however, associations were formed by the knights for farming the revenue, transacting the business of bankers and money-changers, and conducting various commercial enterprises. The trade of Rome B
was entirely passive, no productions either of nature or art being exported to foreign countries. The imports were grain (from Sicily, the province of Africa, Egypt, Syria, Asia Minor, and Pontus), slaves, and, in the latter days of the republic, and under the emperors, various articles of luxury from India, Arabia, Syria, Egypt, &c.

§ 166. *Historico-Geographical View of the Roman Empire.*

A. European countries.

1. Italia, as far as the Rubicon and the Alps, from 732
266. Gallia Cisalpīna, which had been subjugated as early as the year 221, was considered a part of Italy in Cæsar's time (49), but Liguria and the dominions of the Carni, Istri, and Venĕti were not included until the reign of Augustus.

2. Sicilia, with its circumjacent islands. The Cartha- C
ginian portion from 241, the whole island from 210.

3. Sardinia and Corsica from 238.

4. Hispania treated as a province from 206, entirely subjugated in 19, divided into H. citerior or eastern, and H. ulterior or southern. The whole peninsula divided by Augustus into three provinces, Lusitania, Bætica, and Tarraconensis.

5. Gallia Transalpīna. The province or country on D
the southern coast from the Alps to the Pyrenees as early as the year 121; the remainder after the year 51. The

(732) whole country divided by Augustus into four provinces.
A *a.* G. Narbonensis. *b.* G. Aquitanica. *c.* G. Lugdunensis. *d.* G. Belgica. The last of these provinces was subdivided in the time of the empire into three portions, Belgium proper, Germania superior on the Upper Rhine, and Germania inferior on the Lower Rhine.

6. Britannia Romana (or England with southern Scotland), from A. D. 85. Its frontier towards Britannia Barbara or Caledonia often varied, and was protected by walls and mounds. Divided by Septimius Severus into Britannia superior and inferior.

B 7. In north-western Germany the Batāvi, from the time of the campaigns of Drusus, and the Frisii and Chauci, until the Batavian war of liberation, were subject to the Romans, who reckoned also the Chatti and Cherusci among their vassals, until the defeat of Varus.

733 In south-western Germany. The Mattiaci between the Main and Taunus, and the inhabitants of the decumates agri were Roman vassals.

The agri extended eastwards from the upper Danube, and the lower Main to the limes transrhenanus, or great Roman line of fortification (a ditch protected by palisades), which ran from the Main across the Jaxt and Kocher, and joined the limes Rhæticus (devil's wall). This territory was perhaps acquired in Domitian's campaign against the Chatti, A. D. 84.

C 8. Rhætia (with Vindelicia), from the year 15.

9. Noricum, from 15.

10. Pannonia, conquered in 33, reduced to the condition of a province probably by Tiberius, divided into P. superior and inferior.

11. Mœsia, from 29, divided into M. superior and inferior.

12. Thracia, after its subjugation in the year 74, was still governed by tributary kings, until the reign of Claudius or Vespasian, when it became a Roman province.

D 13. Illyricum or Dalmatia. A part of the Illyrian coast was subdued in 228, and the whole country in 168 became a dependency of Rome. To this province were added the dominions of the Japydæ and Dalmatians (conquered in 33), and of the Liburni, who, it would appear, submitted voluntarily to the Romans.

734 The whole district was called the province of Dalmatia, from the name of that nation which had withstood the Romans longer than

any other. At a later period it was denominated Illyria. The (734)
southern portion, or Illyria Græca, belonged to the province of Ma- A
cedonia.

14. Macedonia, conquered in 168, a province in 148. Thessaly and Illyria added.

15. Epirus from 167.

16. Achaia, or central Greece, and the Peloponnesus, from 146.

17. Dacia, from A. D. 106 to 270.

18. Creta, 66, formed a province in conjunction with the empire of Cyrene, conquered in 96.

B. Countries in Asia.

1. Asia Proconsularis, from 130, comprised Mysia, 735
Lydia, Caria, and the greater part of Phrygia. B

2. Pamphylia, with the southern portion of Pisidia, from about 78. Lycia was added to this province by the emperor Claudius.

3. Cilicia (proper or eastern), from 75.

4. Cappadocia, from A. D. 18, to which was added the greater part of Pontus (governed until the reign of Nero by its own tributary kings), together with Armenia minor (by Tiberius).

5. Galatia (from 25), to which Augustus annexed C
almost the whole of Paphlagonia.

6. Bithynia, from 75, to which Pompey added the districts of Pontus and Augustus, the western portion of Paphlagonia.

7. Armenia major, from A. D. 106—117, then under tributary kings until A. D. 363.

8. Mesopotamia, A. D. 106—117, then again 165—363.

9. Assyria, A. D. 106—117.

10. Syria with Phœnice from 64, and Commagēnē D
from the time of Tiberius. To this province was added Palæstīna (dependent from the year 63), as a part of the Roman province of Syria under procurators uninterruptedly from the year of our Lord 44. Also Arabia Petræa, from A. D. 105.

11. Cyprus from 58.

12. The provincia insularum comprised, from the time of Vespasian, the islands of Lesbos, Samos, Chios, and Rhodes.

736 To the Romans were subject also the kings of Colchis
A (or Lazica), and of the empire of the Bospŏrus, on the Tauric Chersonēsus, after the conclusion of the third Mithridatic war, as well as the kings of Iberia, at least from the time of Trajan.

C. African Countries.

737 1. Ægyptus, with the sandy line of coast, as far westward as Cyrēnē (from 30).

2. Africa propria with Numidia. The Carthaginian portion (Zeugitana and Byzacium) from 146. Numidia (eastwards as far as the altars of the Philæni) from 46. The former was termed Old, the other New, Africa.

B 3. Mauretania, or Mauritania, a province from the time of Claudius, divided into M. Tingitana (so named from the city of Tingis), and M. Cæsariensis, which derived its name from its ancient capital Cæsarea.

CHRONOLOGICAL TABLE.

FIRST PERIOD.—*From the rise of the most ancient states to the reign of Cyrus,* B. C. 2000—558.

2000—1000.

B. C.

About 2000 } ABRAHAM. Nimrod. Nimus. Semiramis. Invasion of Egypt by Hyksos.

About 1500 } MOSES. *Return of the Israelites from Egypt to Palestine.* Sesostris.

1194—1184. *The Trojan War.*

1104. *Migration af the Dorians,* or Heraclidæ, to Peloponnesus.

1095—975. MONARCHY IN PALESTINE. Saul, David, Solomon.

1068. Abolition of monarchy at Athens. Archons.

1000—900.

975. *Division of Palestine into the kingdoms of Judah and Israel.*

900—800.

880. *Lycurgus.* Carthage founded.

800—700.

776. First Olympiad.

753. ROME FOUNDED.

747. Æra of Nabonassar. The Babylonians and Medes throw off the Assyrian yoke.

722. Conquest of the kingdom of Israel by Salmanassar [Shalmaneser].

700—600.

656. Psammetichus sole monarch in Egypt.

624. Dracon legislator at Athens.

604. *Dissolution of the Assyrian Empire.* Defeat of Necho nea. Circesium.

600—500.

594. *Solon* legislator at Athens.

586. Jerusalem destroyed by Nebuchadnezzar.

560. Pisistratus at Athens.

558. END OF THE MEDIAN, AND ESTABLISHMENT OF THE PERSIAN EMPIRE, BY CYRUS.

SECOND PERIOD.—*From Cyrus to the death of Alexander the Great,* B. C. 558—323.

B. C.
558—529. Cyrus.
538. Babylonia a Persian province.
529—522. Cambyses.
525. Egypt a Persian province.
522. Pseudosmerdis.
521—485. Darius I.
510. Expulsion of the Pisistratidæ from Athens. Clisthenes.
509—30. ROME A REPUBLIC.
500—449. Insurrection of the Ionians.

500—400.

494. Secession of the plebs from Rome.
492—479. *Defensive war of the Greeks against the Persians.*
490. Victory of Miltiades at Marathon.
485—465. Xerxes I.
480. Battles of *Thermopylæ*, Artemisium, *Salamis*. The Carthaginians defeated by Gelon, near Himera.
479. Battles of *Platææ* and *Mycale*.
478—449. Aggressive war of the Greeks against the Persians.
477 (?). Transfer of the maritime Hegemony from Sparta to Athens.
469. Victory of Cimon on the Eurymedon.
465—424. Artaxerxes I.
465—456. *The third Messenian war.*
451—450. *Legislation of the decemviri at Rome.*
449. Battle at Salamis in Cyprus.
444. Rogations of the tribune C. Canuleius and his colleagues.
431—404. THE PELOPONNESIAN WAR.
430. The plague at Athens.
429. Pericles dies.
428. The island Lesbos revolts from Athens.
424. Xerxes II. Sogdianus.
424—405. Darius II. Nothus.
422. Cleon and Brasidas slain at Amphipolis.
421. Peace of Nicias.
418. Renewal of the war.
415—413. Enterprise of the Athenians against Sicily.
410. Victory of Alcibiades at Cyzicus.
407. Return of Alcibiades to Athens. His disgrace.
406. Callicratidas defeated off the Arginusian islands.
405. Lysander victorious at *Ægospotamos.*
405—362. Artaxerxes II.
404. *Athens taken by Lysander. The thirty tyrants.*
404—395. Last war of the Romans against Veii.
403. Expulsion of the thirty tyrants from Athens.
401. The younger Cyrus slain at Cunaxa.

400—300.

B. C.

394—387. *The Corinthian war.*

394. Lysander slain at Haliartus, Conon victorious at Cnidus.

389. The Romans defeated on the Allia. ROME TAKEN BY THE GAULS.

387. Peace of Antalcidas.

378—362. *War between Sparta and Thebes.*

376. *The Lycinian rogations* accepted in 336.

371. Victory of Epaminondas and Pelopidas at *Leuctra.*

366. The prætura urbana. The curule ædileship.

365. L. Sextius the first plebeian consul.

362. Epaminondas falls at *Mantinea.*

362—338. Artaxerxes III.

359—336. Philip II. of Macedonia.

357—355. War of the confederates against Athens.

355—346. The Phocian, or holy war.

342—340. *First war of Rome with the Samnites.*

339—337. War of Rome with the Latins.

338. Philip II. defeats the Greeks at Chæronea.

336—330. Darius IV. Codomannus.

336—323. ALEXANDER THE GREAT.

334.—Alexander defeats the Persians on the *Granicus.*

333. ——————————— at Issus.

332. ———— conquers Syria, Cyprus, Phœnicia, Palestine, Egypt.

331. ———— vanquishes the Persians at *Gaugamela.*

327—326. Alexander's expedition to Western India.

326—324. Return of Alexander to Babylon.

325—304.—*Second war of Rome with the Samnites.*

323. Death of Alexander.

THIRD PERIOD.—*From the death of Alexander the Great, to the reign of Augustus,* B. C. 323—30.

323—322. The Samian war.

323—321. EGYPT FLOURISHES UNDER THE THREE FIRST PTOLEMIES.

321. Defeat of the Romans at *Caudium.*

314—301. Two wars of Antigonus with the satraps of the west.

312—64. THE SYRIAN EMPIRE UNDER THE SELEUCIDÆ.

309. Victory of Q. Fabius Maximus over the Etruscans at Perusia.

301. *Antigonus defeated at Ipsus.*

300—200.

298—290. *Third war of Rome with the Samnites.*

295. Victory of Q. Fabius Maximus over the Samnites and their allies at Sentinum.

282—272. *War of Rome with Tarentum and Pyrrhus.*

280. Pyrrhus victorious at Heraclea.

— Macedonia and Greece invaded by the Gauls.

— Formation of the Ætolian, and renewal of the Achæan league.

B. C.
279. Pyrrhus victorious at Asculum.
275. ——— defeated at Beneventum.
266. *Italy completely subjected to Rome.*
264—241. First Punic war.
260. First naval victory of the Romans, gained by C. Duilius, off *Mylæ.*
242. Victory of C. Lutatius Catulus at the Ægatian islands.
241. Sicily the first Roman province.
218—201. Second Punic war.
218. Hannibal victorious on the Ticinus and Trebia.
217. ——————————— Trasimene lake.
216. ——————— at *Cannæ.*
212. Syracuse taken.
210. The whole of Sicily Roman.
207. Defeat of Hasdrubal on the Metaurus.
206. Spain a Roman province.
202. *Hannibal defeated at Zama.*

200—100.

200—133. Wars of the Romans in Spain.
197. T. Quinctius Flaminius defeats Philip III. at Cynoscephalæ.
196. T. Quinctius proclaims the freedom of Greece.
192—190. War of the Romans with Antiochus the Great, of Syria.
171—168. War of the Romans with Perseus.
167. Defeat of Perseus at Pydna.
— *The Jews revolt from Antiochus IV.*
167—39. The Jews under the Asmonæans or Maccabees.
150—146. Third Punic war.
148. Macedonia a Roman province.
146. *Carthage destroyed by Scipio Africanus Minor, and Corinth by Mummius.*
133. Numantia destroyed by Scipio Africanus Minor.
— *Agrarian law of Tib. Sempronius Gracchus.*
123—121. *C. Sempronius Gracchus.*
113. Invasion of Illyria by the *Cimbri.*
112—106. War of the Romans with Jugurtha.
102. Marius defeats the Teutŏnes at Aquæ Sextiæ.
101. —————— the Cimbri at Vercellæ.

From 100 to the birth of our Lord.

91—88. The Marsian war, or *war of the Confederates.*
88—82. Civil war between Marius and Sulla.
87—84. First war against Mithridates.
83. Return of Sulla to Rome.
82—79. *Sulla's dictatorship.*
74—64. Third war against Mithridates.
66—62. Catiline's conspiracy.
64. Syria a Roman province.
63 Catiline's conspiracy crushed by the consul, M. Tullius Cicero.
60 Cæsar, Pompey, and Crassus establish the first triumvirate.

B. C.

58—51. *Cæsar conquers Gaul,* crosses the Rhine twice, visits Britain twice.
49—48. CIVIL WAR BETWEEN CÆSAR AND POMPEY.
48. Cæsar defeats Pompey at ***Pharsalus.***
48—47. Cæsar's Alexandrian war.
47. Cæsar's war against Pharnaces.
46. Cæsar defeats the partisans of Pompey at Thapsus.
——— the sons of Pompey at Munda.
44. CÆSAR ASSASSINATED.
44—43. The civil war of Mutina against Antony.
43. SECOND TRIUMVIRATE BETWEEN OCTAVIAN, ANTONY AND LEPIDUS.
42. Brutus and Cassius defeated at Philippi.
39—A. D. 70. The Jews under the Herodians.
31—30. *War between Octavian and Antony.*
31. *Battle of Actium.*
30. AUGUSTUS EMPEROR.

FOURTH PERIOD.—*From the reign of Augustus to the fall of the western empire,* B. C. 30—A. D. 476.

30—A. D. 14. *C. Julius Cæsar Octavianus Augustus.*
4 (?) or 6. CHRIST BORN.
9. *Herman defeats Varus in the Teutoburgian forest.*
14—37. Tiberius.
37—41. Caligula.
41—54. Claudius.
54—68. Nero. Conflagration of Rome.
68—69. Galba, Otho, Vitellius.
69—79. Vespasian. Complete subjugation of Britain.
70. *Jerusalem destroyed by Titus.*
79—81. Titus. Eruption of Vesuvius, Herculaneum, and Pompeii destroyed.
81—96. Domitian.
96—98. Nerva.
98—117. Trajan. Greatest extension of the Roman empire.
117—138. Hadrian. Restoration of Trajan's Asiatic conquests.
138—161. Antoninus Pius.
161—180. M. Aurelius Philosophus.
166—180. War of the Romans with the Marcomanni.
180—192. Commodus.
180—284. Decline of the empire under the usurped power of the Prætorian guard.
226—651. The new Persian empire.
284—305. First partition of the empire between Diocletian and Maximian. Two Cæsars.
324—337. CONSTANTINE THE GREAT, SOLE EMPEROR.
25. *The first œcumenical council at Nicæa.*
30 (?) *The imperial residence transferred to Byzantium.*
75. COMMENCEMENT OF MIGRATIONS OCCASIONED BY THE INVASION OF THE HUNS.

A. D.

395. THEODOSIUS DIVIDES THE EMPIRE between his sons Honorius and Arcadius.
410. *Rome sacked by Alaric.*
451. Ætius and Theodoric I. defeat Attila *in the Catalaunian fields*
455. *Rome plundered by the Vandals.*
476. *Romulus Augustulus deposed. Odoacer king of Italy.*

QUESTIONS.

---

* *The most remarkable forms of the year.*

[2] A DESCRIBE the variable solar year of the *Egyptians*. What
C *form* of year are the *Chaldeans* and *Babylonians* generally sup-
posed to have adopted ? Into what kind of months did all
D the Semitic nations probably divide their years? Did the
Athenian year consist of *lunar* or *solar* months? What *in-
tercalations* took place? Are the Athenians the only Greek
nation with whose chronology we are fully acquainted?
How was their month divided? When did their day begin?
What form of the year did the Romans use under Romulus?
A What under Numa? How often was an intercalary month
added? When and by whose authority was the solar year
adopted by the Romans? How was the Roman month subdivided? How were the days of a Roman month reckoned?
B What were Nundĭnæ? When did the day begin? What calendar did the Christians use? What division of time did the
Christians borrow from the Jews? What did the council of
Nicæa decide with respect to Easter? In the middle ages was
C the beginning of the year uniform in different nations? When was
the 1st of January made the invariable commencement? By
whom was the Julian calendar amended? What amount of
error had accumulated, when the '*new style*' was adopted?
What Christian nations still reckon their time according to the
D Julian calendar (the old style)? How do the *Mahometans*
reckon their time? Describe their year. Do they reckon the
day from sunset or from sunrise? Describe the *Republican
calendar of the French.*

* *The most important historical æras.*

[3] What was the æra of Nabonassar? Give the dates of the
A destruction of the first Temple, the Seleucian æra, that of the
Maccabees, and the æra of the world. What is meant by an
Olympiad? With what year B.C. does the beginning of the first
Olympiad coincide? When did this mode of computing time
come into general use among the Greeks? Did it supersede the
B more ancient mode of naming the year after some person in
authority? After whom was the year named at Sparta?
at Athens? Among the *Romans* what was the only æra
recognized in public proceedings? When did the æra *ab*

urba conditâ come into general use? Give the *Varronian* and
the *Catonian* date of the founders of Rome. What was the
C æra of the Seluecidæ? Amongst whom is this æra still in use?
How did the *Christians of the West* in the first centuries dis-
tinguish the year? On what was the Indiction-Cycle founded?
D Who invented the æra *from the birth of* CHRIST? What
amount of error was probably made in fixing the year of our
LORD's birth? What æra is still in use among the Coptic and
E Abyssinian Christians? Among the *Mahometans* what æra is
used? With *what day* of *what year* does this æra commence?
A What method of computation has been in general use since the
middle of the eighteenth century?

§ 6. History of the Israelities.

I. *From Adam to Noah.*

[11] Give the probable date of the creation. By what was the
B sentence of our first parents' expulsion from Paradise alle-
C viated? How did the sons of Adam employ themselves? Who
first offered sacrifice? and what was the probable origin of that
rite? How was the union of the first family dissolved? Who
A built the first city? By what is the Bible account of the deluge
confirmed? Who escaped the otherwise universal destruction
B of the flood? How were these persons saved?

II. *From Noah to Abraham.*

[12] Where did Noah's descendants settle? What caused their
C dispersion? Over what countries did the descendants of Shem
spread themselves? What countries were peopled by the descendants of *Japheth?* What by the children of *Ham?* What
was the only family in which the knowledge and worship of the
one true God were not entirely lost? From whom was Abraham
descended? What was the first command that Abraham received from God? What was promised on the condition of his
D obedience? What was the land of his fathers, which he quitted?
In what respect did the original promise of a Saviour now become more *definite?*

III. *From Abraham to the Conquest of Palestine.*

13] With whom did Abraham enter the land of Canaan? What
B circumstances soon compelled them to a separation? Where did
Lot settle? What cities were overthrown by GOD, as a monu-
ment of his vengeance against sinners? When these guilty
cities were overthrown, what did the plain in which they stood
C become? Who was ancestor of the idolatrous *Moabites* and
Ammonites? Who were the parents of *Ishmael?* Why was
Isaac called *the son of promise?* What great and mysterious
D trial of his faith did Abraham undergo? How was his faith
rewarded? By what rite was every male of Abraham's family
to be incorporated into the covenant made between him and
GOD? What became of Ishmael? Who became the heir of
A Abraham's possessions? Who were Isaac's children? Of
what profane act was Esau guilty? Of whom did he becom

the ancestor? After Isaac's death who became the head of the
Israelitish family? Give the history of his favorite son Joseph.
B Into what country, and into what district of that country did
Jacob migrate with his family? Under whose command, and
D when did the Israelites quit Egypt? Give an account of
Moses. Who was Aaron? How was the army of the Israelites
A guided? How did the Israelites cross the Red Sea? Where
did Moses deliver to the people a code of laws? How did God
punish their faithlessness and disobedience? How were Moses
and Aaron punished for having on one occasion failed to *sanctify
Jehovah before the people?*

* *The Mosaic Laws.*

[14] By whom were the Mosaic Laws given to Moses? * What
B parts are especially mentioned as having been so given? * What
confirmations of ancient patriarchal usages do the Mosaic laws
contain? * What is the first principle of religious worship as
C laid down in the laws of Moses? * How was the *presence* of the
Almighty indicated to the Jews? * In what way might that
presence not be represented? * Describe generally the tabernacle. * What tribe were charged with the administration of
all that related to public worship? * To what family was the
D priesthood itself confined? * Who discharged the lowest offices
connected with public worship? * What duties were performed
by the Levites besides those that related to the *ceremonial* worship? * Where did the Levites dwell? and how were they sup-
A ported? * Who was the supreme judge? * What did the
High Priest do on the great Day of Atonement? * What was
the object of the *Sabbath?* * Explain the terms *Sabbatical
Year* and the year of *Jubilee.* * What took place in the year
B of Jubilee? * At what three annual festivals were all the
males required to visit the place where the ark of God was deposited? * Describe the object, &c. of *the Passover (Passah).*
* Of *the Feast of Weeks,* or πεντηκοστῆ. * Of the *Feast of
C Tabernacles.* * By what yearly penitential observance was their
dependence on Jehovah especially recalled? * What was the
Feast of Trumpets? * Where were the *sacrifices* offered? * And
into what *kinds* were they divided? * Besides these sacrifices,
what were the Israelites required to bring before the Lord?
D * Mention some other religious observances. * What was the
political constitution of the Israelites? * How were the people
divided? * How were the tribes governed? and what did *each
tribe* form? * To whom was the whole nation subject? * Who
governed it as his visible representative? * On what extraordinary occasions were the people called together? * For what
case was a special provision found in the Mosaic law? * Describe the administration of justice after the conquest of Pales-
A tine. * For what offences was the punishment of *death* inflicted? * How was this punishment inflicted? * Mention the
other punishments and penalties inflicted by the Jewish code.
* Was any (and, if so, what) escape provided for one who had
killed his neighbor without malice prepense? * Who were

required to serve in the army? * How was it divided? * What
B regulations were made with respect to sieges? * What regulation was made for the avoidance of idolatry? * What
C life were the Israelites required to lead? * What social virtues
were strictly enjoined by the law?

Who succeeded Moses, and how was his commission ratified?
How many princes of the Canaanites did this leader subdue?
How was the land of Canaan divided? After whom were the
tribes named?

IV. *From the Conquest of Palestine to the establishment of the Monarchy. Period of the Judges.*

[15] How were the twelve tribes united into one federal common-
A wealth? Where was the tabernacle first pitched in Canaan?
Where was the general assembly held? What great command
B of GOD was in a great measure disregarded? Who were the
Judges? Mention some of them. Who founded the Schools
C of the Prophets? How came the Israelites to desire to have a
visible king? Who was highly displeased at this request? Did
D GOD accede to their demand? Who was anointed to be king
over Israel?

V. *From the establishment of the Monarchy to the separation of the two kingdoms.*

[16] What oath did Saul take when he received the homage of
A the Israelites? What tribes did he subdue? What prohibition
did he disregard in the case of the Amalekites? Of what previous violation of GOD's law had he been guilty? Who was
then privately anointed to be the future king of Israel? Give
some account of this future king's youth. How came he to be
B persecuted by the jealousy of the king? How did Saul end his
life? Was David at once acknowledged by all the tribes?
C What city did David choose to be the royal residence? Where
was the ark of the covenant now placed? For what purpose was
the booty taken in David's wars set aside? Did he execute his
plan? Describe David's conquests and the extent of his king-
D dom. Describe the splendor of his court and monarchy.
A What were the distinguishing characteristics of David's personal
religion? What grievous sins did he commit? What sentence
of punishment was pronounced against him because he had
given occasion to the enemies of the LORD to blaspheme? Who
B deposed David? What was this leader's fate? In whose favor
did David abdicate before his death? Who was the *mother* of
his successor?

[17] How was the *wisdom* of Solomon displayed? What was his
C great work? By what artisans, and in what time was the
temple finished? How was it divided? What did Solomon
build besides the temple? With whom did Solomon renew a
D *commercial league?* What countries did his fleet probably visit?
In what did his *love of magnificence and luxury* manifest itself?
A How did Solomon alienate the affections of his people? By
whom was a conspiracy organized against him? What countries
fell off from Solomon?

[18] What schism took place under Rehoboam? What tribes
B formed the kingdom of Judah? and what the kingdom of
Israel? What modes of false worship did the Israelites generally adopt?

VI. *The Kingdoms of Judah and Israel.*

[19] What was the capital of the kingdom of Israel? To what
D year did it last, and under how many kings? By whom were
the idolatrous kings opposed? What Assyrian king took most
A of the cities of Israel by storm? Who put an end to the kingdom of Israel? What mixture of tribes produced the Samaritans? To what year and under how many princes did the
B kingdom of Judah last? Mention the country or countries to
which the kingdom of Judah became tributary.

VII. *The Israelites under the rule of the Persians.*

[20] By whom and after how many years of exile were the Jews
D permitted to return to their own land? What other favor did
this prince show them? How many at first returned to Palestine?
To whom was the administration of civil affairs principally left?
During the reigns of Cambyses and Smerdis, was any (and if
A so, what) progress made in building of the Temple? Under
whose reign was the second Temple completed? By whom and
under what leaders was the colony established in Judæa?

§ 7. *Literature, Arts, and Sciences.*

[21] To whom was the *learning* of the Hebrews in early times
B confined? In what did it consist? In what does the poetry of
C the Israelites differ from all other national poetry? Into what
D classes, as to *form*, may their poems be divided? What *arts* did
A not flourish among the Jews? What art did flourish? Had
the Jews any *foreign trade?*

§ 9. *Fragments of the Ancient History of India.*

[29] What Indian expeditions are quite legendary? What is
D known of India before the time of Alexander? What forms of
government did Alexander find in the Punjâb? What go-
A vernors did he place over the conquered provinces? What
native prince expelled the governors appointed by Alexander?
What extent of empire did this prince found? By whom was
it finally destroyed? Enumerate the other nations or tribes
who established dynasties in India.

§ 10. *Religion, political Condition, Literature, &c. of the ancient Indians.*

[30] In what principles does the Brahminical religion appear to
C consist? What are the two forms of popular worship which
arose in Northern India with Brahmaism?

* What are the so-called deities that form the Trinity of Indian
D mythology? * Which of the Indian deities is said to have assumed the human form? * How many *incarnations* of this sup-

posed deity are asserted to have occurred? * What are the
religious observances of the followers of Brahman? * Amongst
whom does the practice of burning widows prevail?
[31] What is the date of the *Buddhist* reformation? Who
A effected this reformation? What was believed concerning him?
B What institutions or practices did he reject? Give some
general account of the progress of the *Buddhist* reformation.
[32] What form of government prevailed amongst the Hindoos?
Was the sovereignty hereditary or elective? Describe the
D *tenure* of land. * State generally what is known with respect
to the administration of the government.
[33] Enumerate, each in its order, the four castes into which the
A people were divided. Describe the privileges of the first caste.
What office could only be held by one who belonged, by birth,
to the second *caste?*
[34] Under what title are *the sacred writings* of the Hindoos com-
prehended? What compositions stand at the head of these?
C Of what do the remainder treat? With what do the sacred
D writings conclude? * What is known of the progress of the
Hindoos in science? * For what are we indebted to them?
A * Name their most famous *epics*. * What is known of the
Indian drama? * Who was the most renowned dramatic
writer? * About what time did he flourish?
[35] ART.—*Architecture.* What are the principal monuments of
B Indian architecture? What are the most famous subterra-
C neous temples? and rock-temples? In what respects do the
ancient buildings of India *often*, and in what *nearly always*,
D surpass the monuments of Egypt? By what law was the
attainment of excellence in *sculpture* rendered almost impossible? What is known of their progress in *painting?* What of
their attainments in *music?*
[36] COMMERCE.—How was the *home traffic* of the Hindoos carried
on? What were the principal markets for domestic produce?
B Give a general notion of their *foreign trade:* 1, to the *North-*
C *East;* 2, to the *East;* 3, to the *West.* * What were the principal exports?

§ 12. *History of the Babylonians.*

[42] Which was the more ancient state, Babylon or Assyria?
C Who was the founder of Babylon? About what period was it
founded? * Whom do the *Greeks* mention as the founders of
the Babylonian and Assyrian empires respectively?
43] How many dynasties were there from the deluge to the
D Persian conquest? What was the duration of the sixth? Does
the statement of Berosus with regard to the sixth receive any
A support from Herodotus? By whose assistance were the Babylonians delivered from the Assyrian domination? When did
the æra of Nabonassar begin? Did the Assyrians attempt to
B repossess themselves of Babylon? Who put an end to the
Assyrian empire? What countries were comprehended in the
western portion of the empire? Who overthrew the invader
Necho near Carchemish? What city is supposed to be the

Carchemish of the Scriptures? Who succeeded Nabopolassar?
C In his pursuit of the *Eygptians*, how far did this monarch advance? Why did Nebuchadnezzar lay siege to the city of Jerusalem? How long did the city withstand him? Give the date of the city's destruction. Who was the king of Judah at this time? How were he and his captive subjects treated?
D What became of those who remained in Judah? Why did Nebuchadnezzar wage war against the *Phœnicians?* What great undertakings did he enter upon after his return?

[44] * During Nebuchadnezzar's madness by whom was the government administered? * In what way did this queen show
A her activity and ambition? Who was the last king of Babylon, and what is the name given to him by Herodotus? What means did Cyrus employ to effect the fall of Babylon? To what condition was Babylon reduced?

§ 13. *Religion, Literature, &c. of the Babylonians.*

[45] What was the religion of the Shemites, and of the ancient
B Asiatics generally? What is meant by the religion of nature? How does the religion of the Hebrews differ from that of
C nature? What is the most common idea of the Godhead among Asiatic nations, who profess the religion of nature? Which is the active and which the passive power of nature? What seems to have occasioned the grammatical distinction of genders,
D as applied to inanimate objects? What may be considered a
A later step in the development of material religion? What is the last step in this notion? Who were generally the guardian deities of cities? Who held the first rank among the Shemitic
B divinities? Give the signification of the word Babel.

[46] * Of the five planets, which were considered beneficent
C powers? * which destructive? and which varied according to his position? * Did the Chaldæans place great reliance on their position, rising, and setting?

[47] What honors did the king of kings receive from his people?
D Did he govern responsibly? How was the empire divided, and how governed? Who were termed pre-eminently "Chaldæans?" Who were the sole possessors of all the learning of those days? How was it communicated to members of their own caste?

[48] What were the advantages of Babylon as a place of trade?
A * How was the *land trade* carried on? * with what countries *eastward* and *westward?* * What were their exports to these countries? * How was the *trade on the Euphrates* carried on? * How was the *maritime commerce* carried on? * and with what countries?

[49] What were the principal arts and manufactures of the Babylonians?

§ 15. *History of the Assyrians.*

[52] Who was the founder of the Assyrian empire? About what
B period was the Assyrian empire founded? How far did Semi-

C ramis push her conquests? * What was the amount of the
forces which she marched against the Indians, and what the
result of the expedition?

[53] Who succeeded Semiramis? When did Sardanapalus ascend
A the throne? What was the result of the insurrection of the
Babylonians and Medes against this monarch? Did the Assy-
B rian empire still continue to subsist? Does there exist any
record of the kings who succeeded Sardanapalus? * Who com-
pelled the Israelites to pay tribute?

[54] Under what king, and about what period, did the Babylonians
revolt? How were the Assyrians indemnified for this loss?
C Why did Salmanassar destroy the kingdom of Israel? What
became of the Israelites afterwards? What was the next conquest of this king? Was the siege of Tyre successfully conducted? * Does the historian Ctesias's account of the dissolution
of the Assyrian empire correspond with that given in the Bible?
A About what period did Sennacherib ascend the throne? What
success had Sennacherib against Judah? Who succeeded
B Sennacherib? About what period? Who was the last king of
Assyria? Who formed an alliance against Assyria? and with
what success? How long did the Scythians keep possession
of Media? About what time was Nineveh utterly destroyed?

§ 16. *Religion, Literature, &c. of the Assyrians.*

[55] Were the Assyrians remarkable for their civilization? How
A far did their religion resemble that of the Babylonians? What
political constitution did the Assyrian constitution resemble?

§ 18. *History of the Medes.*

[59] In what author is the earliest mention of the Medes found?
A In whose reign did the Medes emancipate themselves from the
dominion of the Assyrians, to whom they had become subject?
Who first became king of the whole nation? How long did he
reign? What city did he build? Who succeeded Deioces?
What nation did he subdue? What became of him? Who
B succeeded Phraortes? What improvements did this prince in-
troduce in the army? With what king did he form an alliance?
C Who defeated Cyaxares? How far did their conquests extend?
* Whilst the Scythians were dominant in Asia, against whom
was Cyaxares carrying on a war? What was the pretence for
this aggression? How was the war terminated?

[60] Against whom did Cyaxares turn his arms at the departure
D of the Scythians? Who succeeded Cyaxares? How did he
A lose Persia? Was he successful against the rebels?

[61] Give Herodotus's account of the relation which Cyrus bore to
B Astyages. According to Ctesias, was Cyrus related to Astyages? How did Cyrus treat Astyages? What is Xenophon's
account? What confirmation do we receive of this account?

§ 19. *Religion, Literature, &c. of the Medes.*

[62] What was the religion of the Medes? Who was the author
C of this doctrine? Into how many parts was the Zend-Avesta
divided? How many have reached us?
[63] What are *the principal doctrines taught in the Zend-Avesta?*
B State the *moral precepts* taught in the Zend-Avesta. Into how
many castes were the people divided? Name them. Was there
any limit to the king's power?
[64] To whose care was the code of laws intrusted? How can
the great influence of these persons be accounted for? Had
C they any temples? Could the king's ordinances be recalled?
* For what were the Median stuffs celebrated? * With whom
were they the favorite dress?

§ 21. *History of the Persians.*

[75] On what account were the Persians partly Nomades and
C partly agriculturists? How many castes does Herodotus enumerate,
as governing the inferior castes and supplying the higher
offices of state? Which was the most distinguished of these castes?
After the Persians had been subdued by the Median king Phraortes,
did they retain their own kings? Name the first king.
Who was the father, and who the grandfather of Cyrus?
[76] What was the original name of Cyrus? How did he become
D lord of the whole Persian empire? Who was king of Lydia at
that time? What success had Crœsus in his attempt to avenge
himself on Cyrus for the expulsion of his brother-in-law, Asty-
A ages? Whom did Cyrus send to subdue *the Greek cities on the
coast of Asia Minor?* On what terms were these cities ready to
pay tribute? Did all the Greek cities receive tyrants? What
B became of the Phocæans? Was Harpagus successful in this
expedition against the Greek cities?
[77] What were the triumphs of Cyrus himself? What liberty
C was granted by Cyrus to the Jews? * How many different accounts
are there of the death of Cyrus? * State the substance
of them. Who was nominated the successor of Cyrus? Who
was appointed viceroy of the eastern portion of the empire?
Where was Cyrus buried?
[78] When did Cambyses begin to reign? How long did his reign
A last? What additions did Cambyses make to the countries
already subdued by his father? * Why did he undertake the
expedition against Egypt and Libya? * What king did he take
prisoner, and how did he treat him? * What nations surrendered
themselves voluntarily to the conqueror?
[79] How was the plan of Cambyses for extending his conquests
B in Africa rendered abortive? What became of the forces which
C he had raised for this purpose? * On his return to Memphis,
what insult did he offer to the worshippers of the god Apis?
* How did he treat his brother Smerdis? Give an account of
D his other extravagant acts. Where did he die?
[80] Who succeeded Cambyses? Who was the Pseudo-Smerdis
or False-Smerdis? How did he endeavor to render his usurpa-

A tion popular? How was the usurper's reign put an end to?
What festival was instituted in commemoration of this event?
[81] How came Darius to be king of Persia? Whose son was
B he? Trace the pedigree of Darius up to Cyrus the great-grandson of Achæmĕnes. What improvements did Darius introduce
into the government?
[82] * What were the duties of the satraps? * By whom were
they assisted? * How do you account for the rapidity of royal
mandates? * How were the civil and military administration of
each province, as well as the cultivation of the land, managed?
C * How was the tribute paid? * What were the sources of the
A revenue? * How did the inferior officials receive their remuneration? * How were those of higher rank rewarded? * How
were the wants of the most exalted personages supplied? In
what direction did Darius extend his conquests? and why?
* To whom did Darius grant the power of liberating Samos?
[83] Give an account of *the reduction of the revolted province of*
B *Babylon?* What reward did Zopyrus receive for his services?
C Describe *the expedition against the Scythians?* Who were left
in charge of the bridge over the Ister? What service did Histiæus render Darius? What submission did Amyntas offer to
D Megabazus? Where did Darius next turn his arms? Who
was previously dispatched into that country?
[84] About what period did the Persian wars with Greece com-
A mence? How did Histiæus become an object of suspicion to
the king? On his recall to Susa, who was appointed tyrant of
Miletus? What rendered the security of this appointment precarious? What success attended the combined efforts of Ari-
B stagoras and Histiæus against the Persian government? What
circumstance hastened the commencement of the Persian
war?
[85] Who conducted *the first expedition* of the Persians *against*
C *Greece?* What happened to this commander's fleet and army?
Did Darius invade Greece a second time? Under whose advice
did he act? Who commanded the expedition? What was its
date? Where did they first sail? Where was the battle fought
between the generals of Darius and the Athenians? What were
A the numbers of the respective forces? Who commanded the
Athenians? What was the result of the battle? Did Darius
attempt to invade Greece a third time? Who did? Where did
B his land and naval forces assemble? * Give a summary of the
principal events during the march of this vast army.
[86] Where did Xerxes first encounter a firm resistance? Who
withstood him? Who betrayed this brave band? How did
C Xerxes wreak his vengeance on Athens? What was the result
D of the battle of Artemisium? Where was the Persian fleet
totally defeated? Give the date of this battle. What became
of Xerxes? Who was left in charge of the Persian army?
[87] What battles were fought? With what success? In which
A was Mardonius slain? In these two engagements who com-
B manded the Athenians and Lacedæmonians respectively?
After these successess what course did the Greeks take? Who

C won the battle of Eurymĕdon? How did Xerxes meet with his
end? Who succeeded him?
[88] Give an account of the Persian *war with the Egyptians and*
D *Greeks.* Who commanded the Grecian fleet?
[89] Why did Megabyzus throw off his allegiance to Artaxerxes?
A Account for the frequent revolts of the satraps. What tended
B to extinguish the once martial spirit of the Persians? Who
succeeded Xerxes? How long did he reign? Who succeeded
C Xerxes II.? Who succeeded Sogdianus? Why was his reign
marked by repeated revolts of the satraps? How long did the
Egyptians retain the independence which they asserted successfully in this reign? Who succeeded Darius II.?
[90] Who endeavored to establish his right to the succession?
On what grounds? Under what pretext did he march against
D the reigning monarch? Who supported him? Who warned
Artaxerxes of Cyrus's real intentions? What battle was fought?
A In what year? What became of the Greek auxiliaries? Who
commanded them in their retreat?
[91] What was the reward of Tissaphernes for his timely information to the king? Who made considerable progress in the
liberation of the Asiatic Greeks? How were his plans frus-
B trated? What was his policy? What Spartan general fell at
Haliartus? Who took the command in the Corinthian war?
Where did Conon defeat the Lacedæmonians? What became
C of the Greeks of Asia Minor during the *peace of Antalcidas?*
* Why did the attempt to reconquer Egypt miscarry? * Who
poisoned Artaxerxes II? * and who succeeded Artaxerxes II.?
[92] Did this prince succeed in suppressing the revolt of of the Phœ-
A nicians and Egyptians? Who was king of Egypt? What became
of him? Who poisoned Artaxerxes and all his sons except one?
B Who succeeded him? What was his fate? Who succeeded
Arses? What was the fate of Bagoas? Enumerate the three
great victories of Alexander over Darius. Give the three dates
respectively. Who murdered Darius? * What were the causes
of the decline of the Persian empire?
[93] Give some account of the ***religion of the Persians.***
[94] From whom was the Persian constitution borrowed? What
was its character! Was there any limit to the power of the
A "Great King?" From whom did he receive tribute? Where were
his palaces situated? Through whom were all communications
conveyed to the king? Who exercised an influence over the administration of public affairs, and even over the succession to the
B throne? What was deemed necessary to secure the possession
of conquered countries? Was the constitution allowed to remain unchanged? How was their dependence on Persia recognized?
[95] To what was the Persian literature confined? Have any re-
C mains of Persian architecture been discovered?

§ 25. *Fragments of Phœnician History.*

[101] To what race did the Phœnicians belong? Who alone with-
A stood the invasions of the Nomadic tribes and the **Israelites?**

B Who was king of Tyre in the days of Solomon? When did
Tyre and Sidon become separated?

[102] * What mention is made of Sidon by Homer? * For what
C was it famous and also notorious? * Name its earliest foreign
settlements. * Why did Nebuchadnezzar destroy Sidon? * Did
it become again prosperous? * What led to its ruin a second
time?

[103] * Was Tyre or Sidon the older city? * At how early a
D period did Tyre become remarkable for its wealth and power?
* To whom was Solomon indebted for assistance in building the
Temple? * Who founded Carthage? * About what time?
* Against whom did Tyre maintain its independence?

[104] Under the Persian dominion did the Phœnician cities retain
A their own kings? If so, on what conditions? Did the Phœnicians
assist in any of the Persian and Grecian wars? What
effect had the fame of Alexander's arms on the cities of Phœnicia
generally? How long did Tyre hold out against Alexander?
What damaged the future prosperity of Tyre?

§ 26. *Religion, &c. of the Phœnicians.*

[105] Why are we to consider the religion of the Phœnicians as a
B subject of unusual importance? Describe their religion. Why
C were the sun and moon worshipped? What names did they
give to the sun? What suggested to them the idea of separate
D deities? How did they believe that the supreme Being go-
A verned the world? Who was this manifestation of Baal?

[106] Enumerate some of the principal inventions of the Phœnicians.

[107] Was their *maritime trade* extensive? What was this owing
B to? Name the chief goals of their maritime enterprise. What
C were the chief imports? Which of their voyages were kept
secret? What voyage did the king of Egypt prevail on them
to undertake? * What obstructed the commercial intercourse of
the Greeks and Phœnicians? * What Phœnician articles were
D imported by the Greeks? * Give a general account of their
Arabian and Egyptian land traffic. * What was imported by
A them from Palestine and Syria? * what from Armenia and the
Caucasian countries? * By what means was the trade of Phœnicia
principally carried on?

[108] What are we to understand by the term Tyrian purple?
B For what other manufactures were the Tyrians celebrated?

§ 28. *History of the Kingdom of Lydia.*

[119] Who were the original inhabitants of Lydia? Into how
D many dynasties is the history of the Lydian sovereigns divided?
State the extent of the conquests of Crœsus. What caused the
ruin of this monarch?

[120] In the conversation between Crœsus and Solon the Athenian,
A whom did the latter pronounce the happiest of men? What
battle took place between Crœsus and Cyrus, and with what
B result? How was the life of Crœsus saved on two occasions?
How, and by whom, was Cyrus advised to secure the subjection
of the Lydians?

[121] What history remains to us of the other states?

AFRICA.

[122] By what name was Africa known to the Greeks? How
C much of it was known to them? Give a general account of the
peculiar features of this quarter of the globe. What are the
A principal disadvantages it has to contend with? What are the
great obstacles to communication with the interior? What progress has Africa made in civilization?

§ 34. *The State of Meroe.*

130] Give a summary account of the history of the ancient state
B of Meroe. How soon did it attain considerable importance?
C What was the advantage of its position? When did the power
of its priests cease? What traces were there of this kingdom
in Nero's time?

[131] What was the character of the Ethiopian religion? How is
A the similarity between the Ethiopian and Egyptian systems of
worship testified? In what respect did the religion of the
Ethiopians resemble the religion of Brahma? Under what constitution did thé Ethiopians live? How was the power of the
B monarch restricted? What ruins of Temples are found in
Ethiopia? What difference is observable in the style of the
ancient and the more recent Ethiopian Temples? Do the
Ethiopian works of art bear any resemblance to the Egyptian?
C For what countries was Meroe the great centre of traffic?
* How was this traffic conducted? * Which were the three
principal establishments of the priestly caste?

§ 36. *History of the Egyptians.*

[142] Who founded the most ancient states of Egypt? Which was
C the most ancient and the mightiest? During the period anterior
to Sesostris how many dynasties are said to have filled the
throne? * Who is generally supposed to have been the first
A king? * Who built Memphis? * How many sovereigns followed
him? * Who was the builder of Thebes and Osimandyas?
* How early did Abraham found a kingdom established in Upper
Egypt? * Where did Joseph probably live when in Egypt?

[143] What was the most important event of the first period?
Who are the Hyksos supposed to have been? What accounts
B for the blank in the early history of Egypt? Who expelled the
Hyksos? * To whom does Herodotus ascribe the excavation of
the lake Mœris and the building of its two pyramids? * What
colonies were established about this period? * Were the
Israelites then in Egypt?

[144] How are the mighty conquests ascribed by tradition to
C Sesostris limited by Herodotus? How did the range of his
A reputation become extended? Mention the chief acts for improving the country introduced by this monarch. Did his successors long retain the territory acquired in Asia and Europe?
How far did the authority of the later Pharaohs extend?

[145] What Egyptian king is mentioned as having made war on
B Rehoboam?

[146] Give the date of Sabaco's invasion of the country. How
C did the warrior-caste treat Sethos, and why? How was the
D invader compelled to raise the siege? How was Egypt gov-
A erned after Sethos? How long did the Dodecarchy last?
Who re-established the monarchy? By whom was he assisted?

[147] How did Psammetichus offend the warrior-caste? What
B was the consequence of this quarrel? From this period who
C formed the flower of the Egyptian army? How long did the
siege of Azotus last? What city became the usual residence of
the sovereign? From whom did the caste of the interpreters
spring?

[148] Who succeeded Psammetichus? What body of troops did
D this prince encourage? What great canal project was attempted
in this reign? What expedition did he undertake, and with what
success? How did he carry out the plans of conquest set on foot
by his father? Who circumnavigated Africa about this time?

[149] Who succeeded Necho? What expedition did he under-
A take?

[150] Who succeeded Psammis? How did he show his warlike
disposition? What accusation was brought against Apries?
B What became of Apries?

[151] Who was then called to the throne? Why was this prince
lightly esteemed? How did he endeavor to propitiate the
C priesthood? How did he establish his authority on a firm basis?
When did he die?

[152] Who succeeded him? What was Egypt reduced to under
this prince?

[153] What excited a spirit of national hatred against the Persians?
A How was it rendered comparatively easy for the Egyptians to
throw off their allegiance to Persia? In whose reigns were the
efforts to throw off the Persian yoke made? What success attended them? When did Egypt become a Macedonian province?

§ 37. *Religion, &c. of the Egyptians.*

[154] Did the ***objects of worship*** differ in different Nomes? Mention
B some of the animals which were objects of worship; and the
care that was taken of them. Name the ***inanimate objects*** of
C worship. Enumerate the ***local divinities.*** Did the religion of the
priests differ from that of the people? On what peculiar notion
A did their belief in the immortality of the soul depend? What
excluded the dead from being admitted into the realms of the
blessed? How was the right to these honors ascertained?
Were there any oracles?

[155] What do the Nomes appear originally to have been?

[156] What were the seven castes? Where had the ***priestly caste***
B its principal stations? How was the hierarchy supplied with
priests? What offices were filled by the priestly caste? How
was their income derived? What do you observe further of them?
C Where were the ***warrior-caste*** settled? and why? Of what
D did the army consist? Where were ***the herdsmen*** settled? What
A is known about the caste of the ***swineherds?*** What did the ***caste***

of tradesmen comprise? Were these employments hereditary or not? What caste was of especial importance? Who formed the medium of communication between the Egyptians and foreigners?

157] What name was common to the kings of Egypt? How was
B their power circumscribed? Name the several residences of their kings. How were their revenues derived? Who commanded the army in time of war? How were judicial questions investigated? How were the proceedings conducted, and sentence given?

158] What were the sciences cultivated by the priestly caste?
C How was *Astronomy* applied? What rendered *Geometry* so necessary a science? What were the restrictions placed on the
A medical profession? In what did the *Historical learning* of the Egyptians consist?

159] Of what do the monuments of Egypt exhibit great proofs? What prevented the Egyptian artists from rising to the representation of the beautiful?

160] How were architecture and sculpture connected?

161] Name the chief objects of art. How were the walls of the
C Temples adorned? Describe the interior of the Catacombs. What was the form of an Obelisk? What was their average height and base? Where were they hewn and polished? How
D were they conveyed to their destination? Where were they placed? * What became of several of these Obelisks? Where
A are the *Pyramids* only found? Describe them. What is the
B name of the largest? What was its height originally, and what is it now? Mention the particulars that are known with regard to this pyramid. How many pyramids are there near Memphis, and what is their position? Which is the most celebrated group?
C For what were these huge masses probably reared? What did a Sphinx represent? What proves the accurate astronomical knowledge of the Egyptians? Where were Sphinxes chiefly found, and in what numbers? Who built the Labyrinth? Give some account of it.

[162] What is our knowledge of the Egyptian inscriptions?

163] How were the hieroglyphical characters employed? How
A many styles or kinds of hieroglyphics were used? How were the hieratic characters employed? how the demotic?

164] What compelled the Egyptians to confine themselves to in-
B land and river traffic? What rendered Egypt the centre of an extensive commerce by means of caravans? How were corn and cloth transported from Egypt into Arabia and Syria? Who
C extended the commercial relations of Egypt? and how? What was the consequence of these arrangements?

165] How is our knowledge of Egyptian handicrafts obtained? Enumerate the principal arts of the Egyptians.

§ 40. *History of the Carthaginians.*

[170] Why did the Phœnicians select the northern coast of Africa
C for the establishment of a colony? When was Carthage founded? By whom?

[171] What is the legendary account of the foundation of Carthage?

[172] How did Carthage extend itself? What important voyages
A were undertaken? Who made an attempt against Carthage?

[173] What was the first step towards the downfall of the Car-
B thaginians? Did the Carthaginians choose an opportune mo-
C ment for the subjugation of Sicily? What success had they?
On what terms was a peace granted?

[174] What occasioned fresh hostilities? Did the Carthaginians
D secure a firmer foot again in the island? Did the Syracusans
attempt to throw off their subjection to the Carthaginians?
What success attended their efforts?

[175] Who was Agathŏcles? Give an account of the war between
C him and the Carthaginians. What course did the Cartha-
ginians take on the death of Agathŏcles? Who was Pyrrhus?
How was he ruined in Sicily?

[176] What was the result of the first war between the Romans
D and Carthaginians? What troops were employed in this war?
Why did these troops mutiny? and what was the result of the
A mutiny? Who brought this insurrection to a satisfactory termination? What possessions did the Romans acquire during this
war? Why were proceedings taking against Hamilcar? How
did the accused repel the charge? What two parties sprang up
about this time? What was the first step towards the destruction of the Carthaginian constitution?

[177] What did Hamilcar do in order to indemnify his country for
B the loss of her best provinces? Who succeeded Hamilcar in
the command? What success had these generals in Spain?
How was a period put to their conquests in that quarter? Who
founded Carthago Nova? What was the fate of Hasdrŭbal?
Who succeeded him in the command?

[178] What occasioned the second war with Rome? Who was to
A have supported Hannibal in a new war with Rome? Who be-
trayed his project? What did Hannibal do? What was his
end? Who now started hostilities with the Carthaginians? Of
B what provinces did he deprive them? To what straits were the
Carthaginians reduced?

[179] How did the third Punic war terminate? * Who founded a new city near the ruins of Carthage? * How did it rise in importance? * When was it destroyed? * What town was built from its ruins?

§ 41. *Religion, &c. of the Carthaginians.*

[180] What was the character of the Carthaginian religion?
D * Who were the chief divinities of the Carthaginians? * Which
was supposed to be the peculiar residence of Melkarth? * How
then did the Carthaginians show their homage? * What sacrifices were offered to Moloch? * Whom did the god Esmûn re-
A semble? * Did the Carthaginians confine themselves to the
worship of the gods of the mother country?

[181] What was the nature of the Carthaginian government?
B How was a difference of opinion between the kings and the
senate settled? What power did the kings possess? Why was

C the council or college of a hundred established? What power
had they? Was there any other college appointed? How were
their magistrates chosen?

[182] * What were the sources of revenue?

[183] * Of how many vessels did their *naval force,* before their
D wars with the Romans, consist? * What amount of naval force
was employed against Regulus? * Of what troops did their
army consist?

[184] What account can you give of Carthaginian literature?
B What sciences attained a high state of perfection? What was
the language of the Carthaginians?

[185] Did the Carthaginians allow an open trade to their colonies?
Why not? How was the intercourse with foreign countries
C facilitated? What was the extent of their navigation? What
trade did they share with the mother country beyond the Pillars
A of Hercules? What coast was secretly visited on the western
side of Africa?

[186] * What were the chief exports and imports of Carthage?
How was the internal traffic conducted? What was brought
from the interior of Africa?

EUROPE.

[187] What advantages does Europe possess over all the other
B quarters of the globe? In what respects is it inferior to Asia
C and America? What compensates for these points of inferiority?
What greatly facilitates its commercial intercourse? How is
Europe indebted to the East? In what respect may Europe be
A considered superior to the rest of the world? How has their
B excellence in arts and arms been displayed? How is Europe
naturally divided? What remarkable distinctions are there
between eastern and western Europe?

§ 53. *The earliest Population of Greece.*

[230] Who were the most ancient inhabitants of Greece? Were
A they spread over any other countries? * How had they,
probably, already acquired a degree of civilization? * Where
B did they send out colonies to? How was the appellation of
Hellēnes used originally? What names were applied to the
people collectively? Who was the founder of the Grecian race,
and of its principal tribes?

[231] How soon are the legendary foreign immigrations said to
B have commenced? Give some account of Cecrops. Who was
Cadmus? Give some account of him. What improvements did
C he introduce into Thebes? Who migrated to Argos? * What
became of the fifty sons of Ægyptus? When did Pelops come
from Phrygia to Arcadia? Who extended his dominion?

§ 54. *Myths concerning the Migrations of the Hellenic Tribes.*

[232] What story is related of Deucalion? Who is said to have
A succeeded Deucalion on the throne? and who Hellen? How did
B the Æolians spread themselves? How did the Dorians spread
themselves? What success attended the youngest son of Hellen?
What sons had he? Name the four phylæ then established.

§ 55. *The Heroic Age.*

[233] What effect did the wanderings of the Hellenic tribes pro-
D duce? What was the natural consequence of political division
A into separate nations? * How is Hercules described in mythical
history? * Who persecuted, and who protected him? * At
whose command does Hercules undertake his *twelve labors?*
C * Enumerate these. * What became of Hercules? * Who was
Theseus? * How does he show himself a benefactor to the
human race? * Who was his protector?

[234] Give an account of the Argonautic expedition. Whence did
A the Hellespont derive its name? Name the most renowned
heroes who accompanied this expedition.

[235] *What led to the exposure of Œdipus on Mount Cithæron?
C What crime did he inadvertently commit? How did he show
his horror on the discovery? Who were his sons? Name the
D heroes who accompanied Polynīces against Thebes. What was
the result of it?

[236] Why was the war of the Epigŏni undertaken?

[237] How did the war against Troy originate? At whose instigation was this contest undertaken? Name the principal leaders
B engaged in it. What was the amount of the forces? What
detained them at Aulis? How were they released? What
C time did the siege last? * What was their mode of warfare?
* Why did Achilles refuse, after a time, to take any part in the
war?

[238] What was the fate of Agamemnon after his return? Give an
D account of Orestes. Where did Menelaus wander? What
A became of Diomedes? What was the form of government that
prevailed in the heroic age? What offices did the kings hold?
How was their revēnue obtained? Who were the counsellors of
B the kings? Why were assemblies of the people called? * In
many of the Grecian states what does the king seem to have
been? * How was Attica divided by Theseus? * How did
aristocratic constitutions arise?

§ 56. *The Migration of the Dorians, or Heraclīdæ.*

[239] Who gave the name of Thessaly to Pelasgicon? What be-
C came of the aborigines of the district afterwards named Bœotia?
A How did they treat the ancient inhabitants? Why was the
conquest of Peloponnesus by the Dorians undertaken? Who
B headed this expedition? What was its success? How were the
conquered districts divided? How happened it that Attica re-
tained her independence? How much of this account seems
C to be historically certain? Were other Doric kingdoms founded?

Who alone continued to occupy their ancient habitations? What was the fate of the Achæans?

§ 57. *The Greek Colonies on the western coast of Asia Minor, and the adjacent islands.*

[240] By what was the movement of the Heraclidæ followed? To
A what country or countries did the expelled Achæans migrate? Enumerate the cities of note founded by them.
[241] Where did the Ionians betake themselves? What was their
B common bond of union? Name the most considerable cities
C they raised. Who burnt the famous temple of Artemis?
[242] Where did the Dorians emigrate? Where was Herodotus
D born?

§ 58. *Origin of Republican Constitutions.*

[243] What caused the absolute sovereignty of individuals to ex-
A pire? What constitutions followed the regal? Where did two kings continue to reign? Where was the monarchical constitution retained? Was Greece united, or split into independent states?
B How were the different independent cities united? What advantage attended this arrangement? What occasioned the establishment of Tyrants? What is meant by the term tyrant?
C How did this kind of tyranny arise in those states which were not exclusively Dorian?
[244] * What changes of constitution were experienced by Co-
D rinth? * What Corinthian colonies were founded during this period? What institutions served to unite the little independent states into which Greece was divided?
[245] What were the Amphictyoniæ? How did they differ from
A the ordinary confederacies? Which was the most celebrated?
B How was the term subsequently used? What altered its original character? What privileges belonged to the Amphic-
C tyons? What oracle obtained influence through its connection with the Amphictyons? How was the Amphictyonia superseded? From this period to what were the duties of the con-
D federacy restricted? Of what avail were its exertions now?
[246] Were the congresses exclusive? Which were the most re-
B nowned of all the games? Who founded them? Who revived them? From what time was a regular record kept of the conquerors? Where were the games celebrated? and how? How
C was the ceremonial closed? * Name the exercises of the Pentathlon. * What was meant by Pancration? * What rendered the Olympic Panegyris favorable for public advertisements, and the exhibition of works of art? * How were the victors re-
D warded on the spot? and how at home? Name the other great national games. Where were they severally kept, and in honor of whom?

§ 59. *Sparta.*

[247] How was the throne of Sparta always occupied? How long did the contest with the Achæans continue? Which was of all

these struggles the most obstinate? What character did the
C population of Laconia assume? Who were the Helots? Give
D some account of them. Who was Lycurgus? At whose request did Lycurgus give his native city a constitution? Were
A the kings retained? What were their functions? What privileges did they enjoy? How was the government administered? How were they elected? What were the duties of this council?
[248] What power had the popular assembly? How were the
C Ephŏri chosen? What were their duties? How did Lycurgus apportion the lands?
[249] To what were the regulations of Lycurgus with respect to
A education and domestic life directed? How were the strong
B children brought up? Why did Lycurgus institute public meals? What was the only circulating medium allowed? What was the chief occupation of the free citizen? How were the Periœci employed? and the Helots? What course did Lycurgus take to secure permanence to his laws?

§ 60. *The two first Messenian Wars.*

[250] Narrate the legend concerning the cause of the first Messe-
A nian war. How did the Spartans commence the war? Who assisted the Messenians in this struggle? Who commanded the Messenians? What followed his death? * What became of the Parthenii?
[251] What roused the next generation of Messenians to insurrec-
C tion? Who assisted them? Who commanded the forces on each side? How long did they keep possession of the fortress
D of Ira? How did Aristomĕnes escape from prison? Why were the Messenians compelled to abandon their post? What was the plan of Aristomenes? What became of most of the Messenians?

§ 61. *Athens.*

[252] Is the catalogue of Athenian sovereigns until the reign of
A Theseus of any value? When does the historical period of Athens begin? What arrangements of the people did he intro-
B duce? Who was Melanthus? Who were the sons of Codrus? What afforded the Eupatridæ an opportunity of abolishing the kingly office? What became of Neleus? Who were made chief magistrates? To whom were they responsible? Under what title?
[254] How long did the Archonship remain in the family of
C Codrus?
[255] When were nine annual Archons first elected? What title
D had the first of these? the second? the third? How were the remaining six named? Why was a system of written laws
A called for by the people or commonalty? Who was commissioned to draw up a code of laws?
[256] * Who attempted to make himself absolute at Athens? * Who put to death the partisans of Cylon? * Why were the Alcmæonidæ compelled to quit the city?
[257] * What measures did Solon introduce in order to re-

move the misunderstanding between the Eupatrids and the
C Demos? How was Salamis recovered to the Athenians?
How was its possession finally secured to his countrymen?
D What caused *the first Sacred War?* How were the Crisæans
punished? What factions now sprung up in Attica? What
A forms of government did these factions respectively advocate?
Why was the sovereign authority offered to Solon? What followed his refusal?

[258] What were the measures adopted by Solon?

[259] * Who were the persons excluded from civil rights? * What
B was the condition of the μέτοικοι? * How was the condition of
the slaves improved?

[260] How was a democratic character given to the constitution of
C Solon? How were the citizens divided? Which class was
eligible to the Archonship? Were the other offices of state
A open to the other classes? What was the effect of Solon's
measures? * What classes served in the cavalry? * What as
heavy and light armed troops?

[261] From what class were the Archons chosen? What exam-
B ination were they required to undergo before entering on their
office?

[262] What number of members constituted the senate at different periods? How were they chosen? What were their various functions?

[263] How often was the assembly of the people held? What
C was the nature of the questions they decided? How did they
vote?

[264] Who composed the court of Areopagus? Where were its
A sittings held? What duties were committed to this court?
B * How were the lower courts of justice formed? What respect
was shown to Solon's laws? Did his measures allay the factious
spirit of his time?

[265] What means did Pisistratus use to become absolute in Athens? Did he obtain the confidence of the people?

[266] How was the government afterwards carried on? Who
C assassinated Hipparchus? From what motives? How was
the administration conducted after this event? Who expelled
Hippias? Where did Hippias seek an asylum?

[267] Who now established the democracy? How did he en-
A deavor to obliterate all historical family reminiscences? Who
attempted to overthrow the new constitution? Who supported
B him? Why? Did this attempt succeed? What was Ostracism? What power did it give the democratic party?

§ 62. *The Grecian Colonies.*

[268] Where were colonies established during this period? For
C what purposes? What constitution did these settlements adopt?
D Did they degenerate or not? How far did they depend on the
mother country?

[270] Name the Dorian colonies in Lower Italy.

[271] What Achæan colonies were in Lower Italy? What hap-

A pened to Sybaris? * Who founded Metapontum and Poseidonia?

[272] What name had the peninsula between the Thermaic and Strymonic gulfs? Mention the Chalcidian settlements on the
B Thracian coast. Which was the most ancient of all the Grecian settlements in the west? in *Lower Italy?* and in *Sicily?* How was Zancle afterwards named?

[273] Name the Dorian colonies in *Sicily?* What other settle-
C ments had they *on the coast of the Ionian sea?* Had they any
D *on the Thracian coast and Bosporus?* * Did Syracuse undergo any (and if so, *many* or *few*) changes of constitution? * How long did the *Aristocratic* constitution last? * In whose hands was the supreme authority lodged during this period? * Name
A the three *Tyrants* of Syracuse. * Why was the last deposed? * When was Hiero II. chosen king? and why? * Who succeeded him? * What alliance occasioned the capture of Syracuse?

[274] Name the colonies of Milētus *on the Hellespont—on the Pro-*
B *pontis—and on the Pontus Euxīnus.*

[275] What colonies had the Phocæans?

[276] Mention the colony of Zacynthus.

§ 63. *The Persian Wars.*

[277] What caused the Persian wars?

[278] Who was at the head of the *first campaign* against the Greeks? Who was at the head of the *second?* When was the
A battle of Marathon fought? After that battle what design did Miltiades form? How far did this project succeed? What followed his failure at Paros? Who ruled Athens after the
B decease of Miltiades? How did Themistocles obtain the ostracism of his rival? What decree did he prevail on the people to
C pass? What was the real intention of this measure?

[279] What was the date of the third campaign of the Persians?
D Who sided with them? Who opposed them? Who defended the pass of *Thermopylæ?* Who betrayed Leonidas? What
A did he then do? Did the Persian army advance? State the names and events of the three naval engagements which were fought.

[280] How was Xerxes induced to hasten his return into Asia?
B What army did he leave behind him? When did Mardonius invade Attica? Where did the Athenians flee for refuge?
C Where was Mardonius utterly defeated? By what forces? What became of the Medizing Thebans? What other victory was gained on the same day? Which was the first aggressive
A movement on the part of the Greeks? How was the vigor of Themistocles's administration shown? What popular enactment did Aristīdes obtain?

[281] With what view did the allied fleet commence operation?
B Why was Pausanias superseded in the command? How did
C the Spartans take this? * In what did the Hegemony of Sparta over the other Peloponnesian states consist? What were the duties of the allied powers under the protection of Athens?

[282] What fierce antagonism commences about this period?
A Who procured the banishment of Themistocles? by what
B means? To what city or country did Themistocles retire in the
first instance? Whose protection did he afterwards seek?
What was his reception? What was the fate of Pausanias?
How did Aristides end his days? What leaders now rose into
C importance? What policy was pursued? Who was appointed
commander-in-chief of the army? What success attended his
arms? How was the booty expended?

§ 64. *The Third Messenian War.*

[283] What checked the Spartan invasion of A tica? Who
D attempted at this time to throw off the Spartan oppression?
A Who opposed them? To what place did they retreat? Who
B afforded aid to the Spartans? What led to Cimon's banishment by ostracism? Where were the Messenians allowed to
retire to?

§ 65. *The Age of Pericles.*

[284] When did the democratic supremacy commence at Athens?
C Who was the most powerful of all the Athenian popular leaders?
Who was he? How was he enabled to carry on his various in-
D novations? State the use (or abuse) that the Athenians now
A made of the contingents of the allies. What increase was made
to their allies? What further burdens were imposed on them?
B How did Pericles employ the resources at his disposal? Who
introduced the practice of paying the army? What institution
was now the sole remaining representative of aristocratic interests? How did Pericles abridge the rights of this institution?
[286] How did the participation of the Athenians in the insurrec-
C. tion of the Egyptians and of the satrap Inarus end?
[287] What was the real intention of the Spartans in sending an
D army into central Greece? Who were victorious at Tanagra?
A and what neutralized the advantages there gained? Who now
joined the Athenian confederacy? Why did Pericles consent to
the recall of Cimon? What was obtained through Cimon's intervention?
[288] At whose instance was a fresh campaign against the Persians undertaken? Describe the fortunes of the commander and
his fleet.
[289] When was the battle at Coronea fought? by whom, and
B with what result? Why did the Peloponnesians invade Attica
on the conclusion of the armistice? For how long a period did
C the Athenian commander conclude a truce? What were the
conditions of this treaty? What arrangement laid the foundation of fresh disputes?

§ 66. *The Peloponnesian War.*

290] Give the date of the Peloponnesian war. What were the
D causes that led to it? What were the most prominent signs of
A the *jealousy* between Athens and Sparta? How was this feeling aggravated?

[291] How did *the war between Corcyra and Corinth* originate?
C How did it terminate? What occasioned the *revolt of Potidæa*
from Athens? Who supported the Potidæans? Who were the
instigators of the war against Athens?
[292] * What states were the allies *of Athens*? * What *of Sparta*?

I. *Ten Years' War* [ὁ δεκαετὴς πόλεμος] *to the Fifty Years' Truce of Nicias.*

[293] How did the Peloponnesians commence the war? What
A retaliation was made by the Athenians? What prevented
either party from obtaining any decided advantage? What
calamity overtook the Athenians? Who was carried off?
What change now took place in the government? When was
B Potidæa reduced? Why were the Lesbians compelled to surrender at discretion? What was the advice of Cleon? How
was it executed?
[295] What success had the Athenians in 424? What ill fortune
D followed? Who was dispatched for the purpose of reconquer-
A ing the lost cities? Who fell in the engagement at Amphipolis? What peace was then made? On what terms?

II. *From the Renewal of the War to the Issue of the Expedition against Sicily.*

[296] * What states were dissatisfied with the peace of Nicias?
* How was their opposition manifested? * Who persuaded the
Athenians to renounce their alliance with Sparta? * How was
the peace respected? * Was Sparta able or not to prevent a
renewal of the treaty between Argos and Athens?
[297] What gave rise to the expedition against Sicily? Of the
B Athenian statesmen, who *advised* and who *opposed* the expedition?
What generals commanded the expedition? Which of the
Athenian generals was recalled? What charge was preferred
C against him? To what city did he escape? What Sicilian
general prevented Nicias from taking Syracuse? Who commanded the reinforcements sent to Nicias? By whose advice
did a Spartan fleet sail to assist the Syracusans? Who commanded the Spartan fleet? Who now opposed the Athenians?
A What success was obtained against the Athenian fleet? Describe the failure of the last attempt of the Athenians, and the
fate of their army and its commanders.

III. *The Decelean War.*

298] How was the war continued by the Spartans? Who joined
C them? What grievance occasioned the revolt of many of the
Athenian allies in Asia Minor? From whom did Sparta receive subsidies for the war? What change took place in the
D government of Athens? How was the authority of the people
limited? What support did the democratical part of the constitution now obtain? Who was now recalled? On whose
advice? Who persuaded Tissaphernes to renounce the league
A with Sparta? How long did the oligarchical faction last?

What hastened their overthrow? Who now regained the supreme authority?

[299] Describe the successes of Alcibiades against the Lacedæmo-
B nians. Describe his return to Athens. Why was he deprived
C of his unlimited command? Who were appointed to succeed
him? Who succeeded Lysander? Where was he defeated?
* On what charge were the Athenian generals condemned to
death? * How many were executed?

[300] Describe the successes of Lysander. Where was the naval
D power of Athens annihilated? How many ships escaped?
A What was the perilous position of Athens at this time? On what
humiliating terms did Athens surrender? When did the democratic principle perish?

§ 67. *The Hegemony of Sparta.*

[301] Why did the Hegemony of Sparta prove odious and oppres-
B sive? Why did Thebes and Corinth take a part in the war?
What did they never intend? How far did they change their
political creed?

[302] Give the *date* and duration of the supremacy of ***the thirty.***
A What change did Lysander introduce into the government?
Describe the conduct of the Thirty. Which of their number
was put to death by his colleagues? On what grounds?
B Describe the death of Alcibiades. Narrate the proceedings of
Thrasybulus. What success attended him? How were the
C places of the Thirty supplied? What were the changes made
by Pausanias in co-operation with Thrasybulus?

[303] What were the causes of the war of the Spartans with the
D Persians?

[304] How did Tithraustes divert the war from Persia? Did the
A Athenians join the confederacy? What was the pretext for the
B war? Where did Lysander fall? Why was Agesilaus recalled
C from Asia? Where did Conon defeat the Lacedæmonians?
What followed his victory? Where did Agesilaus obtain a
victory? What did Conon and Pharnabazus next effect?
D What proposals did the Spartans make in order to withdraw
the Persians from their alliance with Athens? When was the
peace of Antalcidas concluded? What did Sparta gain by it?
A * What islands did the Athenians continue to hold?

[305] * Give a general account of the Olynthian war.

§ 68. *The War between Thebes and Sparta.*

[306] Who were now at the head of Theban affairs? Of what
B dishonorable action was Phœbidas guilty? What was the fate
of Ismenias? Where did the other democrats betake them-
C selves to? Describe the course of Pelopidas and his companions.
D How was the Spartan garrison treated? What fresh attempts
A were made by Sparta? With what success? What victories
were gained by the Athenians? Under what commanders?
What was now the policy of Athens? What impediment was
B presented? Who now rose into importance? What victory
did this leader obtain over Sparta? Who was killed? What

C ambitious design was formed by Thebes? How was this promoted? Who joined the Thebans? Why were they compelled to abandon their attempt on Sparta itself? What plan did Thebes form in order to restrain the Spartans from any further encroachments on Peloponnesus? Why was the Theban army
D compelled to retire? * What did the second and third invasions of Peloponnesus effect?

[307] Why did the Thebans attack the tyrant of Pheræ? With
A what success? Where did Pelopidas fall? What dissensions induced Epaminondas to undertake a fourth campaign in Pelo-
B ponnesus? What was the nature of these dissensions? Where did Epaminondas fall? Give the date of his death. Why did Sparta refuse to accede to a general peace? Why was Agesilaus sent into Egypt?

§ 69. *The War of the Confederates against Athens.*

[308] Why did the allies renounce their allegiance to Athens?
C Why were the Athenians compelled to recognize the independence of their revolted allies, and remit the tribute?

§ 70. *The Phocian or Sacred War.*

[309] What caused the Phocian or Sacred war? What had the
B Phocians done? Why did the Spartans join the Phocians?
C What measures were taken by the Spartans and Phocians? Who united in the cause of the Thebans?

[310] Who was chosen general of the Phocians? How did Philomelus avoid falling into the hands of the enemy? Who succeeded him in the command? How was he enabled to continue
D the war? Which was the principal theatre of hostilities? why? Why were the Phocians compelled to yield? How was
A Onomarchus slain? Against whom were hostilities still carried on? Why were the Thebans compelled to call in Philip II. of
B Macedonia? What was the termination of the war? Wha was the decree of the Amphictyonic council?

§ 71. *The War against Philip II. of Macedonia.*

[311] With what view had Philip captured Amphipolis and Pydna?
C Why did he give up Potidæa to the Olynthians?

[312] What was Philip's first pretext for interfering in the affairs
D of Greece? Did Philip comply with the request of the tyrants of Pheræ? Why did he permit the tyrants to remain? Who came to their aid? How did Philip then act?

[313] What was the policy of Philip with regard to the Grecian
B states generally? To what did Philip now direct his chief attention? What city offered the most obstinate resistance? Who sent them assistance? How did Philip favor the Messenians?
C Who was his bribed orator? What cities did he blockade on recommencing his plans of conquest? How was the capture of these cities prevented?

[314] How did Philip get a fresh excuse for marching an army into
A Greece? Did any thing he did indicate ulterior objects?

[315] Who had the courage to oppose Philip? How did this great
B man show his activity? Where was the allied army defeated?

In what year? How was the fortune of the day decided? Did Thebes surrender? What appointment did Philip receive?

§ 72. *Religion, Literature, &c. of the Greeks.*

[316] * How was the notion formed that Greek civilization
C was derived from Egypt? * Do we find any traces in proof of this?

[317] Give some account of the religion of the Greeks. What
A traces do we find of a belief in one supreme being? Where
B was the residence of Zeus and the other deities? How were the national divinities amalgamated at a very early period? Name the twelve principal deities.

[318] * Give some account of Zeus. * What was Juno named by
C the Dorians and Ionians? * Who was Persephŏne? * What
D is her history? * Who were the deities of light? * Give an account of Athēne. * Whose children were Apollo and Arte-
A mis? * Where were they born? * How is Apollo also named?
B * Mention his attributes and epithets. * What does *Poseidōn* denote? * What gave occasion to the fable of Vulcan's being the cup-bearer of the gods? * Why was he represented as a
C blacksmith? * Give an account of Mercury: of Vesta. * Who was Mars? * Who was Venus? * Describe the manner in which Bacchus was represented. What were his epithets?

[319] What inferior classes of deities were there? Who were the
A Dæmŏnes? What is meant by *heroes?* What notion produced the deities of the lower world? Name these. How were
B the gods approached? What were their offerings? In what other modes did the Greeks honor the gods? Which of all the sorts of divination was held in the greatest esteem? Which were the most renowned oracles? Name the other sorts of divination.

[320] What necessities were pressed on the Greeks when they
A became engaged in wars with Persia? At Athens who restored the constitution of Solon? Where was democracy introduced? Where did oligarchy prevail? When were these two
B forms of government placed in a state of antagonism? When was the oligarchical system at its greatest height? What was
C the signal for a general rising against Sparta? How was Greece prepared to receive the yoke of a foreign master?

[321] Where did epic, lyric, and dramatic poetry first develope themselves?

[322] What was the character of epic poetry before the days of
D Homer? How did Homer improve the plan of the epic? How were the *Iliad* and *Odyssey* made known to the world?
A Who composed the Homeric hymns? Had Homer any
B imitators? Where was the school of the Homeridæ? Who was at the head of the rival school? What peoms of his are extant?

[323] When did lyric poetry develope itself? To whom is the
D elegiac measure ascribed? Who was the last of the great elegiac poets? How was the elegiac metre most commonly employed? How did Simonides distinguish himself in this

A way? Who invented the Iambic? How did it differ from the
epic and elegiac? How was the *lyric poetry* of the Greeks
B divided? Distinguish the two. How did the subject matter
C vary? Who were the most distinguished poets of the Æolic
school? Name them. Under whom did the Doric choral
poetry develope itself, and attain perfection? What compositions of Pindar's are extant? What is their character?

[324] When did the choral hymns first assume the form of tra-
A gedy? Who introduced a second actor on the stage? How did
Æschylus excite the astonishment and delight of the Greeks?
Who introduced a third actor? What was the chief object in
this addition? What number of tragedies were Æschylus and
B Sophocles accustomed to bring forward at one representation?
C Where was Euripides born? What innovations did he intro-
duce? How did Euripides differ from Æschylus and Sophocles
in the treatment of his heroes?

[325] How did this form of composition arise, and what was its
A character? What specimen have we left of the Satyric drama?
Whence did the Old Comedy derive its origin? Who moulded
it into a more artistical form? When did Aristophanes flourish?
How many of his comedies remain? What representation have
B we in them of Athenian manners? When was all satirical
notice of living characters strictly prohibited? What was the
result of this injunction? What was the object of the Middle
Comedy?

[326] How can we account for the Greeks being so many centuries
C without accurate historical records? Who first broke the ground?
With what did the compilers of history antecedent to Hero-
D dotus content themselves? Describe the character of Hero-
A dotus as an historian. Describe the great historical work of
Thucydides. What unfounded charge has been made against
Xenophon?

[327] Where alone was eloquence cultivated as a political science?
B Characterize the orations of Pericles. Who originally culti-
C vated rhetoric as an art? What combination produced the
elaborate eloquence of the senate and the bar? How was the
D eloquence of Lysias distinguished? [1] Who was a famous teacher
of oratory? What orator was the great opponent of Demosthenes? Did Demosthenes exert all the resources of his
eloquence?

328] Where was philosophy first cultivated? Who was at the
A head of the Ionic school? Upon what does the reputation of
the '*seven wise men*' seem to have been founded? What was
B principally taught by the Sophists? Who resisted their abuse of
this art? How did he attempt to stem the torrent of immo-
C rality? Who held him up to ridicule? Why was he sentenced
to death? Who has preserved his doctrines? What school did

---

1 [What is said in the text gives a false notion of this orator. The *Epitaphios* is probably not a genuine work of his. His pleadings are mostly on private causes, and are exceedingly clear, correct, and nervous, though plain.]

D Plato found? Who founded the Peripatetic school? * Where
are the earliest traces of mathematical science found? * Who
made an attempt to introduce medicine into ordinary life?
* Who was the real founder of the healing art?

[329] Describe the Cyclopian style of architecture. What remains have we of this style? Who has described the palaces
B of the heroic age? What are the most important architectural
monuments of antiquity? How were the fronts of Grecian
C temples ornamented? Where are the most ancient of the architectural monuments still in existence found? Where may those
of the most flourishing period of Grecian architecture be seen?

[330] What ornamental works in *sculpture* were produced? When
D was the period of their greatest perfection? What ornaments
A decorated the temples? Who was the most distinguished
master in sculpture? What were his chief works? Name the
other celebrated masters.

[331] To what was *painting* for a long time confined? How long
B was it considered subordinate to sculpture? Who were the
principal painters of note? Who attained the highest degree
of perfection? Of what did his works consist?

[332] What trade did the Phœnicians carry on with the Greeks?
C Who were notorious for their acts of piracy? Which were the
chief commercial states of Greece?

[333] * Name the *principal branches of Greek commerce.* * What
A were the *principal articles* of import? of export?

§ 74. *History of Macedonia to the Reign of Philip II.*

[340] What traditions exist respecting the establishment of the
C Macedonian monarchy? When do the first continuous notices
D of Macedonian history commence? How did the Macedonian
A Alexander serve Xerxes? Why did Perdiccas II. break with
B the Athenians? Whom did he support? Enumerate the improvements Archelaus introduced into his country. What was
its condition after his death?

[341] * What was the nature of the constitution of Macedonia
C during this period?

§ 75. *Philip II.*

[342] How was the disputed succession in Macedonia settled?
A Who was sent as a hostage to Thebes? How did he benefit
by his residence there? How did Philip obtain the throne?
B What was this prince's grand object? How did he increase
the efficiency of his army? Wherein did its great power consist? Why did he endeavor to make himself master of the
C coasts of Thrace? Who assassinated Philip? why?

§ 76. *Alexander the Great.*

[343] When was Alexander the Great born? What remarkable
A event took place on the night of his birth? Who conducted his
education? What were the first acts of his reign? Who
opposed the Hegemony of Alexander? Who was chosen
commander-in-chief of the forces destined to act against the
Persians?

[344] What expedition did Alexander now undertake? What false
c report was raised? How did Alexander treat the Thebans?

[345] Who was left as regent in Macedonia? What was the state
D of the Persian empire at this time? What forces had Alex-
A ander? Which was his first battle? Who favored the designs of Alexander? Who offered resistance? Who was the favorite
B general of Alexander? What was assigned to him? Why did he *cut* the famous knot at Gordium? How was Alexander's march interrupted? Between whom was the battle of Issus
C fought? when? with what result? What fell into the hands of Parmenio? On what terms was Darius anxious to purchase a peace?

[346] Enumerate the conquests which followed. How was Tyre
D taken? How long did the siege of Gaza last? How did Alexander perpetuate his name in Egypt?

[347] Describe his visit to the temple of Zeus Ammon. What
A advantage attended his conquest of Phœnicia and Cyprus?
B Where did he again overthrow Darius? Where did the defeated monarch fly to for refuge? What provinces did Alexander take possession of? Who murdered Darius?

[348] How did the death of Darius assist the schemes of Alex-
C ander? How was the rapid subjugation of the eastern portion of the empire effected?

[349] What was the fate of Bessus? With what view did he
A undertake an expedition against the Scythians, &c.? Why did he retrace his steps?

[350] * Where did discontent manifest itself? * Why were the
B Macedonians discontented? * Name some of the most distinguished Macedonians who refused Alexander divine homage. * What caused disturbances in Greece? * Who supported Agis II.?

[351] Who composed the Indian army of Alexander? Why did
D Porus submit to Alexander? How was Alexander induced to
A return? Who commanded the fleet? Describe its course.
B How did Alexander return to Persia?

[352] Why did Alexander keep in sight of his fleet? How did he
C proceed after this became impracticable? How were the last years of his life spent?

[353] * How were the oppressive barbarian satraps treated?
D * In what way did Alexander still further conciliate the barbarians? * How did he alienate his own veteran soldiers?

[354] Where and when did Alexander die? What caused his
A death?

§ 77. *Partition of the Persico-Macedonian Empire.*

[355] Who was to be proclaimed the successor of Alexander?
B Who was to govern as regent? in Asia? in Europe? Whom did the army recognize as king? Who obtained the satrapy of Egypt? of Phrygia? of Caria? What province fell to Antigonus? to Eumenes? to Lysimachus?

[356] What were the plans of Perdiccas? How were they
C frustrated? Who succeeded to the regency? When did he die? Who next obtained the guardianship of the two young

A kings? What followed this arrangement? What led to a confederacy against Antigonus? Who comprised this confederacy?
B Who was the son of Antigonus? When and where was Antigonus defeated? Who shared his dominions?

[357] * What was the policy of Antigonus? * How did he
C attempt to weaken Cassander of Macedonia? * What prevented his crossing into Europe? * What did he do in order to reconquer the east?

[358] * How did the war break out afresh? * Who was now com-
A missioned to effect the liberation of Greece? * How was he rewarded for this service? * What victory did Demetrius now obtain? * What titles did he and his father now assume? * Who imitated them? * Why did Demetrius attack Rhodes?
B * What were his exertions? * Were they successful? * Who solicited the aid of Demetrius? * What alliance was then formed? * How were the territories of Antigonus divided?

§ 78. *Macedonia and Greece.*

[359] How did the Greeks receive the intelligence of Alexander's
A death? Who was appointed commander-in-chief of the allied army? To what country did he transfer the theatre of war?
B What success attended the allied army? On what condition was peace granted to Athens? What was the fate of Hyperides and Demosthenes?

[360] How did the kings of the new Macedonian empire content
B themselves? How were their plans continually rendered abortive? What was another obstacle to the complete subjugation of Greece? What Greek province alone remained to Macedonia? What relation did the other states bear to Macedonia?

[361] When were Macedonia and Greece invaded by the Gauls?
A What hordes of barbarians made an irruption into Greece? Whom did the first horde overthrow? Who drove them subsequently out of the country? Under whom did the second
B horde march to Delphi? Describe their repulse. Where did they settle?

[362] What had the Ætolian and Achæan confederacy for their
C object? Where was the *Ætolian confederacy* held? Who gave
D importance to the Achæan confederacy? How were the Athenians persuaded to join it?

[363] What struggle took place between the two confederacies?

[364] * In the *Cleomenian war*, who formed an alliance with Sparta?
A * With what intent? * Who prevented the Achæans from sub-
B mitting to Sparta? How? * How was Cleomenes vanquished? * How did the *war of the confederates* arise? * What was the success of Philip III.? * What made him think of attacking Rome?

[365] What was the object of *New Comedy?* Who was the
C most successful writer of this description of comedy? For
D whom did he furnish a model? Where was eloquence chiefly cultivated? Name the five philosophic schools.

[366] * Who founded the *Peripatetic?* * What was the teaching
A of the *Epicurean* school? * Who founded the *Stoic?* * What

was the character of its teaching? * Who founded the *Skeptic?* * What was its teaching? * Who founded the *New Academy?* * To what school was it opposed?

[367] Name the principal commercial places after the decline of Grecian freedom.

§ 79. *Egypt under the Ptolemies.*

[368] Who received the smallest division of the Macedonian
B monarchy? What advantages attended the allotment of the
C Ptolemies? Give the surnames of the three first Ptolemies.
What was their policy with respect to Egypt, and particularly
A Alexandria? What proof have we of their injudicious foreign
policy? What was the consequence of their obstinate perseverance?

[369] * How did Ptolemy Philadelphus facilitate the commerce
B between India and the Mediterranean? * Why was this mode
of communication but little used? * Which was the great emporium for the Indian and Arabian trade?

[370] When does the decline of the Egyptian empire date its com-
C mencement? What was the character of succeeding sovereigns? How did the people submit to their oppression? How
D did the Romans find an opportunity for intervention? What
A wars followed with the Romans? When did Egypt begin to
take the place of Athens as the seat of learning? What difference was there in the character of the Alexandrian and Grecian literature?

[372] Where do the Alexandrian poets fail? Who excelled in
B lyric poetry? in epic and didactic poetry? Have we any fragments of Theocritus?

[373] Who raised *philology* to the position of a substantive science? What was the plan of these literati? Who were the most celebrated grammarians?

[374] * What great mathematicians flourished at this period? * What philosophic sect sprung up here in the second century?

§ 80. *The Syrian Empire under the Seleucidæ.*

[375] Relate the victories of Seleucus. What was the extent of
B his dominion? What bad policy did the Seleucidæ adopt?
C What would have been their better course? What was the
result of their system of government?

[376] Who averted the ruin of the declining empire for a time?
A What was his first attempt? Whose independence was Antio-
chus compelled to recognize? What was his conviction with
regard to the north-western portion of the Persian empire?
B What war was now successfully renewed? Who interrupted
Antiochus in his career of victory? How did the Romans seek
C war with Syria? For what purpose did Antiochus visit Greece?
A Who deceived him? Who declared war against him? Under
these circumstances how did Antiochus act? Where did the
Romans gain a second battle at? To what condition was
B Antiochus obliged to submit? Who then renounced their alle-
giance to the Seleucidæ?

[377] On the death of Antiochus III., what causes undermined
D the empire of the Seleucidæ? How did Antiochus IV. show
his ignorance of his real position? Who compelled Antiochus
A to disgorge his Egyptian conquest? What occasioned the defection of the Israelites from the Syrian monarchy? How was this empire shaken to its foundation? Who reduced it to the condition of a Roman province? At what date? •

§ 81. *Kingdoms which revolted from the Syrian dominion.*

[378] Who supported the Romans in their war against Antiochus
B III.? What was his reward? Who was the founder of the
C celebrated library of Pergamus? To whom did Attalus III. bequeath his kingdom? Who overthrew Aristonĭcus?
[379] How did Nicomedes treat the Gallic tribes? Who migrated
A to Asia Minor? How did Cæsar favor Deiotărus? Who assassinated Agathocles? What was the extent of the kingdom of Parthia afterwards? Who deposed Arsaces XXX.? Of what
B provinces did the emperor Galerius deprive Narses?
[381] What notices have we of Bactria?
[382] When was Armenia divided? What misfortune attended the alliance of Tigranes with his father-in-law Mithridates VI.? Enumerate the successive changes in the government of Armenia. Who ruled the *Lesser Armenia?*
[383] Who acquired Palestine on the death of Alexander the
B Great? What was the Greek translation of the Old Testament called? How long did the Jews remain subject to the Seleucidæ? What occasioned their revolt?
[384] How long did they maintain their independence? Who was
C recognized by Demetrius as high-priest and independent prince of Judæa? What struggles prepared the way for the dependence of their country on Rome? How did the leader of the Pharisaic party obtain promotion to the high-priesthood?
[385] * How did the Pharisees and Sadducees differ in doctrine?
A * Who were the Essenes? What was the consequence of the new high-priest's neglect of public affairs? Whose son was Herod? How was he enabled to bid defiance to the enmity of the Pharisees?
[386] Why was the government of Herod the Great hateful to
B every Jewish patriot? What was Herod's policy? When was JESUS CHRIST born? Of what province did Judæa form a part? Who was its most notorious procurator? What happened during his government?
[387] * Did Palestine again become a kingdom? * Under whom? Who destroyed Jerusalem? When? How many Jews lost their lives? Where was the seat of government now trans-
A ferred? What occasioned another general insurrection of the Jews? What new city rose on the ruins of Jerusalem?

§ 82. *The Kingdom of Pontus.*

[388] When did Pontus become independent? To whom did
B Mithridates II. submit? Who expelled Antigonus from Pontus? Describe the career of Mithridates VI. On whom was
C Pontus conferred at a later period?

§ 83. *Bithynia and Cappadocia.*

[389] Who are the best known of the Bithynian kings?
D Who inveigled him to Rome? Who was the last king of Cappadocia?

§ 91. *Legend concerning the Immigration of the Trojans into Latium.*

[447] Who visited Latium previously to the Trojan immigration?
A What did he do? Where did Æneas land? Whom did he marry? How was the first settlement in Italy named by the
B Trojans? What city did they found afterwards? * What was the fate of Turnus, king of the Rutuli? * What becomes of Æneas? * Who was his son?
[448] Who founded the city of Alba Longa? * On what grounds
C would you doubt the catalogue of kings from Ascanius to Amulius?

§ 92. *Legend concerning the Building of Rome.*

[449] * Under what two forms is the legend concerning the build- of Rome known?

§ 93. *Romulus.*

[450] How long did Romulus reign? How was the new city of
C Rome soon peopled? How did Romulus act when his matrimonial proposals were rejected? What wars did this give rise
A to? How were they terminated? What became of Romulus?

§ 94. *Numa Pompilius.*

[451] How long did Numa Pompilius reign? Who was he?
B Name the different orders who formed his religious establishment. What were his other remarkable acts?

§ 95. *Niebuhr's view of the origin of the earliest Inhabitants of Rome.*

[452] Why have we the term Quirites associated with that of
C Populus Romanus?
[453] Of what did the Roman people consist before the formation
A of the plebs? How did this distinction originate? What was the nature of the connection between client and patron?
[454] Who were styled gentes minores? Name the three tribes of
C the Roman people. How were these subdivided? Who pre-
A sided over a tribe? curia? gens? Who formed the senate?

§ 96. *The earliest Constitution of Rome under Servius Tullius.*

[455] How was the supreme authority divided? How was the king
C chosen? What was the nature of his authority? How was his revenue derived?
[456] Of what numbers did the senate consist at different periods?
[457] What was the comitia curiata? Who acted as interreges?
A For how long time did each rule?

§ 97. *Tullus Hostilius.*

[458] How long did Tullus Hostilius reign? How was the war
B with Alba Longa decided? How was the attempted desertion
C of Mettius Fuffetius punished? What was the fate of Tullus?

§ 98. *Ancus Marcius.*

[459] How long did Ancus Marcius reign? What were his prin-
D cipal public works?

§ 99. *L. Tarquinius Priscus.*

[460] How long did L. Tarquinius Priscus reign? Who was he?
A Mention his great architectural labors. What changes did he
effect in the constitution? What was Tarquin's fate?

§ 100. *Servius Tullius.*

[461] How long did Servius Tullius reign? What was his origin?
B How did he come to the throne? What temple did he build?
Who murdered him? Who supported Servius Tullius?

§ 101. *The Constitution of Servius Tullius.*

[462] What new order in the state was now become influential?
C Describe the origin and progress of this order. What was the
chief object of the constitution of Servius Tullius? What was
A his policy with regard to the plebs? How did he commence his
reforms?

[463] What new division of the inhabitants did he introduce?
C How many *equites* or knights were there? How were those who
served on foot divided? What amount of property was to be
D possessed by these classes respectively? What class or classes
comprehended the third part of the whole? Name the centuries
of this part.

[464] How was the voting conducting? What connection existed
A between the military and civil constitutions of the kingdom?
B Who were the ærarii?

[465] * How was the property qualification settled? * How often
was a census made? * What items did it comprehend? * To
whom was the administration of the public exchequer intrusted?

[466] Who formed the comitia centuriata? What privileges were
C conferred on this assembly by Servius? How was its power
A limited in elections and legislation? To whom were the judicia
capitis committed?

[467] * What state allowances were granted to the knights? * How
B were the classes divided? * Of how many men did the Roman
legion consist originally? * How were the classes armed?
* What was the office of the *accensi* and *velati*? * When were
the *proletarii* armed?

§ 102. *L. Tarquinius Superbus.*

[468] How long did L. Tarquinius Superbus reign? How came he
C to ascend the throne? What oppressive measures did he adopt?

[469] How was he enabled to build the Capitoline temple of

D Jupiter, and the temples of Juno and Minerva? How were the
A Sibylline books obtained? Who preserved them?
[471] What was the dispute between the sons of the king and L.
B Tarquinius? What was the fate of Lucretia? and who avenged
C her death? Who were the first consuls? * What inconsistencies occur in the chronology of this period?

§ 103. *The Consuls.*

[472] What was the *original* title of the Consuls? How long did
A they retain it? When did plebeians first become eligible to the office of consul? What were the necessary qualifications for the consulship? * How was the election made and sanctioned? * When did the consuls enter on office?
[473] To whom were the priestly duties committed? How was
B the great power of the consuls gradually circumscribed? When were the consuls invested with unlimited powers? How long did the consulship nominally exist?

§ 104. *Consequences of the Expulsion of the Tarquins.*

[474] Who was at the head of a conspiracy to restore the Tar-
C quins? Who succeeded Collatinus as consul? How had the number of senators been diminished? Who were now admitted in their number?
[475] * How was the battle between Aruns and Brutus decided?
A * What important law did P. Valerius obtain for the plebeians?
[476] What heroic deeds did the war with Porsenna produce?
B On what terms were the Romans compelled to conclude a peace with Porsenna?
[477] What power had *the Dictator?* How long did his office last?
C When was the first dictator appointed? What was the advantage of such an office? * From what class was the dictator chosen?

§ 105. *Secession of the Plebs,* 494.

[479] When did the patrician party begin to press heavily on the
B plebeians? With what view was the dictatorship created? How
C had the plebeians been ruined? To whom was the term *nexus* applied? What became of those who failed to redeem their pledge within a given time?
[480] Why did the people refuse to serve in the army? Who
D persuaded them to take the field? What did the people do when they found the promises of their commanders unfulfilled?
A Who brought about a peace? How were the tribunes chosen?
B What was the *object* of their appointment? What power did they possess? How were questions decided in the college of
C tribunes? To what *comitia* could they summon the people? Where was this assembly held? Whom did the resolutions there adopted affect? What were such resolutions called?
[481] What duties were intrusted to the ædiles plebeii?
[482] * Who attempted to obtain for the plebs a share of the ager publicus? * Was his law adopted? * What charge did Genucius make against the consuls?

§ 106. *Wars to the period of the Decemvirate.*

483] How did Cn. Marcius obtain the surname of Coriolanus?
B Why was he condemned by the comitia tributa? What step did he take? What demands did he make when before the city of Rome? How was he induced to raise the siege? What became of him afterwards?
[484] With what view was the war against Veii undertaken?
[485] * What success had the Fabii against the Veientines?
[486] How far had the Ausonian tribes (Æqui and Volsci) ex-
A tended their authority? Who rescued the Romans when beaten on the Algidus?

§ 107. *Struggle of the Plebeians with the Patricians for equality of Civil Rights.*

[485] Who proposed the formation of a code of written laws?
C why? What advantages would the plebeians gain by these laws? Why did the patricians attempt to render this "rogatio"
D ineffective? How did the struggle terminate? * On what grounds has it been supposed that the Roman code was derived from that of Athens?
[488] Who were appointed to frame the new code of written laws?
B What was the result of this commission? How long did these laws form the groundwork of Roman legislation? What most important change was consequent on the formation of this code?
[489] How did the second decemvirate act? How was the discon-
D tent of the people blown into a flame? By whose means was
A peace restored? On what terms? Who impeached the decemviri? What was their fate? What became of their property?
[490] What was the first endeavor of the newly-elected consuls?
B In order to this what laws were enacted?
[491] What essential change in the constitution was effected by C.
C Canuleius? What other changes were introduced by his colleagues? What was the number of the Military Tribunes? What law was passed yearly with regard to the appointment of chief magistrates?
[492] From what order were the Censors chosen? How long did
A their office continue? What were their functions?
[493] * How was the generosity of Sp. Mælius rewarded? * How
C was the senate now recruited?
[494] How had all questions hitherto been decided in the college
D of Tribunes? What enactment was now made? Was this serviceable to any order in the state? What practice was now introduced in the army? What was set aside for this purpose?

§ 108. *The last War against Veii.*

[495] What wars preceded the last against Veii?
[496] What led to the war with Veii? How was Veii taken?
B What dependence is to be placed on the account of its capture?

[497] * What did the oracle and aruspex announce about Veii?
c * What was done in consequence?
[498] How was the Veientine territory disposed of? What charge was made against Camillus? What was his punishment?

§ 109. *War with the Gauls*, 389.

[499] Who now crossed the Alps and entered Italy? Who com-
A manded the Italian division? What amount of forces were
B engaged on the Allia? When was this battle fought? With what event? On what conditions did the Gauls consent to withdraw from Rome? Who interfered at this juncture?
C What followed? Why was Camillus surnamed the second founder of the city? Who re-peopled Veii?
[500] * How were many persons reduced to insolvency at this
A. time? * What was the conduct of M. Manlius? * How was he treated?

§ 110. *Termination of the struggle between the Patricians and Plebeians by the Licinian Rogations.*

[501] Who attempted to relieve the continued embarrassment of
C the plebeians? What laws did they propose? Who stopped the reading of these rogations? When were they adopted?
D To what condition were they made subject? Why was the prætura urbana established? Who held the curule ædileship? Who was nominated the first plebeian consul?
[502] Who was the Prætor Urbanus? What was his principal
B duty? How was his authority indicated? What guide had he for his decisions in cases to which the law did not extend? On
C what did he sit? What other prætor was now appointed? Why was the appointment made necessary? Were the number of prætors further increased? How were they increased by Sulla and Cæsar?
[503] What were the duties of the Curule Ædiles? How long was
A it before the plebeians were established in the possession of their newly-acquired rights? How was the election of Consuls frequently interrupted?

§ 111. *Their Wars—to the Samnite Wars.*

[504] With what nation or tribe had the Romans several wars
B about this time? How were they decided?

§ 112. *First War with the Samnites.*

[506] What was the extent of the Samnite dominion? Was the
D population of this territory large? Who applied to the Romans for aid against the Samnites? Who were consuls at this time?
A What engagements took place? What booty fell into the hands of the Romans? Who gained the victory at Suessŭla? What was the condition of peace between the Romans and Samnites?

§ 113. *War with the Latins*, 339—337.

[507] When was the alliance between Rome and Latium renewed?
C What led to the complete subjugation of the Latins? Where

did the Romans meet the Latins in conflict? Under whose
command? How and why did Manlius punish his son? Where
was a second victory gained? What followed this victory?

[508] * How were the inhabitants of the subdued cities treated?

§ 114. *Second War with the Samnites.*

[509] * What were the causes of the second Samnite war?

[510] How did the Romans divide the forces of the Samnites?
B How many times were the Samnites defeated? Under whom?
Where was a Roman force intercepted and beaten? On what
C terms did they capitulate? * How long did the war with the
Samnites last? * In whose favor did it terminate?

[511] With what states did the Romans now maintain war suc-
A cessfully? What favorable opportunity did the Etruscans
seize to re-establish their ancient boundaries? Who opposed
them? Where were they defeated? How was the conqueror
rewarded? Who obtained the victory near Longula? What
B success attended Fabius as proconsul? Over whom did the
consuls of the ensuing year gain victories? What other battles
were fought? Did the Samnites afterwards recognize the
supremacy of Rome? On what terms was a peace concluded?

[512] * How were the revolted cities of the Hernicans treated?
C how the Volscians and Æquians who had afforded assistance to
the Samnites?

§ 115. *Third War with the Samnites.*

[513] What gave rise to the third war with the Samnites? By
A what alliance did the Samnites seek to strengthen themselves?
Where were they defeated? By whom? Who checked the
advance of the Gauls? What victories did the Romans gain?
B What was the fate of C. Pontius? Who terminated the war
with the Samnites? * How far did the sovereignty of Rome
now extend?

§ 116. *War with Tarentum and with Pyrrhus of Epirus.*

[514] What caused the war with Tarentum?

[515] Whom did the people of Tarentum call to their assistance?
A What victory did this ally gain? On what terms did he offer
peace to the Romans? By whose advice was this proposal rejected?

[516] What battle was won by Pyrrhus in the following year?
C What induced Pyrrhus to conclude an armistice with Rome?
Why did Pyrrhus quit Italy?

[517] When was he compelled to abandon Sicily? Why did he
D return into Italy? Who defeated his mercenaries? where?
What did Pyrrhus then do? What was his fate? Who deli-
vered up Tarentum to the Romans?

§ 117. *Complete Subjugation of Italy.*

[518] Who now opposed the Romans? Who was sent against
A them? With what success? What became of the Etruscan
cities?

[519] What states were now compelled to receive Roman colo-
B nists?
[520] Where were the Picentians sent? why?
[522] * What was the connection of the conquered States with
C Rome?
[523] * What privileges belonged to the Municipia? * What usage
A had the Romans for the purpose of retaining a conquered
people in a state of dependence? * What lands were assigned
B to the colonists? * Who had the administration of public
affairs? * What advantage attended this plan of colonizing?
C * By whose order were colonies established? * What were the
præfecturæ?

§ 118. *Domestic History of Rome during this period.*

[524] When did the importance of the patrician order begin to
decline?
[525] Who took the first decided step towards a complete equaliza-
D tion of the two orders? What were the three laws that he pro-
A posed in order to achieve this? What was gained by the lex
B Ogulnia? What was the object of the lex Mænia? What led
to the complete establishment of democracy?
[526] * With what view did Appius Claudius admit the libertini
C into the plebs? * Who set aside this arrangement? * What
privilege did this office confer? * Why were three censors
deemed necessary?

§ 119. *The First Punic War.*

[527] When did the first Punic war break out? Why did the
Carthaginians support the Tarentines in their struggles against
A Rome? What led to the introduction of Roman troops into
Sicily? Where were the Romans admitted? Who blockaded
B them? Who relieved Messana? How many cities submitted
to the Romans? Did Hiero make peace with the invaders?
What did the Romans now do? What was the fate of Agri-
gentum?
[528] With what view did the Romans create a naval force?
C How soon was a fleet equipped? Who conquered the Cartha-
D ginians by sea? Where? What honorable distinction was
granted to this commander? What was the next bold step of
A the Romans? Who commanded the Romans when the war was
transferred to Africa? Where did Regulus defeat the Carthaginians? What were the number of ships on each side?
529] Give an account of the campaign in Africa. Who was
B placed in command of the Carthaginians? What contributed
to the defeat of the Romans? What became of Regulus?
Where was the naval force of the Carthaginians annihilated?
C Where was the fleet lost?
[530] What success attended a second Roman fleet? What de-
A termination did the disaster lead to? Whom did the Carthaginians send to Rome to sue for peace? How were the endeavors of the Romans to obtain possession of Lilybæum and
B Drepanum rendered abortive? Why did the Romans deter-

mine again to abandon naval warfare? Who commanded the
Carthaginians in Sicily? What decisive victory was at length
gained by the Romans? On what terms was a peace con-
C cluded? In what year did the first Punic war end?
[531] What opportunity did the Romans take to get possession of
Sardinia and Corsica?

§ 120. *War with the Illyrians.*

[532] On what ground did the Romans declare war against the
A Illyrians? On what terms was a peace concluded?
[533] What privileges did the Greeks confer on the Romans in
B gratitude for their deliverance from Illyrian piracy?

§ 121. *Conquest of Cisalpine Gaul.*

[534] What tribes of either *cisalpine* or transalpine Gaul now rose up against Rome? What occasioned this rising? How did the rebellion terminate? What plans did the Romans adopt for the security of the newly-acquired territory?

§ 122. *Second Punic War.*

[536] Give the pedigree of the Scipios. With what view did
B Hamilcar commence the subjugation of Spain? How was this
C intention frustrated? Who besieged Saguntum? What was
the result of this act of aggression? What natural obstacles did
Hannibal overcome on his march towards Italy? What
victories did he gain on his way? What amount of forces had
he on arriving in Italy?
[537] * How did the Romans resolve to carry on this war?
D * Who was dispatched into Sicily? and with what further
orders? * Who marched into Spain? * Why was this plan
altered?
[538] What victories did Hannibal gain, and over whom? What
A fatal error did Hannibal commit after the battle of Trasimenus?
B Where did he march? With what hope? What was the plan
of Fabius? Whence his surname? What was the issue of the
C battle of Cannæ? What most important result followed?
What success attended the fresh army of the Romans?
[539] What city was Hannibal now occupied in besieging?
A * Where did he establish his head-quarters? * What did he
do after failing in his attempts to reduce the citadel of Tarentum? * What success had Marcellus over Hannibal? * What
was his fate?
[540] Why was Hannibal compelled to seek assistance from foreign
B powers? How were the Macedonians and Syracusans pre-
C vented from aiding him? In what year did the whole of Sicily
become a Roman province? Who commanded the Cartha-
D ginian troops in Spain? Where was Hasdrubal defeated? By
whom? How long did Mago struggle against the Romans?
A Who was recalled with him? What was his end?
[541] How did Cn. Scipio open the campaign? Who was sent
B into Spain to his assistance? Who joined Hasdrubal? What
was the career of the Scipios in Spain? How did it terminate?

C Who was now sent out against the Carthaginians? Mention the
victories of this commander. How was Spain divided? How
named? What appointment did C. Scipio receive on his return
to Rome? What permission was granted to him?

[542] Who joined Scipio on his landing in Africa? What plan of
B attack did Syphax and the Carthaginians form? How was it
defeated? Why did the Carthaginian government deem it
advisable to recall Hannibal and Mago from Italy? Where
were the Carthaginians finally defeated? when? On what
terms were they compelled to accept peace?

[543] * How was Masinissa rewarded? * What honors were
C conferred on Scipio? * How were the revolted states of Italy
treated?

§ 123. *The Two Wars against Philip III., king of Macedonia.*

[544] What pretext had the Romans for commencing a struggle for
D preponderance in the east?

[545] * Why did the Romans endeavor to defeat Philip's
A ambitious projects in Illyria? * Not attaining this object,
whose friendship did they court? * How did the war between
Philip and the Ætolians terminate?

[546] How did Philip make aggressions on the Romans? What
B opportunity did the Romans take of punishing him? Who
C prosecuted the war with vigor? What battle put an end to
the war? Its date? To what terms was Philip obliged to
submit? When were the Greek districts proclaimed free?

[547] * How did Flaminius limit the power of Nabis? * Why did
D he allow it to remain?

§ 124. *War with Antiochus III. of Syria.*

[548] * What occasioned the revolt of the Ætolians? * Who
A subdued them? * What charges were made against the two
Scipios? * By whom? * To what country or place did Publius
B retire? * How was Lucius punished? * What was the end of
Hannibal?

§ 125. *Third Macedonian War.*

[549] How was Philip occupied when death stopped his projects?
C Who carried them forward? How did this prince strengthen
himself? How was he often defeated? How was the breaking
D out of war precipitated? What battle decided the fate of the
A Macedonian monarchy? What became of Perseus? How did
the Romans prepare the country for submission to their sovereign
rule? What advantage did the Roman people derive from
these conquests? How did they prove injurious to their
liberties?

550] How was Illyria punished for its alliance with Perseus?
B How were the cities and inhabitants of Epirus treated? How
C were the 1000 falsely accused Achæans treated? What was
the policy of Rome with regard to the Grecian states?

[551] * Who compelled Antiochus IV. [*Antiochus Epiphanes*] to abandon his warlike designs on Egypt? * Who was detained at Rome as a hostage? * Why was Antiochus V. placed on the throne? * Did Demetrius escape? * With what view did the Romans divide Egypt?

§ 126. *The last Wars with Macedonia and Greece.*

[552] Who made an attempt to re-establish the Macedonian
A monarchy? Who defeated the impostor? How was Macedonia
punished for its revolt?

[553] How many of the thousand Achæans who had been sent to
B Rome returned? Who of these endeavored to persuade their
countrymen to resist the Romans? Who proclaimed war
C against Sparta? Who defeated him? where? Who persisted
in carrying on the war? Who superseded Metellus? What
victory did he gain? Mention his other acts. When was
Greece proclaimed a Roman province? Under what name?

§ 127. *The Third Punic War.*

[554] What interrupted the peace between the Romans and Car-
A thaginians? On whose motion was the peace declared at an
end? What unreasonable demand did the Romans make, which
B led to the third war? How was the city taken? By whom was
it destroyed? Under what name was Carthage made a Roman
province?

§ 128. *Further Wars in Spain.*

[555] When did the Romans first consider Spain as one of their
C provinces? How long was it before they got quiet possession of
the peninsula? What period were they perpetually occupied in
putting down revolts of the Spanish tribes? Who gained a
brilliant victory over the Celtiberi? What command did he
D give the inhabitants of all the towns? Who was Viriăthus?
A What was his fate? Who took Numantia? How long did the
siege last? Whence Scipio's surname of Numantinus?

§ 129. *Wars against the Gauls, Ligurians, Carnians, and Istrians.*

[556] What was the result of the disputes with the Cisalpine Gauls
B and Ligurians?

[557] * How long were the Gallic and Ligurian campaigns carried
C on? * What territory was denominated pre-eminently "provincia?" What other conquests did they make?

§ 130. *First Insurrection of the Slaves in Sicily.*

[558] What led to an insurrection of the slaves in Sicily? Who
D was invited to become their king? How many troops had he?
How was an end put to the insurrection?

§ 131. *Domestic History during this period.*

[559] When did the distinction between patricians and plebeians
A become obsolete? What struggles were consequently at an end? What did the term "Populus" now comprehend? Who
B composed the new order of nobility? Who were termed *ignobiles* or *obscuri?* Who were *homines novi?* What ambition had the nobles with regard to the offices of state?

[560] * How were the expenses of the public games defrayed?
C * Which was the first step to the higher offices of state? * To whom was the equestrian dignity confined? * Who were obliged to take part with the nobles? why?

[561] Why was a second prætor appointed? Why were four
A other prætors soon added? when? Why did these magistrates remain at Rome? What titles did the prætors assume in the second year? How were provinces assigned to them? * Mention the four quæstiones perpetuæ.

[562] * What was the *meaning of the term "province?"* * How
C did the provinces generally receive their constitution? * What was the duty of the provincial governor? * How were taxes imposed in the provinces? * Who collected them? * How were the provincial garrisons furnished with soldiers?

[563] * What was the nature of the relations of Rome with other
D free States?

[564] What attempts were made to check the progress of luxury
A and the increasing adoption of foreign manners? Who was the most conspicuous of the censors?

§ 132. *The Two Gracchi.*

[565] What was the condition of the population of Rome at this
C time? Who revived the agrarian law of Licinius? What was the object of this law? Who had been persuaded by the senate to interpose his veto to it? How did Tiberius wish to dispose of the treasures bequeathed to the Roman people by Attalus III.?
A At whose instigation was Tiberius assassinated? What became of Scipio Nasica?

[566] * How far did the commissioners for carrying out the agrarian law of Gracchus succeed? * What proposal did Papirius Carbo make with regard to the tribunes? * Who resisted it? * What was his fate?

[567] What advantages did Caius Sempronius Gracchus obtain for
C the people? Who appeared as a rival tribune to C. Gracchus? Where was Gracchus sent? What law did he propose on his return? Who resisted this law? What was the end of Gracchus?

[568] * How did the Optimates use this victory over the com-
A mons? * What was the lex Thoria? * How were the pauper citizens now principally supported? * Who came to the assistance of the people?

§ 133. *The War with Jugurtha.*

[569] How had Micipsa divided his kingdom? How did Jugurtha
B treat Hiempsal and Adherbal? Who proposed a partition of

the kingdom? Did Jugurtha accept this proposition? Who induced the Romans to declare war against Jugurtha? What
C daring act did he now perform? Who overthrew Jugurtha?
D Where did he fly for refuge? Who induced Bocchus to deliver
up Jugurtha? Who was now rising into importance? In
whose triumphal procession was he exhibited? What was his
A fate? How was Numidia divided?

§ 134. *War with the Cimbri and Teutones.*

[570] Who were the Cimbri? Describe their advance. What was
B their demand? What was their success? Who cut them off?
C Where were they defeated? How was Marius rewarded?

§ 135. *Second Insurrection of the Slaves in Sicily.*

[571] What occasioned a second insurrection of the slaves in
D Sicily? How was it terminated?

§ 136. *To the Social War.*

[572] What ambitious views did Marius entertain? What was
A his first step? Who opposed this proposal? Who lost their
B lives? Why was the commencement of actual hostilities de-
ferred? Whose quarrels occasioned a civil war?

[573] * How did Marius attempt to sustain his declining influence?
* How did Sulla become a rival of Marius?

§ 137. *The Marsic or Social War.*

[574] What ground of complaint had the Italian nations against
C the Romans? What aroused the Italian confederates to deliver
themselves from the Roman yoke?

[575] * Mention the immediate causes of the war. * What was
A the project of Drusus? * Did it become law? * What was
his end?

[576] Who now formed themselves into a confederacy against
B Rome? What was their plan? What was the lex Julia?
C Name the three theatres of war. Who commanded in each of
D these? What was done to prevent the new citizens from gain-
ing a preponderance over the old?

§ 138. *Civil War between Marius and Sulla,* 88—82; *and First War against Mithridates,* 87—84.

[577] When was Sulla elected consul? What command did he
B receive? How did Marius supplant Sulla? What became of
C Sulpicius? Who was Cinna? With whom did he act in con-
cert? Did the army favor them? What was done? Who
nominated themselves to the consulship? Who succeeded
Marius?

[578] What plan did Mithridates adopt for checking the progress
A of the Roman arms in Asia? What was his first step towards
the accomplishment of this mighty project? How was he
furnished with an occasion? Where was Archelaus sent?
B How was his arrival in Italy prevented? What splendid

victories did Sulla obtain? Who had now the conduct of the Mithridatic war? Who murdered him? On what terms was a peace concluded?

[579] * Describe and account for the death of Fimbria. * Did
C Cinna oppose Sulla's return to Rome?

[580] Describe Sulla's return to Rome. Where did C. Marius
A retire after his defeat? Who blockaded him? What attempt
B was made by the Samnites? With what success? How were the Samnites and Prænestines treated? What was the fate of Marius?

[581] Who were now proscribed? What opportunity did this
C afford Sulla? How did he show his authority? When did he lay down his power? Where did he die?

[582] Who undertook the annihilation of the Marian party? * Relate his successes.

§ 139. *Changes effected in the Constitution by Sulla.*

583] What was the nature of the changes introduced into the
B constitution by Sulla? What was his first plan? What did he do in order to secure a popular party? How were these new citizens named? How was the *tribunitial power* restrained? What was the only privilege which the tribunes were allowed to
C retain? How did he endeavor to raise the *senate?* Who were
D declared ex officio members of the senate? Why was their number augmented to twenty? What other plan did he adopt for strengthening the aristocracy? and his own party? What did he do in order to diminish the influence of the people in the
A courts of justice?

[584] * What was settled by the lex annalis? * What criminal laws were re-enacted by Sulla?

[585] Who proposed the repeal of all Sulla's laws? Who opposed
B the measure? What was the first step? Who effected the restoration of the tribunitial power in its fullest extent? What other enactment did he procure?

§ 140. *The War against Sertorius.*

[586] Who was Q. Sertorius? Who chose him as their leader?
C Who supported him? Whom did he make head against?
A Who concluded an alliance with Sertorius? Who assassinated Sertorius? What was the fate of his murderer? Did this victory put an end to the war?

§ 141. *The Servile War; or War of the Gladiators and Slaves.*

[587] Give an account of the war of the gladiators. By whom
B were they headed? Who defeated them? Who utterly destroyed them?

[588] * Who claimed the merit of putting an end to the servile
C war? * What means did Pompey take to secure popular favor? * What command was conferred upon him?

§ 142. *War against the Pirates.*

[589] Mention the causes of the power of the pirates in Cilicia and
A Isauria. Give an account of the ravages committed by the
B pirates. Who fell into their hands? What scourge visited Rome in consequence of their depredations? Who defeated these pirates? How long did his campaigns last? How did he
C dispose of the pirates? How long did Crete hold out? Who subdued it?

§ 143. *The two last Wars against Mithridates.*

[590] * Did Mithridates observe the terms of the peace? * Who resisted him? * With what success?

[591] Who bequeathed his dominions to the Romans? What
A alliance did Mithridates form? Whom did he overthrow? where? Give an account of the successes of Lucullus against
B Mithridates. What prevented Lucullus from profiting by his victories? By whom was Lucullus superseded in his command?
C why? Where did Mithridates fly to? How did Pompey treat Tigranes? What portion of his dominions did he surrender?
D How far did Pompey pursue Mithridates? On his return what did he do in Pontus, Syria, and Palestine?

[592] * What became of Mithridates? * Who succeeded him?
A * How was Pompey hailed at Rome?

§ 144. *Catiline's Conspiracy.*

[593] What conspiracy was set on foot by Catiline? Why had he been rejected as a candidate for the consulship? Who favored
B the project of Catiline? By whom was his conspiracy detected? Who rendered all further attempts of the conspirators fruitless?
C How was Catiline driven from the city? Where did he go? How were some of the conspirators discovered? How were they treated? What battle was fought? Who routed the rebel forces? Who fell in the battle?

§ 145. *The First Triumvirate.*

[594] What discovery did Cæsar make with regard to the republic?
A What resolution did he form in consequence of this discovery?

[595] * How did he follow out his plan? * What popular measures did he support? * What subjected him to the suspicion of being concerned in Catiline's conspiracy?

[596] What demand did Pompey make on his return to Rome?
B Who resisted Cæsar as candidate for the consulship? Who was chosen his colleague? Who effected a reconciliation be-
C tween Pompey and Crassus? What was '*the first triumvirate?*' What was the aim of each of its members? What measure did Cæsar carry in defiance of all opposition from the senate?
A Who obtained his only daughter in marriage? What appointment did he procure for himself? How did the senate meet
B this last usurpation of their rights? By whose means did Cæsar get Cato and Cicero out of the way? Where was Cato sent?

What was assigned to him? How was Cæsar treated? When was he recalled? On whose proposal?
[597] * Where did the triumviri hold a meeting? * What was agreed at it? * Who supplied Cæsar with fresh legions?

§ 146. *Cæsar's War in Gaul.*

[598] With what view did Cæsar form a standing army?
[599] * How did the subjugation of Gaul differ from that of the
A east?
[600] Where did the Helvetii come from? Whose territories did
B they plunder? Who checked them? Where were the Ger-
C mans defeated? Who commanded them? What reputation had the Belgians? What was the amount of their forces? How did Cæsar overcome them? Who offered the stoutest resistance to the arms of Cæsar?
[601] * Who vanquished the Veneti? the Aquitani? * How much
D of Gaul was now subjugated?
[602] What tribes had been driven by the Suevi across the Lower Rhine into Belgium? Who compelled them to return? How did Cæsar now find employment for his legions? Were Cæsar's expeditions to Britain attended by any important results?
[603] What grievances, besides the loss of their freedom, induced the Gauls to make repeated attempts to throw off the Roman
A yoke? Who headed the insurrection? Did it succeed? Who
B surrendered? By what means did Cæsar succeed in tranquillizing the Gauls?

§ 147. *The Civil War between Cæsar and Pompey.*

[604] What province was assigned to Crassus? What was his
C fate? Who was appointed to the two Spains? Who governed them? Why did Pompey remain at Rome? Why did he defer the election of consuls?
[605] * What was the first step taken by the senate to reduce
A Cæsar's power? * What did they next require? * What was Cæsar's offer? * How was it treated?
[606] What did Cæsar determine to do? What measure did
B Pompey adopt? Describe the success of Cæsar. How did he employ his time till vessels were built to transport his troops?
C Who appointed him dictator? How soon did he resign this office? * What advantage did Pompey gain? * How was this lost?
[607] Where was the decisive battle fought between Pompey and
A Cæsar? with what result? What forces met on each side? What became of Pompey?
[608] * Why did Cæsar dispatch M. Antonius into Italy? * How far did he succeed in his object?

§ 148. *Cæsar's Wars in the East.*

[609] In what state did Cæsar find Egypt on his arrival there? What was the consequence of his interference? Whom did Cæsar make queen of Egypt?
[610] Who availed himself of the disruption of the Roman re-
C public to extend the limits of his empire? How far did his

A attempt succeed? Who checked and defeated him? What
was his end?

§ 149. *Cæsar's last Wars against the Partisans of Pompey.*

[611] What party was formed against Cæsar in Africa? Where
B were they overthrown? What were the losses on both sides?
What was the fate of Cato?

[612] * What honors awaited Cæsar at Rome? * How were the
C people and soldiers treated? * What measures did Cæsar take
for the restoration of order? * Who assisted him in his reformation of the calendar?

[613] Where had the sons of Pompey collected a considerable
A force? Where was the decisive battle fought? Who was
victorious? Did he obtain an easy victory? How many of
Pompey's adherents were slain? What was the fate of Cn.
Pompey? what of Sextus? How was Cæsar honored on his
return?

§ 150. *Death of Cæsar.*

[614] Enumerate the offices to which Cæsar was appointed by the
B senate, and the honors that were heaped upon him. What act
C was a formal recognition of his supremacy? How was Cæsar
D occupied during the last months of his life? What were his
military plans? Why did he refuse the diadem when presented
to him? When were the Sibylline books destroyed? What
A prophecy was discovered in the forged books? What demand
was then made? Who formed a conspiracy against Cæsar?
Describe the death of Cæsar.

§ 151. *Consequences of Cæsar's Assassination.*

[615] How did his murderers proceed after his death? Who re-
B fused to sanction the acts of the senate? How did Antony
C drive the assassins from the city? What powers did Antony
D assume? Who resisted him? What was his course?

[616] What occasioned the civil war of Mutina? Why was
A Antony denounced by the senate? Who marched to the assistance of Brutus? Where was Antony defeated? What was
the present plan of Octavian as to Antony?

§ 152. *The Second Triumvirate.*

[617] How did Octavian obtain the consulship? Who formed the
second triumvirate? Who were required to confirm the triumviri in their office? For how long a period?

[618] How did the triumviri proceed before they commenced war
C against the assassins of Cæsar? Who was among these victims?
A Where were Brutus and Cassius defeated? What was their
B fate? Where did the victors proceed? Who was summoned
to Tarsus by Antony? why?

[619] * Who occasioned the Perusian civil war? * Give an account of this war.

[620] What smoothed the way for a reconciliation between Antony
C and Octavian? How was the empire divided among the trium-

viri? How was the friendship of Antony and Octavian cemented? Who blockaded Italy? On what terms was an armistice concluded?

[621] What occasioned a renewal of the war between Octavian and
A S. Pompeius? Where was Pompey defeated? What was his end? How was Lepidus defeated in his design on Sicily?

§ 153. *Foreign Wars of Antony and Octavian.*

[622] What countries were overrun by the Parthians? Who
B drove them across the Euphrates? What portion of the Roman possessions in Asia was presented to Cleopatra? What expedition was undertaken by Antony in conjunction with Arta-
C vasdes? Why was he compelled to retreat? Who was declared to be the legitimate son of Cæsar? why?

623] What expeditions were now undertaken by Octavian? why?
A Who were now subjected to the authority of Rome?

§ 154. *The War between Octavian and Antony.*

[624] When did the term of the triumviral league cease? Against
B whom did the senate declare war? What was the immediate cause of hostilities?

[625] * How did Antony meet his opponents?

[626] Describe the battle of Actium and its result. Where did Oc-
D tavian then proceed? * What became of Antony? * What of Cleopatra?

§ 155. *C. Julius Cæsar Octavianus Augustus.*

[627] When did Octavian return to Rome? What victories were
A celebrated by a triple triumph? What took place in consequence
B of the general peace that now prevailed? How did Octavian seek to establish his authority? How far, if at all, was the old constitution respected? When was the title of Augustus conferred on Octavian? Who bore this title afterwards?

[628] * What did the imperial prerogative comprehend? * How
C was the election of a successor conducted?

[629] * How did Octavian limit the number of the senate? * How
A were members of the senate now appointed? * Could any but *Romans* be appointed? * If so, on what terms? * Who were the advisers of the Imperator? * When did the people cease to have any share in legislation? * How were their decisions superseded?

[630] * What was the power of *the ancient magistrates?* * What
B *new officers* were appointed? * What was the duty of the Præfectus urbi? of the Præfecti prætorio? of the Præfectus annonæ? * Who exercised considerable influence over these appointments? * When were they taken entirely in their own hands by the emperors?

[631] * How were Rome and Italy divided? * How were the
C other cities distinguished? * Who presided over the population of these cities?

[632] * How were the provinces divided by Octavian?

[633] * From what sources was the *military ærarium* raised?

* By what kind of troops were the frontiers protected? * Where were they quartered?

[634] What was the main object of the wars of Augustus? How
B was the eastern frontier of the empire secured? Who were
sent to protect Italy and Gaul against the invasions of the
Germanic tribes? How were the people of lower Germany
won? How did the Romans treat the country from the Rhine
C to the Elbe? What occasioned an insurrection of the tribes of
Lower Germany? How was Varus misled? What was the
consequence?

635] * How were the remaining days of Augustus rendered
D miserable? * Where did the emperor die? * At what age?

§ 156. *Four Emperors of the House of Livia.*

[636] What were the chief traits in the character of Tiberius?
A Whom did he adopt? by whose persuasion? Why did Tiberius
recall Germanicus from Germany? What successes had he ob-
B tained there? What did he achieve in the east? What was
his fate? What measure did Tiberius take for the security of
his person? Who was Sejanus? Why did Tiberius retire from
C Rome? What ambitious project did Sejanus form? How did
Tiberius die?

[637] Who succeeded Tiberius? Give some account of him. What
D form of government did the senate wish to re-establish? Who
A resisted them?

[638] Who succeeded Caligula? How did this prince conduct
A himself? What important conquest began in this reign?
* What was the character of Agrippina?

[639] How did Nero begin his reign? Under whose direction was
B he? What horrible murders did he perpetrate? When did he
let loose his ferocious disposition? What inconsistencies was
C he guilty of? On whom did Nero throw the blame of having
set Rome on fire? Who was supposed to be the real criminal?
Describe the situation of his palace. What occasioned a general insurrection throughout the empire? Who was proclaimed
emperor in his place? What was the fate of Nero?

§ 157. *Three Emperors proclaimed by the Legions.*

[640] How did Sulpicius Galba render himself odious? Who put
A him to death?

[641] Who was Otho? Who disputed his appointment? How
B did he die?

[642] Who proclaimed Vespasian?

§ 158. *The Three Flavii.*

[643] Enumerate the measures of Vespasian. What was his
C character? Who was appointed to crush the revolt of the
Jews? When was Jerusalem stormed? Who suppressed the
A insurrection of the Batavi? Who commenced afresh the war
in Britain? What was the character of his administration?

[644] What was the surname of Titus? why? What occurred
during his reign?

[645] Who was Domitian? How did he commence his reign?
B What was his chief amusement? How did he expose his
C vanity? Why was Agricola recalled from Britain? How did
he appease the Dacians? How was this expedition celebrated?
What was the fate of Domitian?

§ 159. *The most flourishing period of the Empire.*

[646] Who succeeded Domitian? How did he give discontent?
D How did he avoid the vengeance of the Prætorians?
[647] Who was Trajanus? How did he exert himself? What
A success had he against the Dacians? How are these events
represented? How did his campaigns against the Parthians
B terminate? Why was he compelled to retreat?
[648] Who succeeded him? What was his character? To what
C was his *attention exclusively directed?* How was this object
D promoted? What occasioned a *terrible insurrection in this*
A *reign?* How was it suppressed? Who succeeded Hadrian?
[649] What was the character of his reign? How was a portion
of his time occupied?
[650] Who succeeded Antoninus? Who ascended the throne
B with him? At whose desire? Who undertook a war against
the Parthians? Who had the management of the campaign?
C What occasioned the great war of the Marcomanni? Who
conducted it? With what success?

§ 160. *Decline of the Empire under the Prætorians.*

[651] Who succeeded M. Aurelius? On what terms did he grant
A peace to the Marcomanni and Quadi? To whom was the
government intrusted? How did the emperor conduct himself?
What was the consequence?
[652] Who was Pertinax? How long did he reign? How did
B Didius Julianus obtain the throne? Who set Julianus aside?
[654] What were the measures of Severus? Who assisted him in
C the amendment of the legal code? What expedition did Severus
undertake in his old age? Where did he die? Whose ingratitude occasioned his death?
[655] * How did Caracalla begin his reign? * Who was among
D the victims? * What did he do in order to satisfy the greediness of his soldiers, and procure sufficient funds for his own
A prodigal expenditures? * What characters did he assume in
Macedonia and Asia? * Who murdered him?
[656] * Who succeeded Caracalla? * How did he make peace
B with the Parthians?
[657] * What led to the promotion of Heliogabalus to the throne?
* Who was he? * What was his character? * How did he forfeit his life?
[658] What was the character of Alexander Severus's reign?
D What new empire was now founded? How far did the new
sovereign advance? Who gained important advantages over
him? What led to the death of Alexander Severus? Who
accompanied him in all his expeditions?
[659] What was the condition of the empire under the successors

A of Alexander Severus? How did the nine emperors who
reigned during this period of thirty-five years generally lose
their lives?
[660] * Who was *Maximinus?* * Whom did the senate now nom-
B inate to the imperial dignity? * What was their fate? what
that of Maximinus?
[661] * How did Gordianus govern?
[662] * What was the reign of Philippus celebrated for?
[663] * Who was Decius? * Where was he slain?
[664] * Why was Gallus deposed and murdered? * By whom?
[665] * Who put Æmilianus to death?
[666] * Who invaded the Roman dominions during the reign of
D Valerianus? * Who took the emperor prisoner?
[667] * How many rivals had Gallienus? * Who maintained his
position in Gaul and Spain? * Who obtained with Gallienus
the sovereignty of the east? * Under whom did Palmyra be-
A come a most flourishing city? * How did Gallienus meet with
his death? * Who succeeded him?
[668] With what success did Claudius II. begin his reign? * What
victories did he gain over the barbarians? * What was his
death? * Who succeeded him?
[669] What obtained for Aurelianus the surname of restitutor
B patriæ? What province was abandoned? What tribes were
driven back into their own country? Who was Zenobia? Give
C an account of Aurelian's victories over Zenobia. Why was she
conveyed to Rome? How were Palmyra and its inhabitants
treated? What were Aurelian's next victories? Why was the
emperor become odious? At whose instigation was he assassinated?
[670] * How long did Tacitus and Florianus reign? What were
A the questions of Probus on ascending the throne? How far did
he succeed? What plan did the emperor put in execution for
re-peopling the deserted provinces? What occasioned the dis
content of his soldiers? How did they show it? Who was
chosen as his successor?
[671] * Who were appointed his co-regents? * How did he lose
his life?
[672] * Who succeeded Carus? * What was the fate of Carinus
C and Numerianus?

§ 161. *Period occupied by partitions of the Empire, until the reign of Constantine.*

[673] Who succeeded Carinus and Numerianus? To whom was
committed the administration of the western district? Where
did Diocletian establish his residence? Where did his colleague
D reside? Why were the emperors compelled to appoint colleagues? Who were they? What was their task? What rival
A emperors established themselves? What were the successes of
B Galerius? How were the Christians treated? Which of the
emperors abdicated? why? How did he spend the rest of his
days?
[674] When did the death of Constantius happen? Who was pro-

claimed emperor in Britain? In what year did Constantinus become sole occupant of the imperial throne?

[675] * How many emperors were there in the year 308?
C * Name them.

[676] * What became of Constantine's competitors?

§ 162. *Constantine the Great, sole Emperor.*

[677] What induced Constantine to embrace Christianity? Who
A assembled the first œcumenical council? where? What doctrine was discussed? What was the result of the council?

[678] How did Constantine lay the foundation of a future division
B of the empire? How was the new capital named at its dedication? How afterwards? Were the capitals placed on an equal footing? How was the empire divided? Who was at the head
C of the state? What titles did he receive? How many præfecti prætorio were appointed? Why did Constantine increase their
A number? Name their districts. To whom was the military command transferred? How were the dioceses administered? and the provinces? What were the commanders of the troops termed?

[679] * Enumerate the seven chief court offices. * What were
B the duties of these respectively? * Who composed the council of the emperor? * What institutions of former days were retained? * How were the civil and military officers designated?

[680] * What taxes were imposed?

[681] To whom did Constantine give assistance towards the end of his reign? What people did he settle in the Roman province on the Danube? What was the fate of his eldest son? and his wife?

§ 163. *The successors of Constantine the Great to the permanent division of the Empire.*

[682] Of Constantine's sons who became at last sole emperor?
A What became of the others?

[684] Who invaded Gaul? To whom did Constantius intrust the
B defence of that province? What excited the envy of the emperor? Why did he withdraw several legions from Julian? Did the legions obey?

[685] How was Julian perverted to paganism? How did he show
C his hatred against Christianity? Did he restore the temple at Jerusalem? What military expedition did he undertake?
A With what success? What caused his death? Who succeeded him?

[686] Did Jovianus accept the conditions of peace offered by the Persians? What were they? Who was chosen his successor

[687] Who was appointed by Valentinianus to be his co-regent?
B What part of the empire was assigned to this co-regent?

688] * How was Valentinian occupied during the whole of his reign? * What occasioned his death? * Who ravaged Britain at this time? * Who re-conquered it? * How far did he extend the frontier? * Give an account of Valens. * How did Procopius secure his election? * What was his fate? * What wars did Valens carry on?

[689] Who attacked the Goths? Where did Valens grant them
A settlements? What drove them to revolt? Where did they defeat Valens?

[690] Who succeeded Valens? How did Theodosius terminate the
B war? Who were his sons?

§ 164. *The Western Roman Empire—to its Fall.*

[692] Who had the guardianship of Honorius? Where was the
A imperial residence fixed?

[693] Give an account of the war with Alaric, king of the West
A Goths [or Visigoths]. Where was he defeated? By whom?

[695] Why were the legions quartered in Britain and on the Rhine recalled? What tribes overran the western provinces without opposition? Where did these settle? Who occupied the tracts of country which the invaders had quitted?

[696] On what ground was Stilicho condemned to death? Why
C did Alaric persuade Attalus the præf. urbi to accept the im-
D perial dignity? Was he soon deposed? In what year was
A Rome besieged and taken? Where did Alaric die? Who succeeded Alaric? Did he conclude a peace with Honorius? Where did he lead the Visigoths?

[697] * What was the state of the western empire? * Who attempted to depose Honorius?

[698] Who was guardian of Valentinian III.? What appointment did Aetius receive? What troubles did the intrigues of
C this minister involve his mistress in? To whom did Bonifacius
D apply for aid? How did the barbarians behave? What was the then state of Britain? Whose aid did a British prince solicit?
A Who commanded the expedition? What kingdoms did they establish? Who formed an alliance against the West Goths and Latins? Of what nations were the forces composed? Who defeated them? where? Describe the progress of Attila.
B What was the ambition of Aetius? Who murdered him? Who assassinated Valentinian?

[699] Who was next called to the throne? How did Eudoxia
C show her indignation at being compelled to marry Maximus? What was the fate of Maximus?

[700] How was the empire ruled after the death of Maximus?
D What authority did these persons possess?

[701] * Who was the immediate successor of Maximus? * Who was he? * What was his fate? * Who was regarded as regent during the interregnum? * Who assumed the imperial title? * Describe the chief events of his reign. * Who occasioned his death? * Who now exercised sovereign power?
B * Who governed the western empire after the death of Severus? * By whose consent was Anthemius appointed emperor? * Why was Anicius Olybrius proclaimed emperor? * What
C caused the death of Olybrius and Ricimer? * Why was Glycerius soon compelled to resign his throne? * Who followed him?

[702] Who had ruled Italy since the death of Ricimer? How did Odoacer get possession of the throne? In what year?

§ 165. *Religion, &c. of the Romans.*

[703] To whom were the Romans accustomed to ascribe the esta-
A blishment of their religion? What was the original element of
the Roman national religion? What was afterwards added?
B What Greek deities correspond to Jupiter, Juno, and
Minerva? To what circumstances may the decline of the
Roman religion at the commencement of the first century be
attributed? What was the condition of religion in the last years
C of the republic? What opposition had Christians to contend
with before Christianity became the religion of the empire?

[704] * Name *the three Capitoline divinities.* * How was Jupiter
D regarded? * Which were the most remarkable festivals celebrated in his honor? * What was under the special protection
A of Juno? * What was Juno's office? * Who was the patroness
of arts and manufactures? * Who supplicated her aid?

[705] * Which *of the planets* were invoked as deities?

[706] * Who were *the deities of the lower world?*

[707] * Name *the deities of the elements.*

[708] * Name *the deities who presided over agriculture and the rearing of cattle.* * To whom did the Latins attribute the first
establishment of civilization? * Who was worshipped on earth
C under the title of Demeter? * What were the Saturnalia?
* Who was the protectress of the flocks? * When was her feast
held? why? * What was the rank of Mars among the Roman
gods? * Where was the census held?

[709] * Mention *the oracular deities* of the Latins. * In what way
D were the responses of Faunus given? * How was Fauna
styled? * To what class did she confine her oracles?

[710] * What *deities presided over physical and moral events?*
A * Give an account of Janus. * Who were the Parcæ? who
Fortuna? * From what did the worship of Venus derive its
B importance? * To what personifications of abtract ideas and
moral qualities were divine honors paid? * Who was the god
of trade? who of war?

[711] * How were *life, death, and existence after death* represented in the Roman religion?

[712] * Who were the Pontifices? * Who was the president of
C their college? * What were his duties? * How did the Augurs
D ascertain the will of the gods? * Who conducted the inspec-
tion of victims? * What is the difference between auguria and
auspicia? * What duties were assigned to the inspectors of the
A Sibylline books? * Who were the Fetiales? * Who chose the
Vestal Virgins? * What was their number? * How was their
time employed? * Why were the Salii Palatini established?

[713] * How were *the priests of particular deities* termed? * What priests belonged to the order of Flamines? * Who discharged the duty of offering public sacrifices after the expulsion of the Tarquins?

[714] * What were the holy places? * Of what did the sacred usages consist?

[715] Did the Romans cultivate the art of war with success?

c What citizens served in the army? At what age? Who were exempt?

716] * How was the legion originally divided? * What was the
D division at a later period? * How many legions composed a consular army?

[717] Who were excused from military service towards the end of
A the republic? What were the ten cohortes prætorianæ? Who commanded the army at different periods? Who were at the head of each legion? Who were under them? Whom did Constantine place in command of his forces? When was the practice of giving regular pay to each legionary introduced?
B What rewards were distributed for military service?

[718] Who composed *the maritime force?* Describe the Roman vessels.

[719] Into how many periods may the history of Roman literature
c be divided? When did the first begin? Have we any thing of the period antecedent to this date? When was the foundation
D of Roman literature, properly so called, laid? Which was the
A second period? What was the character of this age? When did *the silver age* commence? when terminate? What was its
B character? What period did the *brazen age* include? What was its character?

[720] What were the first attempts of the Romans in Epic poetry?
c What epic history did Ennius compile? Who cultivated the historical, and who the didactic epos? Give a list of Ovid's works.

[721] Who distinguished themselves as translators or imitators of
A Greek models? Who were the principal representatives of New Comedy? * How does it appear that they had a Roman drama, strictly so called? * What was the character of the Mimes? * How did these degenerate?

[722] When did *lyric poetry* develope itself? What was its character? What were the most remarkable performances in this department?

723] What was the origin of *Satire?* Who raised it to the rank
B of a literary production? Who gave a more polished character to it? What was the character of the Satires of Juvenal and Persius?

[724] * When was *the epigram* introduced? * What collection or
c collections of the kind is still extant?

[725] * Whom did Phædrus imitate? Whom did Virgil imitate?

[726] Which was the most distinguished and influential branch of Roman literature? Who first cultivated it? Which was the surest road to honor and influence? Who were the most distinguished orators?

[727] * When did oratory lose its influence over the government?
B * Where was it retained? * Where have we it in its most debased character? * Who were the great teachers of eloquence? * On what accounts are the letters of Pliny and Cicero valu-
c able? To what systems did the Romans confine themselves in the study of philosophy? On what ground do the philosophical writings of Cicero entitle him to the highest praise?

[728] * Which was the most attractive system in the earlier days
of the monarchy? * To what system did Stoicism give place?
D * What was the great work of the elder Pliny? * When did
the science of jurisprudence attain its highest degree of excellence? * Of what compilations were their writings the
groundwork?

[729] In what great architectural works were the Romans assisted
A by the Etruscans? What were the great architectural changes
C from the time of Sulla to that of Constantine? Give some
account of Roman sculpture.

[730] For how long a time were the professors of the art of *paint-*
A *ing* almost exclusively Greeks?

[731] How were trade and manufactures regarded by the Romans?
What associations were formed in the latter days of the repub-
B lic? What was the character of Roman trade? What were
the imports?

SERIES OF READING BOOKS

BY HENRY MANDEVILLE, D. D.

COMPRISING

PRIMARY READING BOOK. 1 vol. 16mo. . . .	Price,	$0 10
SECOND READER. 1 vol. 16mo.	"	17
THIRD READER. 1 vol. 16mo.	"	25
FOURTH READER. 1 vol. 12mo. . . .	"	38
COURSE OF READING, OR FIFTH READER. 12mo.	"	75
ELEMENTS OF READING AND ORATORY. 1 vol. large 12mo.	"	1 00

Great pains have been taken to make these books superior to any other reading-books in use, by reducing them to a complete practical system, founded on the nature of the language, by which the proper delivery of all sentences may be determined, and Reading elevated to the rank of a science. The proper and thorough use of these books places it in the power of every pupil to become an accomplished reader. The selections will be found to contain some of the finest gems in the language, which cannot fail of interesting the pupil, and cultivate a literary taste.

THE FIRST AND SECOND READERS introduce successively the different parts of speech, and are designed to combine a knowledge of their grammatical functions with the meaning and pronunciation of words.

THE THIRD AND FOURTH READERS commence with a series of exercises on articulation and modulation, containing numerous examples for practice on the elementary sounds (including errors to be corrected), and on the different movements of the voice produced by sentential structure, by emphasis, and by the passions.

THE COURSE OF READING comprises three parts: the *first part* containing a more elaborate description of elementary sounds and of the parts of speech grammatically considered, than was deemed necessary in the preceding works; *part second*, a complete classification and description of every sentence to be found in the English, or in any other language; *part third*, paragraphs; or sentences in their connection unfolding general thoughts, as in the common reading-books.

The ELEMENTS OF READING AND ORATORY closes the series with an exhibition of the whole theory and art of Elocution exclusive of gesture. It contains, besides the classification of sentences, the laws of punctuation and delivery deduced from it, the whole followed by carefully selected pieces for sentential analysis and vocal practice.

RECOMMENDATIONS OF MANDEVILLE'S SERIES OF READERS.

That the series is eminently practical and highly approved is shown by the following testimonials, selected from the thousands that have been received from public educators, who have tested them by thorough examination or actual use.

From WALTER BAILEY, *Supt. Public Schools, Fourth District, New Orleans, May 24th*, 1852.

"I have examined, with much care and interest, Professor Mandeville's series of Readers, and am much gratified to observe that he has reduced the subject of punctuation and delivery to a complete system; and they possess such superior advantages over any others that I have ever examined, that I have adopted them as text-books in the public schools under my supervision."

*** In July, 1852, Mandeville's Reading books were adopted and introduced in all the Public Schools of New Orleans.

The following Resolution was unanimously adopted by the Board of Education of St. Louis, October, 12th, 1852.

Resolved, That Professor Mandeville's Series of Readers be substituted as text-books for Swan's Readers in the Public Schools of this city."

From the late S. L. HOLMES, *City Superintendent of Schools, Brooklyn.*

"Mandeville's Reading Books are used in all of the Public Schools of Brooklyn, and with great satisfaction and profit, both to teacher and pupil. As mere reading books they are probably unsurpassed either in matter or system; but as a means of disclosing the true structure of our language, and pointing out the proper mode of parsing it, this series is believed to be altogether unequalled."

PROF. MANDEVILLE'S LECTURES.—"The Committee to whom was intrusted the preparation of an expression of the sentiments of the Teachers of the Public, Ward, Corporate and Private Schools of the City of New York, who have attended Prof. Mandeville's Lectures, in his course on Elocution, respectfully report the following resolutions:

"*Resolved*, That the course of Lectures on Elocution, by Prof. Mandeville, which we have attended, has been to us a source of much gratification and profit.

"*Resolved*, That his system, based upon sound Philosophical principles, is an easy, progressive, natural, and eminently original method of attaining a knowledge of the classification and structure of every kind of sentence in the English language, with it appropriate punctuation and delivery: and we are happy to say unhesitatingly, that in our opinion, his course, if faithfully carried out by teachers as he recommends, is better calculated to make good readers than any other with which we have been acquainted."

The following is signed by all the Principles of the Syracuse Public Schools, except one.

"We, the undersigned. Principals of Public Schools in the City of Syracuse, having formed some acquaintance with Mandeville's System of Reading and Oratory, take occasion cheerfully to express our unfeigned approval and admiration of the same, as the only truly Scientific System known to us, and our belief that its universal introduction into the Public Schools of our country, would prove a very valuable accession to the present educational facilities."

THE SHAKSPEARIAN READER.

BY J. W. S. HOWS.

12mo. 447 pages. Price $1 25.

This work is prepared expressly for the use of Classes in schools and the reading circle, and contains a Collection of the most approved Plays of Shakspeare, carefully revised, with introductory and explanatory notes.

"This is a very handsome volume, and it will prove, we believe, a very popular one. Probably no man living is better qualified for the task of preparing a work of this kind than Prof. Hows, who has long been a teacher of elocution, and from his lectures on Shakspeare, has acquired a high reputation for his masterly analysis of the great dramatist. The only fault that we find with his book is that he has left out the comic parts, and has given nothing of Falstaff. But his reasons for the omission are sound and discriminating."—*New York Mirror.*

PRIMARY SPELLER AND READER.

BY ALBERT D. WRIGHT.

Price 12½ Cents.

This little volume of 144 pages combines a Primary Spelling-book and Reader, happily illustrated with numerous cuts, intended to attract the attention of the young, and to suggest thought for oral instruction and conversation.

It is confidently believed, that the proper use of this little book will obviate most of the difficulties experienced at the commencement of a child's education.

As fast as the letters are learned, an application is immediately made of them.

No word is given in which a letter occurs that has not been previously learned.

The capital letters are taught one at a time, and by review in reading lessons.

The words are systematically presented, being classified by their vowel sounds and terminating consonants; and generally, at the end of each class, they are arranged into little spelling lessons.

The learner is immediately initiated into reading lessons, composed of words of two or three letters, and is then led progressively into more difficult words.

"This is an excellent little book for children, and an improvement on all other Primary Lessons."—*N. Y. Observer.*

"We most heartily commend it to the favorable regard of teachers and parents."—*Teachers' Advocate.*

CLASS-BOOK OF POETRY.

BY ELIZA ROBBINS.

Containing a judicious, beautiful, and interesting Collection of Poetry for the Use of Children in Schools, and private reading. 12mo. 16mo. 252 pages. Price 75 cents.

Extract from the Author's Preface.

"In no way is a graceful and refined style of speech so naturally formed as by poetic language made thoroughly familiar to the young. 'I do not like poetry; I cannot understand it,' often say half-taught children. Give them the poetry of good writers, with a little necessary comment, and you will remove all obscurity from the most instructive and effective poetry, and all distaste to it. I have endeavored to do this in the following collection, and I trust that while it exhibits 'only things pure,' 'lovely, and of good report,' it may also give much pleasure, and be serviceable accordingly."

GUIDE TO KNOWLEDGE.

By Eliza Robbins. 16mo. 400 pages. Price 63 cents.

This contains a large amount of useful information, communicated in an entertaining and easy style of familiar questions and answers on every-day subjects, such as children are constantly asking questions about.

"The basis of this work is the 'Child's Guide to Knowledge—an elementary book which has been much used in England for many years, and is particularly adapted to our own country and nation. It commences with questions and answers on those elementary topics which occupy the attention of the young mind, and ranges over the complete circle of useful knowledge. It is a storehouse of various information for the young. We know of no elementary book, that with the necessary aid of judicious instructors, and suitable illustrative helps, can be made more useful to youth. Accompanying, is a dictionary of technical terms. We cordially recommend it to the notice of teachers."—*Journal and Messenger.*

CLASS-BOOK OF ZOOLOGY.

By Prof. B. Jaeger. 18mo. Price 42 cents.

This work is designed to afford to pupils in common schools and academies a knowledge of the Animal Kingdom, not by making it a tiresome study, overloaded with incomprehensible technical terms taken from Latin and Greek, but as a scientific, amusing, instructive, and useful occupation for the juvenile mind, imparting a taste for collecting and preserving zoological specimens, and furnishing subjects for interesting and elevated observation.

THE CHILD'S FIRST HISTORY OF ROME.

BY MISS E. M. SEWELL.

18mo. 255 pages. Price 50 Cents.

In the preparation of this work for the use of children, the authoress has drawn her materials from the most reliable sources, and incorporated them into a narrative at once unostentatious, perspicuous, and graphic, aiming to be understood by those for whom she wrote, and to impress deeply and permanently on their minds the historical facts contained in the book. The entire work is clothed in a style at once pleasing and comprehensible to the juvenile mind.

"The author of this work has been very successful in her style of narration, as well as gone to the best sources accessible for her facts. While there is nothing light and trivial in her manner, there is all the vivacity of the most lively fireside story-teller; and those things, "of which it is a shame to speak," she gets over with great judgment, delicacy and tact. While it is eminently a child's book, we greatly misjudge if it should not prove a favorite with adults, especially that class who cannot command time to read protracted histories."—*Christian Mirror.*

A FIRST HISTORY OF GREECE.

BY MISS E. M. SEWELL.

18mo. 355 pages. Price 63 Cents.

This work is designed to impart to young people a more clear and understandable knowledge of Grecian history than is attainable through any of the numerous works on that subject that have been accumulating during the last century. By selecting and presenting clearly and concisely only prominent characters and events, and not overloading and rendering their perusal irksome by a mass of minor details, the authoress has rendered an essential service to the youth of our country.

"Miss Sewell is eminently successful in this attempt to set forth the history of Greece in a manner suited to the instruction of the young. The chronology is lucid, the events are well selected, and the narrative is perspicuous and simple. The facts and the method of presenting them are taken mainly from the work of Bishop Thirlwall, an excellent authority, and the work as a whole is the best with which we are acquainted for the use of children in their lessons of Grecian History, whether in the school-room or the family circle."—*Providence Journal.*

"She has faithfully condensed her subject, from the Siege of Troy, B. C. 1184, to the destruction of Corinth, and the annexation of Greece, as a province to the Roman Empire, B. C. 141; forming a most excellent outline, to be filled up by the future acquisitions of the reader. The chronological table of cotemporary events attached is a valuable addition.—*Cincinnati Daily Times.*

HISTORICAL AND MISCELLANEOUS QUESTIONS.

BY RICHARD MAGNALL. REVISED BY MRS. LAURENCE.

12mo. 396 pages. Price $1 00.

The American authoress of this excellent book has made it peculiarly well adapted to the schools of this country by adding to it a chapter on the history and constitution of the United States, and by large additions on the elements of mythology, astronomy, architecture, heraldry, &c., &c. This edition is embellished by numerous cuts, a large portion of the work is devoted to judicious questions and answers on ancient and modern history, which must be very serviceable to teachers and pupils.

"This is an admirable work to aid both teachers and parents in instructing children and youth, and there is no work of the kind that we have seen that is so well calculated to 'awaken a spirit of laudable curiosity in young minds,' and to satisfy that curiosity when awakened."—*Commercial Advertiser.*

HISTORY OF THE MIDDLE AGES.

BY GEO. W. GREENE.

1 Vol. 12mo. 450 pages. Price $1 00.

This work will be found to contain a clear and satisfactory exposition of the revolutions of the middle ages, with such general views of literature, society, and manners, as are required to explain the passages from ancient to modern history.

Instead of a single list of sovereigns, the author has given ful genealogical tables, which are much clearer and infinitely more satisfactory.

GENERAL HISTORY OF CIVILIZATION IN EUROPE.

BY M. GUIZOT

1 Vol. 316 pages. 12mo. Price $1 00.

This work embraces a period from the fall of the Roman empire to the French revolution, and has been edited from the second English edition, by Prof. C. S. Henry, who has added a few notes. The whole work is made attractive by the clear and lively style of the author.

HISTORY OF ROME.

BY DR. THOMAS ARNOLD.

Three Volumes in One. 8vo. 670 pages. $£ 00

Arnold's History of Rome is a well-known standard work, as full and accurate as Niebuhr, but much more readable and attractive; more copious and exact than Keightley or Schmitz, and more reliable than Michelet, it has assumed a rank second to none in value and importance. Its style is admirable, and it is every where imbued with the truth-loving spirit for which Dr. Arnold was pre-eminent. For Colleges and Schools this history is invaluable; and for private, as well as public libraries, it is indispensable.

LECTURES ON MODERN HISTORY.

BY DR. THOMAS ARNOLD.

Large 12mo. 428 pages. Price $1 25.

Edited from the second London edition, with a preface and notes of Henry Reed, M. A., Professor of English Literature in the University of Pennsylvania.

"These lectures, eight in number, furnish the best possible introduction to a philosophical study of modern history. Prof. Reed has added greatly to the worth and interest of the volume, by appending to each lecture such extracts from Dr. Arnold's other writings as would more fully illustrate its prominent points. The notes and appendix which he has thus furnished are exceedingly valuable."—*Evening Post.*

MANUAL OF ANCIENT AND MODERN HISTORY.

BY W. C. TAYLOR, LL. D., M. R. A. S.

Part I.—Containing the Political History, Geographical Position, and Social State of the Principal Nations of Antiquity, carefully digested from the Ancient Writers, and illustrated by the discoveries of Modern Scholars and Travellers.

Part II.—Containing the Rise and Progress of the Principal European Nations, their Political History, and the Changes in their Social Condition; with a History of the Colonies founded by Europeans. Revised by C. S. Taylor, D. D. 8vo. $2 50.

FIRST LESSONS IN ENGLISH COMPOSITION.

BY G. P. QUACKENBOS, A. M.

12mo. Price 45 Cents.

These "First Lessons" are intended for beginners in Grammar and Composition, and should be placed in their hands at whatever age it may be deemed best for them to commence these branches—say from nine to twelve years. In the first fifty pages, by means of lessons on the inductive system, and copious exercises under each, the pupil is made familiar with the nature and *use* of the different parts of speech, so as to be able to recognize them at once. He is then led to consider the different kinds of clauses and sentences, and is thus prepared for Punctuation, on which subject he is furnished with well considered rules, arranged on a new and simple plan. Directions for the use of capital letters follow. Next come rules, explanations and examples, for the purpose of enabling the pupil to form and spell correctly such derivative words as *having*, *debarring*, *pinning*, and the like, which are not to be found in ordinary dictionaries, and regarding which the pupil is apt to be led astray by the fact that a change is made in the primitive word before the addition of the suffix. This done, the scholar is prepared to express thoughts in his own language, and is now required to write sentences of every kind, a word being given to suggest an idea for each; he is taught to vary them by means of different arrangements and modes of expression; to analyze compound sentences into simple ones, and to combine simple ones into compound. Several lessons are then devoted to Style. The essential properties, purity, propriety, precision, clearness, strength, harmony, and unity, are next treated, examples for correction being presented under each. The different kinds of composition follow; and, specimens having been first given, the pupil is required to compose successively letters, descriptions, narrations, biographical sketches, essays, and argumentative discourses. After this, the principal figures receive attention; and the work closes with a list of subjects carefully selected, arranged under their proper heads, and in such a way that the increase in difficulty is very gradual. The work has received the universal approval of Teachers and the Press throughout the Union.

QUACKENBOS'

ADVANCED LESSONS IN COMPOSITION AND RHETORIC.

(NEARLY READY.)

www.ingramcontent.com/pod-product-compliance
Lightning Source LLC
LaVergne TN
LVHW011149110826
845150LV00006B/1193